From
Ace to Zamboni

101 More Dust Bin Stories

Also, by the author. . .

2005
Whistler's Gold: The Secret at Nizhoni Toh
A romance-mystery set on the Navajo Reservation

2015
Stories from History's Dust Bin, Volume 1
121 Stories for Jan 1 thru Apr 30

Stories from History's Dust Bin, Volume 2
123 Stories for May 1 through Aug 31

Stories from History's Dust Bin, Volume 3
122 Stories for Sept 1 through Dec 31

From
Ace to Zamboni

101 More Dust Bin Stories

A collection of unusual or forgotten stories, and more,
from the lives of the famous, infamous, and the obscure.

Wayne Winterton, Ph.D.

Introduction by Slim Randles, syndicated newspaper columnist
and host of the nationally-broadcast radio show, *Home Country*.

Wayne Winterton, PhD

To my wonderful grandchildren

Heather and Weston,
Morgan, Adrian, and Jackson,
Elizabeth and Elijah,
and
great-grandchildren,
Veronykah and Daeton

Cover Artist

Joan Johnson is an award-winning artist, best known for her portraits and scenes of the American west. Born and raised in Studio City, California, she attended Brigham Young University in Utah where she met and married her ever-supportive husband, Steve. They are the parents of two married children and the grandparents of four.

Introduction

"Sit down and I'll tell you a story."

These are very often the most welcomed words of a night around a campfire, or in a cabin in the trees, or just relaxing around the dining room table. We love hearing stories. And we've loved hearing stories since man first learned to talk.

In ancient Ireland, one of the highlights of the year on a distant farm was a visit from the *seanachie,* or storyteller. It's pronounced SHAWN – a- key, by the way, and this was a special job for very special people. The *seanachie* not only told the farm family the news he'd gathered on his travels, but reached back into history for legends of the people themselves.

And a storyteller, by any name, comes up in the legends and history of every country. The farmer, or the people in the small village, had a duty to put him up for the night and feed him. In exchange, they were transported to the days of heroes and villains and kingdoms that rose and fell, and armies and navies and remarkable leaders.

It's accurate to say the *seanachie* was a storyteller, because he was. He was able to mix facts, such as the news of the day, with enough storytelling ability to hold an entire village transfixed for hours.

So, it was really a skillful blending of truth and drama. And one such rare individual is Wayne Winterton, who wrote this book. It has been my pleasure to know Wayne both professionally and personally for a number of years now, and I'm proud to call him a friend.

In this book, Wayne takes you behind the scenes of history. His long career as an educator gave him the tools for research, and decades of appreciation for a good story gave him the gift of the bard.

And so, the teacher not only teaches us, with each of these historical gems, but also entertains us by telling us a story … a true story … that we'll never forget.

His well-received three-volume collection called *Stories from History's Dust Bin,* when it hasn't been busy winning awards, has been gluing readers to its pages for several years now. But what happened was, the printer ran out of ink before Wayne Winterton ran out of stories, and so we will now be able to immerse ourselves in *From Ace to Zamboni, 101 More Dust Bin Stories.* It's a glorious ride about the famous and the not-so-famous.

There's the 1899 story about the newspaper reporter who challenged the fictional Phileas Fogg's record-setting 80-day trip around the world. With Joseph Pulitzer and the *New York World's* blessing, the reporter went around the world in 72 days, eight fewer days than Mr. Fogg, and she (yes, she!) did it <horrors!> without a chaperone, and the newspaper reporter, Nellie Bly, became famous.

Have you ever wondered, duh! How the whole dumb blond thing got started? There's a story about Rosalie Duthé (1748-1830), the world's first officially recognized dumb blonde.

And what about the abandoned single mom from Texas whose invention sold for nearly $50 million and who was also the mother of a rock music star? Oh yes ... it's here, too.

There are 101 of these fascinating people who are kept alive here, with their achievements, their failures, their loves and their secrets. These aren't the stories we learned in our history classes, but now they're the stories a unique and talented writer and retired educator gives us.

Enjoy, because everyone loves a good story.

> Slim Randles, syndicated newspaper
> columnist and host of the nationally-
> broadcast radio show "Home Country."

From the Author

The three-volume *Stories from History's Dust Bin* did well when published in 2015, but receiving the prestigious *Arizona Book of the Year Award** for 2016 has elevated the stature and popularity of the series. If you're a first-time reader of the *Dust Bin* books, welcome aboard or, if you're adding to your collection of *Dust Bin* stories, I guarantee you're going to love what you'll discover inside.

As with *Stories from History's Dust Bin,* there is no "right way" to read *From Ace to Zamboni.* You can start at the beginning and read to the end, or you can pick and choose the stories that interest you most, taking an occasional side trip to expand your knowledge when you're feeling adventuresome.

The book opens with a story about Johnny Ace who may have been America's first Rock 'n' Roll star had he lived beyond his 25th year; and closes with Frank Zamboni, the man behind the machine that resurfaces the ice between hockey periods.

Between the Ace-to-Zamboni bookends, are ninety-nine more easy-to-read stories, often surprising, always interesting, perfect for curled-up nighttime reading, convalescing, or when traveling for work or vacation, whenever a good read is in order.

With special thanks to Sheri and Rob Dailey, Joe and Linda Galetovic, Tami Winterton, and William and Darcy Winterton for their story reviews; to artist Joan Johnson for the caricature of the author on the cover; to Katie Simpson for her helpful word-processing and formatting expertise; and to Jana Lee Winterton, an outstanding grammarian for her role in the book's final, tedious, time-consuming, line-by-line editing.

I couldn't have done it without the help of all of you.

Wayne A. Winterton, PhD
Phoenix, Arizona

* Awarded by the Arizona Authors' Association whose annual competition is open worldwide to all authors of English-language books.

Table of Contents

Note: Some footnotes refer to the author's *Stories from History's Dust Bin* series. For example, on page 57, the 7th paragraph, the term "Electoral College" is followed by a superscript (^{1}) linked to a footnote at the bottom of the page. Footnotes that begin with the words, "*Stories from History's Dust Bin*," reference the author's three-volume series of the same name in which the stories are organized according to a meaningful date, in chronological order.

[1] *Stories from History's Dust Bin* (additional reading):
    Vol 1, Apr 4:   Electoral College with William Henry Harrison
    Vol 3, Oct 4:   Electoral College with Rutherford B. Hayes
    Vol 3, Dec 14:   Electoral College with Joseph Lane

Johnny Ace

Born: John Marshall Alexander, Jr.
On track as America's first rock 'n' roll star, and then . . .
June 9, 1929 (Memphis TN) - Dec 25, 1954 (Houston TX)

A S OFTEN HAPPENS when something sensational shocks the conscience of the nation, half-baked reports become news, whether factual or not. Such was the case in the death of rising rock star Johnny Ace.

There was a tabloid story that an executive from Duke Records, with whom Ace was negotiating a new contract, had shot the young musician; and there was a news report that suggested he committed suicide. The tabloid report was quickly dismissed, but speculation about a suicide lingered.

So, what happened at Houston's City Auditorium on that Christmas day in 1954.

Johnny Ace, born John Marshall Alexander, Jr., was the son of a fundamentalist preacher and a strong-willed mother whose word was law, and this included restricting music in the home to gospel music only.

Growing up, John Alexander's talent as a musical performer was well-known. It was evident that whether hitting the high notes in the church choir or accompanying a group on the piano, Johnny's presence always made the performance better.

As you might expect, mom's strict rule at home gave rise to teenage rebellion. Thus, when John's parents were away at a tent meeting preaching the good news of old time religion; John was either at home playing the sharps and flats of old-time boogie-woogie, or singing the blues like no one else in town, mournful, plaintive blues steeped in rich African tradition.

Not yet, but within a decade, the combination of boogie-woogie and the blues would meld into a new musical genre called rock 'n' roll. It was precisely the sound that might have resulted in John Alexander's name being chiseled onto the timeless tablets of rock and roll music, but it wasn't going to happen.

John's independent attitude also affected his education and without the work ethic needed for serious book learning, he dropped out of high school and joined the navy.

It was the time of the Korean War and Johnny was sure that what he might miss in the classroom, would be offset by seeing the world on Uncle Sam's dime.

But, in the navy he made a habit of taking shore leave to play the piano at local honky-tonks, and too often he was still pounding the ivories and belting out songs well past bed-check.

Now, if he thought his mother's rules at home were tough, he soon found the navy even more restrictive and less forgiving, and before long he had worn out his military welcome. After too many missed roll-calls, searches, and lock-ups by the Shore Patrol, John was sent home to Memphis.

But, in typical John Alexander style, he landed on his feet and was soon playing piano and singing backup with the *Beale Streeters,* a group led by guitarist B. B. King with Bobby Bland on vocals.

In 1951, B. B. King was offered a solo contract with Modern Records and he scored big with his first release, the "Three O'Clock Blues." With King gone, John assumed leadership of the band, but the group was so talent-rich it wasn't long before others were being offered auditions to break out on their own.

One of those opportunities came when David Mattis, the owner of Duke Records, set up a recording try-out for vocalist Bobby Bland.

The entire band, thrilled with Bobby's chance to cut a solo record, showed up at the recording studio to watch and cheer.

But when Mattis handed the singer a copy of sheet music to review before starting the session, Bobby admitted he couldn't read a note of music, and Mattis lost interest.

With studio time already paid for, Mattis looked around to see how he might recover from a potentially costly situation.

In a corner, accompanying himself at an out-of-tune piano sat John Alexander. Mattis liked John's voice and delivery and told him if he could come up with an original melody and lyrics, he'd let him take Bobby's place.

John went to work and in no time at all, he had altered the melody of an old Ruth Brown hit, "So Long," gave it a new set of lyrics and called it, "My Song."

It was 1952 and the song soared to number #1 on the charts and stayed there for nine long weeks! With that hit, Mattis decided John needed a stage name, something imaginative with just the right ring.

Remembering his mother's unforgiving attitude toward non-gospel music, John told Mattis, "Just call me Ace, but don't tell my momma because the first thing she'll want to know is, 'What's an ace?'"

That's when John Alexander, Jr., literally the son of a preacher man, became Johnny Ace, a budding rock star standing on the threshold of what the future would soon herald as the beginning of the golden age of rock 'n' roll.

Mattis, with a potential platinum mine on his hands, signed Johnny to a contract and during the next two years, Johnny didn't disappoint, scoring an amazing eight hits in a row,[1] several of which, unfortunately, were released posthumously, after the incident alluded to in the opening of the story.

A year of successful touring was almost over, and Johnny Ace had become a red-hot commodity.

His concerts were sellouts and teenyboppers were jumping up and down and screaming at the tops of their lungs every time he walked on stage.

It was Christmas Day, 1954. The group, having just finished its first set at Houston's City Auditorium, was relaxing back stage awaiting the curtain call for the next performance.

During the year-long tour, Johnny had carried a .22-caliber handgun with him and sometimes, while traveling in the wide-open spaces he would shoot at cans, critters, and highway signs.

Then, while everyone was munching chips, sipping sodas, and talking about the next set, a shot rang out and Big Mama Thornton, one of the group's vocalists screamed, "Johnny just killed himself! Johnny just killed himself!"

The scream was overheard by a handful of reporters who filed the story, giving rise to the claim of a Johnny Ace suicide.

Later, bass player Curtis Tillman, who had been in the same room as Johnny and Big Mama Thornton and had witnessed the event, told everyone the following:

> *I'll tell you exactly what happened! Johnny had been drinking and he had this pistol and he was waving it around the table and someone said, "Be careful with that thing . . ." and Johnny said, "It's okay! Gun's not loaded. See . . . ." and he pointed the gun at himself with a big smile on his face, and "Bang!"*

Johnny Ace was twenty-five years old.

It was 1954, the same year that Bill Haley and His Comets[2] recorded "Rock Around the Clock," America's first truly big rock 'n' roll song.

There's no telling how far Johnny Ace might have gone in the golden era of rock 'n' roll had he not tempted fate with an "unloaded" gun.

---

[1] Johnny Ace's eight hits in a row: My Song, Cross My Heart, The Clock, Saving My Love for You, Please Forgive Me, Never Let Me Go, Pledging My Love, and Anymore.

[2] See Bill Haley in this book, pages 119-121, to learn more about the roots of rock 'n' roll music.

> *Everybody wants to go to Heaven,*
> *but no one wants to die to get there.*
> B. B. King (1925-2015) Singer, songwriter

Roy Chapman Andrews

Was he the inspiration for Indiana Jones?
Jan 26, 1884 (Beloit WI) – Mar 11, 1960 (Carmel CA)

H AVE YOU EVER wondered how many of your favorite fictional characters, good and evil, were inspired by people who once walked among us?

Bram Stoker's horror novel, *Dracula,* was drawn from the real life of Vlad III Drăculea,[1] a psychopathic ruler who killed thousands of perceived and real enemies by impaling them on pointed stakes.

His infamous nickname?

Vlad the Impaler.

The very real Vlad, who made Stoker's Count Dracula seem like a schoolboy, was the ruler of Wallachia (current day Romania) from 1448 until his death in 1476.

Sir Arthur Conan Doyle's[2] character, Sherlock Holmes, was based on Dr. Joseph Bell, a Scottish physician and master of observation and deduction.

As a lecturing physician at the University of Edinburgh, Bell had random strangers brought into the classroom. Then, by observation and deduction he would determine their habits, occupations, and sometimes even their most recent whereabouts with hardly a word spoken.

Doyle, a medical student at the time, never forgot Bell's lectures and he would endow his literary detective with a deductive mind as sharp as Dr. Bell's.

Robert Louis Stevenson's peg-legged Long John Silver of *Treasure Island* fame, was similar in physical appearance to Stevenson's literary editor William Henley.

Henley, an amputee since childhood, was well-known for his hearty laugh and full, red beard. In fact, Stevenson once told Henley, "It was the sight of your maimed strength and masterfulness that begot Long John Silver…. The idea of a maimed man, ruling and dreaded was taken entirely from you."[4]

And there are others. Popeye was inspired by a man named Frank Fiegal, a ruffian who grew up in cartoonist E. C. Segar's[3] hometown of Chester, Illinois. When Fiegal died in 1947, engraved into his tombstone were the words, "Inspiration for Popeye the Sailor Man."

Rocky Balboa, the protagonist in the *Rocky* movies starring Sylvester Stallone, was inspired by boxer Chuck Wepner, who once put Muhammad Ali on the canvas.

Charles Dickens' penny-pinching Ebenezer Scrooge was inspired by England's most miserly Member of Parliament, John Elwes, a man of considerable wealth who ate moldy food, wore pitiful clothing, and went to bed at sundown to avoid the expense of lighting a candle.

We could go on and on, but we need to get back to the story at hand.

Indiana Jones, the fictional character created by George Lucas, could easily have been inspired by one of four men, or a composite of them. Only Lucas knows, and he's not talking.

But the names that surface most often include Otto Rahn, a German writer, archaeologist, and searcher of the Holy Grail; Hiram Bingham III, a Princeton University history professor and amateur archaeologist who, in 1911, discovered the Inca city of Machu Picchu; Percival Fawcett, an explorer and archaeologist who disappeared in the jungles of Brazil in 1925 while searching for the lost city of El Dorado; and Roy Chapman Andrews, the subject of this vignette.

Roy Chapman Andrews knew exactly what he wanted out of life, and he knew exactly where he wanted to do it.

After graduating from Beloit College in 1906, he caught the next train to New York and walked into the American Museum of Natural History. When told there were no jobs available, he offered to scrub the museum floor – for nothing.

The interviewer, doubting the young man's sincerity, offered him a janitorial position. Andrews never blinked and his first job after graduating from college was mopping the floors of the museum's Taxidermy Department. But it wouldn't be his last! In twenty-nine years (1935), Roy Chapman Andrews would become the museum's director.

But back to the early years of Andrews' love affair with the museum.

He didn't remain a janitor for long. His work ethic and enthusiasm to tackle any task assigned, without complaint, quickly brought him to the attention of the museum's leadership.

When a dead whale turned up on a Long Island, New York beach, Andrews and a youthful colleague were asked to retrieve as many whale bones as they could.

Expectations were low for the two novices as whale bones are heavy and quickly disappear in the sand. Imagine the astonishment of the museum's director when the pair returned with every skeletal bone of the great mammal.

More assignments followed, leading to expeditions into the Arctic, China, Indonesia, Japan, Korea, and Mongolia, to name a few.

Of his many assignments, Andrews is best known for his expeditions into the Gobi Desert of Mongolia. Using a fleet of Dodge vans supported by a caravan of camels, Andrews led safaris into unexplored parts the Gobi from 1922 to 1930.

On the team's first trip into the Gobi, they discovered the fossil of a giant hornless rhinoceros (*Indricotherium*) along with several complete dinosaur skeletons, the first ever discovered north of the Himalayas.

During their second expedition, Andrews' team uncovered a small skull next to a dinosaur skeleton and sent the skull to the museum to determine from which reptile family it belonged.

The skull turned out to be one of Andrews most significant finds. It was not a reptile skull at all, but the skull of a mammal, proving that dinosaurs and mammals had once coexisted.

Subsequent expeditions turned up the world's first discovery of dinosaur eggs (*Oviraptor*), confirming the method by which dinosaurs reproduced. Numerous new species of dinosaurs were discovered, including one named in Andrew Chapman's honor (*Andrewsarchus*).

In 1930, the expeditions had to be abandoned due to political instability in the region.

Then, five years later Chapman was named the museum's director. He had accomplished the goal he had set for himself in college, and he did it the old-fashioned way. He earned it.

Should you question whether Chapman's life was worthy of the adventures that made Indiana Jones famous, here is an excerpt from his book, *On the Trail of Ancient Man:*[5]

> *In fifteen years* (of field work) *I can remember just ten times when I had really narrow escapes from death. Two were from drowning in typhoons, one was when our boat was charged by a wounded whale, once my wife and I were nearly eaten by wild dogs, once we were in great danger from fanatical Lama priests, two were close calls when I fell over cliffs, once I was nearly caught by a huge python, and twice I might have been killed by bandits.*

Was Roy Chapman Andrews the inspiration behind the archaeology-minded character of Dr. Henry "Indiana" Jones? There are many who believe that he was.

Andrews died March 11, 1960, of heart failure.

He is buried in Oakwood Cemetery, in the town of his birth, Beloit, Wisconsin.

---

[1] See Vlad III, Prince of Wallachia in this book, pages 356-358, to learn more about the man that served as the inspiration for *Dracula.*

Stories from History's Dust Bin (additional reading):
[2] Vol 2, May 22:   Featuring Arthur Conan Doyle
[3] Vol 3, Oct 13:   Featuring E. C. Segar

[4] Stevenson, Robert Louis, "The Voyage," (1883) p. 316.

[5] Andrews, Roy Chapman, *On the Trail of Ancient Man: A Narrative of the Field Work of the Central Asiatic Expeditions,* (G. P. Putnam, 1930).

> *An archaeologist is the best husband a woman can have.*
> *The older she gets, the more interested he is in her.*
> Agatha Christie (1890-1976) Novelist

Marshall Applewhite

Born: Marshall Herff Applewhite, Jr.
A 17.29-million-mile trip with 38 friends.
May 17, 1931 (Spur TX) – Mar 26, 1997 (Rancho Santa Fe CA)

MARSHALL APPLEWHITE WAS born May 17, 1931, in Spur, Texas. His "spiritual" message was light years removed from every other theology on the planet. He even authored a pamphlet claiming that Christ had been reincarnated as a Texan (believable, perhaps, but only to Texans), and the text, while lacking in specificity, leaves the reader with the eerie impression that he, Marshall Applewhite, just might be that Texan.

He espoused a mystical doctrine he called Human Individual Metamorphosis, claiming that his personal existence was at an evolutionary level above human. If that seems a little hard to swallow, don't worry, you're not alone. But to better understand Applewhite, we need to travel back in time.

In 1972, divorced and estranged from his wife and children, Applewhite met divorcée Bonnie Lu Nettles. Nettles was a registered nurse whose best friend was a deceased, but talkative 19th-century monk named Brother Francis. Nettles also dabbled in astrology, the pseudo-scientific study of the influence of heavenly bodies on human life.

She confided to Applewhite that she had been told by an extraterrestrial that the two of them were predestined to meet, and that he, Applewhite, had been chosen to fulfill a divine mission.

After doing an astrological reading for Applewhite in which she found their stars to be in perfect alignment, Applewhite shared his belief about other-worldly places and futures. The pair, believing they had been foreordained by some esoteric power of the cosmos, were inseparable until her death in 1985.

But, we're getting ahead of the story.

Applewhite and Nettles began traveling together, viewing themselves as divine messengers in search of an undefined *Awakening.*

One of their first awakenings, unfortunately, and one they would have preferred never happened, took place in Missouri. That's where, despite Applewhite's pleadings to the court that God had divinely authorized him to steal a rental car, the judge failed to be swayed, and a dual conviction of auto theft and credit card fraud landed him in the slammer for six months.

After Applewhite served his time, the pair continued their quest for the elusive awakening, believing now that they were the two witnesses spoken of in Revelation, Chapter 11, Verse 3: "And I will give power unto my two witnesses, and they shall prophesy a thousand two hundred and threescore days, clothed in sackcloth."

Calculating they had 1,260 days, or three-and-a-half years of preaching to do, they began referring to themselves as *the Two,* meaning the two witnesses. Individually, Applewhite became *Bo* and Nettles became *Peep* and some well-intentioned, albeit disillusioned earthlings became followers, and no one dressed in sackcloth.

The pair taught that the body was a container for the soul, and that a mothership would soon arrive from somewhere in the universe to gather the true believers in preparation for (a) a recycling of the earth, and (b) the elusive awakening, which by now had been revealed to them as the *Spiritual Awakening.*

Then, in 1985, Bonnie Lu Nettles died of cancer.

Applewhite assured his followers that she had simply ascended to the next level of her existence.

The group now known as the Heaven's Gate cult, after years of a nomadic lifestyle came into a small fortune, likely the inheritance of one of its followers. They rented a $7,200 per month, 9,200 square-foot mansion in an upscale San Diego community. The membership of the group totaled thirty-nine, including Applewhite.

It's now the mid-1990s and time to learn about something that took place elsewhere, just as the Heaven's Gate crew was unpacking boxes and measuring their new digs for drapes.

On July 23, 1995, astronomer Dr. Alan Hale was at home in Cloudcroft, New Mexico, peering through his telescope when he saw a fuzzy object not on his star charts.

After confirming the absence of other deep-sky objects in his viewing area, and assured that the object was indeed moving relative to the background stars, he emailed the details of his discovery to the Central Bureau for Astronomical Telegrams (CBAT), the clearing house for astronomical anomalies.

That same night, 450 miles west of Dr. Hale's location, amateur astronomer Thomas Bopp was with like-minded friends about ninety miles south of Phoenix in the Arizona desert.

There, while looking through the telescope of a close friend, Jim Stevens, Bopp saw what Dr. Hale had seen, a fuzzy object that hadn't been there two weeks earlier. He checked his star charts for a new deep-sky object, and like Hale, found nothing. Also, like Hale, but via telegram rather than email, he alerted CBAT to his discovery.

By the time Bopp's telegram hit the desk of CBAT director Brian G. Marsden, Marsden had already received Hale's initial email, plus two more with updated location coordinates.

Within days, the independent discoveries of Alan Hale and Thomas Bopp were confirmed, and the world was introduced to a new comet.

Dr. Alan Hale and Thomas Bopp were not the first to see the comet that now carries their names as the comet Hale-Bopp was observed by the ancient Egyptians following the reign of the Pharaoh Pepi I (2332-2283 BC).[1]

Returning now to the Heaven's Gate mansion where all is well, including an ever-present air of anticipation as to when the great *Spiritual Awakening* will begin.

Then, it happened!

The date was January 17, 1994.

The awakening arrived in the form of a powerful earthquake that rocked California's San Fernando Valley, killing 57 and injuring 8,700. It was, Applewhite boldly proclaimed, a sign the end was near.

Then, Applewhite predicted there would be a second sign.

And a year-and-a-half later he got it!

The date was July 23, 1995.

It was the date that the newswires reported that astronomers Dr. Alan Hale and Thomas Bopp had independently identified a previously unknown comet in deep space, traveling in an orbit that would take it past the earth and back into deep space.

Inside the comet's tail, Applewhite assured his followers, was the promised mother ship with Bonnie on board, anxiously awaiting their reunion.

With the comet and its tail visible in the night sky for a record-breaking eighteen months, Applewhite and his followers had plenty of time to prepare to leave Earth for galaxies unknown. They even made video and audio tapes, recording final messages to be given to their families after their departure.

Then, on March 26, 1997, an anonymous call to the Rancho Santa Fe Sheriff's Office led law enforcement to the Heaven's Gate mansion.

Inside were thirty-nine bodies, each lying neatly atop their assigned bunk beds, each face covered with a purple cloth, and each dressed in a black uniform with a shoulder patch reading, "Heaven's Gate Away Team."

Each body also wore matching Nike® shoes, and each had exactly $5.75 in a pocket, toll fare for their interplanetary travel.

Their containers (bodies) remained on Earth and were duly cared for, but there's no telling where the Heaven's Gate crew is today.

Hale-Bopp's 17.29-million mile, 926,639-day orbit won't pass by Earth again until the year 4380, longer than most of us are willing to wait.

---

[1] Hieroglyphics found in Pepi I's burial pyramid at Saqqara, Egypt, mention a "long-haired star" as a companion of the deceased Pharaoh Pepi I. The ancient Egyptian sighting of the comet known today as Hale-Bopp is plausible because according to modern astronomical projections, the comet traveled past the earth roughly 40 to 50 years after the death of Pepi I in 2283 BC.

How bright and beautiful a comet is as it flies past
our planet, provided it does fly past it.
Isaac Asimov (1920-1992) Author

E. C. Bentley

Born: Edmund Clerihew Bentley
The Father of the Clerihew
July 10, 1875 (London, England) – Mar 30, 1956 (London, England)

A FTER DOING A LITTLE research on E.C. Bentley, the author couldn't resist trying his hand at writing one of those four-line biographical verses known as a clerihew:

Edmund Clerihew Bentley,
Gave to literature and quite contently,
Two couplets, no more, the length of his verse
And the use of his name for better or worse.

E. C. Bentley had planned to study law, but soon discovered he preferred journalism, and as it turned out, changing majors was a good decision.

After graduating from the University of Oxford he went on to become a popular English novelist and one of the earliest authors of detective novels. His story, *Trent's Last Case,*[1] published in 1913 is today considered a literary classic.

However, Bentley isn't remembered for his novels, but for his novel verse, a unique form of poetry that has come to be known as a "clerihew," in honor of his unusual middle name.

If you're interested in such things, or about to look up the definition of clerihew, here's a well-accepted one:

Clerihew: An irregular form of light verse, with lines of uneven length and irregular meter, forming two couplets, the first line of which usually provides the name of the subject of the verse, most typically the name of a known person.

Many dictionaries and other reference sources often include Bentley's name alongside the definition by adding something similar to:

The clerihew is named for Edmund Clerihew Bentley
who first described the poetic form in a book published
in 1906 under the pen-name, E. Clerihew.

You're rolling your eyes! So, poetry has never been your cup of English tea? That's okay, but don't be so quick to give up on this little story. You might even learn something. Or maybe not, depending on your attitude. But now is a perfect time to insert a couple of Bentley's clerihews.

For instance:

> Lewis Carroll[2]
> Bought sumptuous apparel
> And built an enormous palace
> Out of the profits of Alice.

"Alice" as you likely know, refers to Lewis Carroll's curious little girl, the same one who followed a harried, time-conscious white rabbit through a portal and into Wonderland.

Here's another:

> I believe it was admitted by Scott
> That some of his novels were rot.
> How different was he from Lytton
> Who admired everything he had written!

What? You liked the clerihew about Lewis Carroll and Alice better? That's fine. It's a good one. The second clerihew, however, was selected to serve an educational purpose.

In the second clerihew, "Scott" refers F. Scott Fitzgerald, and few people know that the author's full name was Francis Scott Key Fitzgerald. He was named for a cousin, Francis Scott Key,[3] the patriot who penned the poem that became America's national anthem, the "Star-Spangled Banner."

But, what do you know about "Lytton," which, by the way, rhymes with "written?" Lytton, as you surely sensed from the clerihew, was someone whom Bentley viewed as rather self-absorbed, a person as they say, "full of himself."

Lytton's full name was Edward George Earle Lytton Bulwer-Lytton. He was better known as Lord Lytton, an English novelist, poet, and playwright who wrote twenty-eight novels, a few pieces of poetry, and several theatrical plays.

He is also credited as the originator of several well-worn phrases that you've undoubtedly heard, such as "in pursuit of the almighty dollar," and "the pen is mightier than the sword."

And who isn't familiar with the words, "It was a dark and stormy night . . . ," the opening phrase of Snoopy's perpetually forthcoming great American novel.

But, what few Snoopy fans know is that he plagiarized those seven words from the first sentence of Edward Bulwer-Lytton's 1830s novel, *Paul Clifford,* the story of a man living two lives.

Over a hundred years before Charles Schulz first inked the tip of Snoopy's nose, Edward Bulwer-Lytton began his story about Paul Clifford with the words: *It was a dark and stormy night; the rain fell in torrents – except at occasional . . . .*

And for whatever reason, those seven introductory words first used by Edward Bulwer-Lytton has given America's favorite beagle the worst case of writer's block the world has ever known.

And thousands of authors, and author-wannabees have chuckled, and commiserated with Snoopy, reflecting on their own mental blocks.

Here are a couple of clerihews with some little-known facts:

John James Audubon
Painted birds with great distinction;
He shot them first, not uncommon,
To save them, he said, from extinction.

You didn't know that Audubon killed the birds he painted?

How do you think he got those birds to sit still while he painted their portraits? You can't just say to a bird, "Hey bird, sit up straight! I'll let you know when you can begin preening!"

He invented a skeletal wiring device to hold the deceased birds in realistic positions, so he could paint them, and he also made a fair amount of money selling animal skins (he was also a taxidermist), enough to offset his painting costs.

And then there's . . .

Galileo Galilei
Committed a revolutionary heresy
When he said the earth was not at rest
Though he was under house arrest.

You might recall from your world history class that Galileo was kept under lock-and-key for the final five years of his life. Why?

Because he refused to back down from his belief that the planets revolved around the sun, when about 97% of the world's scientists were certain the Earth was the center of the universe.

There's a lesson in there for all of us, and it's this.

We should be wary of anyone who claims that 97% of the world's scientists can agree on anything, whether it be the Hollow Earth Theory,[4] the iffy notion of global warming, or the number of angels that can dance on the head of a pin.

And finally, the author's favorite:

Beethoven
Was noted for often
Turning a deaf ear
To advice from a peer.

Thus, as you can see, some clerihews are funnier than others.

[1] Bentley, E. C. *Trent's Last Case,* (Century Company, 1st ed., 1913).

Stories from History's Dust Bin (additional reading):
  [2] Vol 2, May 4:   Lewis Carroll with Alice Liddell
  [3] Vol 2, May 3:   Francis Scott Key with Daniel Sickles
  [4] Vol 3, Dec 22:   Featuring Cyrus Reed Teed

The art of biography
is different from geography.
Geography is about maps,
but biography is about chaps.
Edmund Clerihew Bentley (1875-1956) Humorist, poet

Nellie Bly

Born: Elizabeth Jane Cochran
America's first female investigative reporter.
May 5, 1864 (Cochran's Mills PA) – Jan 27, 1922 (New York NY)

I N 1850, STEPHEN FOSTER, the man known as the *Father of American Music*, wrote a snappy light-hearted ditty about a lady who loved to dance. He named her Nelly Bly,[1] and you may sing along if you like. It begins like this:

Nelly Bly! Nelly Bly! Bring the broom along,
We'll sweep the kitchen clean, my dear, and have a little song.

Fourteen years after Foster set Nelly Bly to music, a baby girl was born to Michael and Mary Cochran of Cochran's Mills, Pennsylvania. They named her Elizabeth Jane, and a little later in the story you'll learn the connection between Foster's "Nelly Bly" and Elizabeth Jane Cochran.

Elizabeth Jane was not your typical female of the 1800s.

Her father was the founder of the town and the owner of the mill that bears the family name, Cochran's Mill. He had ten children by his first wife, and following her passing, remarried and fathered five more. Elizabeth was third from the end of that string of fifteen, and all fourteen of her siblings would agree she was the family rebel.

Elizabeth was never one to beat about the bush when a question arose, or a problem needed solved.

She told it like it was!

In 1870, Michael Cochran died without leaving a will and his assets were auctioned to pay his debts. Elizabeth's mother, in need of financial and emotional security, made a desperate decision and married John Jackson Ford, an abusive and violent alcoholic.

The marriage ended, first with a separation in 1878, then a court hearing in 1879, in which 15-year-old Elizabeth took the stand. The youthful and very articulate Elizabeth explained to the judge – in devastating detail – exactly what life had been like with John Jackson Ford in the house.

Down went the judge's gavel.

Bam.

Divorce granted!

In 1880, the family moved to Pittsburgh and what happened there two years later defined the rest of Elizabeth's life, and made her a national celebrity.

Picking up a copy of the *Pittsburgh Dispatch* she read Erasmus Wilson's "Quiet Observer" column titled, "What Girls are Good For." Wilson wrote that "women belonged in the home doing domestic chores," even calling women who worked outside the home, "monstrosities."

When 18-year-old Elizabeth had all of the Quiet Observer she could stomach, she wrote an angry rebuttal to the editor, sharing her thoughts in fiery, descriptive terms that required no interpretation. When it came time to sign her response she stiffened, and not wanting to embarrass her family, signed it simply, Lonely Orphan Girl.

Erasmus Wilson's reaction to the Lonely Orphan Girl's response to his column is unknown, but George Madden, the newspaper's editor loved it, especially the straight-forward, tell-it-like-it-is style of writing from a woman. With a little detective work he tracked down the Lonely Orphan Girl, and offered the teenaged Elizabeth a reporter's job.

She wrote her first article for the newspaper on the topic of "Working Women in Pittsburgh," and used the Lonely Orphan Girl byline.

Madden might have felt Elizabeth's byline lacked authority, or dignity, or seemed immature. But whatever the reason, when he asked for a follow-up article on divorce – and you can be sure Elizabeth had an opinion on that topic – he asked her to come up with a new byline. And that's when the Lonely Orphan Girl chose the name of the dancing lady from Stephen Foster's popular song, "Nelly Bly."

Madden either purposely changed Foster's spelling of "Nelly" to "Nellie" to avoid copyright conflict with the song, or he unwittingly misspelled "Nelly" as "Nellie" when the newspaper went to press. Regardless, Elizabeth Cochran became Nellie Bly, and Nellie Bly became the toast of Pittsburgh as her news stories and writing style soon won the hearts of the city's readers.

Nellie, who had never been a run-of-the-mill anything, wouldn't become a run-of-the-mill reporter either, and it wasn't long before she was doing what is known these days as investigative reporting.

In fact, she may have been America's first investigative reporter, and if she wasn't the first, she was certainly the nation's first female investigative reporter.

In 1887 Nellie quit the *Pittsburgh Dispatch* and walked into the offices of the *New York World,* a newspaper owned by Joseph Pulitzer.[2]

There, she agreed to feign insanity to investigate reports of brutality at the Women's Lunatic Asylum on Blackwell's Island, New York.

After perfecting some deranged expressions by evaluating them in a mirror, and adopting some other observable symptoms of insanity, she checked into a boardinghouse and using today's vernacular, she went nuts!

It didn't take long before she was committed to the above-mentioned lunatic asylum where she found conditions worse than either she, or Joseph Pulitzer, expected.

Nellie's outstanding undercover news reports became the book sensation, *Ten Days in a Mad-House,* and launched a full investigation into the New York Department of Public Charities and Corrections.

But what really captured the public's imagination, was her decision to travel around the world, and to do it in fewer days than it took the fictional Phileas Fogg to do it in Jules Verne's[3] classic novel, *Around the World in 80 Days.*

And in 1889 she did just that!

Sponsored by Pulitzer and the *New York World*, she traveled around the globe and she did it, <*horrors!*> without a chaperone, shocking America's sensibilities.

Just as amazing was what she took with her. Her wardrobe consisted of one dress, an overcoat, a few changes of underwear, £200 in English bank notes, and a single small travel bag with essential ladies' toiletries! That was it!

The *New York World* sponsored a contest in which the reader who estimated to the second, the closest time it would take Miss Bly to complete the 24,889-mile trip, won a fully-paid trip to Europe including spending money.

Nellie made the around-the-world trip, traveling alone in a variety of standard and unconventional conveyances: ships, horses, flat-bottomed sampans, railroad cars, burros, rickshaws, whatever was available, and she did it in exactly 72 days, 6 hours, 11 minutes, and 14 seconds, setting a world record at the time.

Nellie could have clocked even better time had she not taken a side trip to Amiens, France, to visit with none other than Jules Verne and his wife Honorine.

Verne was generous in his praise of Bly and wished her the best in her attempt to beat the 80-day record held by his fictional balloonist, Phileas Fogg.

And that, dear readers, is a thumbnail-sized account of the non-fictional, very attractive, investigative reporter, Nellie Bly.

Nellie died of pneumonia in New York in 1922 at the age of fifty-seven.

She is buried at Woodlawn Cemetery in The Bronx, New York.

Stories from History's Dust Bin (additional reading):
[1] Vol 1, Jan 27:   Nellie Bly with The Last Great Race on Earth
[2] Vol 1, Apr 10:   Featuring Joseph Pulitzer
[3] Vol 1, Feb 19:   Jules Verne with Homer Hickam

I have never written a word that did not come from my heart.
I never shall.
Nellie Bly (1864-1922) Journalist

Tycho Brahe

Born: Tyge Ottesen Brahe
His nose may have been the death of him.
Dec 14, 1546 (Scania, Denmark) – Oct 24, 1601 (Prague)

A VAILABLE ON THE INTERNET is a portrait of Danish astronomer Tycho Brahe, a man with an egg-shaped face, a pair of deer-in-the-headlight eyes, and one of the strangest mustaches you've ever seen, guaranteed.

But what the painting does not show is Brahe's face as he saw it in the mirror each morning. Oh, he always knew what he was going to see, and it was never going to look right. And emotionally, it would forever be a reminder of one particularly poor decision on his part.

Fortunately for Brahe, he had the financial resources to mitigate the problem, at least to some degree. But unfortunately, his means of mitigation may have unwittingly contributed to his early death. The cause of which is only now – over four-hundred years after his death – beginning to be examined.

Tycho Brahe, highly intelligent, was raised by an uncle who saw to it that he received a top-flight education, and he did, becoming a highly respected astronomer whose astronomical observations and interpretations, without the benefit of a modern telescope, are mind-boggling.

But, as a young man and despite his brilliant scientific mind, he could be driven by ego and given to rashness, especially when his ideas and intellect were challenged.

And that's exactly what happened when he quarreled with his cousin, Manderup Parsberg, over a complex and unproven mathematical equation.

You would be hard-pressed these days to find two twenty-year-old cousins, or anyone for that matter, who would choose to settle the issue of a questionable mathematical equation by fighting a duel with real swords, but that's exactly what Tycho and Manderup decided to do.

Here's how it all started.

On December 10, 1566, the two cousins, who had been invited to attend a wedding dance at the home of Professor Lucas Bachmeister, caused quite a scene when they engaged in a noisy and unrelenting quarrel over the merits of the disputed equation.

You might think that getting steamed over some numbers, when everyone else was having fun toasting the bride and groom, would be just a little "over-the-top" of good taste. But with cousins Brahe and Parsberg, it happened twice!

The argument that took place at the above wedding dance was but a warm-up for an even more heated debate seventeen days later, December 27, 1566.

The two cousins were at it again, locked in serious cerebral combat, with neither able to bring the other to his intellectual knees using analytics, mathematics, or over-powering argument.

So, what's a person to do under such circumstances.

They decided if they couldn't resolve the argument with logic, they would resolve it by seeing who was the better swordsman.

That seems reasonable, right?

And besides, who hasn't at one time or another, considered using the "thrust and parry" method of problem resolution?

A decision was made to hold the duel on Sunday, December 29, 1566, and to make the contest even more challenging, it would take place at night.

Fortunately, neither man died during the ensuing clinking of metal-on-metal in the darkness, but Tycho lost the bridge of his nose, sliced off as cleanly as a butcher trimming fat from a pork roast. With that unfortunate ending, Parsberg was declared the winner and Brahe the loser – by a nose.

For any twenty-year-old man in the 1500s – or during any century for that matter – the loss of the upper-half length of one's nose means it's going to be more and more difficult to find a date to the Renaissance Faire, regardless of one's intellectual genius.

But because he had his whole life before him, and since money was no object, Brahe did the only thing he could do. He had a prosthetic nose made from metal to alleviate the problem.

To make the new nose as inconspicuous as possible, he had it created from a mixture of gold, silver, and according to some historians, copper and other metals as well. With considerable experimentation, the metals were blended to his complexion, and as much as possible, built to resemble the contour of his original nose.

The prosthetic was worn over his nasal cavity and held in place by an adhesive balm that required frequent re-application.

Over the years, Brahe had several metal noses made for himself, each turning out slightly different in appearance and color, but all things considered, life was good.

In 1560, his witnessing of a solar eclipse inspired him to become an astronomer, and he not only achieved his goal, but assembled one of the largest bodies of astronomical data to that point in history.

He was also known for his highly accurate observations and he has been described as "the first competent mind in modern astronomy to feel ardently the passion for exact empirical facts."[1]

When he discovered that the Copernican tables (named for astronomer Nicolaus Copernicus) were several days off in predicting the overlap of Jupiter and Saturn, he devoted a considerable amount of his life to correcting them.

Without benefit of a telescope, being the last of the major naked eye[2] astronomers, he conducted a full study of the solar system and accurately plotted the positions of approximately 800 stars.

Brahe's observations also formed the basis for Johannes Kepler's *Laws of Planetary Motion*, published in 1609. In fact, during the early part of his career, Kepler was an assistant to Brahe before being named the imperial mathematician to the Austrian Emperor Rudolf II.

Then, at the age of fifty-four, after attending a banquet in Prague, Brahe suddenly came down with a bladder or kidney infection that resulted in a serious retention of urine. The infection was aggressive and non-responsive to treatments of the day and on October 24, 1601, only eleven days after first stricken, Brahe died.

The medical consensus in 1601 was that he died of a strained bladder. It was considered rude during that era to exit a banquet before its conclusion, and some believe it was his faithful attention to this highly uncomfortable societal expectation that caused his death.

Then, in 1901, exactly three hundred years after his death, Brahe's body was exhumed for burial relocation.

While he was above ground, samples of his moustache hair and body tissues were secured for scientific purposes, and early 1900's testing indicated he likely died of kidney failure.

But more recent tests have suggested his death may have been caused by mercury poisoning, as highly toxic levels of mercury have been found in the hair and hair-roots of his moustache.

Although the results have yet to be proven conclusively, it's probable that the source of the mercury poisoning came from amalgams of mercury reacting with the various metals used in the prosthetic noses he wore daily for the last thirty-four years of his life.

Today, Tycho Brahe's body is interred in a tomb near the famed Astronomical Clock in Prague, Czechoslovakia.

[1] Edwin Arthur Burtt, *The Metaphysical Foundations of Modern Physical Science: A Historical and Critical Essay* (1925)

[2] In astronomy, *naked eye* observation refers to observing astronomical events without equipment, such as an astronomical conjunction, the passage of a comet, a meteor shower, and in some cases, asteroids.

Those who study the stars have God for a teacher.
Tycho Brahe (1546-1601) Astronomer

Jim Bridger

Born: James Felix Bridger
A youthful mistake – forgiven.
Mar 17, 1804 (Richmond VA) – July 17, 1881 (Kansas City MO)

JIM BRIDGER BEGAN his career as a mountain man when he was 17-years-old by serving as the youngest member of William Ashley's Upper Missouri Expedition, the purpose of which was to locate the headwaters of the Missouri River.

Bridger would live to the age of seventy-seven years, and become a living American legend in the process, but it was not without one major regret.

Ashley's expedition included others who would become major historical figures, such as Jedediah Smith, the first American to enter California from the East; fur traders William and Milton Sublette; David Edward Jackson for whom Jackson Hole, Wyoming, is named; and Jim Beckwourth,[1] an African-American born into slavery, freed by his master, and who at one time – believe it or not – was the Chief of the Crow Nation.

In addition, there were ninety-four others on that expedition, a group known at the time as Ashley's One Hundred.

Oh, and lest we forget, the man behind Jim Bridger's earlier mentioned regret, frontiersman Hugh Glass, whose incredible tale of survival in the wilderness has been the subject of two Hollywood movies.[2]

Bridger's achievements during his lifetime include being one of the first white men to see what is now Yellowstone Park with its remarkable scenic beauty, numerous geysers, and colorful hot pots.

He may also have been the first non-Native American to see the Great Salt Lake (around 1824), but he shares the claim with French-Canadian trapper Étienne Provost, who may have been first, but proof has been elusive.

In 1843, Jim Bridger and Pierre Luis Vasquez from St. Louis, Missouri built Fort Bridger, one of the earliest trading posts in Wyoming to serve westward-bound pioneers and the U.S. military.

The place known as South Pass is the lowest point on the Continental Divide. It's where the Oregon, California, and Mormon trails converge before once again going their separate ways. Thousands of pioneers and immigrants used that pass during their westward movements.

In 1850, Army Captain Howard Stanbury stopped at Fort Bridger to inquire if there might be a shorter way through the Rockies.

Bridger went looking and found one, a more southerly route known today as Bridger's Pass. It shaved sixty miles off the original Oregon Trail and became the route for the Union Pacific Railroad, and much later, the route for U.S. Interstate 80.

Bridger was successful in blazing the Bridger Trail through Wyoming to the Montana gold fields. He was also a successful army scout during Red Cloud's War. But, he was unsuccessful in collecting back rent from the federal government for its use of Fort Bridger, proving once again that some things never change.

Besides being one of America's most prolific trail blazers, Bridger was a masterful story teller. He could be convincing, as he was when telling gullible Easterners about places where petrified trees graced the sides of glass mountains. "And would you believe," he would say in a voice oozing credibility, "that there were petrified birds in the petrified trees warbling petrified songs."

He loved stringing children and adults along by telling of the time he was pursued by an angry Cheyenne war party only to find himself hopelessly trapped in a box canyon with hundreds of tomahawk-wielding, whooping, hollerin' Indians, drawing ever, ever, ever, ever, closer. Then he'd suddenly stop as if in deep thought and wait for someone to ask the inevitable, "What happened next, Mr. Bridger?" To which, without so much as a wink, he'd reply, "They killed me."

But there was one story that Jim Bridger never told, nor liked to be asked about. A true story that he relived over and over in his mind until the day he died. It happened during that first expedition when mountain man Hugh Glass, almost died, but didn't.

Early in the expedition as Glass was scouting ahead of the main party, he surprised a mother grizzly with two cubs. The instant he stepped into her territory, she charged, slamming him to the ground, and then she began tearing flesh from his body to feed to her cubs. Glass instinctively grabbed the knife from his belt and tried to fight back.

Each time Glass stabbed at the massive bear, she raked him with her claws, and for a man armed with only a knife, no matter how determined, the outcome will always favor the grizzly.

Glass was badly mauled and barely conscious when Andrew Henry, John Fitzgerald, and Jim Bridger arrived on the scene and killed the grizzly.

Henry, an experienced explorer was certain that Glass's death was inevitable. He asked Fitzgerald and Bridger to remain with their fellow mountain man until he died and could be buried. The two agreed, skinned the grizzly for a burial shroud, dug a grave and waited.

But Glass, although unconscious, continued to breathe.

On the morning of the third day, Fitzgerald and Bridger watched as an Arikara war party appeared in the distance and began moving in their direction.

As the war party drew uncomfortably close, the two men panicked, rolled Glass's still breathing body into the fresh grave, covered him with the bearskin, and kicked dirt and leaves over the grave to hide its presence. Then they hightailed it to the main camp taking Glass's rifle and knife with them, telling everyone that Glass had died.

But Glass didn't die.

Undiscovered by the war party, he eventually regained consciousness and rolled out of his grave.

With some skin over his scalp gone and a few ribs exposed, he set and splinted a broken leg. Then he wrapped the bearskin around his body, and without his gun or knife for protection, he began an amazing 200-mile hobbling-crawl back to Fort Kiowa.

All he could think about, he would later say, was finding the men who had left him to die.

During the trek, he told of awakening to find a grizzly licking his maggot-infested wounds before moving on. Some believe the bear's dining on the maggots may have saved his life by removing or lessening some of the infection.

During the ordeal with no way to kill a deer, or small game, Glass lived on berries, roots and whatever else he could find.

It took him two months to make it to the Cheyenne River where he constructed a raft and floated downstream to Fort Kiowa where he finally received medical help.

Sometime later, Glass came upon Bridger near the mouth of the Bighorn River. The confrontation, as recorded by Philip St. George Cooke[3] in 1830, reads:

> (As Glass) *leaned upon his rifle; his thoughts took a sudden turn. The more guilty object of his revenge had escaped; the pitiful being before him was perhaps the unwilling and persuaded accomplice of his much older companion. Glass said to the boy, 'You have nothing to fear from me, go – you are free – for your youth I forgive you.'*

Bridger died on his farm near Kansas City, Missouri, on July 17, 1881. He is interred at the Mount Washington Cemetery in Independence, Missouri.

---

[1] There is no doubt that Beckwourth once served as the chief of the Crow nation. He claimed that while trapping, he was mistaken for the lost son of a Crow chief, taken to the appropriate Crow village where he stayed, married the daughter a Crow chief, and eventually became the highest-ranking chief of the Crow nation.

[2] The two movies are: *A Man in the Wilderness* (1971), starring Richard Harris, and *The Revenant* (2015), starring Leonardo DiCaprio. The 1971 movie, although based on the story of Hugh Glass, had to use alias names [Hugh Glass = Zack Bass] due to pending litigation at the time.

[3] Cooke, Philip St. George, *Scenes and Adventures*, 1830, p. 139.

The idea of wilderness needs no defense,
it only needs defenders.
Edward Abbey (1927-1989) Environmentalist

John Burns

Born: John Lawrence Burns
One tough ol' bird.
Sept 5, 1793 (Burlington NJ) – Feb 4, 1872 (New York NY)

J OHN BURNS WAS HEAD-STRONG and the subject of an 1864 Bret Harte poem, *John Burns of Gettysburg,* that begins:

> *Have you heard of a story that gossips tell*
> *Of Burns of Gettysburg? No? Ah, well:*
> *Brief is the glory that hero earns,*
> *Briefer the story of poor John Burns:*
> *He was the fellow who won renown –*
> *The only man who didn't back down.*

Burns claimed to be a direct descendant of the Scottish poet, Robert Burns. The claim, whether true or not, was enough to evoke some good-natured teasing by the townsfolk that John typically dismissed with a smile.

But it was also possible to fan the fire inside John's belly, and the townsfolk knew just how far they could needle the old man and remain on his good side.

At nineteen, he fought in the War of 1812.

At the age of fifty-three (1846), he fought in the Mexican-American War.

And now, in the spring of 1863 with the Civil War beginning its third year and John approaching his 70th birthday, he had no trouble telling anyone who would listen that, "Johnny Reb better not step foot in Gettysburg, or else!"

Burns didn't like growing old.

He tried to volunteer for duty with the Union's first call to arms in 1861, right after the opening volleys rattled the dawn at Fort Sumter, but he was told to go home because of his age.

But, instead of going home he traveled to West Chester, Pennsylvania and tried to enlist there, but they sent him packing for the same reason. *John, you crazy ol' buzzard, you're too old for this war. Go home. Get some sleep.*

The Gettysburg town fathers tried to satisfy his urge to fight by handing him the constable's badge. But a few weeks later he was in Washington D.C., once again begging to enlist.

Someone in Washington offered to let him drive a supply wagon, but gee-hawing a wagon in friendly territory wasn't what Burns had in mind. He declined, returned home, and reluctantly pinned the constable badge to his vest.

In June of 1863, Burns was incensed when Confederate Major Jubal A. Early and his troops marched into Gettysburg.

Burns became such a thorn in the side of the Confederates that Major Early had him carried to his own jail and locked up just to get "the ol' coot" out of the way. When the Confederate troops marched out of Gettysburg a few days later, Major Early set Burns free.

Out of jail, but fuming over being jailed by a Confederate Major, Burns arrested every lingering Confederate soldier he could find and dared anyone to try and set them free.

In the early morning hours of July 1, 1863, Burns heard the opening shots of what would become the Battle of Gettysburg, and he knew his town was not going to escape the war.

He had no uniform, so while enduring a blistering rant from his wife, he pulled on his best blue trousers, a waistcoat (vest), a swallow-tail coat with brass buttons, and a high black silk hat.

Thus, dressed as if he were going to church, he threw the strap of his powder horn over his shoulder, grabbed his outdated flintlock musket, told his sobbing wife goodbye, and fell into step with the first Union regiment that came through town, the 150th Pennsylvania Infantry.

During their first marching break, Burns walked up to the commanding officer, Colonel Langhorne Wister, who stared at Burns in his Sunday best and shook his head. Burns returned the stare before asking if he could join the regiment.

"Can you shoot?" asked Colonel Wister.

"Give me a target and you'll soon find out," shot back Burns.

Amidst some good-natured taunting from the soldiers, Colonel Wister told Burns to go to the edge of a wooded area near McPherson's Farm and take up a position.

The Colonel's intent was to get the old man out of the sun and far enough away from the action that he wouldn't get hurt.

It wasn't long before Confederate Colonel Joseph Shelby's Iron Brigade could be heard approaching.

Then, just as the first wave of rebel soldiers crested a distant hill ....

Bam!

The shot came from Burn's old flintlock, and way off in the distance, a Confederate officer leading a group of men slumped in his saddle and rolled slowly from his horse onto the ground.

Burns smiled, licked his thumb, and started to reload his old flintlock when one of the men took it away from him – and handed him a new rifle – one recently taken from a dead Confederate soldier. It was a handsome rifle, custom inlaid with silver along the cheek-piece.

The elderly, oddly-dressed Burns, high black silk hat and all, had proven his worth to the men of the 150th Pennsylvania, and the teasing quietly turned to respect.

During the skirmish with the Iron Brigade, Colonel Wister designated Burns a sharpshooter and he didn't disappoint.

But when a portion of the Union lines gave way to the Confederates, Burns received minor injuries to an arm and leg, preventing him from keeping up with the other men.

Now, isolated from the 150th, he was spotted by several Confederate soldiers who began walking toward him. He buried his rifle and cartridges, made a mental note of his location, and began babbling incoherently.

Clothed in his Sunday best and that tall black silk hat, it didn't take much to convince the rebels he was just a sorry old geezer trying to find the grave of his deceased wife. The soldiers took Burns to their surgeon who patched up his wounds and sent him on his way.

Burns returned to where he buried his rifle and cartridges and hooked up with another Union outfit, the 7th Wisconsin Regiment. With the 7th, he continued his march into the history books as one of the stranger stories of the Civil War.

When Lincoln arrived in Gettysburg on November 19, 1863 to deliver his famous address, he asked to meet with Burns.

The President took the old man by the arm and the two took a brief walk, chattering away like a couple of magpies.

The walk with the president that day assured that Burns' fame would go well beyond Gettysburg.

That's because a year later, poet Bret Harte would write a poem as you now know, about the stubborn old Scotsman from Gettysburg, and in the next to last verse, reminiscent of the Roman patriot-citizen, Lucius Quinctius Cincinnatus,[1] he wrote:

> *So raged the battle. You know the rest:*
> *How the rebels, beaten and backward pressed.*
> *Broke at the final charge, and ran.*
> *At which John Burns – a practical man –*
> *Shouldered his rifle, unbent his brows,*
> *And then went back to his bees and cows.*

There is a statue of John Burns standing proudly atop a battlefield boulder at Gettysburg National Military Park. It shows Burns with a tightly clenched left fist, a defiant look, and in his right hand, a rifle inlaid with silver along the cheek-piece.

John Burns is buried at Gettysburg, one of only two graves at that hallowed cemetery with permission to fly the American flag twenty-four hours a day.

The other grave so honored is that of Virginia "Ginnie" Wade,[2] the only civilian killed during the Battle of Gettysburg.

---

[1] *Stories from History's Dust Bin* (additional reading):
Vol 2, May 13:   Lucius Cincinnatus with the Society of the Cincinnati

[2] For a well-researched and very readable historical novel about Virginia "Ginnie" Wade and others of Gettysburg, pick up *The Calm and the Strife*, co-authored by David J. Sloat and John W. Sloat, published by CCP Publishing, British Columbia, Canada.

> *There is no honorable way to kill,*
> *no gentle way to destroy.*
> Abraham Lincoln (1809-1865) 16th U.S. President

George Carlin

Born: George Denis Patrick Carlin
Prodigious ponderer
May 12, 1937 (Manhattan NY) – June 22, 2008 (Santa Monica CA)

G EORGE CARLIN'S MIND worked differently than everyone else's on the planet, and that's because he saw situations and people in ways that the rest of us just don't think about.

For instance, here's what he had to say about Thomas Edison and the invention of the electric light.

When Thomas Edison worked late into the night on the electric light, he had to do it by gas lamp or candle. I'm sure it made the work seem that much more urgent.

There have been several George Carlin's over the years and that's because Carlin and his comedy wasn't static. Carlin's act was in a constant state of evolution, keeping pace with the times.

There was social critic Carlin, who poked fun at society, blending his several alter-egos together so seamlessly that it didn't matter your politics, he was just plain funny.

Then, there was comedian Carlin who found ways to poke fun at everything, and those who came to see him laughed just as hard as those who paid to see social critic Carlin.

Was he good?

He is second on Comedy Central's list of the 100 greatest stand-up comics, right behind Richard Pryor. He was a frequent guest host for Johnny Carson's *Tonight Show*; he was the first host of *Saturday Night Live* (October 11, 1975); he received a Hollywood Walk of Fame star in 1987; he was inducted into the Comedy Hall of Fame in 1994; and in 2008 he received the Mark Twain Prize for American Humor.

Unfortunately, George died four days after his selection was announced, making him the only honoree to receive the award posthumously.

After three lackluster starts at three Catholic high schools in New York, he shelved his high school education.

Then, as soon as he was old enough to do so, he joined the U.S. Air Force, received training as a radar technician, and was sent to Barksdale Air Force Base in Louisiana for duty.

Now, and this may be hard to believe, but his military record is even less distinguished than his high school record.

Not long after arriving at Barksdale, he walked off the base and into a Shreveport radio station, applied for a job, got it, was soon designated an unproductive airman by the military and discharged.

During his incredibly brief stint in the military, he stood before three military courts for breaches of military discipline and was the recipient of more non-judicial punishments than we have time – or space – or interest – to list here.

Out of kindness, let's just say the military wasn't a good career fit for George.

In 1959, he and disk jockey Jack Burns formed a comedy team, and they found immediate success in one of Fort Worth's coffeehouses, *The Cellar.* A couple of years later, the duo headed for California. There, they honed their offbeat comedy in beatnik[1] coffeehouses and by working at radio station KDAY in Hollywood. After a couple of successful years, Carlin and Burns parted on friendly terms to pursue alternative goals.

Carlin appeared on several television variety shows, and as the old saying goes, the rest is history. Folks old enough to remember 1960s – 70s television will recall the nasal monotone voice of one of Carlin's best-known characters, Al Sleet, the hippy-dippy weatherman:

The weather forecast for tonight: Dark. Continued dark overnight with widely scattered light by morning.

Sometime during the 1970's, Carlin's dress and routines changed, and he took on the edgy persona of the hip generation.[2]

While many comedians of the era (Flip Wilson,[3] the Smothers Brothers, Dan Rowan, Dick Martin, Jerry Seinfeld, and others) generally appeared in relatively conservative attire,

Carlin strolled to the microphone in faded blue jeans, long hair and beard, beads and earrings, and an oddly detached psyche.

Today's grandparents will remember the weird vacant look in Carlin's eyes when he appeared on television.

Sometimes his humor was sharp-edged and tipped with venom, and at other times it was just very, very funny, but always spot on with the times and the culture.

For instance, about bumper stickers, he said he would like to see one that said: *We are the proud parents of a child whose self-esteem is sufficient that he doesn't need us promoting his minor scholastic achievements on the bumper of our car.*

It wasn't just the absurdity of a very long bumper sticker that made Carlin's message funny; it was that he said aloud, what everyone else only imagined themselves saying.

He made us smile and laugh at ourselves.

Carlin's comedy covered hundreds of daily situations, each simmered to perfection in the cauldron of his unique genius.

Here's a dozen thoughts from the matchless mind of George Carlin:

- Think of how stupid the average person is, and then realize that half of them are even stupider than that.
- I was thinking about how people read the Bible a whole lot more the older they get; then it dawned on me. They're cramming for finals.
- Atheism is a non-prophet religion.
- The reason Santa is so jolly is because he knows where all the bad girls live.
- Ever wonder about those people who spend $2 apiece on those little bottles of Evian water? Try spelling Evian backwards.
- I went into a bookstore and asked the saleswoman, 'Where's the self-help section?' She said that if she told me, it would defeat the purpose.
- One can never know for sure what a deserted island looks like.
- I'm always relieved when someone is delivering a eulogy and I'm listening to it.

- Was George Washington's brother, Lawrence, the Uncle of Our Country?
- No one who has had 'Taps' played for them has ever been able to hear it.
- The Golden Gate Bridge should have a long bungee cord for people who aren't quite ready to commit suicide, but want to get in a little practice.
- Here's the main reason we can't have the *Ten Commandments* posted in a courthouse: You cannot post, 'Thou shalt not steal,' 'Thou shalt not commit adultery,' and 'Thou shalt not lie' in a building full of lawyers, judges, and politicians, as it creates a hostile work environment.

George Carlin died June 22, 2008 of heart failure.

He had performed the previous week at the Orleans Hotel and Casino in Las Vegas.

In accordance with his last wishes, his body was cremated, and his ashes scattered in front of various nightclubs in New York and elsewhere.

---

[1] beatnik: a member of the *Beat Generation,* recognizable by long, unkempt hair, ill-fitting clothes, communal living, and a contempt for regular work.

[2] hip generation: slang, from the *hippie* subculture, often defined as someone with a defiant attitude toward established values, expressed externally by displaying beads, well-worn clothing, headbands, and a detached-from-reality attitude.

[3] *Stories from History's Dust Bin* (additional reading):
    Vol 3, Dec 8:   Featuring Flip Wilson

Trying to be happy by accumulating possessions is like trying to satisfy hunger by taping sandwiches all over your body.
George Carlin (1937-2008) Comedian

Joshua Chamberlain

Born: Joshua Lawrence Chamberlain
The knightliest soldier of the Civil War.
Sept 8, 1828 (Brewer ME) – Feb 24, 1914 (Portland ME)

P RESENT ON THE horrific killing field known as Little
Round Top, just two miles from the battle at
Gettysburg, stood Joshua Chamberlain, a general in the Union
Army. Except for the fact that he seemed impossible to kill, he
is best remembered for something he did around noon on April
12, 1865.

That one thing had nothing to do with the Congressional
Medal of Honor he received for his defense of Little Round Top;
nor for the strategy he employed to delay Confederate General
John B. Hood from continuing his march toward Washington.

Neither did it have anything to do with the fact that,
depending on which historian you read, he had from three to six
horses shot out from under him in battle, or anything to do with
the six wounds he sustained in battle.

Nor did it have anything to do with three different Joshua
Chamberlain obituaries, appearing on three different dates, two
of which were premature.

Instead, that one thing was for something that happened just
minutes before Lee surrendered to Grant.[1] Something that most
of Chamberlain's men didn't want to do, but did because he
ordered them to do it. Something that has required the passage
of time to fully appreciate. It was also something that when
viewed through the lens of great military decisions, has elevated
Chamberlain's stature as a man of remarkable sensitivity and
vision.

Although born with a speech impediment, Chamberlain was
a highly respected professor of languages at Bowdoin College
in Brunswick, Maine. He was also known for the awareness he
had of his personal limitations, a quality not always associated
with college professors or military generals.

He was a thoughtful decision-maker, and when he decided
on a course of action, he was difficult to dissuade. Some called

the trait "mule-headedness," while Chamberlain would prefer something along the lines of "being determine and steadfast."

Such was the case with the Civil War in which his intellect told him the cause of the Union was just, and he wrote a letter to Governor Israel Washburn of Maine, which read in part:

> *I fear, this war, so costly of blood and treasure, will not cease until men of the North are willing to leave good positions, and sacrifice the dearest personal interests, to rescue our country from desolation, and defend the national existence against treachery.*

His letter to Governor Washburn, which was shared with Bowdoin's president, wasn't appreciated. And when he asked the college president for a leave of absence from his professorship to join the Union Army, he got his leave of absence all right, but not to join the army. He was told to travel abroad for two years, ostensibly to refine his knowledge of foreign languages. He spoke ten fluently.

Chamberlain, always the gentleman, thanked the college president for his time, and quietly closed the door behind him.

Then he walked briskly from the college campus to the recruiting office. There, when offered the rank of a full colonel in the Union army, he turned it down. According to his biographer, John J. Pullen, the reason for his declination was to allow himself time to "start a little lower and learn the (military) business first."

The decision was typical Chamberlain.

Once enlisted, he buried himself in a study of military protocol and war strategies and on August 8, 1862, he was promoted to Lieutenant Colonel of the 20th Regiment. It was a rank below what the fellow at the recruiting office had offered, but as was his approach to life, he accepted the rank with a smile, and without further discussion or question.

The 20th Regiment went on to fight twenty campaigns from the Battle of Fredericksburg (December 11-15, 1862), where he and his men survived by stacking the bodies of frozen comrades to form a shelter against the sub-zero weather; to the Battle of

Gettysburg where estimates of casualties for both sides range from 46,000 to 51,000.

In 1864, during the Siege of Petersburg, Lieutenant Colonel Chamberlain was shot through both hips, a wound that should have taken his life. As he lay on the ground bleeding, General Ulysses S. Grant, not believing his officer could survive his wounds, granted him a field-promotion to Brigadier General.

Chamberlain, however, did survive and with his new rank, was assigned to lead the 1st Brigade of the 1st Division of V Corps.

Incidentally this event, with everyone including General Grant certain that Chamberlain's death was imminent, led to the first of three newspaper obituaries of his death.

On a second occasion, a rebel soldier had Chamberlain in his sights and pulled the trigger. The instant the hammer struck the powder, Chamberlain's horse reared, and the ball passed through the horse's neck, striking a leather-bound book and mirror that Chamberlain kept in his breast pocket. Although slowed down by the book and mirror, the ball continued through Chamberlain's ribcage and exited his back without hitting a single vital organ, ending its flight with a dull *thwack* against the sidearm of his military aide.

Chamberlain, who had fallen with his horse, slowly regained his composure laying – and then sitting up – in a deep pool of horse blood.

Aware that his men needed help, he urged the fatally-wounded animal to its feet, remounted, and rode until the horse literally ran out of blood and toppled over, dead.

When Chamberlain looked up, he was surrounded by three Confederate soldiers with fixed bayonets.

Without missing a beat, and with a uniform so thoroughly soaked in horse blood that it was unrecognizable, he stood up and yelled to his captors, "Don't you know who I am? Don't you see those Yanks that are almost upon us?" And with that, he led the three rebels into the Union lines where they were taken captive.

This incident of last being seen lying in a pool of blood beneath his horse found its way to the press where it became his second obituary.

But the thing mentioned up front, for which Chamberlain would be most remembered by history, an event that invoked the ire of most of his men at the time of Lee's surrender to Grant, was this . . . .

As General Lee lined up his exhausted men, men who expected the ultimate in humiliation, to march with their heads held high toward Appomattox Court House and to surrender themselves and their weapons, General Chamberlain had already ordered his men to stand smartly at attention, and to hold a salute[2] until the last of the defeated Confederate soldiers had marched past.

It was an act that led Confederate General John B. Gordon to refer to Union General Joshua Chamberlain in his memoirs[3] as "one of the knightliest soldiers of the federal army."

General Chamberlain's third and final obituary appeared when his body finally gave out in Portland, Maine, on February 24, 1914, at the age of eighty-five.

---

[1] *Stories from History's Dust Bin* (additional reading):
>   Vol 1, Mar 26:   U. S. Grant with Old Abe, the War Bird
>   Vol 1, Apr 27:   Featuring Ulysses S. Grant
>   Vol 2, Jun 25:   U. S. Grant with George A. Custer
>   Vol 2, Jul 3:   U. S. Grant with James I. Waddell

[2] Some accounts simply state a "salute," or "military salute," others refer to the salute as being either a "marching salute," or a "carry arms salute," the latter two types meaning a salute in which a soldier's rifle is held in his right hand and positioned perpendicular to the right shoulder.

[3] Gordon, John Brown, *Reminiscences of the Civil War,* (Scribner/Martin & Hoyt, 1904). Reprints widely available from internet book sellers.

We fought no better, perhaps, than they.
We exhibited, perhaps, no higher individual qualities.
Joshua Chamberlain (1828-1914) General

Christmas Eve Truce, A

There'll be no killing at my house!
Dec 24, 1944 (Ardennes Forest, German-Belgium border)

THERE'S A WELL-KNOWN STORY about a Christmas Day truce that took place in 1914, just six months into World War I, when thousands of German and Allied (British, Belgium, and French) troops were engaged in a ferocious battle along the war's Western Front.[1]

That unofficial truce is recognized as a wartime miracle, an extraordinary event that brought a day of peace into a conflict that would eventually claim over ten million lives. Although not all historians agree as to what brought the warring factions together, most accounts suggest it started with the singing of hymns.

One account tells of a squad of British soldiers gathering their dead and hearing German soldiers in the distance singing "Stille Nacht" (Silent Night). Then, after returning with their deceased comrades, of themselves singing "O Come, All Ye Faithful," and then hearing the same hymn sung by Germans in the original Latin, "Adeste Fideles."

Cautiously at first, soldiers from both sides began singing together, and by daybreak, German and Allied soldiers up and down the Western Front were exchanging token gifts and even playing soccer together. When nightfall came, the men returned to their respective lines and the fighting resumed.

That event, and the hundreds of stories that grew out of that one-day unofficial truce, has been the subject of many books, a few movies, and even a memorial.

The 1969 film *Oh! What a Lovely War* includes a scene showing British and German soldiers enjoying the Christmas truce. The 2005 French film, *Joyeux Noël,* tells the story of the truce through the eyes of British, French, and German soldiers; and in 2008, a memorial to the Christmas truce was dedicated in Frelinghien, France.

Then, exactly thirty years later there was another unofficial Christmas truce, this one near the end of World War II. But unlike the event of 1914 that involved roughly 100,000 soldiers, the truce of 1944 involved only seven soldiers, a woman, a small boy, and a warm miracle on a cold night.

This is that story.

On Christmas Eve, 1944, Elisabeth Vincken's husband, a cook in the German army, left his wife and young son Fritz in a small shack well-hidden in the heavily-wooded Ardennes Forest near the Belgium-German border. Elisabeth had already lost her eldest son in the Battle of Stalingrad and the hurt from his death was never far from her heart.

Only a few miles from that small shack raged one of the deadliest battles of World War II, the infamous forty-day *Battle of the Bulge* that cost a combined total of 36,528 Allied and German lives and left 84,493 wounded soldiers in its wake.

There was no love between the two warring factions.

The night was bitter cold, the forest dense, and the terrain difficult, a combination of factors that caused soldiers on both sides of the conflict to become lost, as happened that night.

That's when Elisabeth heard a knock at the door.

Cautiously opening the door and peering into the darkness, she saw two very cold American soldiers on the porch, and a third, a severely injured soldier shivering uncontrollably in the snow.

The soldiers asked if they could come inside.

Contrary to explicit German orders, which included a summary execution for anyone found harboring the enemy, Elisabeth ushered them in and asked her son, Fritz, to bring Hermann, the family rooster inside.

Hermann would be their Christmas Eve dinner, she implied, sending Fritz on a second errand to return with five potatoes.

As Elisabeth was working in the kitchen, there came another knock at the door. With his mother busy, and assuming it was more lost Americans, Fritz opened the door.

Standing on the porch were four cold German soldiers who, like the Americans, had become separated from their unit. They asked Fritz if they could come in.

Elisabeth, hearing German being spoken, rushed past Fritz and into the doorway. The soldiers told Elisabeth they were lost and hungry, asking if they could come inside to get warm.

Elisabeth said, "Yes, but others are inside that you will not consider friends."

The Germans, who knew the enemy had been seen in the area, asked sharply, "Americans?"

Elisabeth didn't hesitate, but responded in the affirmative.

The atmosphere was tense with the Americans inside the home, but out of sight of the Germans, and both groups armed and wary of what could happen. That's when Elisabeth firmly ordered everyone to lay down their weapons.

When it was apparent that one of the Germans was reluctant to comply, Elisabeth said, sharply: "Es ist die Heilige Nacht und es warden keine tötung hier!" meaning, *It is the Holy Night and there will be no killing in my house!*

Amazingly, everyone, including the reluctant German soldier complied with the woman's demand, stacking their weapons where they stood. The Americans stacking theirs near the kitchen; the Germans stacking theirs near the front door.

Elisabeth, not satisfied with the arrangement, told both groups to mix their weapons together in a single pile, giving neither side an advantage.

Although the men grudgingly complied, it was the smell of Hermann roasting in the oven that brought about a change in attitude and the differently-uniformed men began to relax.

One of the Americans opened a pack of cigarettes, offering one to each of the Germans before taking one for himself. That was followed by one of the Germans asking others of his group to remove some rations from their backpacks. The gathered rations were handed to Elisabeth with instructions that they be added to the dinner under preparation.

The initial concern on both sides soon lessened and the once stern faces gradually melted into friendly smiles. One of the Germans, a medic, went to where the wounded American was lying on the floor and quietly began rendering medical aid.

The others gathered to watch and help when they could.

Elisabeth waited until the medic had finished bandaging his patient before she announced that dinner was ready.

The meal wasn't served until Elisabeth prayed over the food, and it's a good guess that her eyes weren't the only ones bleary with tears as she asked the Lord to bless her family, the food, and her Christmas guests – all of them.

Before the night was over, everyone had sung Christmas carols, jointly in English and German before falling asleep under the same roof.

In the morning two of the German soldiers went outside, and with branches cut from a tree, constructed a sturdy litter for carrying the injured American soldier.

When it was time for the soldiers to leave, the German's being more familiar with the area, not only marked up an American map with the safest route to return to their lines, but gave the Americans a compass as well.

Both groups thanked and hugged Elisabeth and Fritz for their hospitality, then together they retrieved their weapons and parted ways.

The unofficial truce of 1944 was over, but not before the humanity within each human soul was once again revealed, if only for a night.

[1] *Stories from History's Dust Bin* (additional reading):
    Vol 3, Dec 25:   Featuring an Unofficial Christmas Day Truce

> *Peace on earth will come to stay,*
> *when we live Christmas every day.*
> Helen Steiner Rice (1900-1981) Author

Grover Cleveland

Born: Stephen Grover Cleveland
A president of firsts – and a few oddities.
Mar 18, 1837 (Caldwell NJ) – June 24, 1908 (Princeton NJ)

T HERE WAS A TIME in American politics when a candidate's moral fiber and integrity were considered important assets for the highest office in the land.

When Grover Cleveland was presented the opportunity to purchase documents with compromising information on James G. Blaine, his political opponent, he bought them, but only on the condition there were no remaining copies, and then he personally set fire to them.

Grover Cleveland was a president of integrity.

He was also a president of *firsts* and *onlys*.

He was the *first* Democrat to become president after the Civil War, a party drought of twenty-eight years: Lincoln (Rep), Johnson (Nat'l Union), Grant (Rep), Hayes (Rep), Garfield (Rep), Arthur (Rep), Cleveland (Dem).

He was the *only* president to win the popular vote during three consecutive elections, in 1884, 1888, and 1892.

However, although he won the popular vote in 1888, he failed to win the all-important electoral college,[1] and thus lost to his opponent, Benjamin Harrison.

In 1892, he made a third bid for the White House, this time defeating Harrison by winning both the popular vote and the electoral college and thus the election.

Cleveland is the *only* president to serve two non-consecutive terms as president, making him the 22nd (1884) and 24th (1892) president.

He was the *first* president to use that new-fangled invention, the telephone, in the White House.

He is the *only* U.S. president to have personally carried out an execution, and he carried out two of them.[2] The executions were for two men convicted of murder, and were performed by hanging during his time as the sheriff of Erie County, New York, prior to his election to the presidency.

Cleveland's trip to the White House was most unusual.

He was elected with the combined support of Democrats and the reform wing of the Republican Party, political activists known as the Mugwumps,[3] who refused to support their own party's nominee, James G. Blaine.

Cleveland, a bachelor when he was elected president, was accustomed to a single man's uncomplicated way doing things.

If he could have done so, he would have eliminated most of the amenities associated with his 1600 Pennsylvania Avenue residence.

He once sent a letter to a long-time friend in which he complained, "I must go now to dinner. But I wish it was to eat a pickled herring on a Swiss cheese sandwich and a chop at Louie's, instead of the French stuff I shall find on my table."

As a 49-year-old bachelor when elected to his first term, he was the *first* and thus far, the *only* president to be married in the White House. His bride was Frances Folsom, a girl who had lived with the Cleveland family following the death of her father when she was a child of eleven.

Later, when it came time for her to graduate from Wells College, she and Grover announced their engagement.

Five days later, the couple exchanged vows inside the White House at a small ceremony attended by relatives, a few close friends, and members of the cabinet and their wives.

At the age of twenty-one, Frances Folsom Cleveland became the youngest-ever First Lady.

Grover Cleveland may have been a Democrat and he may have had some unusual Republican friends, but he wasn't afraid to anger either side. He was his own man and he didn't mind letting people know where he stood.

He supported a minority group that called themselves the Bourbon Democrats, a pro-business group opposed to high protective tariffs, much to the disdain of his party.

He also opposed farm subsidies and vigorously worked to bar special favors to any economic group.

He once vetoed a bill to appropriate $10,000 to distribute seed to drought-stricken farmers in Texas, explaining his actions by saying, "Federal aid encourages the expectation of paternal care on the part of the government and weakens the sturdiness of our national character."

He vetoed numerous private pension bills to Civil War veterans whose claims he believed were fraudulent, and when Congress passed a bill to provide pensions for veterans with non-military service disabilities, Cleveland vetoed that bill as well.

He angered the railroads by ordering an investigation of western lands held by federal grants and, based on its findings, he forced the railroads to return 81 million acres back to the states.

He riled the unions. When striking railroad employees violated an injunction, Cleveland sent federal troops in to enforce it. "If it takes the entire army and navy of the United States to deliver a single postcard to Chicago," he thundered, "that card will be delivered!"

In 1887, he asked Congress to reduce the country's high trade tariffs. His own party raised a fuss that doing so would give the Republicans an effective issue for the campaign of 1888. His face reddened and nearly exploded with anger, "What's the use of being elected or re-elected unless you stand for something?"

The people loved Cleveland's "plain talk" even if politicians from both sides of the Washington swamp, didn't.

But, the tariff issue cost Cleveland the 1888 election, primarily because of heavy voter turnout in the industrial states who believed a lower tariff would cost them their jobs.

Although Cleveland won the popular vote (49% to 47%), the electoral college-rich Northeast carried Benjamin Harrison into the White House.

On the way out the door, First Lady Frances Cleveland suggested to the White House staff – and thus surreptitiously to the incoming president – that they not make any bold changes to the décor as she and Grover would be back.

She was right.

Four years later Cleveland faced Harrison in a rematch and won.

[1] *Stories from History's Dust Bin* (additional reading):

Vol 1, Apr 4:	Electoral College with William Henry Harrison
Vol 3, Oct 4:	Electoral College with Rutherford B. Hayes
Vol 3, Dec 14:	Electoral College with Joseph Lane

[2] In 1872, Cleveland executed Patrick Morrissey, who was convicted of stabbing his widowed mother to death; and a year later he executed John Gaffney, who was convicted of killing a man during a drunken rage.

[3] Mugwump: Historically, a term referring to independent voters, depicted in cartoons as a bird "sitting on the fence" with its *mug* on one side, and its *wump* on the other.

The ship of Democracy, which has weathered all storms,
may sink through the mutiny of those aboard.
Grover Cleveland (1837-1908) 22nd and 24th U.S. President

Bob Cummings

Born: Charles Clarence Cummings, Jr.
Pilot, patriot, and Hollywood icon
June 9, 1910 (Joplin MO) – Dec 2, 1990 (Woodland Hills CA)

BORN JUST SEVEN YEARS after Orville Wright[1] made history as the first to successfully fly a powered, heavier-than-air aircraft, Bob Cummings would enjoy a lifelong feeling of kinship with the aviation pioneer. In fact, and in a very personal way, Orville Wright would become a part of Bob Cummings' persona, and interestingly, the relationship began before Bob was born.

It happened when Orville Wright arrived in Joplin, Missouri, in early 1910 with a case of "barber's itch," a folksy term for an irritating staph infection caused when the shaved hairs of the face curl into the skin, instead of outward.

Orville couldn't have chosen a better doctor.

Dr. Charles Clarence Cummings was one of the earliest physicians to realize the efficacy of treating skin diseases with ultraviolet rays. His 1910's high-tech treatment cured Orville's infection and a bond was formed between America's most famous aviator and the small-town physician.

A few months later, Ruth Cummings gave birth to Charles Clarence Cummings, Jr., who would someday become a skilled pilot like his father's famous friend. He would also become one of America's most recognizable Hollywood personalities as actor Bob Cummings.

But the transition from *Charles* Cummings Jr. to actor *Bob* Cummings was still decades away.

Charles grew up listening to his father talk about Orville and dreaming about becoming a pilot. The dream grew wings when Joplin plumber James Cooper asked if Mr. Henley's high school auto mechanics class would be interested in overhauling the engine of his TravelAir biplane. They were, and they did.

When finished with the project, Mr. Cooper treated Charles to a flight and with money earned selling sodas at a local drug store, Charles paid the Joplin plumber to teach him to fly.

On March 3, 1927, after only 3¼ hours of flight instruction, Cooper told Charles to "take 'er up alone, you're ready."

Charles taxied up and down the runway several times to gain a feel for the controls and to build up his courage. Then, turning into the wind at the far end of the runway, he revved the engine, released the brake, and seconds later pulled back on the stick to discover the thrill of solo flight that pilot/poet John Gillespie Magee[2] would describe fourteen years later, *Oh! I have slipped the surly bonds of Earth and danced the skies on laughter-silvered wings....*

After graduating from high school in 1928, Charles briefly attended Joplin Business College and Drury College, both in Springfield, Missouri, before enrolling at the Carnegie Institute of Technology in Pittsburgh, Pennsylvania, to study mechanical engineering.

Then came the stock market crash of 1929, destroying his family's financial resources and dashing his hopes of becoming an engineer.

His roommate at Carnegie was Frank Crenshaw, an aspiring actor. When Frank asked Charles to drive him to New York to audition for acceptance at the American Academy of Dramatic Arts, Charles did so.

While Frank was auditioning, Charles was approached and invited to audition as well. The Academy, having signed a full complement of aspiring actresses, needed additional male students to balance the enrollment numbers. To sweeten the deal, the Academy offered $14 per week to defray student costs, a godsend to Charles who was broke without a job.

After two years at the Academy, and with Broadway in need of British actors, Charles went to England to study speech inflections and cultural mannerisms, returning to America as Blade Stanhope Conway.

When Broadway didn't need a Brit, as with the *Ziegfeld Follies of 1934,* he became American actor Brice Hutchins.

And when he moved to Hollywood, believing that neither of his alter-egos were quite right for the movies, he *<ahhh>* developed a drawl, adopted a few western *<ahhh shucks>* idiosyncrasies, and *<yup>* marketed himself as Bruce Hutchins from the great state of Texas.

But, after a few bit-parts, Bruce went the way of Brice and Blade, and Charles Clarence Cummings Jr., *legally* changed his given name to Robert, becoming *Bob Cummings*. Make a mental note of this *legal* action as you'll soon learn there was yet another element to Cummings' name change.

His film debut in 1935 as Judge Davis's hotheaded stepson in *The Virginia Judge,* proved to Hollywood that Cummings wasn't just another actor, but one with potential star power.

In 1939, he achieved bona fide star status with the release of *Three Smart Girls Grow Up,* where he played the love interest of Hollywood darling Deanna Durbin.

In 1942, like thespian patriots Eddie Albert, Martha Raye,[3] Robert Stack, Jimmy Stewart, and others, he enlisted in the military, where he served as a pilot and flight instructor.

In 1952, he began a long career on television.

It started with *My Hero,* a comedy in which he played a well-meaning but bumbling real-estate agent named Robert Beanblossom who required constant rescuing by his secretary.

Then, in the for-television version of *Twelve Angry Men,* he played Juror #8, the role made famous by Henry Fonda in the film version, and Cummings won an Emmy for his performance as a lead actor.

From 1955 to 1962, he starred in *The Bob Cummings Show,* a sitcom that played for years afterward in reruns titled *Love That Bob.* Cummings played bachelor Bob Collins, a former World War II pilot turned professional photographer. The show featured an endless stream of lovely ladies and flirtatious situations that gently pushed the boundaries of 1950s television.

In the mid-1960s, Cummings co-starred with Julie Newmar in *My Living Doll,* the story of a womanizing Air Force psychiatrist whose mission it was to teach a naïve female robot (Newmar) how to act like a woman, without letting the world in on the secret.

Now, remember when we said that Bob Cummings enjoyed a lifelong feeling of kinship with Orville Wright, and in a very personal way became one with him?

Well, when Charles Clarence Cummings Jr. *legally* became Robert "Bob" Cummings back in the 1930s, he had the court change his middle name as well, to Robert Orville Cummings, in honor of his father's friend, and his personal hero, Orville Wright.

Was Bob Cummings a pilot worthy of Orville's name? In 1938, the first year of flight instructor licensing, the very first civilian flight instructor certificate (No. 00001) was issued to 28-year-old Robert O. Cummings.

Bob Cummings became an American icon. He was part of Disneyland's grand opening in 1955; he hosted the 15th Anniversary Celebration of Walt Disney World in 1986; and his final public appearance was at Disneyland's 35th Anniversary Special in 1990.

His personal life was dotted with five marriages and seven children, two of whom have stretched their wings in the theater.

His son Tony is an actor and writer, known for *Another World* (1964), *Santa Barbara* (1984), and *3 Geezers* (2013).

His daughter Melinda starred in the Latter-day Saint (Mormon) Church production of *Pioneers and Petticoats* (1969). She afterward forewent an acting career to marry college professor Dr. Kim Cameron and to raise a family.

Cummings died on December 2, 1990, at the Motion Picture and Television Hospital in Woodland Hills, California.

He was eighty years young.

[1] *Stories from History's Dust Bin* (additional reading):
  Vol 1, Feb 8:   Orville Wright with Thomas E. Selfridge
  Vol 2, Aug 22:   Orville Wright with Raymonde de Laroche
  Vol 3, Dec 3:   Orville Wright with Richard Pearse

[2] John Gillespie Magee (1922-1941), Royal Canadian Air Force pilot and author of the sonnet, *High Flight*.

[3] When near death, a special act allowed Martha Raye a burial at Arlington, but her preference was Fort Bragg, where she was laid to rest with full military honors as an *honorary colonel* in the U.S. Marines, and as an *honorary lieutenant colonel* in the U.S. Army. She is the only civilian buried at Ft. Bragg to receive military honors each Veterans' Day.

Family is not an important thing. It's everything.
Michael J. Fox (1961-) Actor

Rodney Dangerfield
Born: Jacob Cohen
He lacked respect, but lived with a lot of it.
Nov 22, 1921 (Deer Park NY) – Oct 5, 2004 (Westwood CA)

IF EVER THERE was a guy who "never got no respect," it was aluminum-siding salesman turned stand-up comedian Rodney Dangerfield.[1]

That's right, Dangerfield reportedly sold aluminum-siding before molding his carefully crafted alter-ego into America's best-known nobody and launching himself into a long and successful career as a lonely loser.

But like many others who made it big in show business, his was neither a comfortable childhood nor an easy trip into the overcrowded world of entertainment.

When I was born, I was so ugly the doctor slapped my mother.

Dangerfield, born Jacob Cohen, was the son of vaudevillian Philip Cohen (stage name: Phil Roy) and Hungarian immigrant, Dorothy "Dotty" Teitelbaum, but his wasn't much of a family. Curious about his ancestors, he conducted genealogical research into his family background.

I once checked my family tree and found three dogs using it.

Not satisfied with the results of his personal efforts, he hired an independent research firm to dig deeper into his family lines. That's when his worst fear was confirmed.

I've just learned I'm the sap in the family tree.

His only memory of a family vacation was when, as a young lad, his parents took him to the beach. It was wonderful, he recalled, until he realized he was hopelessly lost. He was relieved to see a lifeguard approaching him.

Do you think we'll ever find my mommy and daddy?
I don't know, replied the lifeguard,
there are so many places they can hide.

Jacob and his sister Marion rarely saw their father, and after becoming successful, Dangerfield admitted to his audience that he only saw his father once or twice a year before the old man stopped coming around altogether.

I once asked my father if I could go ice-skating on the lake.
He told me, let's wait 'til it gets warmer.

At fifteen, Jacob was earning extra money selling gags to a couple of local comics. He also worked as a singing waiter in a restaurant, and he performed, when he could get a gig, as a stand-up comedian using the stage name Jack Roy.

He joked with his audiences about his obscurity as a comedian, and how far out of town he had to go to find work.

I played one nightclub that was so far out,
my act was reviewed in 'Field & Stream.'

The review apparently served as a wake-up call. That's when he realized his future as an entertainer was going nowhere. So, he quit show business to sell paint.

That's when he realized he had become a has-been without ever becoming a somebody.

I dropped out of show business once, but nobody noticed.

In 1949, he married his first wife, Joyce, and they had two children. They divorced in 1962 and remarried in 1963.

About the relationship, he once confided to his audience the lengths that he and Joyce had taken to save their marriage:

We sleep in separate rooms, we have dinner apart,
and we take separate vacations.
We're doing everything we can to keep our marriage together.

But the marriage didn't stay together, and Jacob and Joyce divorced a second time in 1970. That's when he took a long hard look at his act and determined it was pretty much like everyone else's stand-up act, and he concluded that ....

My problem is that I appeal to everyone
that can do me absolutely no good.

.... and that's when he decided it was time to make some changes. He needed to become someone with whom everyone could relate.

Tucked away in the back of his mind was an old Jack Benny[2] radio show he remembered listening to, in which an uninspiring wannabe cowboy complained that all he wanted out of life was a little respect.

That's when Jacob Cohen, who early in his career performed as Jack Roy, officially became Rodney Dangerfield, a nervous-appearing comedian who claimed he "never got no respect."

I told my doctor that when I wake up in the morning
I can't stand looking at myself in the mirror.
He said, 'Well, at least we know your vision is perfect.'

Dangerfield's big break came on March 5, 1967, when the Ed Sullivan Show needed a last-minute replacement for an act that had been delayed and wouldn't arrive in time to appear. The previously unknown Dangerfield became an overnight sensation with lines like:

Last week my tie caught on fire.
Some guy tried to put it out with an axe.

In the 1970s, Dangerfield opened his own club in Manhattan named, what else, but "Dangerfield's." Knowing the difficulties in making it big in show business, he was generous to the extreme in providing a venue for unknown comedians. Some of those who got their starts on Dangerfield's stage included Jim Carrey, Jerry Seinfeld, Adam Sandler, and Roseanne Barr.

I told my dentist my teeth are going yellow.
He told me to wear a brown tie.

Today, you'd be hard pressed to find anyone who doesn't love the man who parlayed a self-proclaimed lack of respect into one of the most respectable comedians of the 20th century.

'Yeah, I know I'm ugly,' I said to the bartender,
'Make me a Zombie.'
He said, 'I'm sorry, but God beat me to it.'

In 1982, Dangerfield was honored by the Smithsonian Institution by displaying one of his famously-worn red neckties. As he handed the tie to the museum's curator, Rodney joked:

I have a feeling you're going to use this
to clean Lindbergh's[3] plane.

Success in the field of entertainment can be stressful, so he tried his best to keep his new wife, Joan, informed regarding the professional help he was receiving:

I told my wife the truth.
I told her I was seeing a psychiatrist.
Then she told me the truth.
That she was seeing a psychiatrist,
two plumbers, and a bartender.

In August 2004, Rodney underwent heart valve replacement surgery. Arriving at the hospital in advance of the surgery, a reporter asked how long he expected to be in the hospital. In a typical Dangerfield one-liner, he told the reporter:

If all goes well, about a week;
if not, about an hour and a half.

Unfortunately, the surgery wasn't successful, and Rodney slipped into a coma, regaining consciousness only one time, but long enough to smile and kiss his wife before he passed away.

Even after he was laid to rest in October 2004, the ever-resourceful Rodney Dangerfield found one last way to poke fun at himself with a final self-deprecating joke.

His tombstone, in Los Angeles' fashionable Westwood Village Memorial Park Cemetery, in accordance with his last wishes, contains only his name, and a single sentence:

Rodney Dangerfield
There goes the neighborhood.

[1] Mr. Dangerfield's personal life, career, and death have been presented in the same self-deprecating style he used in his comedy act, and although drawn from several biographical sources, may be somewhat less than 100% historically accurate.

Stories from History's Dust Bin (additional reading):
  [2] Vol 2, Jul 26:   Jack Benny with Gracie Allen
  [3] Vol 2, May 27   Charles Lindbergh with Robert Ripley

I haven't spoken to my wife in years.
I didn't want to interrupt her.
Rodney Dangerfield (1921-2004) Comedian

Andy Devine

Born: Andrew Vabre Devine
Cowboy sidekick with a frog in his throat
Oct 7, 1905 (Flagstaff AZ) – Feb 18, 1977 (Orange CT)

W ERE ANDY DEVINE to drive Interstate 40 today, along
the southern edge of Kingman, Arizona, he would
stare in disbelief at the large freeway sign that alerts motorists
to an upcoming off-ramp for Andy Devine Avenue, Kingman's
widest street.

Andy might think to himself, "How could this be?" knowing
that by his own admission he was, at one time, Kingman's most
mischievous and unrepentant young citizen.

To answer the question of *How could this be?* we'll begin
by turning back the calendar to when the town of Kingman and
the youthful Andy Devine were growing up together during the
early 1900s.

You see, the history of Kingman, and the coming-of-age of
Andy Devine, are both tied to a town landmark known as the
Beale Hotel. The Beale still stands today (2018), where it has
stood since its construction in 1899, one-hundred and nineteen
years ago, on Beale Street. Only today, the hotel languishes sad
and abandoned, a largely forgotten reminder of Kingman's (and
Andy Devine's) long-past glory days.

Let's take a trip back in time, back to the establishment of
the town of Kingman.

In 1857, President James Buchanan appointed surveyor-
explorer Edward Beale to build approximately a thousand miles
of wagon trail west from Fort Defiance, Arizona to the Arizona-
Nevada border.

During construction of *Beale's Wagon Road,* as the road
became known, and roughly three-quarters of the way to the
Nevada border, a marvelous flowing spring used for centuries
by Native Americans was named Beale Springs, in honor of the
head of the survey crew, Edward Beale.

Twenty-three years later (1880), Lewis Kingman surveyed a
route for the Santa Fe Railroad from Albuquerque, New Mexico

to Needles, California, which followed much of *Beale's Wagon Road* through Arizona. Later, Lewis Kingman became the supervisor for the laying of railroad track from Winslow, Arizona to Beale Springs.

Two years later (1882), a few early pioneers homesteaded the Beale Springs area, which had been used primarily by the military, by clearing land and fencing pastures. At some point, the settlement became Kingman, in honor of Lewis Kingman.

Those same pioneers, mindful of the man who built the first wagon train, and the name-sake for their water-source, named the town's main street, Beale Street.

Then, in 1899, the Beale Hotel was built on Kingman's main street, providing travelers a place to stay overnight, or for a few days, depending on when the next stagecoach would arrive, or later, when the next train would stop on its way through town.

Six years later (1905) and approximately 150 miles east of Kingman, in the small town of Flagstaff, Arizona, a son was born to Tom and Amy Devine. They named him Andrew.

Soon after Andrew's birth, a work-related accident cost Tom one of his legs and he received a sizeable cash settlement from the railroad. Needing a new way to make a living, Tom and Amy bought the Beale Hotel and moved to Kingman.

Young Andrew (Andy) grew up working for his parents at the Beale, but he was best known around town for his reckless energy, a nice way of saying he was one rowdy youngster.

In 1908, the *Mohave Miner* newspaper reported that, "Andrew, the three-year-old child of Mr. & Mrs. Thomas Devine, fell from the rear porch of the Beale Hotel to the ground, a distance of thirteen feet, sustaining a fracture of the left arm and sundry cuts and bruises."

Later, according to *Mohave Memories* writer Karin Goudy, during a World War I Liberty Bond drive, twelve-year-old Andy climbed onto the back of a two-man military tank and "rode all over town much to the amusement of the townsfolk, and the dismay of the tank driver, who couldn't get him off and drive the tank at the same time."

Many Kingman stories abound about the rascally Andy, including the time he nailed the satchels of some traveling salesmen to the floor of the hotel. The salesmen, playing billiards in a private room while awaiting the train, suddenly heard a voice yelling, "Train's a leaving! Train's a leaving!"

Making a frantic dash from the billiard tables to the front door of the hotel, they grabbed their satchels on the run, ripping out the bottoms and leaving trails of sales supplies and literature all the way to the tracks.

It was this same kind of spirited youthful vigor and lack of common sense that caused Andy to suffer a serious accident, one that might have compelled anyone else on the planet to withdraw into depression. Yet, the result of this accident would be the very thing that would eventually elevate Andy to Hollywood stardom.

There are differing versions regarding the accident. But all agree it was the combined effect of Andy's endless energy and an ordinary curtain rod that did the damage.

One version has Andy carrying a curtain rod from one hotel room to another, stumbling and then falling, accidentally driving one end of the curtain rod into the roof of his mouth.

Another has Andy jumping up and down on a sofa with the end of a curtain rod in his mouth, falling to the floor, and driving the rod into his vocal cords.

Regardless of how it happened, falling or jumping on a sofa with a curtain rod in one's mouth is never a good thing, except that . . . somehow . . . . in Andy's case . . . . . well, you be the judge.

After the accident, it took Andy a year to speak without stammering, and when he did speak, it was with a strange two-tone voice that fluctuated from bass to soprano, sometimes within the same word.

In 1926, twenty-one-year old Andy moved to Hollywood to try his hand at becoming an actor, and he landed some bit parts in a few silent films. Although everyone knew the day of the talkies was coming, he couldn't imagine himself surviving as an actor with his other-worldly voice.

One of the final silent movies Andy made was a two-reeler titled *The Collegians* where he was cast – to perfection – as a hefty football player.

When talkies replaced silent movies, someone remembered Andy from his football-playing role in *The Collegians* and he was cast to play another football player, Truck McCall in the 1931 movie, *The Spirit of Notre Dame.*

But roles for scratchy-voiced actors in the new era of talkies were in low demand. In fact, on one occasion when he was out of luck, money, and ideas all at the same time, he became so despondent that he attempted suicide, only to discover the gas to his apartment had been turned off earlier the same day for non-payment.

But then roles started coming in. A few at first, then more, and the uniquely strange voice that he once thought would keep him out of the movies, became his ticket to movie-making stardom as one of America's best loved cowboy sidekicks.[1]

Thus today, not only is Kingman's widest street named after Andy, but the town hosts an annual Andy Devine Days Festival complete with a parade, a queen, and a rodeo at the Mohave County Fairgrounds.

As Andy might say, were he alive today, *sometimes it's our shortcomings, the very things that set us apart from everyone else, that makes us uniquely fitted for success.*

It most certainly was for Andy, the youthful hell-raiser from Kingman turned Hollywood's favorite cowboy sidekick.

Andy died in 1977 of leukemia.

He was seventy-one years old.

---

[1] Andy's final film, *The Mouse and His Child,* where he lends his voice to that of the frog, is a good one to rent if you want to hear Andy's "other-worldly" voice.

Asked if he had strange nodes on his vocal cords, Andy replied:
I've got the same nodes as Bing Crosby, only his are in tune.
Andy Devine (1905-1977) Actor

Earle Dickson

Born: Earle Ensign Dickson
The secret to his success – a klutzy wife.
Oct 10, 1892 (Grandview TN) – Sept 21, 1961 (Kitchener, Ontario)

I N 1917, EARLE DICKSON married the lovely but accident-prone Josephine Knight. She enjoyed everything about being married to Earle, except for the hot surfaces and sharp objects in the kitchen, and accidents yet to happen elsewhere in the house.

A wonderful wife, she never failed to have a hot meal ready when Earle returned from work, and he, a loving and observant husband, never failed to notice another cut, burn, scrape, or scratch on his winsome wife. It would be Earle's attentiveness to Josephine's medical needs that would bring him success.

Earle was an excellent employee, a cotton-buyer for the Chicopee Company of Massachusetts, a subsidiary of Johnson & Johnson. When Chicopee went out of business in 1915, the well-respected Dickson was added to the payroll of the parent company in New Brunswick, New Jersey.

It would be there, inspired by the needs of his wife, that he would come up with one of the world's truly great ideas, a self-applied bandage.

It may be difficult to appreciate such a dilemma these days, but a serious problem of a hundred or so years ago was the lack of an easy way to bandage one's own minor injuries.

Earle, who always carried some cotton samples in his salesman's tote, would sit down with Josephine whenever she needed patched. He would first cut a length of adhesive tape, take a small cotton fluff from his tote, attach the cotton to the center of the tape, cover the injury, and get a hug from Josephine who would soon be as good as new.

That was, until she started another meal, picked some fruit, or did a little sewing. Paring knives! Tree branches! Scissors! They all meant trouble to this lovely lady.

Day-after-day, Earle went through the same routine, cut a length of adhesive tape, add a cotton fluff, cover the injured area and hug Josephine; cut a length of adhesive tape, add a cotton fluff, cover the injured area and hug Josephine.

Then, one day, he came up with a solution to the problem, a way that Josephine could bandage herself.

Instead of making homemade bandages one at a time, he took a roll of adhesive tape, unrolled an arm's length of it and placed a cotton fluff every few inches along the length at regular intervals. Then, most ingenious of all, he would cut a piece of crinoline to the width and length of the adhesive strip, and use the easy-to-remove crinoline to keep the tape from sticking to itself as he rolled it up.

Josephine loved her husband's inventive mind, and when she got a little too close to something sharp, she could unroll a few inches of tape, snip off one of the cotton-fluffed sections, peel away the crinoline and bandage herself.

And best of all, at least from Earle's point of view, he would still get his hug when he returned from work.

The more Josephine was able to bandage her litany of cuts and scratches, the more convinced Earle became that his "bandages on a roll" idea had merit.

By the time Earle had come up with a solution to his wife's klutziness, Johnson & Johnson had already made a name for itself with its fresh-smelling *Johnson's Baby Powder*. Also, the company was well on its way to cornering the market for the manufacture and sanitized packaging of large gauze and cotton bandages for hospital use.

And for those of you interested in curious but useless trivia, Johnson & Johnson could just as easily have been named, Johnson, Johnson, & Johnson as it was run by three brothers, Robert, James, and Edward.

Earle waited until the time was right to make a pitch for his bandage-on-a-roll idea, and when the opportunity came, as it did in 1920, Earle didn't hesitate.

While in the company of James Johnson, he snipped a bandage from his roll of bandages, peeled the crinoline from the sticky side of the tape to expose the cotton fluff, and deftly stuck the bandage to his own forearm. The light in James Johnson's head came on and he knew that Johnson & Johnson had a new first-aid product, but it wasn't a winner at first.

The first generation of do-it-yourself bandages were a one-size fits all, two-inch wide bandage, fine for hospitals, but not for ladies like Josephine, or tiny tots with tiny-bandage needs.

Over time, the bandages on a roll gave way to individual bandages. Then came the replacement of the cotton fluff with a gauze pad, and later yet, aeration holes were stamped above the gauze pad to speed the healing process, and finally, each Band-Aid® was wrapped inside a sanitary package.

But, let's return to those early days of development.

At first, sales were virtually non-existent, with the company realizing only $3,000 in sales and zero profit during the product's first year on the market. Then, under the direction of the company's head of research and marketing, Dr. Frederick Kilmer,[1] three very smart and far-reaching decisions were made.

First, Dr. Kilmer wrote a series of articles for physicians and the public, touting Band-Aids as an excellent way to prevent infection.

Next, the company sent a free box of Band-Aids to every Boy Scout troop in America.

And lastly, they sent a selection of Band-Aids to those who work in the nation's most cut-prone occupation, butchering.

Well, you know how the story ends, and who hasn't taken care of a cut finger, scuffed knee, or even the hurt feelings of a five-year-old by sticking a Band-Aid somewhere near the *owie*?

Earle Dickson became a vice-president of the company and a longtime member of its Board of Directors.

And, at least in this instance, it can be said without fear of contradiction, that it was Earle's klutzy wife Josephine and her numerous cuts scrapes and endless supply of hugs, who provided the inspiration for the inspiration.

---

[1] Dr. Frederick Kilmer, the head of Johnson & Johnson's marketing division, was the father of poet Joyce Kilmer, best known for his famous poem, *Trees.*

If you want to cut your own throat, don't come to me for a bandage.
Margaret Thatcher (1925-2013) Politician

Rosalie Duthé

Born: Catherine-Rosalie Gerard Duthé
The world's first official dumb blonde. Duh!
1748 (Unknown) – Sept 25, 1830 (Paris, France)

A BRUNETTE GOES to the doctor complaining that her body hurts whenever she touches it. "Hmmm," says the doctor, "show me what you mean." The brunette presses her finger against her hip and screams. Then she pushes her finger against her knee and tears of pain run down her cheeks. Finally, she pokes her finger deep into her tummy and crumples like a rag doll to the floor. The doctor, having seen enough, tells her to sit, relax, and take a deep breath. Then, in his best doctor-patient manner, he asks, "Are you a true brunette?" "No," the teary-eyed woman confesses, "I'm actually a blonde, but I dyed my hair last week." The doctor nods and says, "Just as I thought, you have a broken finger."

Now, if you happen to be blonde and female you've been the target of too many blonde jokes. *So*, you may have wondered during a time of personal reflection: *Where did it all begin?*

Never have you been so fortunate, as you are holding in your hand the best book available to enlighten yourself regarding facts that have long been relegated to the dust bin of history, such as who was the dumb blonde that started the whole dumb blonde thing.

Catherine-Rosalie Gerard Duthé, born in 1748, is the world's first officially recorded dumb blonde.

Life for Rosalie started out wholesome enough, entering a French convent in her youth. What is not clear is why she left. Was it of her own accord or was she shown the door for breaking one or more of the convent's rules?

What is clear is that soon after the doors of the convent slammed shut behind her, she entered the world of a wealthy English banker named George Wyndham, the 3rd Earl of Egremont. Without specifics, it's said she ruined the Earl, but in what manner, financially, socially, or both, is not known.

Vivacious and light on her feet, she became a dancer at the Paris Opera Ballet where she met numerous French noblemen, most notably, a young Comte d'Artois who in 1824 would become King Charles X of France. Heady company for a youthful ingénue, especially one with few, if any qualms about pushing the limits of 19th century moral decorum.

Indeed, one incident is indicative of Mlle. Duthé's relaxed approach to proper Parisian protocol. In 1788, Louis Philippe II, the Duke of Orléans, introduced his 15-year-old son, also named Louis Philippe to Duthé with instructions that she educate young Philippe in the social arts.

Then, at some point during the educational process, Rosalie was seen in the company of the young Louis Philippe as they rode around the Champs-Élysées in a royal carriage. It was an event that ruffled some royal feathers as French culture dictated only royalty ride in royal coaches! And to the best of anyone's knowledge, the alluring and flirtatious Mlle. Duthé had nary a drop of royal blood in her standard-issue veins.

To disparage Duthé and to embarrass the family of the Duke of Orléans, someone with a wicked sense of humor and a wickeder way with words, gave new meaning to a popular French song.

The song's once family-friendly lyrics were replaced with lyrics of such lecherous meaning they will not be presented here. But know that the new lyrics, sung lustfully in the taverns and streets of Paris, ridiculed the real or imagined nature of the relationship between young Philippe and his social arts teacher.

The song, however, failed to change the course of history and Louis Philippe, the son of the Duke of Orléans would in 1830 become King Louis Philippe I, and from the bawdy side of French life, he would forever be remembered as a notch on the handle of Mademoiselle Duthé's parasol.

Besides her dalliances with the prominent men of her era, Duthé is best known these days for the many portraits she sat, stood, and reclined for, many of which still exist in private collections and museums.

She was an unapologetic artist's model, painted by some of France's most notable artists, attired in everything from full neck-to-ankle period dresses to her birthday suit.

Among those who captured her in oils were François-Hubert Drouais, whose portrait of Rosalie is owned by the Rothschild family of England; Lié Louis Périn-Salbreux who painted a nude of Rosalie at her bath for Comte d'Artois, the suitor who later became King Charles X; and Henri-Pierre Danloux who painted a portrait of Rosalie for the noted French banker, Frédéric Perregaux.

By the way, when he was near death, Perregaux had the painting brought to his bedside so the last image he would gaze upon before death would be that of Mlle. Duthé's beauty.

And now, duh! for the cherry on top of Rosalie's story.

Rosalie was known for something else, a personality trait that solidifies her reputation as a dumb blonde. It's not known if the trait was a genuine facet of her personality, or if it was an exaggerated acquired trait. But, she had this habit of coyly pausing for extended periods of time before speaking, almost as if she were "dumb" in the literal "deaf-and-dumb" sense.

Her real (or feigned) dumbness was such an expected part of her personality that in 1775 it inspired a one-act theatrical satire, *Les Curiosités de la Foire* (The Curiosities of the Fair) that reportedly kept Paris laughing for weeks.

A few dumb blondes assuredly duhhed their way through history before Rosalie, but with no name and no certifiable evidence of ditziness available, cultural historian Joanna Pitman is comfortable in stating that, "Rosalie Duthé has acquired the dubious honor of being the first officially recorded dumb blonde."[1]

Duthé died in 1830 at the age of eighty-two and is buried at Père Lachaise Cemetery in Paris, the most visited cemetery in the world, with 3.5 million annual visitors.

---

[1] Joanna Pitman: *On Blondes,* (Bloomsbury USA, March 3, 2003).

Why does it say "TGIF" inside blondes' shoes?
"Toes Go in First"
From the warped mind of a brunette or redhead.

Cliff Edwards

Born: Clifton Avon Edwards
He went from rags to riches to rags to respect.
June 14, 1895 (Hannibal MO) – July 17, 1971 (Hollywood CA)

W HEN CLIFF EDWARDS died a pauper in 1971, Walt
Disney[1] provided a headstone for his final resting
place, inscribed as follows:

Cliff Edwards
1895-1971
In Loving Memory of Ukulele Ike

Cliff Edwards was a musical artist from an earlier era whose
name you probably won't recognize. But if you have enough
years under your belt, you'll recognize some of the music and
voices he made famous from the late 1920s into the 1950s.

His is the classic story of a likable, talented man who came
from nowhere, found the perfect niche for himself in the
entertainment business, sold millions of records, made a lot of
money, and then became a casualty of poor choices, too many
past-due alimony payments, an endless litany of problems with
the Internal Revenue Service, and the inevitable downward
spiral brought on by alcoholism and drug addiction.

Cliff's once-bright star began to fade in the late 1950s and
as Cliff stumbled, his star tumbled, and his life fell apart.

He became a forgotten man, earning a few bucks now and
then as a movie extra, or by doing the voice-over for a cartoon
character. Any movie. Any cartoon. But soon, even those
infrequent short-term opportunities dried up.

Alcohol and drugs are job killers, and thus, people killers.

His became a nondescript face against a background of
penniless obscurity, flop houses, soup kitchens and welfare,
until he ended up a charity patient at the Virgil Convalescent
Hospital in Hollywood where he died of cardiac arrest in 1971.

When news of Cliff's hospitalization became known, Walt Disney Productions covered most of his medical expenses, a fact not generally known by the public until after his death.

When the Actors' Fund of America and the Motion Picture and Television Relief Fund learned that Edwards had passed away, and that his body was to be sent to the UCLA medical school as a research cadaver, the two organizations took ownership of his remains.

Cliff's body was then interred, with dignity and with friends present, at the Valhalla Memorial Park in Burbank.

So, who was Cliff Edwards and why would Disney and others cover his final expenses and provide him a decent resting place?

Cliff, born in 1895 in Hannibal, Missouri, quit school at fourteen and followed the Mississippi River south to St. Louis where he found work singing in saloons.

Discovering that honky-tonk pianos were the worst cared for musical instruments on the planet, he stopped at a pawn shop and bought a ukulele because "it was the cheapest instrument in the store."

He mastered the chords, became his own accompanist, and when a saloon owner who couldn't remember his name, introduced him as "Ukulele Ike," the name stuck.

Fast forward nine lean years to 1918 when Cliff got a break at the Arsonia Café in Chicago, performing a song written by the club's pianist, Bob Carleton, titled, *Ja-Da* (Ja-Da, Ja-Da, Jing, Jing, Jing!). Cliff and the catchy song caught the attention of Joe Frisco, a Vaudeville star headlining at New York's Palace Theater.

Frisco loved what he saw in Cliff and wrote him into his Palace act, and together they elevated the popularity of an already crowd-pleasing vaudeville show to new heights.

Following their successful run at the Palace, the duo became headliners at the Ziegfeld Follies.

Now, in case you're wondering if Cliff Edwards (Ukulele Ike) was the real deal, talent wise, the answer is yes! Edwards had a three-octave vocal range and a unique sound that he called the *Effin* sound (like jazz's scat singing). And, best of all, he had the stage presence and personality to work the unique sound into his solos, and the public loved both him and his singing.

Following his stint with the Follies, Edwards signed a recording contract with Pathé Records, and his entertainment world expanded beyond New York.

He became one of America's most popular singers with appearances in several Broadway hits. His star continued to soar, and his popularity, music, and his ukulele made him a trendsetter among the college set.

Woe to the Roarin' Twenties' collegian who didn't have an ukulele to strum to his doe-eyed darling, while wearing baggy pants and a knee-length Lord Chesterfield coat.

For those during the *Roaring '20s* who "knew their onions," Ukulele Ike was "the cat's pajamas!"[2]

When his contract with Pathé Records was over, Edwards again toured the Vaudeville circuit, followed by more popularity and even more breaks.

In 1924, he appeared in George Gershwin's hit Broadway show, *Lady Be Good,* where he introduced the song "Fascinatin' Rhythm."

In the *Hollywood Review of 1929* he scored big with his rendition of "Singin' in the Rain," and he went from being just another actor who could carry a tune to a genuine star, appearing in over 100 movies.

His third hit and the biggest of his career came when he was cast as the voice of Jiminy Cricket in Walt Disney's *Pinocchio.* Jiminy's song, "When You Wish Upon a Star," as sung by Cliff Edwards won the Oscar for the best song of 1940.

If you've a computer handy, take a break. Get on the internet and listen to one or more of Cliff's songs: "Singin' in the Rain," "When You Wish Upon a Star," "Give a Little Whistle," or "It's Only a Paper Moon." Any of his hits will do, but don't forget to come back to the book and finish the story.

You'll be rewarded.

Then, as fast as Cliff's star had risen, it imploded, taking Cliff and his fame with it. With all his success, the 100-plus movies, Broadway shows, and countless singing engagements, having recorded over 120 record sides with an estimated 74 million records sold, he went bankrupt for the reasons stated at the beginning of the story.

But, rather than end on a sad note, here's the follow-up to Cliff Edwards Oscar winning song, "When You Wish Upon a Star."

The song has since become the theme song of the Disney Corporation.

It's ranked by the American Film Institute as number seven in their listing of the 100 Greatest Songs in Film History.

It was once the #1 song in Billboard's Record Buying Guide based on retail sales.

It has been recorded more times than you can count, from Glenn Miller to Guy Lombardo, and even by Alvin and the Chipmunks who, as you might suppose, tinkered with the lyrics to come up with "When You Wish Upon a Chipmunk."

And perhaps the greatest tribute of all, was the decision of the Disney Cruise Line to use the first seven notes of the song's melody as their horn signals.

So, Cliff, or Ukulele Ike, which ever name you're known by among the stars, know that you left behind a star for the rest of us to wish upon, and for that, America is grateful.

Stories from History's Dust Bin (additional reading):
   [1] Vol 1, Feb 16:   Walt Disney with James Baskett
   [1] Vol 1, Apr 22:   Walt Disney with Margaret Winkler
   [1] Vol 3, Oct 22:   Walt Disney with Annette Funicello
   [2] Vol 1, Apr 29:   Featuring Tad Dorgan

To this day, if I ever meet grownups who play ukulele, I love 'em.
Paul McCartney (1942-) Singer, songwriter

W. C. Fields

Born: William Claude Dukenfield
If there's a will, prosperity can't be far behind.
Jan 29, 1880 (Darby PA) - Dec 25, 1946 (Pasadena CA)

T HE STORY IS TOLD THAT . . .
While sitting alone, engrossed in a book in an empty train station, W. C. Fields was spotted by a reporter. As the reporter walked toward the entertainer, he was surprised to see the book that Fields was reading was a Bible.

He stopped some distance away and watched as the famous man, unaware of his presence, ran his fingers down page-after-page, halting at times to do a little reading, or stopping to highlight the text with a stubby red pencil before continuing.

Suddenly, sensing he was not alone, Fields looked up, acknowledged the reporter by wiggling his fingers as he often did in his movies and explained, "I'm looking for loopholes."

Admittedly, the chances of that being a true story falls somewhere between nil and none. But, it is illustrative of the persona that Fields' cultivated for himself. That of an irreverent quick-thinking curmudgeon who was always on the hunt for an easy way out.

As a child, William Claude Dukenfield worked with his oft-abusive father selling produce, and yet somehow, he found a way to slip four years of formal education into his head.

Around the age of nine, he realized a talent for juggling. When business was slow, he drew attention to the produce wagon by juggling heads of lettuce and crook-necked squash while rattling on and on about almost nothing at all.

When things went south with his father, as they invariably did, he ran to the safety of friends or relatives until things cooled off at home.

By twelve, he was spending more time on the street than at home. He worked in an oyster house, and when the need arose, he talked his way into a jail cell to escape inclement weather.

Somewhere along the way he saw a Vaudevillian named James Harrigan, who combined juggling with splashes of comic relief. Harrigan, who billed himself as *Poor James Harrigan, the Original Tramp Juggler*, performed in the torn and tattered tuxedo of a down-and-out hobo.

Harrigan's act renewed Fields' interest in juggling and he adopted a similar stage character, and he did well. It was Fields' ability to blend socially questionable insults into his own brand of peevish prattle that paved his way onto the vaudeville stage and a moderate amount of success.

It wasn't long, however, before Fields' realized he needed to set himself apart from an overcrowded field of run-of-the-mill vaudevillians. He needed a unique personality, and when he decided what it was going to be, he literally went from rags to riches overnight.

He discarded the hobo look in favor of a clean-shaven face, trashed the ill-fitting tuxedo for one with real class, expanded the standard juggler's repertoire of rubber balls and bowling pins to include objects that had no business being juggled, such as bricks, hats, and cigar boxes.

The next thing he did was to discard *William Claude* in favor of the corporate-sounding, *W. C.* and shorten his surname, *Dukenfield*, to *Fields*.

Appearing now as "W. C. Fields, the Eccentric Juggler," he amazed audiences by performing truly mind-boggling tricks with apparent ease, some of which had taken him two, three, or more years to perfect.

For instance, he could stack a top hat, a cigar, and a whisk broom on a slightly elevated foot. *<Polite applause here please.>* Then, flip all three items into the air in such a way that the top hat would rotate once and alight properly on his head, the cigar would go into his mouth, and with a subtle, last-minute, half-twist of his hips, the whisk broom would fall magically into a hip pocket. *<Spontaneous enthusiastic applause.>*

On those occasions when the cigar missed his mouth, or the whisk broom missed his hip pocket, he would berate the objects as if they had performed badly on purpose, sometimes muttering muddled expletives under his breath to the suddenly shocked and startled delight of the audience.

It wasn't long before he was working the more prestigious theaters, sharing billing with some of the big stars of the day, Sarah Bernhardt, Fanny Brice, George Burns, and others.

In 1906, he debuted on Broadway in the *Ham Tree* and in 1915 he joined the Ziegfeld Follies.

He began appearing in a few silent movies, most notably *Sally of the Sawdust* in 1925, but it was with the advent of sound a few years later that Fields truly came into his own.

Among his most memorable talkies were *My Little Chickadee* (1940), *The Bank Dick* (1940), and *Never Give a Sucker an Even Break* (1941), the latter movie title becoming a popular American catchphrase.

Fields was known for his terse one-liners, some from his stage appearances and movies, and others simply attributed to him because they sounded like something he would say. But, all of them consistent with his public image, that of an irascible, womanizing, child-hating, incorrigibly sly and clever alcoholic.

Here are a few of his classic comebacks, and they're even funnier if you can sound like the man himself. So, look up "W. C. Fields" on the internet, listen to a few of his voice inflections, and give it a try.

- When asked, "Do you like children?" His response was, "Sure. I like children. Fried."

- About economics, he complained: "The cost of living has gone up another dollar a quart."

- Regarding alcoholic beverages: "I like to keep a bottle of stimulant handy in case I see a snake, which I also keep handy."

- About women: "Women are like elephants. I enjoy looking at them, but I wouldn't want to own one."

- Also, about women: "It was a woman who drove me to drink. Come to think about it, I never got around to thanking her."

- About Philadelphia: "I spent a year in Philadelphia once. It was on a Sunday, I think."

- On his support of clubs for women: "Yes, but only if every other means of persuasion fails."

- About lavish spending habits: "I spent half of my money on gambling, alcohol, and women. Unfortunately, I wasted the other half."

- On tolerance: "I have no prejudices. I hate everyone equally."

- About overcoming adversity: "There comes a time in the affairs of man when he must take the bull by the tail and face the situation."

Fields died on Christmas Day at the Las Encinas Sanatorium in Pasadena, California where he was being treated for an alcohol-related gastric hemorrhage.

He was sixty-six years old.

After he died, it was reported that his tombstone included the words, "I'd rather be in Philadelphia," a city he often claimed to loathe in his comedy routines.

In truth, his grave marker bears only his stage name and the years of his birth and death.

No doubt exists that all women are crazy;
it's only a question of degree.
W. C. Fields (1880-1946) Vaudevillian, actor

Ham Fisher

Born: Hammond Edward Fisher
In the end, not even Joe Palooka could help him.
Sept 24, 1900 (Wilkes-Barre PA) – Dec 27, 1955 (New York NY)

J OE PALOOKA[1] WAS a comic strip prize-fighter who also fought the Nazis during World War II.

But, while Palooka was slugging it out in the make-believe Sunday funnies, his creator, Ham Fisher, was slugging it out in a real-life courtroom. Fisher's final flailing punch came in the form of an allegation that a rival cartoonist was drawing hidden pornographic images into the backgrounds of his comic strips.

When the allegations were proven false, not even Joe Palooka could rescue the cartoonist who had created him, and you'll be surprised, perhaps even shocked when you learn the identity of the man with whom Fisher fought.

Let's go back to when Hammond "Ham" Fisher quit high school and worked a variety of jobs to stay financially afloat.

At sixteen, he peddled brooms and brushes door to door, drove a delivery truck, sold advertising for the *Wilkes-Barre Record* and then a big break! A chance to try his hand at being a sports reporter.

During those sports reporting days he befriended a young boxer he later described as having a pair of powerful biceps but not much power between the ears. It was from his intellectually-challenged boxer-friend that Fisher got the idea for Joe the Dumbbell, a punch-drunk comic strip pugilist who never made it to the big time, or into the Sunday funnies.

But Fisher, a modestly skilled artist at best, never forgot Joe.

He eventually drew a new character, combining the Dumbbell's prodigious punching power and lack of sophistication with a gifted understanding of the uncomplicated side of life.

The new Joe was self-reliant, clean-minded, and pure-in-heart and spirit. He was also a true-blue patriotic American with a strong work ethic and he hated the Nazis. Fisher named his new comic-strip character, Joe Palooka,[2] and conferred upon him the title of heavyweight champion.

At first, Palooka didn't do any better than Joe the Dumbbell.

After quitting his job at the *Wilkes-Barre Record,* Fisher hit the road as a traveling salesman for the McNaught Syndicate, a carrier of columns by such notables as the homespun Will Rogers, advice to the lovelorn columnist Abigail (Dear Abby) Van Buren, and self-improvement guru Dale Carnegie.

The Syndicate also promoted some of the nation's most successful comic strips such as Charlie Chan, Rube Goldberg, and Mickey Finn, and as their sales representative, the Syndicate allowed Fisher to "test the waters" for newspaper interest in his Joe Palooka comic strip.

In 1928, after getting a "thumbs-up" from a few interested newspapers, the Syndicate agreed to give Palooka a fighting chance at success, and the hard-hitting boxer was a knockout!

The strip enjoyed a long run, lasting well into the 1950s, including spinoffs in comic books, lunch boxes, board games, a movie (*Palooka,* staring Jimmy Durante), and even a short-lived television series.

But while Joe Palooka was slugging it out with the bad guys in the Sunday funnies, a nasty fight was working its way toward a showdown in court.

Fisher's strength had always been in ideas, storylines and situations, but not as an illustrator, and he relied on the talents of several artists to draw the strip.

One of those artists was a fellow named Alfred Caplin. Among the characters that Caplin introduced into the Palooka strip was a hillbilly family, including a powerfully-built, but oafish and intellectually-challenged man named Big Leviticus.

In 1934, Caplin parted ways with Fisher to launch his own comic strip, which featured a well-built hillbilly very much like Big Leviticus in appearance, but blessed with a pure heart, an almost childlike outlook on life, and the patriotic zeal of Joe Palooka. Thus, combining the best qualities of Joe Palooka and Big Leviticus into one character.

Although the cartoon-reading public cared little about the similarities between the two hillbillies, Ham Fisher did care, big time! Thus, began a long and nasty feud between Fisher and

Caplin, a conflict well-known inside the cartooning community, but hardly known – or cared about – by the readers of the Sunday funnies who enjoyed both strips.

Over time, Caplin's strip eclipsed Fisher's in popularity, and that only fueled Fisher's growing frustration.

Attempting to counter the popularity of Caplin's strip, Fisher reintroduced Big Leviticus and his family time-and-again to remind his readers that they were the *original* hillbilly family, but the readers paid little attention. After all, they were just fun-to-read funny-paper characters.

Caplin wasn't above taking a few jabs at Fisher either. After Fisher underwent cosmetic surgery on his nose, Caplin introduced a racehorse into his strip that he named *Ham's Nose Bob*.

Fisher, infuriated, retaliated by accusing Caplin of drawing obscenities into his strip, claiming he had drawn pornographic images and situations into the backgrounds of his strip panels.

Caplin responded by filing a lawsuit, a hearing was held, and the court determined that Fisher's claim was "without merit."

The findings of the court triggered an ethics investigation by the National Cartoonists Society, who afterward expelled Fisher from the Society.

It was the last straw for a depressed Fisher, who felt betrayed by the artist who had once worked for him.

And then it was over.

Two days after Christmas, 1955, Ham Fisher was found dead inside a friend's studio. He had committed suicide and alongside his body were several notes regarding a growing despondency over personal issues.

And now, the promise to reveal the name of the comic strip, and the artist that represented the other side of the feud. Here are a few clues.

It was a comic strip that featured one of the most beautiful cartoon ladies of all times, a voluptuous blonde named Daisy Mae whose wardrobe consisted of two items, a very short skirt and a polka-dot peasant blouse with a missing button.

The strip took place in the town of Dogpatch, USA, where the biggest event of the year was the annual Sadie Hawkins Day race. It was at that event, in 1952, that the long-legged and fleet-footed Daisy Mae finally caught the man of her dreams, a simpleminded country bumpkin named L'il Abner.

The L'il Abner strip was drawn for forty-three years, from 1934 to 1977, by Ham Fisher's long-time nemesis, Alfred Caplin, a man better-known to the American public, and to the world by his pseudonym, Al Capp.

Wal, cuss mah bones! Who'd a knowed that?

[1] Palooka, the surname of Fisher's character has become part of the American lexicon. Although Fisher's *Palooka* was a worthy champion with thoughtful reasoning power, the term *palooka* has come to refer to an oafish and clumsy simpleton [*That's him, the big palooka sitting at the bar*], a street brawler, generally a large man of inferior or average pugilistic skills and a brain to match.

[2] A note of interest. On a hill overlooking Route 37 near the small town of Oolitic, Indiana, stands a ten-foot high limestone statue of Joe Palooka, his boxing robe falling from his back. The statue, carved by George Hitchcock and Harry Easton of the Indiana Limestone Company and donated to the town, shows Palooka clad in boxing trunks and fight shoes, his fists clenched and his face staring straight ahead in solemn resolve. The statue was dedicated by Ham Fisher in 1948, in honor of Palooka's patriotism as the first comic strip character to enlist in the U.S. military where he spent five years of comic strip time fighting Adolf Hitler and the Nazis.

Anyone who can walk to the welfare office can walk to work.
Al Capp (1909-1979) Actor

Alexander Fleming

Sometimes clutter can be a good thing.
Aug 6, 1881 (Ayrshire, Scotland) – Mar 11, 1955 (London, England)

I F YOU'RE A YOUNG person looking for a role model, you'll be pleased to learn about a very smart guy who didn't always clean his room, and because he suffered from *chronic untidyosis*, a made-up malady for sure, he ended up saving millions of lives. Don't say it's too good to be true, because it really happened, and it's quite possible that Dr. Alexander Fleming, when asked how he made the wonderful discovery, said something like: *One sometimes finds what one is not looking for.*

Yes, biologist Fleming suffered from the above-mentioned malady, a symptom of which may be an untidy bedroom, an unkempt closet, or a trashed school locker. Or, as happened in Fleming's research laboratory, a partially eaten sandwich and a bunch of unwashed petri dishes.[1]

Fleming was a brilliant researcher and his accomplishments as one of the scientific community's brightest minds bears that out.

But, perhaps not unlike yourself, he often found it difficult to stop what he was doing, thus failing to allow sufficient time to tidy up his surroundings when day is done.

On a particularly busy day in August of 1928, he had worked up to the last possible second on a challenging project when he suddenly realized he was running late, very late!

The reason for his concern was that he knew the rest of his family would already be packed and anxious for his arrival, so they could leave for a week-long vacation at their summer place on Scotland's beautiful Dhoon Beach.

That's the way it was on that August day in 1928 as Dr. Fleming looked around the laboratory at the array of used petri dishes littering his work area.

So, what did he do?

He gathered up the dirty dishes, some containing old staphylococci cultures, and stacked them near the sink, perhaps tossing the remains of an uneaten sandwich on top of the pile. Then he threw his white biologist's jacket over the pile as if to hide the unsightly dishes from his mind. Finally, he grabbed his jacket, locked the laboratory door at St. Mary's Hospital and began his drive home.

In his laboratory, Dr. Fleming was always busy working on biological pursuits, including ways to combat the effects of harmful bacteria once it gets past the body's first line of defense, the skin. One of the many disappointments of such research was that germ-killing agents were typically as destructive to the good cells as they were to the infected cells.

There remained a mountain of research yet to be done.

But right now, he needed to get away from the frustrations of the lab and clear his mind, and even more importantly, he needed to spend some quality time with his family.

At Dhoon Beach, the white sands were beautiful, and the beach, tucked inside a cove of lush green vegetation, was cool and inviting. Beyond the beach, rested an endless expanse of incredibly blue ocean. At low tide, the remains of an ancient shipwreck added a story-book aura to the place and within its once-upon-a-time charm, Dr. Fleming finally relaxed and became Alexander Fleming, family man.

Then, as happens with all great vacations, it was time to return home and for Dr. Fleming to do what he hadn't allowed time to do before leaving on vacation. Washing, disinfecting, and putting away the items he had covered with his white lab coat, including the petri dishes with old bacteria cultures he had been experimenting with.

The date was Monday, September 3, 1928, and as he was filling the sink and adding disinfectant to the water, a former lab assistant, D. Merlin Pryce, popped in for a casual chat about Fleming's vacation.

The two friends relaxed and engaged in small talk.

Then, as he had often done before, Fleming complained about having to wash his own laboratory dishes, and to underscore his point, he picked up one of the soiled petri dishes and was about to slip it into the sink when he noticed something unusual.

"Hmmm," he mused, handing the dish to Pryce, "what do you make of this?"

It wasn't just the mold in the petri dish that had caught Fleming's attention, it was that some staphylococci bacteria were aggressively growing in the dish, and wherever the mold had encroached into the staphylococci growth, the staphylococci had died.

He tested a sample of the mold and determined it was *penicillin notatum*, a common variety of mold that grows on stale bread.

Based on his observations, he ran some experiments and sure enough, he found that common bread mold, *penicillin notatum*, was toxic to staphylococci bacteria.

He wrote up his findings, including a few ideas for potential uses, and the article found its way into the *British Journal of Experimental Pathology.*

Moving forward now, to the beginning of World War II.

Statistics were bearing out the awful fact that almost as many men were dying from infected battlefield wounds as were dying from enemy firepower.

A powerful new anti-bacterial agent was needed, and fast!

Two scientists from Oxford University, Howard Florey and Ernst B. Chain, in addition to their own research, were scouring previous literature for similar research. That's when they came across Fleming's twelve-year-old article on the anti-bacterial qualities of bread mold, *penicillin notatum.*

Florey and Chain, based on Fleming's discovery, learned how to produce a stable long-lasting anti-bacterial powder from the mold.

The production of medical-quality penicillin went into full gear and its availability saved an unknown number of soldiers' lives. And just as amazing, the *wonder drug* as it was being called, was found to be effective against numerous other medical problems, including diphtheria, gangrene, tuberculosis, syphilis, and pneumonia.

In 1945, all three scientists, Fleming, Florey, and Chain received the Nobel Prize in Medicine with Fleming rightfully credited as the scientist who discovered penicillin.

So, the next time your mom gets on your case for not cleaning your room, tell her about your new hero, Alexander Fleming, and tell her how he saved millions of lives because he, like yourself, suffered from frequent bouts of *chronic untidyosis.*

If she looks at you like you're crazy, you might read to her the quote from the bottom of the opening paragraph that states: *One sometimes finds what one is not looking for.*

If your mother responds by rummaging through your closet, checking the contents of your nightstand drawers, or looking under your mattress, and says to you, "I too have found what I was not looking for," know it's time to put your Nobel Prize acceptance speech on hold, and start cleaning your room.

Now!

---

[1] petri dish: a shallow, circular flat-bottomed glass dish with a loose-fitting cover, used for producing bacteria and other microorganism cultures.

If they can make penicillin out of moldy bread,
they can sure make something out of you.
Muhammad Ali (1942-2016) Boxer

Joseph Friedman

Born: Joseph Bernard Friedman
Inspired by Judith and her milkshake.
Oct 9, 1900 (Cleveland OH) – June 21, 1982 (DeKalb IL)

J OSEPH FRIEDMAN, A FIRST-GENERATION American with an incredibly inventive mind, designed a lighted pencil at the age of fourteen. It was intended to cast a small amount of light on the paper as the writer composed a letter or wrote out a grocery list. He called his idea the "pencilite," and although it never got past the design stage, it was a harbinger of what young Joseph would become, an inventor.

He took his next idea, a writing pen containing a reservoir of ink in the pen's barrel to the U.S. Patent Office, and on April 18, 1922, he received patent number 1,412,930 for his invention.

His next step was to sell the patent.

Friedman spent ten years in search of someone interested in his invention before he found Walter A. Sheaffer, the owner of an art supply company in Fort Madison, Iowa. Walter added a vacuum-creating lever to draw ink up and into the reservoir, eliminating the messy need to fill the reservoir manually, and Sheaffer's *fountain pens* became the industry standard.

Professionally, Friedman was an optician and his work in that field is what fed and clothed his family and kept him in spending money to pursue his first love, inventing new ways to improve on old ideas.

Over the years, he invented or improved on a broad range of items, including household gadgets, hearing aids, and even a few items related to automobile engine components.

In addition to the fountain pen patent that he sold, he held nine other U.S. patents and a handful of foreign patents as well.

And during those times when his income as an optician didn't quite pay the bills, he moonlighted by selling real estate.

Joseph Friedman never sat still, physically or intellectually and he thought about and saw things in ways that most people never imagined.

For instance, take the time that Joseph and his family stopped at the Varsity Sweet Shop in San Francisco, an ice cream parlor run by his brother Alfred. Joseph watched as Judith, his pint-sized daughter, struggled with a milkshake that was almost as big as she was.

When the person behind the counter set the milkshake in front of Judith, the top of the straw was even with her eyebrows, way too high for a little girl to wrap her lips around the straw to draw the deliciously flavored ice cream into her mouth.

Now, if you're a grandparent, a parent, or just a lover of children, you know how magical it is to watch a child enjoy a treat, and Judith wasn't enjoying hers! The very-real fear of tipping the treat all over the counter, or worse, all over her pretty dress, had already spoiled the fun.

Friedman only watched his daughter struggle for a minute or two before he stood up and walked into the backroom of his brother's store, found some dental floss and a small wood-screw about the same width as a paper straw, and returned.

Next, he took a fresh paper straw and tamped the small screw two or three inches deep into the straw.

With the screw positioned where he wanted it, he began wrapping a length of dental floss tightly around the straw at the location of the screw. Then, tightening the floss to near its breaking point, a series of circular impressions began to appear.

After removing the dental floss and working the screw free of the straw, Friedman winked at his daughter who had given up on the milkshake and was now intently watching her father.

Placing the circular impressions of the straw at the rim of Judith's glass, he bent the straw to the perfect angle to reach her lips, making it possible for her to enjoy the treat with little fear of spillage.

The research for this project took about fifteen-minutes from start to finish, and the cost? Zero dollars, unless Judith's Uncle Alfred wanted to charge his brother for the extra straw, and the result was the invention of a lifetime.

But, the next step was the difficult one.

On September 27, 1937, after securing U.S. patent number 2,094,268 for his newly designed "flexible drinking tube," he set about trying to find an individual or a company interested in buying the patent from him. But try as he may, he couldn't find a single willing investor or manufacturer.

In the end, it couldn't have worked out better.

Joe Friedman decided to stop looking for someone to buy his idea. Instead, he decided to manufacture the flexible drinking tube himself. He began by inventing something else, a machine that could do what he had done with the piece of dental floss and a small screw. That is, to make corrugated rings a couple of inches below the top of the drinking straw.

He, his wife, a few family members and a friend, all willing to invest in his "flexible drinking tube," established the Flexible Straw Corporation in 1939.

With the start of World War II, work on the idea proceeded slowly as Friedman returned to working full-time as an optician and moonlighting by selling real estate and life insurance.

By war's end (1945), inventor Friedman was putting the finishing touches on the first version of the flexible straw manufacturing machine, and by the late 1940s he had found a market for the straw with the strangely corrugated circles.

The first sale took place in 1947. The buyer was a hospital that quickly saw value in using flexible paper straws instead of the glass drinking tubes that required constant sterilization. From there, it was business, business, and more business.

The straw was a resounding success for patients who needed a disposable straw that could reach their lips while reclining in a hospital bed, and with the hospital market securely in hand, the company moved into the restaurant and home markets.

On June 20, 1969, the Flexible Straw Company sold all its patents, trademarks, and licensing agreements to the Maryland Cup Corporation.

Today, the Maryland Cup Corporation manufactures and sells over 500-million flexible straws a year, all because Joseph Friedman did something to make it easier for his tiny daughter to enjoy a milkshake at her Uncle Alfred's ice cream parlor.

An essential aspect of creativity is not being afraid to fail.
Edwin Land (1909-1991) Inventor

Karl von Frisch

Born: Karl Ritter von Frisch
He discovered the meaning of the waggle.
Nov 20, 1886 (Vienna, Austria) – June 12, 1982 (Munich, Germany)

T HERE ARE THOSE who don't believe there's seventy years' worth of stuff to know about bees. They suggest that if you know that bees (1) make honey, (2) are armed with tail guns, and (3) prefer condos to single-family dwellings, then you know all you need to know.

Karl von Frisch lived for ninety-five years, with seventy of those years spent in becoming the world's foremost authority on honeybees.

The son of a surgeon, Frisch was a naturally inquisitive youngster who was blessed to have as an uncle, Sigmund Exner (1846-1926), the world's foremost authority on insect vision during his lifetime.

It was Exner who inspired young Karl to study bees, and study he did! He eventually surpassed his uncle's legendary work, extending the world's understanding of bees to include the insect's sense of smell, its interpretation of shapes, and its unique navigational system.

Frisch's seven decades of honeybee research is best known for two major breakthroughs. In 1915, he settled the question as to whether bees viewed the world in color or in shades of gray; and in 1945, he solved the mystery behind the strange dances performed by bees that had confounded biologists and beekeepers for thousands of years.

Regarding the question as to whether bees viewed the world in color or in black-and-white, he borrowed an idea from Ivan Pavlov[1] to solve the puzzle. He used Pavlov's technique of associating the stimuli to be studied with a subsequent reward for food, and the bee gave up its secret.

Frisch began by training bees to eat at a table upon which was placed a single blue card with a small amount of honey. Once the bees were trained to fly to the blue card for a helping of honey, he changed the rules.

He covered the table with gray cards of varied darkness, including grays that matched the color blue when viewed in black and white. Upon one of those randomly-placed gray cards, he spread a small amount of honey. Within the entire field of gray cards, he placed a single blue card similar in all respects to the card that once provided the honey, only this blue card was honey-free.

The hypothesis was simple.

If the eyes of the hungry bees could not distinguish between gray and blue, they would simply fly around until discovering the card with honey.

But if the eyes of the bees could discern blue, which they had been trained to associate with honey, and if they flew immediately to the single blue card (amidst a sea of gray cards), it would prove that bees saw the world in color.

And that's exactly what happened.

As soon as the bees were allowed into the feeding area, they flew directly to the blue card, landed, and were likely frustrated to find the card absent of honey.

Frisch's other well-known study has to do with the two dances that honeybees perform inside the hive – one called the "round dance," the other called the "waggle dance."

The method used to discover the answer might seem simple, but keep in mind it's not easy to track a single bee as they all look alike, so with that in mind, please appreciate the attention that Frisch had to devote to his research to find the answer.

In watching his bees, he determined that once a honeybee found a good source of food, other bees seemed to magically find the same source. He reasoned, correctly, that somehow the first bee on the scene had communicated the location to the other bees, hundreds or thousands of them, each of which could then successfully navigate on their own to the same source.

His research led him to realize that the bee discovering the new source of food could share the location by performing what is now called the waggle dance.

The performing bee begins the waggle dance by running in a figure-8 pattern on the vertical surface of the honeycomb. The central part of the figure-8 is the "straight run," and it is here that the performing bee provides the basic location information.

The angle of the straight run, when measured against the vertical surface of the honeycomb, tells the follower bees the angle they must fly with reference to the sun when they leave the hive. The duration of the dance tells the follower bees the distance, by telling them how long they must fly, to arrive at the new food source.

The waggle dance, which is used to locate destinations of more than fifty yards distance is the most complex form of communication ever discovered in an invertebrate animal.

The other dance, the round dance, directs follower bees to locations less than fifty yards distant.

This dance is different from the waggle dance in that the initiating bee commences to whirl in a narrow circle, changing from clockwise to counter-clockwise in rapid succession – creating a new circle each time.

As the bee dances, the dance becomes like the popular conga-line dance, in which individuals attach themselves to the end of the line and blindly follow the leader. As the initiating bee works at the head of the line, other bees begin joining in until enough bees, at the discretion of the initiating bee, have committed themselves to the project, and off they go, a flying conga line to the food source.

And there is yet another dance, called the tremble dance, in which recruiter bees can direct worker bees in need of an assignment to relieve returning bees of their nectar so the returning bees can turn around and make another collection run.

When someone says you're as busy as a bee, let's hope they consider you as smart as a bee as well.

[1] Ivan Pavlov: Russian psychologist, best known for his work in *classical conditioning*, specifically *conditioned reflex* as related to the salivation of dogs when a stimulus (a bell) indicates the presence of food.

A bee is never as busy as it seems;
it's just that it can't buzz any slower.
Kin Hubbard (1868-1930) Cartoonist, journalist

David George

Born: David Elihu George
Was David George, John Wilkes Booth?
Date unknown – Jan 13, 1903 (Enid OK)

I MMEDIATELY AFTER THE GUNSHOT, a struggle ensued between President Lincoln's guest, Major Henry Rathbone[1] and the assailant. As the attacker shook free of Rathbone's grasp, he struck a heroic theatrical pose and yelled, *Sic semper tyrannis!* (Thus, always to tyrants!)

Then, just as he was swinging himself up and over the railing of the presidential box, Major Rathbone caught the tail of his coat, turning him ever so slightly, but enough that one of his heels (or a spur) snagged the red-white-and-blue bunting, landing him awkwardly and hard on his left foot. The assassin, momentarily stunned, stood up and hobbled as rapidly as he could across the stage floor and out the rear door.

The date was April 14, 1865. The place was Ford's Theater in Washington, D.C. The event was the assassination of President Abraham Lincoln.

On April 26th, assassination co-conspirator David Herold[2] and a man believed to be the assassin, John Wilkes Booth, were trapped in a tobacco barn. Herold surrendered, but the other man yelled, "I prefer to fight!" and with that, the barn was set ablaze.

As the barn burned and filled with smoke, army sergeant Boston Corbett, peering through a crack in the side of the barn saw the man inside make a run for the barn's back door. Corbett rested his gun in the crack, took careful aim and fired. The ball struck the man in the back of the neck, severing his spinal cord. He was then dragged from the barn and died shortly afterward.

That, in five paragraphs, is the story of the assassination of President Lincoln and the death of a man believed by most to have been Booth, the assassin. Except, that for years afterward, there has lingered another story, one that even today, over 150 years since the assassination, resurfaces from time to time.

It goes like this.

In 1871, about six years after Lincoln's death, a man named John St. Helen of Glen Rose, Texas, failed to report to work at a local saloon.

His absence caused saloon owner, F. J. Gordon, to go to the boarding house where St. Helen lived and check on his usually dependable bartender. But St. Helen was nowhere to be found.

John St. Helen had arrived in Glen Rose a year or two earlier from parts unknown. He was a fine-looking, well-dressed man who walked with a limp, friendly but not given to idle talk, and he was active in the town's amateur theater, amazing folks with his ability to quote lengthy passages of Shakespearean dialogue.

Saloon owner Gordon had befriended the stranger when he first arrived, and since he needed help, hired the newcomer as a bartender. St. Helen in return had honored the friendship by being a prompt and dependable employee – until now.

After St. Helen's disappearance, there was talk he had become agitated after seeing the guest list for the wedding of a local politician's daughter, which included a U.S. Marshall and several other law enforcement types as guests, and no one had seen him since.

Then, sometime later, another John St. Helen story emerged, this one from a Texas town about twenty miles northwest of Glen Rose named Granbury.

There, a gravely ill man named John St. Helen, after being told by his physician that his condition was terminal, asked to have his best friend, attorney Finis Langdon Bates brought to his bedside. When Bates arrived, St. Helen confided to his friend that he was not John St. Helen, but John Wilkes Booth, the man who had assassinated Lincoln.

John St. Helen, however, eventually recovered from his illness, and when confronted by Bates about his death-bed confession, was elusive in his response, suggesting that perhaps his mind had been addled by the fever.

And, this John St. Helen, just like the John St. Helen of Glen Rose, was known for quoting lengthy passages of Shakespeare.

Then, just as John St. Helen of Glen Rose had disappeared without saying goodbye, John St. Helen of Granbury left town without saying goodbye and was never seen again.

At least never seen again as John St. Helen.

When St. Helen didn't return, Bates searched his rented room and claimed to have found a derringer of the type used by Lincoln's assassin, wrapped in an 1865 Washington D.C. newspaper with the headline, *Lincoln Assassinated.*

In 1900, Bates, based on his belief that John St. Helen was John Wilkes Booth and that he had recovered the assassination weapon, filed for the $100,000 reward offered by Congress in 1865 for information leading to the capture and arrest of Lincoln's assassin.

The claim was denied.

Three years later, 1903, the trail takes us to Enid, Oklahoma, where we will add yet another name to the story.

This time, it's not someone named John St. Helen, but someone named David E. George, a housepainter known for quoting long Shakespearian passages while he worked, and who on January 13, 1903, is not dying, but is already stone-cold dead.

A few hours earlier and prior to swallowing the strychnine that ended his life, he had confessed to his landlord that he wasn't David E. George, but John Wilkes Booth, adding, "I killed the best man that ever lived."

George had tried to convince a few others of his identity before taking his life, but no one had taken him seriously.

David George's body was taken to Enid's undertaker, William Penniman, for embalming. When no one claimed the body, Penniman dressed the deceased man in black, tied him securely to a chair, and gave him a couple of glass eyes to lend credibility to his interest in the newspaper now resting on his lap.

And there, for a few days, the freshly embalmed body of David George observed the citizenry of Enid through a funeral home window.

Rummaging through David George's personal effects, Penniman found a note containing the name and contact information for Granbury attorney Finis Langdon Bates, and a request by the deceased that Bates be contacted in the event of his death.

Ten days after George's suicide Bates arrived and identified the body in the window as his friend, John St. Helen.

Bates then took possession of the body, eventually renting it to various traveling shows where it was frequently exhibited as the body of John Wilkes Booth.

In 1907, Bates, convinced that his friend John St. Helen (alias David E. George) had been truthful when giving his death-bed confession, published a 309-page book titled, *The Escape and Suicide of John Wilkes Booth*[3].

So, what's the possibility that the man shot in the back of the neck and carried from the burning barn wasn't John Wilkes Booth, but someone as shady as co-conspirator David Herold, but less-willing to be captured?

And what's the possibility that John St. Helen #1, John St. Helen #2, and David E. George are all aliases belonging to one man, John Wilkes Booth, who since 1865 had been living on the lam, but couldn't resist impressing others with his ability to quote long passages of Shakespearean dialogue?

How many bartenders and housepainters do you know who have a penchant for quoting Shakespearean passages at all?

And there are other unanswered clues.

For instance, in 1913, Baltimore mayor William Pegram and a long-time friend of John Wilkes Booth, after viewing the embalmed body of David George, signed a statement that the deceased was indeed that of Booth.

And so that's where we're going to leave this story, non-conclusive, quite unsolvable, but an interesting sidebar to the assassination of one of America's greatest presidents.

Stories from History's Dust Bin (additional reading):
[1] Vol 2, Jul 1:   Featuring Henry Rathbone
[2] Vol 3, Dec 20:   David Herold with Samuel A. Mudd

[3] Bates, Finis Langdon, *The Escape and Suicide of John Wilkes Booth: or, the first true account of Lincoln's assassination, containing a complete confession by Booth*, (J. L. Nichols, Naperville, IL, 1907). Reprints available from the internet.

I have too great a soul to die like a criminal.
John Wilkes Booth (1838-1865) Actor, assassin

Jules Henri Giffard

Born: Baptiste Jules Henri Jacques Giffard
The man who invented the dirigible.
Feb 8, 1825 (Paris, France) – April 14, 1882 (Paris, France)

D ID YOU KNOW that along the row of iron plates that separates the base from the first observation deck of the Eiffel Tower,[1,3] there are the names of seventy-two French citizens, each personally selected by designer-builder Gustave Eiffel to honor their contributions to science?

Well, you're not alone, because neither did the French housepainters who were hired twenty years after the erection of the tower, to apply a coat of paint to protect the iconic monument from rust and the elements.

Interestingly, the "paint over" wasn't corrected with the next painting twenty years later, nor with the next, or the next, or the next. In fact, it wasn't until 1986, eighty years later, when the names were painted a contrasting color, that they were once again readable from ground-level.

Depending upon how much time you spent passing notes to your friends in school, you may recognize the names of some of the honored scientists.

There is Louis Daguerre, the inventor of the daguerreotype photographic process and known as the *Father of Photography*; Jean-Baptiste Dumas, best known for his work relative to the atomic weights of the elements; Léon Foucault, known for the Foucault pendulum that proved the earth rotates on its axis; and André-Marie Ampère, the physicist who founded the science of electromagnetism, and for whom the measurement of electric current, the "amp," is named.

In addition to the four relatively famous names cited above, there are sixty-eight others, some famous and some you've never heard about, but all of whom are worthy of recognition for their contributions to science.

One of the names that will quite assuredly fall into your "never heard about" category would be that of Jules Henri Giffard (1825-1882), who is credited with designing, building, and flying the first powered and steerable lighter-than-air aircraft.

Before continuing, and to make certain we're together with what we're talking about here, Giffard's work in the field of balloon aerodynamics in the 1850s had to do with a powered and steerable *lighter-than-air* aircraft.

That's different than the Wright Brothers,[2] who in 1903 designed, built, and flew the first powered and steerable *heavier-than-air* aircraft.

Now that we've addressed that potentially confusing matter, let's continue.

On September 24, 1852, Giffard flew a 144-foot long lighter-than-air aircraft from the Hippodrome in Paris to the town of Trappes, seventeen miles distant. His top speed during the flight, with a slight tailwind, was about six miles per hour, or roughly twice the walking speed of a human.

It was that slight tailwind that prevented him from flying the seventeen miles back to the Hippodrome, not because he couldn't maneuver the aircraft, but because his 3-horsepower steam engine lacked the *oomph* to push it against a mild headwind.

He did, however, prove the maneuverability of his aircraft by making several turns into the wind to show the crowd below that he was truly in control of the aircraft's direction.

But it was not the breath-taking six miles per hour, nor the seventeen miles that Giffard flew that earned him a place of honor on Gustave Eiffel's tower, although those things were certainly factors. It was his invention of the "steam injector."

You see, in addition to the hydrogen gas inside the balloon's envelope that provided lift, the craft's power and steerability were provided by a huge, 350-pound steam engine.

That's right, in addition to supporting Giffard's weight aloft, the balloon also had to lift a 350-pound steam engine equipped with the above-mentioned steam injector valve. It was that valve that released a jet of steam to (1) turn a propeller at 110 revolutions per minute, and to (2) make possible the right-left steering of the craft using a vertical rudder.

With Giffard's successful demonstration that he did in fact, have control of the direction of his balloon, the term balloon, which had previously referred only to a craft that could ascend and descend, was found to be lacking.

To differentiate between the two types of aircraft, Giffard's *steerable* balloon became a *dirigeable*, the French word for airship. Then, over time, the correctly-spelled *dirigeable* became the Anglicized[4] *dirigible*, the word still in use today when referring to a steerable balloon, such as the ill-fated German *dirigible*, the Hindenburg.

To prepare for flight, once Giffard started the process of having the dirigible's envelope filled with hydrogen, he would start a fire beneath the onboard boiler to heat water into steam. When the envelope was filled, and the craft was straining at its tethers, and as soon as the steam engine was producing a full head of steam, he would signal the ground crew to release the ropes and the ascension would begin.

After lifting off, and by means of his needle-valve, Giffard could divert the steam from the boiler, through the steam injector into the apparatus that turned the propeller.

So, it was on September 24, 1852, that Henri Giffard made the world's first flight in a steam-powered and navigable, lighter-than-air aircraft.

It took a few more years to refine the steam injector, but on May 8, 1858, he was granted a patent, and five years later he was appointed a Chevalier of the Légion d'Honneur, France's highest civilian award for meritorious service.

By 1882, Giffard, who had lost his eyesight to disease, became so deeply depressed that he committed suicide. He left his estate to the French government for use as a humanitarian and scientific center.

By the way, the lift and power of Giffard's dirigible was also sufficient to carry a passenger, making his steam-powered dirigible the world's first controllable, passenger-carrying airship as well.

On your next trip to Paris to buy a pair of shoes, or whatever it is you go to Paris to do, if you're so inclined, check out Jules Henri Giffard's name. It's the sixteenth of eighteen names engraved on the southwest side of the Eiffel Tower.

Stories from History's Dust Bin (additional reading):
  [1] Vol 1, Feb 4:   Eiffel Tower with Franz Reichelt
  [2] Vol 1, Feb 8:   Orville Wright with Thomas E. Selfridge
  [2] Vol 2, Aug 22: Orville Wright with Raymonde de Laroche

[3] See Victor Lustig in this book, pages 184-187, to read about the man known as the "smoothest con artist ever born," who successfully sold the Eiffel Tower once to a French scrap-iron dealer, and almost sold it a second time.

[4] To Anglicize means to adapt a foreign word, or phrase, to English usage, e.g. to anglicize *Juan* to *John.*

For once you have tasted flight you will
walk the earth with your eyes turned skywards,
for there you have been and there you will long to return.
Leonardo da Vinci (1452-1519) Painter, Sculptor

Betty Grable

Born: Elizabeth Ruth Grable
Oh! Those legs! Those lovely legs!
Dec 11, 1916 (St Louis MO) – July 2, 1973 (Los Angeles CA)

A CTRESS BETTY GRABLE was beautiful, she also had a pleasant singing voice and her acting skills were well above par, but it was for something else that she is remembered.

If you've a grandfather old enough to remember the 1940s and '50s, and you wish to re-energize his psyche, ask if he remembers Betty Grable. If he's mentally sound, and if grandma's not around, he'll lean back, close his eyes, smile and whisper, "Oh those legs. Those beautiful legs!"

Along both sides of Hollywood Boulevard and Vine Street is the Hollywood Walk of Fame. It's where movie stars and others have been honored by having their hand and foot prints captured in concrete alongside their signatures, but Betty Grable was memorialized differently.

On February 15, 1943, she was lifted by three soldiers, one from each branch of the service, and laid sideways onto the wet concrete to capture the full profile of one of her legs.

So, just how important were Betty's legs to Hollywood? Twentieth Century Fox had her legs famously insured by Lloyd's of London for a cool million dollars.

Okay, so insuring Betty's legs was mostly a publicity stunt, still, you'd be hard-pressed during that era to find a man who didn't think those legs, bare or sheathed in silk or nylon, were worth at least a million dollars.

And that takes us to another part of this story.

Do you know what is honored each May 15th?

Nylon stockings,[1] that's what.

If you're at your computer, type *Nylon Stockings Day* into your computer's search engine and you'll get plenty of hits, most of which will tell you that May 15th is Nylon Stockings Day, but only a few will tell you the story behind the day.

That's because it's mostly a forgotten day, and the 1940s terminology, *nylon stockings,* has been replaced by the single-word, *nylons,* but they both mean the same thing, near-transparent coverings for lovely feminine legs.

But Nylon Stockings Day was a big deal in the 1940s, and for a decade afterward. That's because prior to May 15, 1940, unless you worked for E. I. DuPont, Inc., or were lucky enough to have seen a sample of the remarkable fabric, you had no idea how something called "nylon" was going to change the face, or rather the legs, of America's ladies.

And like others of that era, you would have been surprised to learn that nylon is made from oil, petroleum polymers that have the elasticity and toughness to be stretched into a thread as fine as frog's hair and nearly invisible to the eye.

Women's magazines called nylon a miracle thread, and a perfect replacement for silk.[2]

So, let's back up and see how all of this came together.

On October 27, 1938, two years before the advent of Nylon Stockings Day, Charles Stine, a vice president of DuPont, announced that a scientist named Wallace Hume Carothers had succeeded in creating a "yet to be named" synthetic super-fiber that he promised would revolutionize the fabric industry.

A year later, Stine unveiled the super-fiber "nylon," not to a gathering of balding scientists, but to a gathering of 3,000 excited women who had been invited to participate in the formal introduction of the discovery. The venue was the New York *Herald-Tribune's* Annual Forum on Current Events.

Stine's speech, "We Enter the World of Tomorrow," was chosen to match the forum's, World of Tomorrow, theme. Everything went off like clockwork and DuPont and America's women were ready for the dawning of the Age of Nylon.

During 1939 and into 1940, spools of nylon thread were shipped to America's hosiery manufacturers, who would later ship cartons of nylon stockings to America's retailers.

To heighten the suspense, DuPont's marketing executives proclaimed May 15, 1940 as *Nylon Stockings Day* and secured promises from retailers to withhold sales until that date, and the retailers honored their promise.

The anticipation alongside the hype generated by magazine, newspaper, and radio advertisements turned the day into a retail sales event like none other up to that time, with an estimated 750,000 pairs of nylon stockings sold on that day alone.

Everything went well, and every American woman who could afford a pair, bought a pair, that was until December 7, 1941, when Japanese warplanes bombed Pearl Harbor.

It was a day that changed America's priorities overnight!

Beginning May 4, 1942, ration books were distributed to every American family, restricting the purchase of rubber tires, leather shoes, clothing, gasoline, flour, in fact, hundreds of items badly needed to sustain America's military forces.

Nylon, no longer available for ladies' legwear, had many military uses, from strengthening the tires on warplanes to making parachutes for the men who jumped out of them.

Women lucky enough to have bought a pair of nylons between May 15, 1940, and May 3, 1942, wore that one pair on special occasions only, as if they were worth a million dollars.

And speaking of million-dollar treasures, Betty Grable, was asked by President Roosevelt to serve as the poster girl for the collection of nylons and other recyclables for the war effort. Betty graciously accepted and life-size cutouts of Betty and her million-dollar legs stood near thousands of collection dumpsters across the nation, reminding Americans to recycle.

After the war (1945), nylon was again turned into nylon stockings. Only a few pair of those bought before the beginning of World War II, outlasted the war.

Those that did had been cared for as if they had been made of gold, which of course is exactly what they were made of, gold, black gold!

---

[1] The term, "nylon stockings," was a replacement term for "silk stockings." The singular term "nylons," came into popular use later.

[2] Silk, produced by the mulberry silkworm, had been used to accentuate lady's legs since the 1500s.

There are two reasons why I'm in show business,
and I'm standing on both of them.
Betty Grable (1916-1973) Actress

Bette Nesmith Graham

Born: Bette Clair McMurray
She had the right solution for the problem.
Mar 23, 1924 (Dallas TX) – May 12, 1980 (Richardson TX)

I F ANYONE FALLS into the category of someone whose name is short of being a household word, it would be Bette Nesmith Graham.

And, as you're about to learn, Bette made more than a few mistakes in her youth and she would acknowledge that. But she more than made up for her mistakes by inventing something that has helped millions of other people correct theirs.

Bette wasn't voted most likely to succeed at Alamo Heights High School in San Antonio, Texas. Instead, had there been a category for the student "most likely to make a few poor choices," she may have nailed that honor on the first vote.

Bette, cute as a button, was a handful for her parents.

She quit school at seventeen to marry her boyfriend, 24-year-old Warren Nesmith, who couldn't run to the local military recruitment office fast enough when Bette told him she was pregnant. With Warren gone, Bette was left on her own with no job skills, morning sickness, and in nine-months, an infant son.

At the end of WWII, Warren returned home, told Bette he didn't see a future with her or his three-year-old son, and just like that, he walked out of their lives.

Bette found work as a secretary, a job she really needed but didn't enjoy because her typing skills were marginal at best. She also worked when she could as a commercial artist, a job she enjoyed, but paid little over the cost of her art supplies. And through it all, she experienced the angst and the loneliness that plagues most single mothers. Her existence was month-to-month, her income barely covering the rent, food for herself and her son, and gas enough to get her back-and-forth from work.

In 1950, her father passed away, leaving some property to Bette in Dallas. That's when she, her pre-teen son Michael, her widowed mother, and a younger sister, Yvonne, all packed up and moved to Dallas.

Once again, the only job available for which Bette had any experience was a secretarial job, and she found a good one at

Texas Bank and Trust. But this time, with help from her family, Bette tackled the job as a woman possessed. Her confidence and typing skills improved swiftly as she worked her way up the secretarial ladder to the position of Executive Secretary.

The 1950s ushered in an era of electric typewriters and when the bank moved to the electrics, the new technology arrived with a few unexpected problems.

For instance, with manual typewriters, corrections were easily made by rolling the paper forward, erasing the error with a standard pencil-tip eraser and retyping. Not so with the electrics. They used carbon-coated ribbons that didn't respond to rubber erasers, leaving smears uglier than the errors, and often requiring the typist to start over with a fresh sheet of paper.

That's when Bette's interest and experience as a commercial artist took over. In explaining how she came up with a solution to the erasing-the-error problem, Bette wrote:

> *An artist never corrects by erasing, but by painting over the error. So, I decided to use what artists use. I put some water-based, white tempera paint in a little bottle and took it and my watercolor brush to the office, and that's what I used to correct (paint over) my mistakes.*

Although her initial mixture needed refined, she knew she was on the right track, so she enlisted the help of her son's chemistry teacher. They perfected the liquid, creating a thin opaque paint, easily applied, and fast drying. Corrections could be made on the fly and they were nearly invisible to the eye.

Bette's correction fluid worked so well that other secretaries at Texas Bank and Trust wanted some, as did the secretaries down the street, and into the next town. That's when she started a home-based business, naming the mixture *Mistake-Out.*

The demand for the white liquid grew, slowly at first, but in direct proportion to the decline of manual typewriters.

Bette was in the fast lane for success!

She and her struggling musician son Michael[1] mixed the solution in the kitchen and she paid his musically-inclined friends to fill the little bottles, affix the labels, and package the product, all of this, hopefully, for turning a profit.

In 1956, she incorporated her fledgling company and then came the boost that propelled her company beyond the borders of Texas. The product was favorably reviewed in a national trade magazine and the General Electric Corporation placed an order so large that she had to hire some full-time employees. That's right. Employees. Plural!

In 1957, she renamed the company, the Liquid Paper Company, and ten years later the company's sales topped the $1-million mark.

Rare indeed was the corporate office, federal agency, school, military installation, residence, church, hospital, home-office, or college dorm room that didn't keep a small bottle of what was informally referred to as "white out" right next to the typewriter.

The one-time Alamo Heights High School cutie, who wasn't the school's academic over-achiever and stood no chance at being honored as the student most likely to succeed, had done just that, in spades.

Bette retired in 1979, selling her business to the Gillette Corporation[2] for a cool $47.5-million. Indeed, she had become successful beyond all expectations.

Bette died on May 12, 1980, at the age of fifty-six, shortly after completing the sale of the business to Gillette.

---

[1] Bette's son Michael Nesmith, became a successful songwriter, actor and philanthropist. You might know him as a member of the pop rock band, *The Monkees,* and co-star of the television series of the same name.

[2] *Stories from History's Dust Bin* (additional reading):
   Vol 1, Jan 5:   Featuring King C. Gillette

> *Anyone who is making progress, faces fear.*
> *Overcoming fear is all there is to success.*
> Bette Nesmith Graham (1924-1980) Secretary, inventor

Sylvester Graham

Born: Sylvester Graham
Sly was a cracker of a guy.
July 5, 1794 (Suffield CT) – Sept 11, 1851 (Northampton MA)

S YLVESTER GRAHAM WAS the seventeenth child of 70-year-old Presbyterian minister John Graham and his wife, Ruth. He was only two years old when his father died, and in a house already packed to the rafters with children, he was raised by various relatives until he was ready to follow in his father's ministerial footsteps.

But, it is not for his service as a man of the cloth that he is remembered, but for something he genuinely believed would prevent people from having impure thoughts, thus making it possible for them to be assigned a harp and ushered into Heaven.

But, as with all attempts by man to alter societal direction, it wasn't going to be easy.

Sylvester enrolled at Amherst Academy around 1820 to study theology. But he never fit in with the other students and after his classmates fabricated a malicious scandal involving his friendship with a woman, he quit college.

Disillusioned with his college experience, he studied the Bible on his own, and in 1828 he became a traveling evangelist.

Around 1830, Graham joined the Philadelphia Temperance Society and worked part-time for the organization. Unlike many temperance societies, this one wasn't run by noisy hellfire and damnation preachers, but by a group of physicians who were concerned about the effects of alcohol on the human body.

Dividing his time between circuit riding and working for the Society, Graham established two important friendships.

First, there was his friendship with William Metcalfe, who had founded a vegetarian church in Philadelphia. Metcalfe claimed that Christ was a vegetarian, and he required his congregation to abstain from meat. He also taught strict temperance values, was opposed to war, and he supported the abolition of slavery, topics he frequently wrote about in two newspapers he published.

The second important friendship came about when Metcalfe introduced Graham to Dr. William Alexander Alcott, and the two of them would, in 1850, become the founding fathers of the American Vegetarian Society.

Alcott, a physician and a vegetarian, was one of America's most prolific writers of the early to mid-1800s, turning out 108 books during his lifetime. Many of his books were about health through vegetarianism, but he also wrote about educational reform, morality, and other social topics.

Regarding morality he wrote about what he termed "free courtship manners," specifically warning young couples about the negative effects of "excitable conversation" and the danger of being "in the presence of exciting books." And you may need to use your imagination here, something he referred to as "unnecessary heat" in courtship. For example, he wrote that dancing more than three times with the same partner may result in unnecessary heat and should be avoided.

The Reverend Graham, adopting ideas from both of his new friends, along with his unique interpretation of the scriptures, soon became a well-known advocate for America's temperance and vegetarianism movements.

In fact, he inspired a following of dietary devotees who became known as "Grahamites," folks who rigorously followed a diet he introduced in 1829 known as the Graham Diet.

Although his publication, the *Graham Journal of Health and Longevity,* may have raised a few eyebrows on occasion, his messages regarding the benefits of eating lots of fresh fruits and vegetables were spot on, and had he stopped there, you would not be reading about him now.

But he didn't stop there, he claimed that not only fruits and vegetables were good for the body, but so were whole grains. He preached that all meats, coffee, cider, tea, all forms of spices (except salt in moderation), butter (if used sparingly) and all chemical additives should be eliminated from the diet.

And there was more. He claimed that a strict vegetarian diet could cure alcoholism, and for individuals lacking sexual self-restraint, his diet was guaranteed to weaken human sexual urges thought by Graham to contribute to blindness and early death.

And for those hoping to gain admission to Heaven, enough veggies could curb (if not cure) lustful thinking and what he termed as "inappropriate intention."

He also taught that although alcohol had medicinal value, it should not be consumed in public or social settings.

The Reverend Graham was such a spellbinding speaker that his lectures on nutrition and the curtailment of sinful habits were sold out affairs, drawing huge crowds of the curious as well as his own flock of faithful Grahamites. It was said that when he mentioned sex and corsets in the same breath during his lectures, some of the women in the audience would faint from shock.

Although Graham touted the benefit of wholesome foods, he became best known for his stand on the virtues of whole wheat bread. He denounced the big-city bakers who used refined flour devoid of the husks, bran, and the dark oily germ of freshly-harvested wheat. And he scorned those who whitened their bread, plied the dough with additives, and baked the loaves too quickly in the interest of fast production and profits.

Graham plowed new ground in the baking industry by inspiring a new type of bread, one made from unsifted flour, dark in appearance, and free from additives. The rather bland flour became known as Graham flour.

The new bread, which was more cracker than bread, was not intended to compete with bakery shop bread or crackers, but to complement the natural elements of his diet. All of this aimed at suppressing the unhealthy sexual appetite of the natural man.

That same cracker with some ingredient adjustments, mainly the addition of sugar or honey as a sweetener, is available today from your favorite grocer.

But, as to the effectiveness of the Graham cracker as a sexual depressant, well, the jury has yet to reach a verdict in the matter.

The doctor of the future will no longer treat the human frame with drugs, but rather will cure and prevent disease with nutrition.
Thomas Edison (1847-1931) Inventor

Bill Haley

Born: William John Clifton Haley
A rock 'n' roll overnight success story.
July 6, 1925 (Highland Park MI) – Feb 9, 1981 (Harlingen TX)

INSIDE A NEW YORK recording studio at precisely 4:30 pm on April 12, 1954, drummer Billy Gussak struck a drumstick smartly against the rim of a drum – twice. Rap! Rap! There was a full second of anticipatory silence before Bill Haley leaned into the microphone and sharply enunciated the timeless cadence-inspired lyrics that literally brought rock 'n' roll[1] music to life: *One-two-three o'clock, four o'clock rock . . . .*

While it is the song that everyone remembers – the song that gave birth to the rock 'n' roll movement – it took more than just the words of the song to bring it all together.

It also required a 1955 black-and-white movie with serious social overtones starring Glenn Ford, Ann Francis, and Sidney Poitier. It's that part of the history of rock 'n' roll that most people have forgotten.

To explore the genre's roots, we need to go back in time, five or six years before April 12, 1954, when Gussak gave the rim of his drum those two sharp raps!

From 1949 to 1953, Bill Haley was the leader of a talented group from Chester, Pennsylvania, who performed as *Bill Haley and the Saddlemen*, with Haley acknowledged as one of America's finest yodeling cowboys.[2]

Always searching for that elusive name to convey the star power that he and his group knew existed somewhere, Haley and the Saddlemen recorded under a host of names, including: *Johnny Clifton and His String Band, Bill Haley and the Four Aces of Western Swing, The Kingsmen*, and *The Lifeguards*.

They even cut a single as *Reno Browne and her Buckaroos*, although B-actress Reno Browne, the wife of western star Lash LaRue, never sung a note, nor strummed a guitar. However, her photo does appear on the sheet music for "My Sweet Little Girl from Nevada," one side of the 45-rpm single.

By 1951, Haley's music had become more rhythm and blues than country-western, and the term "rockabilly" was easing into America's consciousness. The group recorded "Rocket 88," a musical tribute to the Oldsmobile Rocket 88 automobile with the rockabilly sound, and the recording sold moderately well.

A year later they cut another rockabilly record, this one more *rock* than *billy*, titled "Rock the Joint," and Bill Haley and the Saddlemen were "this close," – hold up a hand and show an eighth-inch gap between thumb and index finger – to perfecting the sound that would rock them all the way to the top.

But, their fame wouldn't be as the Saddlemen.

It was time for the group to try yet another identity.

That's when a friend of Haley's suggested that since most people mispronounce "Halley's Comet"[3] (named for English astronomer Edmund Halley[4]) when discussing the famous comet that circles the earth every seventy-five years, that they might capitalize on the spelling similarities of *Haley* and *Halley*.

And so, Larry, Dick, and Harry, and the rest of you from the '50s and '60s, that's how *Bill Haley and the Saddlemen* became *Bill Haley and His Comets*. And yes, the group's name is Bill Haley and *His* Comets, although most everyone refers to them as Bill Haley and *the* Comets.

In 1953, although rarely remembered today, the group recorded what rock 'n' roll purists consider the first song of the new genre, "Crazy Man, Crazy." It was the first to be recorded with the new beat, reaching #15 on the charts.

In 1954, the group recorded what would become their biggest hit (over 25-million records sold), but it took a full year for the song to catch on. The song was "Rock Around the Clock," and for some reason, it lacked traction when first released, clinging precariously to the bottom of the charts for a week before burning out like, well, like a fading comet.

Bill Haley and His Comets fared better with their next recording, their version of a Big Joe Turner hit, "Shake, Rattle and Roll." It was money in the bank, a million records sold.

So, what was it that propelled "Rock Around the Clock" into the history books as the best known, best-selling, and the most famous rock 'n' roll song of all time?

The answer lies in the 1955 movie briefly alluded to in the third paragraph, a movie blessed with a musical score by Max C. Freedman and James E. Myers, the same two gentlemen who three years earlier had co-composed "Rock Around the Clock."

And the name of the movie? *Blackboard Jungle.* It was a dark, violent, racially-charged movie that opened with Billy Gussak's two famous rim shots. Rap! Rap! A second of breathless silence, followed by Bill Haley's sharply enunciated, *One-two-three o'clock, four o'clock rock . . . .*

This time "Rock Around the Clock" shot like a Roman candle to number #1 and stayed there eight consecutive weeks, and the kids of America rocked around the clock that night and the next, and the next, for a decade or more.

In February of 2006, the International Astronomical Union named an asteroid, "79896 Billhaley," in honor of the 25th anniversary of the death of the man who ushered in the golden age of rock 'n' roll. The man who helped a generation of 1950s and '60s teenagers put their glad-rags on, and in broad daylight, rock all the way to seventh heaven, and beyond.

---

[1] Don't confuse the *rock 'n' roll* of the 1950s – '70s, danceable music with a toe-tapping, finger-snapping beat and intelligible lyrics, with the eardrum-busting, profanity-laced "music" of the new millennium. The only thing the two musical genres share is the name, *rock 'n' roll.*

[2] To hear Bill Haley sing a yodeling song, check the internet for his rendition of *Yodel Your Blues Away,* (1949) with the Four Aces of Western Swing.

[2] *Stories from History's Dust Bin* (additional reading):
Vol 3, Nov 30:   Halley's Comet with Mark Twain

[4] To impress your rock 'n' roll friends, *Halley's* (rhymes with *Sally's*) *Comet* is named for English astronomer Edmond Halley (1656–1742). The comet, visible every 75-76 years, will make its next appearance in 2061.

Just let me hear some of that Rock and Roll Music,
Any old way you choose it.
It's got to be Rock and Roll Music,
If you want to dance with me.
Chuck Berry (1926-2017) Singer, songwriter

Alexander Hamilton

Born: Alexander, 10th Duke of Hamilton
History's other Alexander Hamilton.
Oct 3, 1767 (London, England) – Aug 18, 1852 (London, England)

M OST FOLKS KNOW of one historically interesting Alexander Hamilton, but few are aware of a second Alexander Hamilton. The two Hamilton's, each serving as statesmen for their respective countries, were born twelve years apart on opposite sides of the planet.

The senior of the two Hamilton's was born January 11, 1755, in the British West Indies, the child of an adulterous affair between James Hamilton, a Scottish man, and Rachel Faucette, a woman of mixed heritage. It was a tough life for the youngster who later in life would be ingloriously described as "the bastard brat of a Scottish peddler."[1]

The other Alexander Hamilton was born October 3, 1767 in London. He was the child of Archibald Hamilton, the 9th Duke of Hamilton and his wife, Harriet. As a member of an aristocratic Scottish family, he was indulged with all that comes with royal birth, including two honorific titles. He was both the 10th Duke of Hamilton and the 7th Duke of Brandon.

The first Alexander Hamilton, the so-called bastard brat of a Scottish peddler, became one of America's Founding Fathers. He was also the principal author of the Federalist papers, the man behind President Washington's economic policies, America's first Secretary of the Treasury, and today, the man whose portrait graces the ten-dollar bill.

The other Alexander Hamilton, the 10th Duke of Hamilton, 7th Duke of Brandon, served as a Member of Parliament, was an advisor to the Privy Council, and served as Ambassador to Russia for the United Kingdom. He was a Knight of the Garter, a prestigious British honor, and he also had an intense interest in Egyptology, the art of mummification, and from 1834 to 1852, he was the senior trustee of the British Museum.

Where America's Hamilton is one of the best examples of a brilliant roll-up-the-sleeves, no-nonsense workaholic, and so fiercely opinionated he was willing to fight a duel with Aaron Burr and lose his life; the United Kingdom's Hamilton was one of the UK's best examples of what is meant to "keep a stiff upper lip," and, as expected of a British dandy, to "always look your spanking best" regardless of how dire the circumstances.

We will now take leave of America's Hamilton to focus on Britain's Hamilton, a fellow as mentioned, who always looked his best and had a keen interest in Egyptology, especially the science and process of mummification.

Of the 10th Duke of Hamilton, 7th Duke of Brandon, England's Lord Lamington once wrote:

> ... and there never was such a magnifico as the 10th Duke, the Ambassador to the Empress Catherine. When I knew him he was very old, but held himself straight as any grenadier . . . always dressed in a military laced undress coat, tights and Hessian boots, his fingers covered with gold rings.

Hamilton's interest in mummies grew out of his friendship with Egyptologist Thomas Joseph Pettigrew (1791-1865), who was an expert in mummification and known affectionately to his friends and students as "Mummy" Pettigrew.

He was also known for entertaining dinner guests, hopefully after dinner, by bringing mummies into a viewing room, unwrapping them and allowing the guests to observe up close and personal the details of the mummification.

It was probably Hamilton's fascination with mummies and the process by which they could maintain their appearances long after death, that induced him to arrange with Mummy Pettigrew, to have his own body undergo mummification upon his death.

In 1842, Hamilton began the construction of an elaborate domed mausoleum on the royal grounds of the Hamilton Palace at South Lanarkshire, Scotland.

Inside the mausoleum would reside not only his mummified body, but the deceased bodies of the other nine Dukes of Hamilton, who would be relocated from the family vault to alleviate the overcrowded conditions of that resting place.

Hamilton purchased at considerable expense, a genuine Egyptian sarcophagus constructed during the Ptolemaic period (around 330 BC) and had it shipped to Scotland.

On August 18, 1852, at the age of eighty-four and with all the arrangements in place, Alexander Hamilton, the 10th Duke of Hamilton, 7th Duke of Brandon, on the very cusp of death suddenly realized he hadn't been fitted for the sarcophagus. Those present said he opened his eyes and said, "Double me up! Double me up!" And then he departed this life.

His last words were puzzling to those present, except for Mummy Pettigrew who instantly realized that the sarcophagus, perfect in size for nearly any ancient Egyptian king, was likely far too short for nearly any Scottish duke.

After death and mummification, Pettigrew surgically removed Hamilton's legs, and placed the body inside the sarcophagus, afterward placing the legs on each side of the body.

The sarcophagus containing the 10th Duke of Hamilton, and the nine caskets containing the nine other Dukes, were all placed inside the new mausoleum, and there they remained undisturbed for nearly seventy years, 1852 to 1921. That's when Hamilton Palace and the nearby above-ground mausoleum were deemed unsafe due to subsidence and scheduled for demolishment.

Prior to demolition, each of the mausoleum's residents were moved to the Brent Cemetery in Hamilton, Scotland. The first nine Dukes of Hamilton were buried in caskets befitting their royal status. But his excellency, Alexander Hamilton, the 10th Duke of Hamilton, 7th Duke of Brandon, was not buried in a casket, but buried inside his royal sarcophagus, looking good and resting comfortably with his royal legs neatly at his side should he need them to stroll through the Pearly Gates.

---

[1] From a letter dated 1/25/1806, sent from America's 2nd president, John Adams to Dr. Benjamin Rush, making it obvious that Adams and Alexander Hamilton were not close friends.

Probably the saddest thing you'll ever see is a mosquito sucking on a mummy. Forget it, little friend.
Jack Handley (1949-) Humorist

John Hanson

Born: John Hanson
Was he America's first president?
Apr 14, 1721 (Port Tobacco MD) – Nov 15, 1783 (Prince George's MD)

O N NOVEMBER 5, 1781, with the convening of the second *United States in Congress Assembled,* the first order of business under the newly approved Articles of Confederation was the election of the President of the Continental Congress.

In 1781 there was no executive branch of government as we know it today, so whoever served as President of the Congress was, using current terminology, the CEO (Chief Executive Officer) of the United States.

The process of getting to this point in 1781 had been arduous and difficult.

The signing of the Declaration of Independence five years earlier (1776) required that each state ratify the Articles of Confederation, yet, many legislators and their constituents were wary of imposing another layer of government upon themselves.

By 1780, all the states except Maryland had signed the Articles.

The reluctance of Maryland to agree to the Articles of Confederation had to do with something that might be expressed as "size matters." You see, Maryland, just as it is today, was a small state in 1780.

How small?

A look at a map of the United States as it was from 1776 to 1780 will astound you.

For instance, in 1780 Massachusetts was long and narrow. It began at the Mississippi River, then across Lake Michigan, and across Lake Erie including a piece of land between Pennsylvania and Lake Ontario, ending at the Cape Cod hook on the edge of the Atlantic Ocean. And, although it was disputed land, Massachusetts doggedly claimed ownership of a portion of present-day Maine as well.

And, not only did Massachusetts claim land all the way to the Mississippi, so did Connecticut, Georgia, North Carolina, South Carolina, and Virginia.

Thus, small state Maryland steadfastly refused to ratify the Articles until the above-mentioned states were willing to cede their western land claims.

Those states did eventually cede their western holdings and in January of 1781, Maryland's delegate, John Hanson, finally added his signature to the Articles, paving the way for the country to move forward.

With the Articles firmly in place, the first order of business of the second *United States in Congress Assembled,* was the selection of a President. With barely a quorum of states present (7 of 13 states), John Hanson, the last to sign the Articles was elected President.

Although George Washington[1] didn't vote for Hanson, he sent him a personally signed letter that reads, in part: "I congratulate your Excellency on your appointment to fill the most important seat in the United States."

John Hanson, as you now know was stubborn, but stubborn with a vision and blessed with a persuasive personality, and he was foremost a patriot!

During the Revolutionary War, he organized and sent the first southern troops to join Washington's army. When funds were scarce, he paid soldiers from his own pocket; and once, when the army needed shoes, he sent 800 pounds sterling directly to General Washington to buy the needed shoes.

During his administration, President Hanson established the first Treasury Department, the first Foreign Affairs Department, appointed the first Secretary of War, and directed Francis Hopkinson,[2] to create the Great Seal of the United States. He also set aside the fourth Thursday of every November as Thanksgiving. And he accomplished all the above in a single one-year term.

But every so often, there pops up a minor controversy as to who should be recognized as the first President of the United States.

So, let's lay out the contenders.

There were seven different "Presidents of the Continental Congress," *appointed* by their peers to wield the gavel during congressional assemblies prior to John Hanson. There are eight names below because Peyton Randolph served twice, as he was the first and third President of the Congress. Their names and lengths of service were, in order:

Peyton Randolph, 48 days in 1774;
Henry Middleton, 4 days in 1774;
Peyton Randolph, (second term) 14 days in 1775;
John Hancock, 2 years and 5 months (1775-1777);
Henry Laurens, 1 year (1777-1778);
John Jay, 9 months (1778-1779);
Samuel Huntington, 22 months (1779-1781); and
Thomas McKean, 4 months (1781).

And now we come to the seventh man to be called President, John Hanson, who served for one year (1782). But most important, Hanson can claim the distinction of being the first to be *elected* under the Articles of Confederation.

That's when, for the first time, the specific duties of the President were spelled out, including a presidential term of one year, with a second one-year term allowed after a two-year intervening period.

Then, after John Hanson's term, there were six additional men, each being *elected* to serve a one-year term as president.

They were:

Elias Boudinot in 1783;
Thomas Mifflin in 1784;
Richard Henry Lee in 1785;
Nathan Gorman in 1786;
Arthur St. Clair in 1787, and
Cyrus Griffin in 1788.

Only now do we come to George Washington who was elected to a four-year term (1789-1793) and a second four-year term (1793-1797).

Now, you might be asking, what happened to the single one-year term and the provision that required a two-year intervening period before you could be elected to a second term?

In other words, what happened to the process set forth in the Articles of Confederation under John Hanson's presidency?

What happened was that the Articles of Confederation didn't work out as hoped, a fact that took America's earliest legislators six years to come to grips with.

Thus, out of the Articles of Confederation was born the Constitution of the United States, which spelled out in much greater detail the duties of the president, including the allowance of an unlimited number of four-year terms.[3]

Stories from History's Dust Bin (additional reading):
  [1] Vol 1, Jan 1:   George Washington with Betsy Ross
  [1] Vol 1, Feb 22:   Featuring George Washington
  [2] Vol 3, Oct 2:   Featuring Francis Hopkinson

[3] On February 27, 1951, the 22nd Amendment changed the "unlimited number of terms" to a maximum of "two consecutive four-year terms" in office.

Those who own the country ought to govern it.
John Jay (1745-1829) Statesman

Ernest Hemingway

Born: Ernest Miller Hemingway
Suicide runs in the family.
July 21, 1899 (Oak Park IL) – July 2, 1961 (Ketchum ID)

A T SOME POINT before Ernest Miller Hall's death in 1905, he became so noticeably depressed that his son-in-law, Dr. Clarence Hemingway (Ernest Hemingway's father) took the precaution to remove the bullets from his father-in-law's Civil War era .32 caliber revolver.

And it's a good thing he did!

Because not long afterward, Ernest Miller Hall, for whom Ernest Miller Hemingway was named, placed the revolver to his head and tried to end his life, but lived because of his son-in-law's thoughtfulness.

When Ernest Miller Hall died of Bright's disease on May 10, 1905, the .32 caliber revolver became Clarence's, a memento of the time he had saved his father-in-law's life. That same .32 caliber revolver would later be passed on to the original owner's grandson, famed novelist Ernest Miller Hemingway.

Ernest Miller Hemingway was born in Cicero (now Oak Park), Illinois, a suburb of Chicago on July 21, 1899. He was the second of six children, the eldest being a sister, Marcelline, and following Ernest were Ursula, Madalaine, Carol, and a brother, Leicester.

Ernest's father, Clarence, was a successful obstetrician and the man who invented the spinal forceps that are still used today. His mother, Grace Hall-Hemingway had been a budding opera singer who once performed in Madison Square Garden, but gave up an operatic career when she fell in love with Clarence.

In high school Ernest was a sports reporter for the school paper, and after high school, he worked for the *Kansas City Star*. It was there where he began to use words and craft sentences, squeezing the greatest amount of meaning from the fewest number of words. For example, he once described his home town as "a place of wide lawns and narrow minds."

Classic Hemingway!

In 1924, the *Transatlantic Review* published his first short story, *Indian Camp,* and two years later 27-year-old Ernest completed what many regard as his finest work, *The Sun Also Rises,* a novel that has never been out of print.

Following the success of that first novel, he immediately began work on a second, *A Farewell to Arms,* but before he could finish the story, tragedy struck.

On December 6, 1928, Ernest's father Clarence spent the morning at his medical practice, and then entered his home, ate lunch, and burned an unknown number of personal papers in the furnace. Shortly thereafter, he walked into the master bedroom, drew the drapes and with his father-in-law's old Civil War era .32 caliber revolver, shot himself behind the right ear.

The reason for the suicide, at least publicly, had to do with Clarence's poor personal health and some unwise investments. Clarence did, in fact, suffer from diabetes and heart disease, and was prone to severe headaches. The latter, exacerbated by Florida real estate speculation and many poor investments that had put a serious strain on the family fortune.

But secretly some family members felt that Clarence had become mentally ill, and they were aware that the problem had been steadily growing worse.

When Ernest, who had a troubled relationship with his father, refused to attend the funeral, his mother sent him the .32 caliber revolver with which his grandfather had attempted to take his life, and with which his father had successfully taken his. With that, the old Civil War weapon found its way into the hands of the namesake of its original owner.

The Hemingway family would go on to experience an unexplainable number of suicides, and everyone familiar with Ernest, the man and his writings, is aware of Ernest's own suicide in 1961, but here is the back story.

In 1960, Ernest was in Cuba working on a manuscript, but for the first time in his life, he was experiencing serious difficulties in putting words to paper.

A friend and playwright, A. E. Hotchner, traveled to Cuba to see if he could lend a little support and cheer up his fellow novelist, and what he found was disheartening.

Hemingway clearly wasn't himself. Hotchner described him as "unusually hesitant, disorganized, and confused," and suffering badly from failing eyesight.

Following Hotchner's visit, Ernest and his wife Mary left Cuba for good, but Ernest grew more and more despondent about the ragged condition of his manuscript, which Mary had locked in a Cuban bank vault for safekeeping.

Mary took Ernest to Sun Valley, Idaho and there his condition worsened. He became concerned about everything: money, taxes, his unfinished manuscript, personal safety, his deteriorating vision, and more.

In early 1961 Ernest entered the Mayo Clinic in Rochester, Minnesota where he was treated for hypertension.

In April, he and Mary were at their cabin in Ketchum, Idaho where early one morning, his wife found him in the kitchen cleaning a shotgun.

After sedating him, she had him transported to a Sun Valley hospital where he was treated and released.

The date was June 30, 1961.

Then, in the early morning hours of July 2, 1961, he unlocked the basement closet where his guns were kept, and with the shotgun he had recently cleaned, he ended his life. He was nineteen days shy of his sixty-second birthday.

But there is more to the saga of suicide in the Hemingway family.

Five years after Ernest's suicide, his 64-year-old sister Ursula (1902-1966) committed suicide with an intentional drug overdose.

Twenty-one years after Ernest's death, his brother Leicester (1915-1982), a successful author himself, committed suicide by shooting himself in the head.

Thirty-five years after Ernest's death, his granddaughter Margaux (1955-1996), a successful fashion model, actress, and spokesperson for Fabergé jewelry committed suicide with a drug overdose.

And finally, forty years after Ernest's death, his youngest son Gregory (1931-2001), a physician and an author, who also lived a double-life as a woman using the name "Gloria," was found dead in a cell in the women's section of a Miami, Florida jail. The cause of death was hypertension and heart disease.

Today, some researchers believe the Hemingway family suffered from something called *hereditary hemochromatosis,* a disease that leads to mental and physical deterioration and can be genetically transferred within the family.

> *Every man's life ends the same way, it's only the details*
> *of how he died that distinguish one man from another.*
> Ernest Hemingway (1899-1961) Novelist

Walter Hunt

Born: Walter Hunt
A genius with no business cents.
July 29, 1796 (Martinsburg NY) – June 8, 1859 (New York NY)

W ALTER HUNT, BORN in 1796, may be the most prolific inventor you've never heard about. His list of accomplishments is impressive, if only for the sheer variety of his inventions.

For instance, his inventions include a forerunner of the repeating rifle, an efficient flax spinner, the first lockstitch sewing machine, a foot-operated streetcar bell, paper collars, a street sweeper, a swivel-cap bottle stopper, a knife sharpener, a rope-making machine, an early version of the fountain pen, a nail-making machine, the ice plow, the inkstand, artificial stone, the velocipede (a bicycle with a huge wheel in front and a tiny wheel in back), an ice boat, and there are others.

And one of those *others* was Walter's most enduring invention, and one that you have used many times yourself, perhaps even today . . . so please read on.

Walter, the eldest of thirteen children born to Sherman and Rachel Hunt, received his education in a small one-room schoolhouse.

As an adult, he was an expert brick mason, an efficient farmer, and a skilled mechanic. His friends called him a master tinkerer and in addition to inventing things himself, he was always on the lookout for ways to improve on other people's inventions. Take his improvement of an inefficient flax spinner as an example.

Born in Martinsburg, New York, he lived and farmed in nearby Lowville, a town dominated by a large flax mill. When the mill operated at peak efficiency, the town prospered; and when the mill experienced production problems, the people suffered, and that included Walter, his parents, and his twelve brothers and sisters.

In the spring of 1826, when the mill threatened to cut wages to offset a loss in profit, Walter convinced mill owner Willis

Hoskins that the poor bottom line wasn't the fault of the workers, but the fault of an inefficient flax spinner.

Highly motivated with his and his family's earning power in jeopardy, he designed and built an improved flax spinner in a matter of months and installed it in the flax mill, and no one lost their job or had their pay reduced.

After securing a patent (June 22, 1826), he went to New York in search of someone to manufacture his invention. But he quickly learned he was a better inventor than businessman. His heart wasn't in the business end, nor did he understand how to deal with investors. Thus, unable to find a manufacturing company that would build and market his invention, he located an interested investor and simply sold the patent.

Unfortunately, doing the creative work of inventing and patenting something, and then selling the patent to someone else became the *modus operandi* for Walter Hunt's non-existent business plan.

By the way, during that trip to New York he witnessed a child struck by a carriage. Unable to clear the incident from his mind, he invented a device to prevent similar accidents.

Although carriages had horns for warning pedestrians, they were useless when a horse or team was spooked, a situation that generally required both hands to control the animals. Hunt's solution was a "coach alarm," a foot-operated hammer that struck a metal gong.

His coach alarm was patented on July 30, 1827, and yes, when he returned to New York in search of a manufacturer, he ended up selling the patent instead.

In 1827, he packed up his family, moved to New York, and went into the real estate business. But he never lost his zeal for inventing things.

Before long he invented a new-fangled knife-sharpening grindstone. His new grindstone was a small, quick-to-use knife-sharpener with a protective guard, ideal for city folk, for which he received a patent on February 19, 1829.

This time he didn't even go looking for investors, he just sold the patent to an interested party and paid off a few debts.

In 1834, he built the first sewing machine to use an "eye-pointed needle," one that worked in conjunction with a "thread-carrying shuttle" located below the sewing surface. But fearful that his invention would contribute to the unemployment of seamstresses, he didn't patent the machine himself.

Instead, he sold a working prototype of the machine and the rights to his plans to George Arrowsmith, whose initial intention was to apply for a patent and build the machines himself, but he never did.

In 1846, twelve years after Hunt invented his sewing machine, Elias Howe of Spencer, Massachusetts built a machine of similar design, perhaps after purchasing Hunt's original design from George Arrowsmith.

The two machines were nearly identical, both used a curved eye-pointed needle and an arc motion to pass the thread through the fabric and through a looped thread fed from an underneath shuttle to create a lockstitch.

However, unlike Walter Hunt, Elias Howe patented his design, but the story isn't over.

While the above was taking place, the Isaac M. Singer company asked (or paid) for Walter Hunt to build one of his sewing machines for them, which he did. Then, the Singer company tried to use the machine designed and built by Hunt to break the patent held by Elias Howe

A court battle ensued during the early 1850s, finding that Elias Howe was not the originator of the eye-pointed needle sewing machine design, and credit was awarded to Walter Hunt.

Now, the court case gets even more complicated.

Because the court recognized Hunt as the originator of the sewing machine with the eye-pointed needle, the case continued with Singer disputing Elias Howe's patent rights, and because Walter Hunt had never patented his sewing machine, the validity of Howe's patent was upheld by the court in 1854.

Confused?

Just know that Walter Hunt didn't care a fig about the court battle and he simply went on inventing other things. That wasn't the case, however, between Isaac Singer and Elias Howe as they remained on bitter terms until 1867, when Howe passed away and his patent expired.

Now for the invention that was mentioned up front, the Walter Hunt invention that has never gone out of use, an invention that you'll surely recognize.

Hunt called the invention, a dress pin.

Today, we know Hunt's invention as the safety pin.

The story goes that he invented the dress pin while working out the details of a $15 debt owed to a friend. As the two friends were coming to an agreement regarding the debt, Hunt was mindlessly fiddling with a piece of wire he had picked up from the floor (or ground). Suddenly, he came up with an idea for a fastener that could be locked in place, making it safe for a lady to use on a dress.

Then, you guessed it, after making a few refinements he walked his idea and two sample dress pins to a manufacturer named Jonathan Richardson. Richardson liked the idea and purchased the rights to the design for $400.

Walter then called on his friend, smiled, paid his $15 debt, and pocketed a handsome $385 profit.

Selling his idea to Richardson for $400 was what some, in hindsight, might call a pinheaded decision. But not Walter Hunt, who continued to invent other things, ostensibly because there were other things that needed invented.

Walter Hunt died in 1859 at the age of sixty-two.

He is buried in Greenwood Cemetery, Brooklyn, New York.

If you think Abraham Lincoln became famous for inventing the Town Car, it's time to spend a few hours on history.
Bo Bennett (1972-) Businessman

Ivan the Terrible

Born: Ivan IV Vasilyevich
A Tsar is born.
Aug 25, 1530 (Moscow, Russia) – Mar 28, 1584 (Moscow, Russia)

T HE RULE OF IVAN IV, the first Tsar of all Russia, began in 1547 when he was sixteen years old, and ended with his death in 1584 at the age of fifty-three.

During the thirty-seven years of his rule, Ivan's approach to governing was as split as his personality. His early years of governance were marked with sensible laws and attempts at modernization. But, after a stroke and the death of his wife, he became mentally unstable, and his strong-arm indifference towards the lives of others earned him two of history's most infamous nicknames, "Ivan the Fearsome" and "Ivan the Terrible."

We'll begin our story with the birth of Ivan IV in 1530, when what is now the country of Russia was merely a scattered collection of sovereign city-states.

When Ivan was three, his father (Ivan Vasili III) died of blood poisoning from an infected leg. But, before he gimped into the after-life, he did two things. He gave his son the title of *Grand Prince of Moscow* and he named his wife, Elena Glinskaya, his successor, but only until Ivan was old enough to begin his rule of the Sovereign of Moscow, as their city-state was known.

To care for little Ivan, Agrippina Fedorovna Chelyadnina, a widowed and childless Russian noblewoman was chosen to serve as the Grand Prince's royal attendant.

Elena Glinskaya ran Moscow remarkably well and her period of rule generally receives high marks by today's historians. Achievements during Elena's reign included a reform of the currency system and an end to a miserable long-running conflict with neighboring Lithuania. She also enacted immigration reforms and made numerous civic improvements.

In 1538, five years into her administration, Elena was assassinated (poisoned) and there was no shortage of suspects.

Foremost were the brothers, Ivan V. and B. V. Shuysky, members of a rival political family who had never hid their contempt for Elena.

Also accused of the murder was Agrippina Fedorovna Chelyadnina, the widowed care-giver of Elena's son Ivan, the now eight-year-old heir-designate to the throne.

Who poisoned Elena may never be known, but someone had to be brought to justice, and politically it wasn't going to be the Shuysky brothers. That's when care-giver Agrippina was given a rather odd choice. She could become a nun, or else.

Assuming the "or else" was not in her best interest, she became a nun and young Ivan was tossed like a hot potato from one royal family to another.

During the remainder of his childhood and into his teens, Ivan watched as his mother's civic achievements were undone by bickering factions fighting for control of a rudderless Moscow.

Without belaboring Ivan's childhood and youth, everything came together on January 16, 1547. That's when 16-year-old Ivan IV was crowned the *Tsar of All the Russias.*

Within days, and responding to invitations, numerous families of Russian nobility paraded their teenaged daughters before the new Tsar, a smorgasbord of nubile Russian girls, most, if not all, linked to important political alliances.

"I'll take that one," Ivan IV might have said, pointing to Anastasia Romanov, and the royal wedding took place on February 3, 1547, a mere eighteen days after his coronation.

What existed in 1547 as a rag-tag collection of sovereign Russian municipalities with names like the Grand Duchy of Tver and the Principality of Ryazan, Ivan IV would, over time, unify under a single flag as the Tsardom of Russia.

But getting there wouldn't be pretty.

He began his rule by trying to follow in his deceased mother's footsteps, doing what he could to bring about reform and improvements after eight years of royal in-fighting.

As the Grand Prince of Moscow, Ivan had received an excellent education. He had also inherited the magnificent Library of Constantinople that his grandfather, Ivan the Great, had received as a gift from Constantine XI, the last Byzantine emperor.

To that collection, Ivan IV added manuscripts from the ancient Library of Alexandria, plus numerous Greek, Latin, Chinese, and Egyptian writings.

To protect his library, he moved it to a secure location beneath the city of Moscow and directed scholars to begin work on translating the books and documents into Russian.

He also introduced Russia to its first printing press, opened new trade routes, and built beautiful cathedrals. He didn't seem like someone whose name would soon become synonymous with evil.

But as history has repeatedly shown, power corrupts.

In the early 1550s, he became obsessed with expanding the Sovereign of Moscow into a collection of territories under his control.

In 1552, flexing Moscow's military muscle, he annexed Kazan and Astrakhan, former Tatar principalities. He expanded into Siberia and began putting into place the land-holdings that would eventually become the footprint of modern-day Russia.

Then, in 1553 and only twenty-three-years of age, he suffered a stroke and with it, a nasty change in personality. And if that weren't devastating enough, his beautiful Anastasia died before the end of the decade.

With Anastasia's death came the beginning of a sadistic streak that would grow worse over time.

For example, believing that Anastasia had been poisoned by someone from her own family, Ivan had members of the Romanov family arrested, some at random and others with whom he disagreed in the past, and had them publicly executed in horrific and degrading ways.

In 1564, due to the defection of some of his military leaders, Ivan considered stepping down as the head of state. But, as incredible as it sounds, the citizens of Moscow asked him to stay on. He agreed, but only on the condition he be allowed to create an independent territory surrounding Moscow for which he alone would have control.

It was an agreement the Russian people would long rue.

Ivan established an army of 6,000 men known as the Oprichniki, and took control of the outlying towns, confiscating property, and creating serfdoms managed by cruel masters.

He levied taxes and ruthlessly tortured and killed at will, especially those he suspected of disloyalty.

When the town of Novgorod stood up to the Oprichniki, Ivan personally led the attack against the city, torturing and killing at least 10,000 and perhaps as many as 30,000 citizens. Historians are not in agreement with the number of Novgorod deaths.

In keeping with his dual personality, Ivan had architect Postnik Yakoviev design one of the world's most beautiful buildings, St. Basil's Cathedral in the heart of Moscow.

When the construction of the cathedral was completed, Ivan had the architect's eyes removed to prevent him from building another edifice that might challenge the beauty of St. Basil's.

In 1584, Ivan the Terrible collapsed while playing chess.

He was taken to his bed chamber where he asked to be dressed in the robes of a monk. Hoping, perhaps, that he might slip into the hereafter without being recognized.

He died on March 28, 1584, at the age of fifty-three.

Ivan the Terrible ruled Russia with a gory fist.
Known for ordering that his enemies be skinned,
boiled, burned, and broken,
he was the favorite Tsar of Joseph Stalin.
Michael Farquhar (1971-) Author

Andrew Jackson
Born: Andrew Jackson
There's a key in this story.
Mar 15, 1767 (N or S Carolina) – June 8, 1845 (Nashville TN)

O CCASIONALLY, WHEN RESEARCHING a story, a totally unexpected piece of information comes to light. Nothing earth-shattering, and as you may suggest after reading the story, hardly worth mentioning at all.

Well, that's where we're at, you and me, wondering what to do next. Should we plow ahead, or skip and go to the next story?

The story about Andrew Jackson, a very colorful character in American history, is interesting by itself, but if you're not into marginally-useful historical minutia, you may not find the key in the story worth your time.

Okay! You're still here.

So, let's continue.

If you're aware of the toughness of hickory wood, you need only look at the uncompromising countenance of Andrew "Old Hickory" Jackson on a $20-dollar bill to understand the nickname.

However, it was said that despite his tough-as-nails exterior and sometimes over-the-top expectations, he was fair and well-liked by the men who served under him, and who would tell others, "The old man is as tough as old hickory."

He earned the nickname during the War of 1812. After taking command at the Battle of New Orleans with a relatively small army, Jackson delivered a beating to the British they'd not soon forget. It was the most one-sided battle of the war. The British counted over 2,000 casualties, which included 291 dead; the colonists had 71 casualties with 13 dead.

Jackson had proved himself an excellent military strategist and almost overnight, the hard-nosed, hard-driving, seldom smiling Andrew Jackson became an American hero.

Andrew Jackson's father died the year Andrew was born, leaving him and his siblings to be raised by their mother on a piece of land within the yet-to-be-surveyed border between

North and South Carolina. Incidentally, because the family lived on an un-surveyed border, President Jackson is the only Commander-in-Chief whose exact birth state is unknown.

During the Revolutionary War (1775-1783), thirteen-year-old Andrew and a brother joined the Continental Army.

Both were captured by the British and released after only two weeks' captivity. While there is no record of what happened while they were prisoners, knowing Jackson's personality, and assuming his brother was of like disposition, one can only speculate the boys gave their captors all the trouble they could stand. This alone would have made Jackson's victory at New Orleans thirty-six years later, all the sweeter.

Why?

Because Jackson forgot little.

Andrew's mother, Elizabeth, died of cholera in 1781 when Andrew was fourteen years old. Two uncles stepped forward to share in the raising of young Andrew, seeing to it he received an education. Shortly after his twentieth birthday, he announced he was a lawyer, hung out a shingle, and started a law practice.

As one of the founders of the state of Tennessee, Jackson ran for the U.S. House of Representatives and was elected, and then ran for the U.S. Senate, and won again. In both the House and the Senate, he was known as a man with a fiery temper, not given to compromise, and equally feared and respected.

In 1804, he acquired an estate known as the Hermitage where he established a residence, kept a large staff of slaves, farmed the land, and bred fine horses.

In 1806, Jackson and rival horse breeder, Charles Dickinson, long at odds with each other, agreed to a duel, a potentially fatal problem-solving technique not uncommon during the era.

Their differences were two-fold. First, there was an alleged reneged racing bet; and second, they flat-out didn't like each other. And to add fuel to what should have been a resolvable matter, Dickinson knew exactly how to raise Jackson's ire! Disparage his wife, Rachel.

Rachel had been married prior to her marriage to Andrew, and when the marriage failed, a divorce was sought. Rachel filed her divorce papers with the court and married Andrew.

Rachel's estranged husband, however, took a more cavalier approach to filing his paperwork, turning it in much later, sometime after Rachel's marriage to Andrew. Thus, technically, Rachel was briefly married to two men at the same time.

To correct the problem, after making certain all the paperwork was completed, certified, and the decree published, Andrew and Rachel repeated their vows to assure family and neighbors alike that they were indeed, legally married.

But, as fellow horse-breeder Dickinson saw the matter, it wasn't that simple. In his eyes, Rachel was a soiled woman, an adulterer.

Without mincing words, he published his virulent feelings in a local newspaper, stating that Andrew and Rachel "had lived in sin" while awaiting the court's finalization of her divorce.

As you may imagine, Dickinson's letter to the editor didn't set well with the fiery Jackson who sent a letter of his own to the newspaper, including an open challenge to Dickinson to settle the matter with a duel.

Dickinson, well-known for his marksmanship, accepted.

Jackson, no stranger to dueling himself, already had five successful confrontations to his credit. It was obvious to friends, families, business associates, and neighbors alike, that this settling of differences was not going to end well for someone.

On the fateful date, the two men paced away from each other, turned, and only Dickinson fired, striking Jackson in the chest but not killing him.

Under the rules of dueling, since Dickinson had fired, and Jackson had not, Dickinson was required to stand perfectly still while Jackson took his time to aim, which he did, and he did not miss.

Dickinson was dead, and Jackson would live with a bullet lodged in his chest for the remainder of his life, and it would not be the last time he faced a man with a gun.

Andrew Jackson has the distinction of being the first sitting president for which an assassination attempt was made. It took place on May 6, 1833, inside the Capitol Building, following the funeral for Warren Davis, a Representative from South Carolina.

As President Jackson was preparing to leave the building, a man named Richard Lawrence stepped in front of the president, quickly took aim and pulled the trigger.

"Click," the pistol misfired.

Lawrence pulled out a second pistol, aimed and pulled the trigger.

"Click," another misfire.

At that moment, Andrew Jackson, a frail, but feisty sixty-eight years old, mercilessly attacked the assassin with his cane, and as you would expect from Old Hickory, he didn't hold back.

After rescuing the assailant from Jackson's cane and temper, he was put on trial in the case of, "The United States vs Richard Lawrence." The prosecuting attorney stated the government's case and presented overwhelming evidence that Lawrence had indeed attempted to assassinate the president.

The defense called on several doctors who testified that Lawrence was delusional, believed himself King of the United States, and was thus mentally ill and incompetent.

The jury, deliberating only five minutes, found Lawrence *not guilty by reason of insanity*, and committed him to an insane asylum where he remained until his death in 1861.

Now, for the part of the story that, as mentioned up front, is neither earth-shattering nor of serious importance to the above case, but is an interesting piece of historical minutia.

The prosecuting attorney who tried America's first case involving the attempted assassination of an American president was Francis Scott Key,[1] the same man who nineteen years earlier (1814), penned the words that became America's national anthem, "The Star-Spangled Banner."

And that's the "key" to the story. What do you think? Was it worth the read?

---

[1] *Stories from History's Dust Bin* (additional reading):
    Vol 2, May 3:   Francis Scott Key with Daniel Edgar Sickles

> *It's a damn poor mind which can't think of at*
> *least two ways to spell any word.*
> Andrew Jackson (1767-1845) 7th U.S. President

Al Jolson

Born: Asa Yoelson
He broke the sound barrier in 1927.
May 26, 1886 (Seredžius, Lithuania) – Oct 23, 1950 (San Francisco CA)

ASA YOELSON WAS BORN in Lithuania, the youngest of Moses and Naomi Yoelson's four children. Coming from the humblest of beginnings, no one could have known that the little Jewish boy who came to America at the age of eight would one day be acclaimed the "World's Greatest Entertainer."

Yet, time has a way of replacing the world's greatest this and the world's greatest that, remnants from an earlier generation, with a supposedly updated set of world's greatest this and that's, but some things cannot be changed.

In the case of Asa Yoelson, the thing that cannot be changed is his forever link to what has been called, "film entertainment's finest triumph."

Times were difficult in the late 1800s and Moses Yoelson, a rabbi and a cantor, a leader of Jewish congregations in songful prayer, decided to go to America, find work, save his money, and bring his family to the new world.

It took four penny-pinching years, but in 1894, the very frugal Moses brought his family to the nation's capital where he was working as a rabbi. A year later his wife died in childbirth leaving an ill-prepared Moses to raise four children.

In 1895, Asa's older brother Hirsch found sporadic work as an actor and eight-year-old Asa, who idolized his brother, spent his time singing and dancing on the streets of Washington for the few nickels and pennies that were tossed his way.

But show business wasn't what Rabbi Yoelson wanted for his sons, especially Asa, and he fervently prayed that the boy would grow up to become a rabbi like himself. But it wasn't to be, and over time, differences turned into arguments, and arguments into hurtful blowups, and father and son lost their once close relationship.

As Hirsch found success in acting, he changed his given name to the more American-sounding Harry. Asa liked the idea and changed his name from Asa to Al.

In 1897, when Harry was out of work, he could be seen performing on street corners for coins alongside his younger brother, and on days when donations were plentiful, they would splurge and buy tickets to the various musicals staged at Washington's National Theater.

In 1898, the year of the Spanish-American War, Harry and Al found steady work as singing-performers, entertaining the troops that flowed through Washington on their way to new assignments. Also, around this time and fed up with the fighting at home, Harry left his argumentative father and moved to New York.

A year later, Al, now thirteen, left home and moved in with Harry. By this time Harry had already adopted a new surname, exchanging Yoelson for Jolson; and Al, once again following his brother's lead, changed his surname to Jolson as well.

In New York, Al found work as an extra in a Jewish play called *Children of the Ghetto*. When the play ended its run, Harry already had something else going, and so it was for the Jolson brothers, each supporting the other, together managing to keep the wolf on the other side of the door.

In 1901, Harry and fifteen-year-old Al, along with another performer, Joe Palmer, put together a song-and-comedy routine under the banner of Jolson, Palmer, and Jolson. The trio toured the vaudeville circuit with moderate success, not headliners, but good enough to work regularly, continually building on the show's strengths as they went along.

It was during one of those "we've got to do something to 'freshen up' our act" moments that Al applied burnt cork to his face and sang a few minstrel songs.

You might have expected the blackface portion of Jolson, Palmer, and Jolson to have been the inspired piece-of-magic that turned the show into a major vaudeville success, but it didn't. The show continued to be good enough to remain on the circuit, but billing was always in small letters beneath the headliners.

Yet, there was something about that blackface routine, a feeling while performing that Al really liked, and he would be reminded of that feeling a few years in the future.

Blackface didn't originate with Jolson, nor was it a novel idea. Nearly all of vaudeville's minstrels in those days were white men applying burnt cork to their faces.

After several years of Jolson, Palmer, and Jolson, Al left the trio to strike out on his own. During their days as a team, the three performers had stuck closely to a script to prevent someone from stepping on someone else's lines, or being caught off guard. But Al loved to improvise, and it was his ability to do just that, that he redefined himself on stage.

It was during a show at a small, intimate, San Francisco night club that he remembered the blackface routine and how comfortable it had felt to him at the time.

After intermission, and feeling that something needed to be done to energize both himself and the audience, he dug into his make-up bag in search of a container of burnt cork.[1] He applied the cosmetic to his face, stepped onto the stage, and sung a few minstrel songs.

Something happened during that solo performance; maybe it grew from the spontaneous banter that wasn't possible when he had to stay on script. But whatever it was, the audience went wild after each song, calling him back for three encores.

In New York, Jolson appeared at Hammerstein's Victoria Theater, followed by performances at Schubert's Theater.

In 1921, he would introduce his most famous song, "My Mammy," in Broadway's *Bombo*, along with three other songs that would forever be identified with him: "Toot, Toot, Tootsie Goodbye;" "California, Here I Come;" and "April Showers."

Al Jolson would not be second banana to Harry or anyone else for the next forty years because, as he would often stop in mid-performance to tell his audience:

> *Wait a minute!   Wait a minute!   You ain't heard nothin' yet!"*

In the third of those three brief phrases, make note of the operative word, *heard*, as that word would soon take on a whole new meaning in the business of film entertainment. That's because in 1927, Hollywood sound engineers figured out how to record the spoken words of actors and actresses onto the same strip of celluloid that contained the movie's action, and then deliver those sounds to an amplifier inside a movie theater.

It was this achievement of synchronized sound that has been called *film entertainment's finest triumph*, and it was the very thing that would elevate one man, Al Jolson, to incredible heights as the *World's Greatest Entertainer*.

It may seem strange today, to make a big deal out of a talking motion picture.

But, if you were alive in 1927 and went to see Al Jolson in the *Jazz Singer* (the world's first talking motion picture), you may have left the theater feeling much like the Israelites of old after witnessing Moses parting the Red Sea.

Watching images on a screen talk, their lips synchronized to the words they were speaking, seemed no less a miracle, and thus it was Hollywood's sound engineers and Al Jolson's voice that truly broke the "sound barrier" of film entertainment.

---

[1] Burnt cork is a homemade cosmetic used by minstrels of the Vaudeville era. It consists of cork ash mixed with water, and applied directly to the skin. Today, it is a known carcinogen and is no longer used.

A responsive audience is the best encouragement an actor can have.
Al Jolson (1886-1950) Entertainer

John Paul Jones

Born: John Paul[1]
A hero once lost; once again honored.
July 6, 1747 (Kirkbean, Scotland) – July 18, 1792 (Paris, France)

T HERE SHOULDN'T BE an American of teenage years or older who hasn't heard the phrase attributed to John Paul Jones as he stood on the smoldering deck of the 42-gun *USS Bonhomme Richard,* a Colonial warship off the coast of England. The date was September 23, 1779. The event was the American Revolution, and the problem was that 32-year-old Captain Jones was in a battle he couldn't win.

The deck of the *Bonhomme Richard* was already ablaze when the *USS Alliance,* firing at the *HMS Serapis* in a stormy sea, not only struck the *Serapis* with a salvo from its cannon, but it then collided with the *Richard,* further crippling Jones' ship.

The *Richard* began taking on water. That's when one of the ship's officers, believing that Captain Jones had been killed, surrendered the warship to the commander of the *Serapis.*

When the commander of the *Serapis* demanded the American flag be lowered as proof of its surrender, a very much alive Captain Jones suddenly emerged from the black billowing smoke. With flames from the deck licking at his boots, Jones set the British commander straight by yelling, "I have not yet begun to fight!" At least that's how we remember the story.

But, what is remembered in popular history, isn't always what happened, and here is an example.

During the Battle of Mobile Bay in 1864, legend has Admiral David Farragut[2] striking a heroic pose, his body erect and his saber pointing forward as he shouts to the man at the helm: "Damn the torpedoes![3] Full speed ahead!"

The historically accurate account has Admiral Farragut lashed to an upper section of the ship's rigging to give him a secure bird's-eye view of the battle. When his ship, the *USS Brooklyn,* slowed down to approach Mobile Bay, he yelled to a deck hand below, "What's the trouble?" The man responded that torpedoes had been sighted in the Bay. Admiral Farragut then directed Percival Drayton, the officer at the helm with the words, "Damn the torpedoes! Four bells, Captain Drayton, go ahead."

Admittedly, the historically accurate version doesn't carry the same courageous imagery as the saber in the air account conjures. But that's because the "Damn the torpedoes! Full speed ahead!" version is the product of a Hollywood scriptwriter who rewrote history to add visual and audible punch to the script of a 1943 war comedy titled *The More the Merrier* starring Charles Coburn.

But, enough of that, let's return to John Paul Jones' story.

What if John Paul Jones didn't say, "I have not yet begun to fight!" Does it matter?

The *London Evening Post* account of September 30, 1779, said that Jones' response to surrender was, "... that he might if he could; for whenever the Devil was ready to take him, he would obey his summons, (rather) than strike to anyone."

The *Edinburgh Advertiser* wrote that Jones told British Captain Richard Pearson of the *HMS Serapis*, "I may sink, but I'll be damned if I'll strike (my colors)."

A month later, October 12, 1779, the *London Observer* reported Jones as saying, when asked to surrender, "I have not thought of it, but am determined to make you strike."

Regardless, there was a lot of fight left in Captain Jones, and his incessant butt-kicking of the British Navy throughout the Revolutionary War is legendary.

We must never lose sight of the patriots who gave their last full measure of devotion, and those who continue to lay their lives on the line for this great country, and it's also important to remember that a little butt-kicking is necessary from time to time.

It's up to us as citizens to do our part by respecting the flag, taking pride in our veterans, and keeping the memories of our brave patriots from falling through the cracks of history. Because that's exactly what happened to John Paul Jones when he died in France in 1792. He had fallen through the cracks of history.

Here's the little-known back story of Revolutionary War hero John Paul Jones after the colonists won their independence.

When the Revolutionary War was over, Jones entered the service of the Russian Navy as a rear-admiral where he took part in several campaigns against the Turks. Although his naval skills were never questioned, jealousies among Russian officers caused him to be disliked.

In 1788, when told to report to St. Petersburg, he did so believing he was about to receive a new command. Instead, he was told to pack his bags, that his career in the Russian navy was over.

He left Russia and traveled to Paris where he went into retirement.

Four years later he fell ill and on July 18, 1792, at the age of forty-five, he was found in his apartment bed, dead from kidney failure.

A wealthy admirer of Jones, Pierrot François Simmoneau, paid F460 francs for his burial, which included an expensive lead coffin built expressly to preserve a body in alcohol.

Jones, after permission was granted by the French royal family, was then laid to rest in the Saint Louis Cemetery for Foreign Protestants.

Four years and a predictable French revolution later, a new government replaced the old, and the cemetery where Jones was buried, was sold as part of a government housing project.

Because the residents of the cemetery were foreigners with no relatives to monitor conditions, the once attractive cemetery became a cesspool of illegal business transactions, decaying animal carcasses, and a hideaway for gamblers wagering on cock-fights.

One hundred and seven years later (1899), with poor records of who was buried where, and with portions of the cemetery now covered by the government housing project, Horace Porter, the newly appointed American ambassador to France, began an exhaustive search for Jones' remains.

After six years of meticulous research, Porter located the lead-lined, alcohol-filled coffin, inside of which rested the very well-preserved body of John Paul Jones.

That same year, Jones' body was ceremonially transported from Paris to the United States, escorted by three naval cruisers.

Upon approaching the American coastline, seven battleships solemnly joined the procession.

On April 24, 1906, in a ceremony presided over by President Theodore Roosevelt, the lead coffin with Jones' body was temporarily interred in Bancroft Hall at the United States Naval Academy at Annapolis, Maryland.

Seven years later, January 26, 1913, his remains were reinterred in a beautiful bronze and marble sarcophagus at the Naval Academy Chapel.

One of the most respected warriors of the American Revolution had been found, returned home, given a hero's welcome, and laid to rest in a manner befitting a true patriot.

[1] John Paul Jones was born John Paul. He added the "Jones" around 1773 to avoid being caught and charged in the death of a crew member. He later claimed self-defense to avoid an Admiral's Court.

[2] *Stories from History's Dust Bin* (additional reading):
Vol 2, Aug 14:   Featuring David Farragut

[3] A Civil War-era torpedo was not the powered explosive device of today, but rather a floating device designed to detonate when bumped into by an object in the water, such as the hull of a ship.

I wish to have no connection with any ship that does not sail fast;
for I intend to go in harm's way.
John Paul Jones (1747-1792) Naval commander

Buster Keaton

Born: Joseph Frank Keaton
The master of deadpan.
Oct 4, 1895 (Piqua KS) – Feb 1, 1966 (Los Angeles CA)

B USTER KEATON'S LIFE had as many ups-and-downs as his silent movies had *pratfalls*, a word meaning to either fall figuratively, as in being humiliated, or to fall literally, as in landing ingloriously on one's keister.

But it wasn't for his butt-busting theatrical pratfalls that Joseph Frank "Buster" Keaton received his nickname, it was given to him from a close friend of the Keaton family, a person whose name you'll immediately recognize. Guaranteed!

Buster's vaudevillian father, Joe Keaton, and his partner, a Hungarian-born immigrant named Erik Weisz, were co-owners of a traveling show called the Mohawk Indian Medicine Company.

The show was not unlike most of the patent-medicine shows that traveled around the country in the late 1800s and early 1900s. Joe and Erik would either announce their expected arrival in town by pasting posters on lamp posts or to the sides of buildings, or they might arrive unannounced and park their colorful patent-medicine wagon somewhere sure to attract attention.

Before hawking their strange concoctions, they would often put on a brief show in the town's opera house, a hotel ballroom, or simply a public park, anywhere they could draw a crowd.

Then, after some on-stage bantering with clever patter and promises of miraculous cures, they would move the crowd to their medicine wagon.

There, standing amidst a wagon full of home-brewed nostrums and curious mixtures of claimed ancient Egyptian, Far Eastern, or Native American origin, they would tout the medicinal benefits of each colorful bottle, guaranteeing a cure for every ailment from broken bones to a broken heart, from feminine fainting to masculine rejuvenation.

By the way, Joe and Erik didn't confine their sales of home-brewed patent medicines to just one part of the United States. They traveled from state to state, from town to town, and that's how Buster came to be born in the tiny railroad town of Piqua, Kansas.

It seems that Joe Keaton's wife Myra was in her ninth month of pregnancy, and it was just after the traveling roadshow arrived in Piqua that the future Buster Keaton made an unannounced stage appearance of his own. The year was 1895, and it's quite possible the little tyke was literally born inside a vaudeville theater.

Eventually, the Mohawk Indian Medicine Company went the way of all good medicine shows, and Joe and Erik went their own ways as well, but they remained close and visited with each other whenever their paths would cross.

Joe and Myra Keaton became a Vaudeville act and when their son turned three, the act became *The Three Keatons*, with the newest Keaton making his stage debut in Wilmington, Delaware in 1899.

It was a rough act in which the toddler was taught to constantly get in the way of his clueless father. As a result, the senior Keaton would pick up the junior Keaton and throw him into the scenery, into the orchestra pit, and even into the audience. A hidden suitcase handle sewn into the toddler's clothing aided the senior Keaton with the tossing.

When the law showed up to check on stories of child abuse, they were never able to find any bruises or broken bones on the toddler, and in true theatrical form, the show went on.

In later years, Buster explained that his father had worked tirelessly with him, teaching him how to break a fall by becoming limp just before impact, and how to be funny by keeping a straight face. His deadpan expression eventually became his theatrical signature.

In 1917, a chance meeting between 21-year-old Buster Keaton and one of the silent era's biggest stars, Roscoe "Fatty" Arbuckle,[1] changed small time Buster into a Hollywood star.

Arbuckle asked Keaton to do a scene with him in *The Butcher Boy,* and it became the first of more films that you can count, and the start of a lifelong friendship between the two very talented actors.

Successive films were slapstick to the extreme with the smallish Keaton, the master of the pratfall, taking physical abuse after physical abuse from the portly, well-fed Arbuckle, all to the delight of the audience.

From being submerged in a keg of molasses to subjecting himself to the bite of an angry dog, he kept right on taking fall after fall.   And the money was great, collecting a regular paycheck of $40 per week for doing what came naturally to him, and earning considerably more than he was making on the Vaudeville circuit.

In 1920, Keaton struck out on his own as an actor and a filmmaker, and before the decade was over, he had churned out what was destined to become silent-era classics with titles like *Sherlock Jr., Steamboat Bill, The Cameraman,* and a host of others.   He had become more famous than Arbuckle, just as famous as Chaplin, and life was good.

In 1928, he signed with MGM and made a string of comedy "talkies" that never quite carried the punch his silent films enjoyed, and his career appeared to be over.

Then, in the 1950s, he turned up a second time, made a number of movies, most notably *Sunset Boulevard* (1950) with Gloria Swanson where he played himself, and then mostly cameos such as the train conductor in *Around the World in 80 Days* (1956), as 'Jimmy the Crook' in *It's a Mad, Mad, Mad, Mad World* (1963), as a witch doctor in *How to Stuff a Wild Bikini* (1965), and in his final movie, as the senile Roman statesman Erronius in *A Funny Thing Happened on the Way to the Forum* (1966).

He appeared in some television commercials and made a few guest appearances, right up to the time he fell asleep in 1966 to join his buddy, Fatty Arbuckle, who had done the same thing in 1933.   The two of them awaiting the arrival of the third of the big three of silent films, Charlie Chaplin, who joined them on Christmas Day, 1977.

And, oh! Before we forget, the story of how Joseph Frank Keaton became Buster Keaton, and who it was that gave him that name.

It seems that when the little guy was about eighteen months old, he fell down a flight of stairs, hit bottom, sat up on his own, never cried, and seemed to be none the worse for the experience.

His father's old patent medicine partner, Erik Weisz, was visiting when the fall took place, and it was he who picked up the toddler and remarked, "Well, that was some *buster* your baby took!" and Joseph Frank Keaton became Buster Keaton.

Later, Erik Weisz, Joe Keaton's former patent medicine partner would change his name as well, to one you'll certainly recognize, Harry Houdini.[2]

---

[1] Roscoe "Fatty" Arbuckle (1887-1933), was a 13-pound baby who grew up to become, quite literally, one of the silent era's biggest stars, tipping the scales north of 300 lbs. He was a mentor to Charlie Chaplin, and the man credited with having "discovered" Buster Keaton and Bob Hope. He was also the defendant in a highly publicized court case involving the 1921 death of actress Virginia Rappe.

[2] *Stories from History's Dust Bin* (additional reading):
Vol 1, Apr 28:   Harry Houdini with Joseph Dunninger

A comedian does funny things; a good comedian does things funny.
Buster Keaton (1895-1966) Actor

King George V
Born: George Frederick Ernest Albert
The punctual king
June 3, 1865 (London, England) – Jan 20, 1936 (London, England)

I N THE MEL BROOKS movie, *History of the World, Part I,* theater's "fourth wall," that is, the invisible wall that separates the actors from the audience is occasionally "opened" to allow Brooks, as the king, to speak directly to the audience.

In the above-mentioned movie, and after using his status as the King to intimidate – without fear of reprisal – an attractive lady of the court, Brooks slyly turned and faced the camera, and thus the theater audience, and in doing so added this catchphrase to the American lexicon, "It's good to be the king."

But there are times when being the king isn't all it's cracked up to be. This is especially true if those attending the king during his final hours are more concerned that his royal death is politically on schedule, than making sure his final moments are kingfully comfortable.

The royal problem, as understood by the king's royal staff, was a need for royal punctuality. In other words, the British kingdom would be best served, politically, if King George V would be so kind as to die before midnight.

After all, he had lived a good life, albeit one with more than his share of health problems.

In 1915, he was badly injured when thrown from a horse during a review of British troops in France, and for most of his senior years he had suffered from a combination of illnesses, including pulmonary disease, pleurisy, and septicemia.

In addition to those problems, a lifetime of heavy smoking had reduced the ability of his noble lungs to function adequately, requiring periodic administrations of oxygen.

And finally, the death of his sister, Victoria, the previous month had a profound effect on the way he was interacting with others. In other words, the king was royally depressed.

That King George V at seventy-years of age was in the final throes of life was a certainty, but not a problem.

Okay, so it was a problem for King George, but not for the empire where there is always a long line of potential successors waiting in the royal wings.

The problem, if you wish to call it that, was a concern on the part of the kingdom's public relations types, that the king might not be dying fast enough for the news of his demise to make London's morning newspaper, the *Times*.

Inside Buckingham Palace, a royal residence steeped in royal etiquette, there was the very real feeling that no king worth his crown jewels ought to die after the news deadline for the *Times*. To die after the deadline would be an unconscionable act, relegating the word of his passing to Britain's less respected evening journals. Egad! Horrors!

But apparently, such worries were unfounded, because when the British citizenry picked up their morning copy of the *Times* for January 21, 1936, they learned that the very punctual King George V had passed away at precisely 11:55 pm the night before, a mere five minutes ahead of the midnight news deadline and the rolling of the morning presses.

Moving ahead now to 1986.

On the 50th Anniversary of the passing of King George V, the personal notes of the royal physician who had attended His Majesty's final hours, Lord Dawson of Penn, were made public. Here's what the British subjects of 1936 knew, and what they didn't know.

At around 9:30 pm on January 20th, Lord Dawson issued a brief bulletin to the public, stating: "The King's life is moving peacefully toward its close."

Next, according to Dawson's notes, he phoned his wife, explained the situation, and asked her to "advise the *Times* to hold back publication."

Late into the evening, Sir Alan Lascelles, the king's personal secretary, entered the bedroom, stayed for a brief visit, then left. The secretary reported to the press that King George's final words, before smiling and lapsing into a coma, were, "How is the Empire?" It was a phrase that both the press and the people loved. It was so like King George to show more concern for the welfare of the Empire than for himself.

But, according to Lord Dawson's notes, the king's actual final words before receiving a sleep-inducing sedative and lapsing into a coma were a bit more on the blue side of the King's English, and somewhat north of a simple, "Damn you!"

Apparently, it was obvious to King George that he was about to be royally shafted – using a well-worn phrase – but was too weak to resist. So, use your imagination regarding the king's final conversation, but know that it was less "How is the Empire?" and more "What are you doing to me?"

According to Lord Dawson's notes, he reentered the bedroom at 10:30 pm and administered two consecutive lethal cocktails. First, an injection of 750 milligrams of morphine followed by a second injection of a single gram of cocaine.

Then he wrote that what he did was an act to preserve the king's dignity, and to alleviate the strain on the Royal Family so that his death could be properly announced in the morning paper, "rather than in the less appropriate evening journals."

The record will show that King George V was pronounced dead by Lord Dawson at precisely 11:55 pm Sunday evening, January 20, 1936, right on schedule and perfectly timed to allow the *Times* to carry the headline, "A Peaceful Ending at Midnight."

Thus, King George V, noted throughout his life for his strict adherence to punctuality and his great love for the Empire, did not disappoint, and that is the royal truth.

The highest of distinctions is service to others.
King George VI (1895-1952) Son of King George V

Max Kiss

Born: Max Kicsi
The man behind everyone's favorite "Ex."
Unknown (Hungary) – June 22, 1967 (Atlantic Beach NY)

M AX KICSI WAS a pharmacist in a Hungarian town near one of that country's major wine-producing areas. He was aware, as was everyone, that local wineries had long been adding a mild acid, phenolphthalein, to boost the level of tartness required by some wines to give them the perfect amount of swirl-around-the-tongue pucker.

Max was also aware, as was everyone, that too much wine consumed during an evening of fun, frivolity, and flirting could result in a nagging headache, nausea, or the nastiness of up-chucking everything that went down so easily the night before, a condition known as a hangover.

Max also knew, as did his customers, that the worst form of hangover by far was the kind that not only included a nagging headache, nausea, and up-chucking, but what the less socially refined of his customers might describe as *the runs*, a euphemism for Europe's dreaded *Führer's Foxtrot*, or as the condition is known throughout North and South America, *Montezuma's Revenge*.

As a pharmacist, Max was an excellent observer of people, a personable home-spun philosopher some might say, and a thoughtful, natural-born problem-solver.

He would have been a willing listener to his customers' morning-after problems.

He would also have chuckled each time a customer asked if there was anything to the old-fashioned cure known as "the hair of the dog that bit them,"[1] a tongue-in-cheek expression that suggests the best way to cure a hangover is to have another drink.

"Now, there's a solution that makes no sense," Max may have chided the "hair of the dog" customer while reaching for a pharmaceutical consistent with the science of the day, and suggesting that a spoonful of said science, stirred into a glass of water and consumed, might be helpful in returning order to the customer's biologic universe.

And while measuring out a portion of the medication to treat his customers' diarrheal problems, he would ask what kind of wine and how much had they consumed the night before, and he probably learned more than he needed to know about some of his customers' private lives.

But for Max, it was all done in the name of research. It may have seemed like small talk for the sake of conversation to his customers, but for Max, it was small talk with a purpose.

It's not known how long it took Max to determine who of the town's heartier wine drinkers suffered from hangovers only, and who suffered from hangovers exacerbated by an unwelcome case of diarrhea, but he did.

And therein lies the secret to Max Kicsi's success.

Sorting out all the possible combinations of the problem wasn't easy. There was no question the alcohol in the wine caused the headaches, but the diarrhea was another matter.

Too many runs, if we may use that word, to the outhouse could be related to several non-wine causes, including the onset of a cold or the flu, or to something as simple as what someone ate for dinner before leaving for the tavern, or something else altogether.

Mentally sifting through all the possibilities of who-had-what-to-drink with who-ate-what-for-dinner created some interesting preference patterns. Max, with his always friendly manner and casual conversation, finally narrowed the diarrheal problem down to those customers who preferred to drink the tart wines, those that contained the pucker-producing chemical, phenolphthalein.

Thus Max, with his analytical mind, had discovered the potential solutions to two problems that he was often asked about: diarrhea and constipation.

First, for customers complaining of diarrhea and headaches after a long night of drinking the tart, phenolphthalein-laced wines, he might suggest they give the sweeter wines a try to see if that eliminates the diarrheal problem. And he might suggest an aspirin or two to help with the headache.

Second, for customers suffering from constipation, he might suggest a nightly glass of one of the tart, phenolphthalein-laced wines until the customer's biological functions returned to normal.

Then, early in the first decade of the 1900s, Max Kicsi's name rose to the top of America's immigration list and he packed his bags and sailed to New York.

He settled in Brooklyn where he found work as a pharmacist, and like most immigrants of the era, he was anxious to become a *real* American.

So, he anglicized[2] his surname, Kicsi, which meant "small" in Hungarian, to Kiss, which means, well, you know what *kiss* means.

In early 1900s America, what few commercial laxatives were available were nasty-tasting liquids, the discomfort of the constipation often preferable to the taste of the treatment.

That's when Max tried mixing some of the intestine-relaxing phenolphthalein with tasty chocolate and do you know what? It was a heck of a lot easier to swallow than the foul-tasting liquid laxatives on the market.

He called his chocolate-flavored laxative *Bo-Bos,* that was until he happened to be reading a Hungarian newspaper article regarding an on-going parliamentary deadlock, the abbreviation for which is "ex-lax" in Hungarian.

He took a long hard look at the Hungarian abbreviation, thought about it, and decided that it could also serve as the perfect abbreviation for "Excellent Laxative."

Thus, Max Kiss, a newly-minted American pharmacist of Hungarian heritage suddenly knew he had the perfect name for his product. Ex Lax! The year was 1906.

By 1925, Max's product was – dare we say – moving so well that he established his corporate headquarters on New York's Atlantic Avenue.[3]

Max passed away on June 22, 1967.

The date of his birth and thus his age, are unknown.

He is interred at Mount Lebanon Cemetery in Glendale, New York.

[1] *he hair of the dog that bit you (me)* is a dictum of ancient origin, implying that the cause of a problem is also the cure for the problem. For instance, should you be bitten by a dog, the cure for the bite might be to either: (a) pluck a hair from the offending dog and place it into (or onto) the wound, or (b) cut the hair into small pieces and consume it in a cup of tea.

[2] To Anglicize means to adapt a foreign word, or phrase, to English usage, e.g. to anglicize *Juan* to *John.*

[3] Fake news: There is nothing in the historical record to support the rumor that Max once considered moving his corporate headquarters for Ex-Lax to Flushing, New York.

A hangover is the wrath of grapes.
Dorothy Parker (1893-1967) Poet, satirist

John Peake Knight

Born: John Peake Knight
He signaled the way of the future.
Dec 13, 1828 (Nottingham, England) – July 23, 1886 (New York NY)

T HERE'S A CORNER building at 12 Bridge Street in Westminster (London), and attached to that building, facing the intersection, is a circular plaque with black lettering on a green background, that reads:

City of Westminster
John Peake Knight, 1828 – 1886
Inventor of the world's first traffic lights
which were erected here
9th Dec. 1868
J. P. Knight Group Ltd, 1998

"Eighteen-sixty-eight," you remind the author, "was still more than a quarter century before the invention of the first gasoline-powered motorcars." Then you add, "Why would John Peake Knight even think about something like a traffic light in the mid-1800s?

It would be like inventing something today, that we can't envision and won't be useful for another quarter century, and besides, how bad could it have been on the streets of London in, say, 1868, anyway?"

Okay! Your point is well-taken, but let's answer your last question first, that is, "how bad could it have been on the streets of London in 1868?"

Imagine, my friendly but argumentative friend, a thousand horses, hundreds of dogs, and an untold number of goats pulling small carts along London's streets every day.

Then, imagine the stench that would percolate throughout downtown London from the droppings of those horses, dogs, and goats, and so my friend, you tell me how bad the streets of London could have been in 1868.

"Ah hah!" you press, irritated and feeling like your question was ignored, "what's that got to do with Knight's invention of a traffic light, before conveyances were motorized?"

Nothing. It's just that you asked, "how bad could it have been on London's streets in 1868?" And I told you.

But your question about the need for Knight's invention is a good one. "Would a traffic light really be needed to manage the traffic of horse-drawn carriages, push-carts, goat-drawn drays, bicycles, delivery wagons, and other 1800s type vehicles?"

Well, there *was* a problem, and it was this.

Statistics are available for 1866, a mere two years prior to Knight's invention of the traffic signal, and in that year London reported 1,102 traffic-related deaths and 1,334 injuries on city streets. And that was for only one year! It doesn't take a genius to figure out that over 10,000 people were dying every decade in the late 1800s mostly from horse-and-buggy accidents, and even more than that were injured.

That shouldn't make anyone happy except for the dour-faced guys in the undertaking business. It's hard to imagine that someone didn't realize before 1868 that something needed to be done to manage vehicle traffic.

True, there may have been others who recognized the problem, but it would be John Peake Knight, a man with a sixth-grade education, who decided to do something about it.

Knight ended his formal education at the age of twelve when a job came open in the parcel room of the Midland Railway, and he was intelligent, a trait that shined brightly through his skimpy half-dozen years of formal education.

By the age of twenty-five he had worked himself into the position of superintendent of the South-Eastern Railway; and fifteen years later he was named the traffic manager for the Brighton Railway Line.

Part of his success had to do with his approach to running a railroad. He was observant, proactive, and not one to wait until a problem needed fixed – before fixing it.

Knight was the first to introduce gas lighting inside railway carriages, a nighttime safety factor. Then, to make riding the carriages more attractive to the ladies, he introduced the "alarm pull" so the weaker sex (a perfectly acceptable reference to women in the 1800s) could signal the driver that a stop was necessary.

Ladies of the 1800s with their elaborately brocaded dresses, dainty shoes, floppy hats, tiny parasols, and yes, big bustles were a fragile lot those days. Alleviating their fear of traveling at speeds approaching 15-mph (five times the speed of a walking person) went a long way toward curbing their anxieties and preventing fainting spells.

Knight also introduced emergency brake cords as well as the Pullman sleeping car, and it was at about that time, the mid-1860s, that he began to direct his attention to public safety beyond railway travel alone.

In 1865, Knight suggested a dual-use semaphore[1] safety system that consisted of a brightly-painted moveable arm for daytime traffic, and hooks for the placement of red and green gas lamps on the moveable arm for nighttime traffic.

To assure continuous nighttime service, gas for the lamps was fed from an underground gas line. With Knight's system, the moveable arm in horizontal extension meant *stop*; an upward-angled extension meant *caution*; and the full downward position, meant *go*.

The device wasn't the stand-alone signal we have today. It required a constable to manually operate the levers that positioned the arms during daytime, and to rotate the upper-end of the device to change lamp positions at night. But it was an idea on the right track.

The first traffic signal was installed December 9, 1868, near 12 Bridge Street, close to the House of Commons, and it was likely a fascinating topic of conversation by the legislators who nodded approvingly as they safely crossed the street.

It was also appreciated by coachmen and others responsible for horse-drawn conveyances because the driver could look ahead and know whether to slacken the reins for a faster pace, or to pull on the reins to slow down, or to halt the horses altogether.

Then, on January 2, 1869, the device exploded from a faulty gas-line connection, killing the operating constable.

Although John Peake Knight's new-fangled traffic signal was short-lived, a mere twenty-four days, it had been effective.

But in 1869, neither the city of London, nor John Peake Knight had the will to give it another try. No one was willing to risk another gas-line explosion or the loss of another constable or pedestrians who may be standing nearby.

It would be another forty-three years (1912) before Lester Farnsworth Wire (1887-1958), the head of Salt Lake City's first traffic department, would successfully take up the cause and invent the world's first electric traffic light.[2]

---

[1] Semaphore: a word combined from the Greek *'sema'* meaning "sign," and *'phore'* meaning "bearer of."

[2] Lester Wire's 4-way traffic light was mounted on a pole in the middle of the intersection at Main Street and 200 South in the heart of Salt Lake City. It received its power from an overhead trolley line, and required a traffic officer seated in a small, gable-roofed booth on the sidewalk to manually switch the lights from red to green to manage the flow of traffic. The small booth where the officer controlled the device was referred to by the locals as *Wire's pigeon house.*

> *If you haven't seen your wife smile at a traffic cop,*
> *you haven't seen her smile her prettiest.*
> Kim Hubbard (1868-1930) Journalist, cartoonist

Marquis de Lafayette

Born: Marie-Joseph Paul Yves Roch Gilbert du Motier de Lafayette
American freedom fighter from France
Sept 6, 1757 (Chavaniac, France) – May 20, 1834 (Paris, France)

T HE NEXT TIME you're in Washington D.C. do the tourist thing. Take a few pictures of the White House and its beautifully manicured grounds through the protective fence that surrounds the president's residence. *There*, you might say to yourself, *these photos are good enough to show the folks back home*.

But if you want something a cut-above the typical tourist's snapshot of the White House, turn 180-degrees on your heel and face the beautiful park that moments ago, was at your back.

This is the view the President and First Lady see when facing Pennsylvania Avenue from the north portico of the White House. It's called Lafayette Square, seven acres of lush grass, manicured flower beds, freshly-clipped shrubbery, and no less than five historic statues.

Next, walk across Pennsylvania Avenue and onto the park grounds. The statue atop the large white pedestal and central to the park is President Andrew Jackson, "Old Hickory" as he was known, hat-in-hand astride a rearing horse.

The other four statues, one at each corner of the park are unique in that each honor a person from a foreign country who fought heroically on the side of the colonies during the Revolutionary War. They were Comte Jean de Rochambeau of France (SW corner); Friedrich Wilhelm von Steuben of Germany (NW corner); Thaddeus Kościuszko of Poland (NE corner); and the Marquis de Lafayette of France (SE corner), the man for whom Lafayette Square is named.

Turn now and face the White House.

By taking a few steps to either the right or the left, position yourself to where you've got a colorful flower bed in the foreground and either the Lafayette or the Rochambeau statue to one side of the White House. Frame the photo, click the shutter, and you'll have a photograph worthy of Ansel Adams. Okay, almost worthy of Ansel Adams, but light-years ahead of anything the tourists at the iron fence will take home with them.

Although all four of the foreign fighters have a story worthy of their statue, we'll concentrate on the one for whom the park is named, the Marquis de Lafayette.

Among the Marquis' ancestors were Gilbert de Lafayette III, a leader of Joan of Arc's army during the Siege of Orléans in 1429; the Marquis' great-grandfather, Comte de La Rivière, the commander of the Black Musketeers, the famed royal guard for King Louis XIII; and finally, the Marquis' father, also known as the Marquis de Lafayette, who died August 1, 1759, when struck by a British cannonball at the Battle of Minden.

And that brings us to the subject of this vignette, the son of the man killed by the cannonball, whose full birth name (Marie-Joseph Paul Yves Roch Gilbert du Motier de Lafayette) is longer than some folk's memories.[1]

With the passing of his mother (Marie Louise de la Rivière) in 1770, the young Marie-Joseph Paul Yves, et al., became, as his father had become before him, the Marquis de Lafayette. Thus, the very young, newly minted Marquis de Lafayette would inherit a yearly stipend of £120,000 livres, turning the boy into one of France's wealthiest citizens at the age of thirteen.

Being born into a family rich in the heritage of fighting men, the young Marquis was enrolled in military schools to enable him to carry on the family tradition as a musketeer.

To his credit, perhaps because he had been born into such a wealthy family, and a family noted for independent thought and an open scorn of danger, he sensed from an early age it would ultimately be his responsibility to fight for a worthy cause.

The following year (1771), fourteen-year-old Lafayette was commissioned a lieutenant, but since he had not yet finished military school, his commission limited his wearing of the uniform to military parades only.

That same year, a marriage was arranged between Lafayette and the 12-year-old daughter of Jean-Paul François, a French military leader, with nuptials held three years later (1774).

The wedding present to the 17-year-old groom, a captain's commission in the Dragoons.

In 1775, Lafayette, now eighteen and a captain in the Dragoons, became interested in the broiling conflict between Britain and her colonies across the Atlantic.

Acutely aware it was a British-fired cannonball that killed his father at the Battle of Minden, he began to think of ways to enter the fight on behalf of the colonies.

He believed it would be a fight that, if won, would diminish Britain's standing in the world; and perhaps more importantly to him, it would be a personally satisfying way of exacting revenge for the death of his father.

On December 7, 1776, nineteen-year-old Lafayette spoke to American agent Silas Deane about receiving a commission in Washington's Army, and was rewarded with the rank of Major General.

But there was a problem.

Washington's Continental Army didn't have the funds to pay for the young Frenchman's trip to America.

When Lafayette's father-in-law (and commanding officer) learned of Lafayette's plans to leave France to fight for the colonists, he forbade his son-in-law to leave the country.

But Lafayette was very much his own man, albeit a very young and very wealthy young man, so he chartered a sailing ship, the *La Victoire* for £112,000 livres, to make the trip to America.

But, when rumors of Lafayette's decision to travel to America came to the attention of King George of England, King George put the squeeze on King Louis XVI of France, who in turn put the squeeze on the young Marquis de Lafayette.

Lafayette was told in no uncertain terms, that any attempt on his part to fight on behalf of the colonies would ultimately result in his capture and imprisonment.

But Lafayette would not be dissuaded. He traveled first to Spain where he disguised himself as a woman, and then, on April 20, 1777, he began his covert trip to America.

When the ship's captain announced his intention to dock in the West Indies to sell his cargo, Lafayette confided his identity to the captain, and then paid cash for the cargo in exchange for bypassing the West Indies and sailing directly to America.

On June 13, 1777, the ship docked near Georgetown, South Carolina, and that's how it came to pass that the Marquis de Lafayette came to America, disguised as a woman, with enough cash in his pocket to buy a ship's cargo and reroute the ship so he could make himself available as a twenty-year-old general in George Washington's army.

And for this, plus for serving honorably and with distinction during the Revolutionary War, the youthful Marquis de Lafayette was named one of America's foremost foreign heroes, and the namesake of one of Washington's most beautiful parks, one that the occupants of the White House look out upon every day.

[1] Regarding his extremely long birthname, he reportedly stated in his autobiography that it wasn't his fault, that he had been given the name "of every conceivable saint who might offer (him) more protection in battle." [The History Channel website]

Humanity has won its battle. Liberty now has a country.
Marquis de Lafayette (1757-1834) Aristocrat, patriot

William Lear

Born: William Powell Lear
Like Sinatra, he did things, "his way."
June 26, 1902 (Hannibal MO) – May 14, 1978 (Reno NV)

I N 1916, AFTER COMPLETING the eighth grade at Kershaw Grammar School in Chicago, Illinois, William "Bill" Lear enrolled at Englewood High. But, it wasn't long before he was asked to leave for being disrespectful toward his teachers.

It seems he insisted on doing things "his way," as if he were smarter than his teachers, and he was sent home with a note to his mother asking that he not return to Englewood.

The message of that note would become a recurring theme in his life.

With his formal education on hold, he went to work for the Multigraph Company repairing typesetting machines, a complex invention that looked as if it had been invented by newspaper cartoonist Rube Goldberg.[1]

If you've ever watched a noisy clanking too many moving parts all moving at the same time typesetting machine, you'll wonder how a 14-year-old lad could possibly handle such a job. But Bill did, and he was very good at it.

The son of divorced parents, Bill and his mom bounced around, living with relatives in Iowa and friends in Illinois. He also spent a summer with his father in Tulsa, Oklahoma, where the pair worked together to rebuild a Model-T Ford.

When the summer was over, rather than return to his mother in Chicago, he joined the navy and went to radio technician school.

Remember the "his way" problem Bill had in high school?

Well, it happened again.

It was soon apparent that Bill Lear's mind operated under a completely different set of expectations than that of the navy. But the military was kind, giving Bill an early, but honorable discharge, and he left with nothing to show for his brief time in the service, except for a head jammed-full of radio repair skills.

After his discharge, he returned to Tulsa hoping to finish high school.

He enrolled at Tulsa Central High School, took a required academic placement test, and scored so high that a school counselor assured him he wouldn't have any problem graduating in a single year.

Bill signed up for the courses he needed for graduation, added a few interesting electives, smiled broadly, and dug in like there was no tomorrow.

Then!

Déjà vu all over again.

He was expelled before the school year was half-way over for demonstrating a total disregard toward the teaching staff. *He was there to learn*, he was told in no uncertain terms, *not to be a pain in the rear by trying to prove his teachers wrong.*

You may have sensed that Bill wasn't a model student, and you would be right.

But he was highly intelligent, an avid reader, and he could recall everything he read, mentally sorting information and storing it in a steel-trap mind with no apparent limits.

For relaxation, he read books about geniuses like Albert Einstein,[2] Thomas Edison, Nikola Tesla,[3] and others.

In 1919, he took a $40 a week job as a mechanic at Chicago's Grant Park Airport, exchanging his weekly salary for flying lessons. As an unrepentant scholar who twice failed to finish high school, there was no way he could know that those flying lessons, and a pure love of aviation, would one day bring him world-wide fame.

In 1924, twenty-two years old and not sure of what to do, he learned that a man named Clifford Reid in Quincy, Illinois, was planning to expand his auto supply business to include radio. Lear, based on his brief stint in the navy as a *radio technician*, told Reid he was a *radio engineer* and he got the job.

From that point on, Lear took control of his life and what he achieved was remarkable.

While working for Reid, he met a man named Julius Bergen, and the pair founded Quincy Radio Laboratories.

He became involved in broadcasting and helped to establish radio station KVOO in Tulsa, the station that launched the career of Paul Harvey,[4] known for his "Rest of the Story" broadcasts.

He worked for Universal Battery where he invented a *battery eliminator,* a device that converted alternating current to direct current, making it possible to power a standard battery-driven device from a wall socket. Confusing? To non-technical types like you and me perhaps, but it wasn't the least bit confusing to Bill Lear who, when faced with a problem, usually invented his way to a solution.

At the time of his death in 1978, he held over 150 patents.

When Lear and a partner, Ernest Tyrman, got into trouble building and selling radio sets using patented parts and processes they were not licensed to use, Ernest developed ulcers, checked into a hospital, and died following surgery.

What did Lear do? He changed his diet and then patented new parts and invented new processes that didn't infringe on other peoples' patents.

He established Lear Radio Laboratories, one of the first companies to pursue electronic miniaturization.

The company, located in the basement of his old home in Chicago, successfully reduced the size of radio frequency coils from that of a closed fist, to that of a quarter. Zenith Electronics ordered 50,000 units the first time they saw them.

In 1929, he sold Lear Radio Labs to buy one-third interest in Galvin Manufacturing. There, he designed, built and patented the first car radio, and when Paul Galvin and Bill Lear were considering a brand name for the invention, they decided on "Motorola," a made-up name, which at least to Galvin and Lear, implied "sound in motion."

The name immediately became as popular as the radio it represented, and in 1930, Galvin Manufacturing changed its name to the Motorola Corporation.

Bill's mind and his inventiveness never rested.

Whenever he faced a problem or a need, he found a solution, and many of those solutions became inventions. Now, consider these facts about Bill Lear:

He never got beyond the eighth-grade.

He and a friend founded Quincy Radio Laboratories.

He helped to establish radio station KVOO in Tulsa.

He invented numerous electronic components at Universal Battery.

He established Lear Radio Labs and invented miniaturized radio frequency coils.

He owned a third of Galvin Manufacturing, which became the Motorola Corporation after he designed and patented the first automobile radio.

He invented the 8-track stereo player, turning cars into highway concert halls.

And perhaps his most amazing venture was the founding of the Lear Jet Corporation in the late 1950s. The Wichita, Kansas company (now owned by Canadian Bombardier Aerospace), is best-known for small, fast, inexpensive (as jets go) aircraft.[5]

Bill Lear was also known for having a keen, subtle, sense of humor, the proof of which can be found in the name he gave his second daughter, Shandra.

Go ahead. Say her full name aloud, "Shandra Lear" and experience the soft side of Bill Lear, a prolific inventor and brilliant businessman with a mind brighter than the chandelier in your living room.

---

[1] Rube Goldberg (1883-1970), an American cartoonist known for depicting complicated machines for performing simple tasks. He is also the namesake for the Rube Goldberg Machine Contests, challenging high school and college students to build a complicated machine to perform a very simple task requiring at least 25 but no more than 75 actions.

Stories from History's Dust Bin (additional reading):
   [2] Vol 1, Apr 18:   Featuring Albert Einstein
   [3] Vol 2, Jul 10:   Featuring Nicola Tesla
   [4] Vol 3, Sep 4:   Featuring Paul Harvey

[5] Learjet, known for its corporate jets, employed 3,200 workers in 2013, and delivered its 3,000th Learjet in June 2017.

For me, the best of life is the exercise of ingenuity –
in design, in finance, in flying, in business.
William Lear (1902-1978) Inventor, businessman

Thaddeus S. C. Lowe

Born: Thaddeus Sobieski Constantine Lowe
Father of Military Aerial Reconnaissance
Aug 20, 1832 (Jefferson Mills NH) – Jan 16, 1913 (Pasadena CA)

THADDEUS S. C. LOWE'S formal education ended with his completion of the fourth grade, a fact he mentioned often in conversation with others. Yet, he excelled in chemistry and meteorology, and is credited with the invention of an ice-making machine, with which he established the Citizen's Ice Company in Los Angeles. He also owned the Pasadena Grand Opera House and built an observatory with a 16-inch reflective telescope atop Echo Mountain near Los Angeles.

Today, not far from Echo Mountain stands Mt. Lowe, originally Oak Mountain, but renamed in 1893 to honor "Professor" Lowe, who did all the above as he loved to say, "with no more than a fourth-grade education."

Thaddeus S. C. Lowe was foremost an aeronaut, who on at least one occasion prior to the Civil War, suggested to President Lincoln[1] that a hot-air balloon in the service of the Union would be a good thing.

Prior to the Civil War, Lowe considered crossing the Atlantic Ocean in the *City of New York*, a massive balloon he later renamed the *Great Western*.

The *Great Western*, by the way, sported a Venice-style gondola for its passengers instead of the familiar wicker basket, the design of which could have served as the inspiration for the cover of a Jules Verne[2] novel.

Extending out from the gondola were many strange-looking gadgets and just below the opening of the giant balloon were numerous flags. But most unusual, and mounted to the side of the gondola, was a steam-powered paddle wheel in the event the balloon should be forced to ditch in the ocean.

In fact, it's worth taking a break from reading, just to browse the internet for an artist's illustration of Lowe's grand balloon.

The *Great Western's* maiden flight was a successful Philadelphia to New Jersey run on June 28, 1860, after which Lowe announced everything was ready for a transatlantic flight.

The first attempt to cross the ocean was on September 7, 1860, but a strong gust of wind ripped the huge envelope apart before it could be inflated.

After repairs, during an attempt to test the airworthiness of the repaired balloon, a bulge formed where the wind had earlier torn the fabric and the balloon was placed in storage.

On April 19, 1861, two days after Virginia seceded from the Union, Lowe took off in a smaller balloon, the *Enterprise,* to fly from Cincinnati to Maryland.   But, the undependable winds carried him south to Charleston, South Carolina, the heart of the Confederacy, where he was taken prisoner as a Union spy.

After persuasively arguing he wasn't a spy, he returned home to find a letter from President Lincoln asking him to come to Washington.

On July 11, 1861, Lowe met with the president, where he was asked to elaborate on the ways in which a balloon might be helpful to the Union cause.

The following is from the *War Eagle,* an 1861 newspaper, regarding a conversation between President Lincoln and Mr. Lowe, as reported by Wilfrid Dellquest.

> *"I have heard about you," said the President. "You are Thaddeus Lowe. I thought you were going to fly across the Atlantic in your airship, the City of New York?"*
>
> *"I was forced down, sir, by a gale."*
>
> *Lincoln smiled, "You landed in South Carolina, Mr. Lowe, and the natives were going to lynch you. They thought you were the Devil. They should have known better than to think the Devil would come from the sky."*
>
> *"The Sheriff put me in jail to save me from the mob. It was all a misunderstanding."*
>
> *Lincoln closed his eyes for a moment. "You're asking me to equip our Army with balloons to observe*

enemy movements. I should think, Mr. Lowe, that
balloons would make splendid targets."

Lowe, shook his head, "Balloons are not easily
shot down, Mr. President. They would be fixed at
altitudes beyond the range of enemy guns. There
would be nothing to shoot at, except the almost
invisible mooring ropes. The balloons would be
equipped with telegraph wires, and our field
headquarters would receive instant reports of enemy
movements. Not only that, sir, but our own artillery
fire could be directed from the air."

"Mr. Lowe," said President Lincoln, "I have
always been a great hand at playing hunches, and I
have a hunch that something may come out of this idea
of yours.

I may get cussed out for doing it, but I'm going to
appoint you Chief Aeronaut of the United States
Army."

The next day, Lowe, with a balloon named the *Intrepid,* a
telegraph key, and 500-feet of connecting wire, ascended 500-
feet above the White House lawn and sent President Lincoln a
message, which began: "I have the pleasure of sending you this
first dispatch ever telegraphed from an aerial station."

Thaddeus Lowe went on to serve the Union as an aeronaut,
but it wasn't without a few close calls. For instance, his first
outing was to observe the fighting at the First Battle of Bull Run.
It was textbook perfect except for one thing. Those pesky winds
changed direction and he was forced down behind enemy lines
again, this time, badly twisting his ankle upon landing.

Fortunately, he was found by Union soldiers.

Unfortunately, they were unable to transport him back to the
Union lines.

Fortunately, Thaddeus's wife, after being informed of her
husband's predicament, dressed herself as a disgusting hag and
gee-hawed, spit, wheezed, and blew her nose through enemy
lines in a dilapidated wagon containing yards and yards of foul-
smelling canvas.

After finding her husband, she hid him, his balloon, and the gondola under the canvas and continued the charade by once again gee-hawing, spitting, wheezing, and blowing her nose back to the Union side of the war.

Ever the entrepreneur, Lowe retired to Pasadena, California in 1890, built a 24,000-square foot mansion, started a water-gas company, founded a bank, was a partner of the Mount Lowe Railway, opened some ice-making plants, bought the Pasadena Opera House, and we've traveled full circle, returning to the place where we started this story.

Lowe passed away on January 16, 1913 at his daughter's home in Pasadena. He was eighty years old, a member of the U.S. Army Military Intelligence Hall of Fame, an American original, and as he would fondly tell you, he did it all "with no more than a fourth-grade education."

Did we mention that already?

---

[1] *Stories from History's Dust Bin* (additional reading):
   Vol 2, Feb 12:   Featuring Abraham Lincoln

[2] See Jules Verne in this book, pages 352-355, to read about the man who wrote *Five Weeks in a Balloon* and *Around the World in 80 Days*.

I learned a great many years ago,
that in a fight between a husband and a wife,
a third party should never get between
the woman's skillet and the man's ax.
Abraham Lincoln (1809-1865) 16th U.S. President

Percival Lowell

Born: Percival Lawrence Lowell
The man behind the discovery of Pluto.
Mar 13, 1855 (Cambridge MA) - Nov 12, 1916 (Flagstaff AZ)

B ASED ON THE odd deviations he saw in the orbits of Neptune and Uranus, astronomer Percival Lowell was convinced that somewhere beyond Neptune existed another, yet-to-be-discovered, ninth planet. Although he never saw the planet himself, another astronomer, Clyde Tombaugh did, and here's something not commonly known. The name of the new planet, *Pluto,* was suggested by an eleven-year-old girl from England, approved by Tombaugh and his associates – and for a very special reason.

Percival Lowell grew up in a wealthy, prominent Boston family. His brother, Abbott Lowell was president of Harvard University from 1909 to 1933; his sister, Elizabeth Lowell Putnam is the namesake of the Elizabeth Lowell Putnam Prize in Mathematics, still awarded today; and another sister, Amy Lowell, won the Pulitzer Prize for Poetry in 1926.

So, what's a proper Bostonian named Percival to do to set himself apart from his over-achieving siblings? (1) Use his allowance to build a world-class observatory? (2) Perform the groundwork that would lead to the discovery of a new planet fourteen years after his death? (3) Work tirelessly to prove the existence of life on Mars? (4) Take a trip to Venus aboard an alien spaceship piloted by a small, almond-eyed fellow named Murray?

Okay, write-off number 4, the trip to Venus with Murray never happened. But the other three things did.

1. In 1894, in Arizona Territory not far from the small town of Flagstaff, Lowell built an observatory to pursue his interest in the planet Mars. It was the first modern observatory built away from the artificial light of a population center. It also took advantage of the 7,200-foot altitude and crystal-clear Arizona

skies to assure optimal viewing of space, and in 1896, the world's fourth largest telescope, the 24-inch Alvan-Clark refracting telescope, was installed at the observatory.

2. Although not known to Lowell during his lifetime, it would be his untiring work that would lead to the 1930 discovery of a ninth "planet." Although Pluto was initially considered a standard, albeit small planet, its planethood was questioned in 1992, and its designation as a standard planet was downgraded to dwarf planet status in 2006.

3. Lowell would make a cogent case for the existence of canals and intelligent life on Mars, a claim that fascinated the public, but would be discredited during his lifetime and finally put to rest by NASA's Mariner missions to Mars in 1965 and 1972.

Let's begin Percival Lowell's story with his graduation from Harvard in 1876. Honored as one of the commencement speakers, he may have surprised family, friends, and faculty alike when he delivered a speech titled, *The Nebular Hypothesis*, a theoretical presentation on the formation of the solar system, instead of a speech on a topic within his major field of study, business.

That surprising speech was a harbinger of things to come.

For eleven years after graduation, he used his business degree to benefit his family's textile business before tapping into his family's wealth and influence to begin a serious study of astronomy. Of special interest to Lowell was the planet Mars, and it was that interest that led him to Arizona.

Lowell, highly intelligent and wealthy, had the means to probe his personal interests.

He was convinced that Mars had once been home to an advanced race of technologically-advanced *Martians*, his term.

Using his telescope, he produced drawings of what he thought were canals flowing downward from polar ice caps. He believed the canals had been built to provide water to the darker areas on the planet's surface, which he assumed were patches of vegetation.

His speculative enthusiasm for a once-populated Mars quickly fired public imagination. He delivered lectures on the canals and the people he believed constructed them, authoring three books, *Mars* (1895), *Mars and its Canals* (1906), and *Mars as the Abode of Life* (1908).

Lowell's greatest contribution to astronomy, however, came late in life when he went in search of a ninth planet.

The eighth planet, Neptune, had been discovered in 1846 when astronomers observed strange movements known as "perturbations," in the orbit of the seventh planet, Uranus. The perturbations were perceived, correctly, to result from the effects of gravitational pull between the known planet, Uranus and an unknown planet (Neptune).

Lowell was certain that what had held true and resulted in the discovery of Neptune, would hold true for the discovery of a ninth planet as well.

In 1906, Lowell, with his powerful 24-inch telescope and with help from his long-time friend and colleague, William H. Pickering,[1] who shared Lowell's belief in the existence of a ninth planet, began a systematic and carefully planned search to locate the elusive piece of solar real-estate.

The search included the systematic photographing of specific areas of the night sky, typically two or three weeks apart, and then comparing the image plates to determine if any of the heavenly bodies had shifted position. Stars being fixed objects; planets being moving objects.

In 1916, ten years into his research, Percival Lowell died of a cerebral hemorrhage, believing that his work had been in vain.

However, set aside by Lowell for future examination, were two photographic plates, one taken March 19, 1915, and the other April 7, 1915, for which technology didn't exist during his lifetime to credit him with the discovery of Pluto. But the needed technology, a "blink comparator," did exist fifteen-years later (1930) when 23-year-old Clyde Tombaugh worked at the Lowell Observatory.

On February 18, 1930, Tombaugh subjected the two photographs to the blink comparator. With its ability to rapidly shift two photographic images back and forth to determine the movement of light, movement was apparent! And not only was movement apparent, but it was at the exact location in the solar system where Lowell had believed such a planet existed.

The discovery of the new planet, initially called Planet X, was world-wide news, reaching the home of eleven-year-old Venetia Burney of Oxford, England.

Sitting at the kitchen table with her grandfather, Venetia, whose fifth-grade class had been studying Roman mythology, recalled that Pluto, the god of the underworld, lived in a place so far away that light couldn't reach it.

Then, looking at her grandfather, she said something akin to, *I think Pluto would be a good name for Planet X because it's so far away.*

Venetia's grandfather sent a telegram to the Lowell Observatory in Flagstaff that contained the following: "… and for naming the new planet, please consider PLUTO, suggested by small girl Venetia Burney for a dark and gloomy planet."

The folks at the Lowell Observatory loved the suggestion, not only for Venetia's reasons, but because the first two letters of Pluto (PL) were a match for Percival Lowell's initials (PL).

Those initials, unused to designate any other celestial body, were a perfect way of posthumously honoring Percival Lowell for his dedication and persistent in the search for a ninth planet.

Percival Lowell, who passed away on November 12, 1916, was buried on Mars Hill, right next to his observatory.

---

[1] *Stories from History's Dust Bin* (additional reading):
   Vol 2, May 15:   William H. Pickering with Williamina Fleming

That Mars is inhabited by beings of some sort or other, we may consider as certain as it is uncertain what these beings may be.
Percival Lowell (1855-1916) Astronomer

Victor Lustig

Born: Robert V. Miller
The bouncing Czech.
Jan 4, 1890 (Czech Republic) – Mar 11, 1947 (Springfield MO)

F RANCE AND AMERICA were not as lucky as Victor
Lustig's home country of Czechoslovakia. "The
smoothest con man ever born," as he was known throughout his
lifetime of grifting, ran cons in both countries, including aboard
the ocean liners that steamed across the Atlantic.

Aboard ship, he successfully bilked wealthy passengers out
of their money and many of them, when they realized they
should have known better, were too embarrassed to report their
losses.

And he didn't mess around with penny-ante cons. No sir!
He was at his best going after the big money, such as when he
once sold the Eiffel Tower and nearly pulled off the same scam
a second time.

Born Robert V. Miller in Bohemia,[1] he grew up in Hostinne,
Czechoslovakia, where his father was the mayor. As a student,
he was bright but with a penchant for getting into trouble. In his
late teens, he attended the University of Paris and rarely returned
to his home country, a decision for which Czechoslovakian law
officials should be most grateful.

After a year of college, he began committing dozens of
crimes across Europe using almost as many aliases, his favorite
being that of Victor Lustig. And when a prestigious-sounding
European title advanced the con, he was Count Victor Lustig.

Lustig's scamming success on the high seas ended in 1914
when World War I dried up the pleasure cruise business and he
found himself in, of all places, Missouri.

There, learning that a bank had recently repossessed a local
ranch, and using the alias, "Robert Duval," he offered the bank
$22,000 in Liberty Bonds[2] to buy the ranch. The bank saw it as
a good deal and didn't flinch when he proposed to give the bank
another $10,000 in bonds in exchange for cash with which he
could get the ranch back on its feet.

Bank officials were there as Lustig placed $32,000 dollars in Liberty Bonds in an envelope for the bank; and the bank placed $10,000 in cash in another envelope for Lustig. There were broad smiles, lots of friendly handshakes, and the deal was done.

It wasn't until Lustig was gone that the bankers discovered that their envelope, supposedly containing $32,000 in bonds, contained nothing but blank pieces of paper cut to the size of bonds.

Lustig was caught before he could get out of the state, but just how slippery was he? He convinced authorities of the "Show Me" state, without showing anything to anyone, that it was all a big mistake. There were smiles and apologies as he was released from custody, and just that quick, he was gone.

In 1925, while relaxing on a park bench in Paris, Lustig picked up a newspaper and read an article about the difficulty the French government was having in maintaining the Eiffel Tower. The article explained how expensive it had become to keep the famous landmark painted, in addition to hundreds of recurring small-ticket repair needs.

Bingo!

A light went on in Lustig's head and he knew the story had just provided him with all he needed for his greatest con.

He located a counterfeiter who had served prison time, and paid him to create fake government credentials identifying himself as the "Deputy Director General of the Ministère de Postes et Télégraphies."

Next, he invited several local scrap metal dealers to a highly confidential meeting held at the most prestigious hotel in Paris, the Hotel de Crillon.

After the dealers· arrived and were comfortably seated, Lustig spoke at great length and detail regarding the numerous maintenance problems associated with the Tower.

The upkeep, he explained, had become more expensive than the tower's worth. It had outlived its original purpose as a draw to the 1889 Paris Exposition thirty-six years earlier. He took care in explaining, as they already knew, that the structure had never been intended to become a permanent landmark.

Then, the *coup d'grace!* He produced the newspaper article that he was sure each had already read.

He reinforced the points made by the newspaper, adding that the government had covertly decided to sell the eyesore, and that it was his responsibility to quietly carry out the transaction.

He went on to explain that each of them had been invited to today's meeting based on their excellent reputations as honest businessmen. They were also told, "warned" might be a better word, that due to the inevitable public outcry sure to come from those who would petition the government to keep the famous attraction, it was of utmost importance that the transaction be kept confidential.

A ride to the Eiffel Tower in a rented limousine gave Lustig an opportunity to listen as the men talked amongst themselves, and to assess which man was the most gullible and would become the "pigeon" whose offer he would select.

Before the limousine ride had reached the famous landmark, he had selected his pigeon, a man named André Poisson.

Lustig then told the group that bids were to be delivered to him personally the following day.

One day later he advised Poisson of his decision, and asked that they meet at a designated time. But Poisson had become suspicious of why everything was being done in such a hush-hush way.

Sensing a problem, Lustig confided to Poisson that as a government official, his salary was not as high as it needed to be to support the lifestyle he enjoyed, and that he expected Poisson to give him a bribe over and above his bid.

Poisson, who had dealt with French officials before, was suddenly at ease. This was, after all, a government bureaucrat and since all bureaucrats were corrupt . . . of course, how stupid of me to be concerned – a bribe!

And all doubts about the authenticity of the deal were erased. In addition to his bid, he added a sizeable bribe, and Lustig delivered to Poisson a worthless, but official-looking, Bill of Sale.

It wasn't until Poisson went to the Paris equivalent of City Hall to receive the deed to the structure, that he learned he'd been duped and was out his bid and the bribe.

Lustig was nowhere to be found, aboard a train to Vienna.

The scam had worked so well that Lustig returned a month later to run the same con again. Only this time, the gendarmes were onto the scheme and Lustig barely made it out of France, and on his way to America, again.

In America, he conned $5,000 from Al Capone, and he did it by convincing Capone of his (Lustig's) honesty. A few weeks after Capone gave Lustig $5,000 to invest in a double-your-money scheme, Lustig told Capone the investment failed, and that he would not rest until he had repaid ever dime of the gangster's money.

Capone was so impressed that he gave Lustig a generous "reward for his honesty," and forgave the "failed investment."

In 1935, Lustig was finally arrested, turned in by a scorned mistress named Billie May.

He was convicted of counterfeiting and sentenced to twenty years in Alcatraz.

He was later sent to the Missouri State Prison for medical attention where he died on March 11, 1947 of a brain tumor complicated by the effects of pneumonia.

[1] In 1993, the territory of Bohemia officially became a part of the Czech Republic.

[2] Liberty Bond: A "special issue" bond sold in the United States (1917-1918) to help finance World War I. Buying Liberty Bonds was considered an act of patriotism.

Men make counterfeit money;
in many more cases, money makes counterfeit men.
Sydney J. Harris (1917-1986) Journalist

Wilfrid 'Wop' May

Born: Wilfrid Reid May
Pursued by the Red Baron, and lived.
Mar 20, 1896 (Carberry Canada) – June 21, 1952 (American Fork UT)

M ANFRED VON RICHTHOFEN'S red Fokker Triplane was recognizable to every experienced airman during World War I. Known by friend and foe alike as the Red Baron and credited with eighty aerial victories, Richthofen was the most famous and the most feared pilot of his era.

Wilfrid "Wop" May, known only to his family, friends, and a handful of flight instructors, was a lowly pilot-in-training who had just received orders to go to the Royal Naval Air Station at Clairmarais, France, to learn to fly an aircraft known as the Sopwith Camel.[1]

It wouldn't be long before the world's most feared pilot, the Red Baron, and novice-pilot Wop May's paths would cross in the skies above France.

Wilfrid May was born April 20, 1896 at Carberry, Manitoba, Canada.

When he was six, the family moved from Carberry to Edmonton, stopping along the way to visit relatives. His playmate during one of those visits was two-year-old Mary Lumsden. When Mary tried to pronounce Wilfrid's name, it came out "Woppie." The nickname stuck, at least half of it, and Wilfrid May became Wop May, the name he would be known by for the rest of his life.

In 1916, a month before his 20th birthday, Wop joined the Canadian Expeditionary Force, a branch of the Canadian Army, and was trained at Calgary to become a firing range instructor.

When his unit was about to be shipped to Europe in 1917, he applied to England's Royal Flying Corps (RFC), was accepted, and became an RFC airman.

Wop nearly died before his first solo training flight. It happened when another pilot-in-training attempted to land at the same time on the same runway where Wop, his flight instructor, and his plane were waiting preparatory to takeoff. The incoming aircraft struck Wop's plane and both aircraft were destroyed but miraculously, but no one was hurt.

On October 27, 1917, Wop arrived at a London airfield to receive navigational training and flight instruction for flying a Caudron G.3 trainer.

The following month, after a total of 3½-hours of flight instruction, Wop made his first solo flight and received his pilot's wings.

A month later, he was assigned to Hendon, England, for training in aerial photography, bombing, and combat. There, he learned to fly the British Avro 504, an intermediate plane used for preparing pilots to fly the more advanced, more powerful, 50-horsepower Sopwith Pup.

Wop graduated from training at Hendon with 55-hours flying time and the rank of Flight Lieutenant.

On April 1, 1918, England's Royal Flying Corps was renamed the Royal Air Force (RAF), and eight days later, Lieutenant Wop May became a member of the RAF's 209th Squadron.

His log book shows that from April 11th to the 20th, he spent his time in aerial target practice, and on one occasion, received his first taste of combat:

April 11th, 30 minutes looking over ground and getting
used to machine;
April 16th, 30 minutes target practice;
April 20th, First time over the line. Flight got into a
scrap with a triplane ... he crashed. I didn't get a
burst into him.

Then, a day later (April 21, 1918), two newly-trained pilots from opposite sides of the conflict were destined to end up in the same place, at the same time, with the same set of instructions.

One of those pilots was Wop May, who was told by squadron commander Roy Brown to go up and observe the aerial battle from a safe distance, ending his instructions with a firm, "Stay on top and don't get involved! Just watch and learn."

The other pilot was Wolfram von Richthofen, the Red Baron's nephew who, like Wop May, was a novice pilot and had just received similar advice. To get above the fight, stay on top and a safe distance from the action, and watch and learn.

While observing the aerial dogfight that was taking place below and some distance away, Wop spotted Wolfram's aircraft, like himself, flying in circles and observing the action below.

After a few minutes of considering the pros-and-cons of the situation, and disregarding squadron commander Brown's firm instructions Wop decided the German plane might be easy pickings.

When Wolfram saw Wop's plane bearing down on him, he turned and headed straight down and into the dogfight where he knew his Uncle Manfred would be somewhere nearby. Wop, now fully committed and believing he had the German plane on the run, gave chase and suddenly found himself on the edge of some very serious aerial combat.

As soon as the Red Baron saw the situation facing his nephew, he left the dogfight and headed straight for Wop.

What had just become a life-threatening problem for Wop, was not lost on squadron commander Roy Brown.

Brown watched as the Red Baron's distinctive red Fokker Triplane banked and accelerated in pursuit of Wop May, who was in full pursuit of the Baron's nephew.

That's when Brown, concerned only for Wop May's safety, exited the dogfight and headed straight for the Red Baron, a fight with all the potential for a deadly ending for someone.

Diving from above May's Camel, Brown intercepted the Red Baron's Fokker, and here is Wop May's official combat report of what happened next:

> *April 21, 1918*
> *Engaged 15-20 triplanes, claimed one. Blue one.*
> *Several on my tail, came out with red triplane on my tail which followed me down to the ground and over the line on my tail all the time, [he] got several bursts into me but didn't hit me.*
> *When we got across the lines he was shot down by Captain Brown. I saw him crash into side of hill.*
> *Came back with Captain.*

We afterwards found out that the triplane was the famous German airman Baron von Richthofen. He was killed.

There is no dispute that the Red Baron died that day amidst a hail of bullets, fired not only from Commander Brown's Camel, but from army troops on the ground as well.

Although the RAF originally credited Brown with the kill, it is almost certain that the bullet that killed the Red Baron came from ground fire, not from Roy Brown's Camel.[2]

Wop May went on to become a decorated pilot, receiving the Distinguished Flying Cross (1918), the Order of the British Empire (1935), and the U.S. Medal of Freedom (1947).

Years after a distinguished flying career, including countless humanitarian missions, Wop and his son Dennis took a well-earned vacation to do some sightseeing in the United States.

During the steep 1½-mile hike to Timpanogos Cave near the top of Mt. Timpanogos east of American Fork, Utah, Wilfrid 'Wop' May, age 56, suffered a severe stroke and died.

---

[1] Sopwith Camel: Technically, the *Sopwith F-1*. The F-1's guns were housed under a curved sheet of metal that gave the plane's fuselage a distinctive camel-like hump, hence the nickname, *Sopwith Camel.*

[2] Today, most believe the Red Baron was killed from a bullet to the chest, most likely from ground fire. Roy Brown's bullet, fired in pursuit, would have struck Richthofen in the back.

It is a pity that my collection of trophies contains not a single Russian.
Manfred von Richthofen (1892-1918) The Red Baron

John Joseph Merlin

Born: Jean-Joseph Merlin
His inline skates were his downfall.
Sept 17, 1735 (Huy, Belgium) – May 4, 1803 (London, England)

J OHN JOSEPH MERLIN, born in 1735, was a mechanical genius, an amazing eccentric with remarkable ingenuity and light-years ahead of his time.

Living when he did, many of his inventions seemed quite impossible to those who saw them. In fact, most of those that have survived to the present day remain curiously clever and worth a visit to the internet to look at and marvel at the gifted genius of their creator.

Looking back on Merlin's life, he may have been cut from the same bolt of creative cloth as his contemporary, Charles Babbage,[1] the man known today as the *Father of the Computer*.

In fact, Babbage visited Merlin's Mechanical Museum as a young man and wrote about his fascination with a pair of twelve-inch-tall automated nude figures.

He wrote that one was a "singularly graceful" ballet dancer, and the other, a lady, "… in brass and clockwork, capable of performing almost every motion and inclination of the human body … even to the motion of the eyelids, and the lifting up of the hands and fingers to the face."

He went on to say that one of the figures "… used an eyeglass[3] occasionally, and bowed frequently as if recognizing her acquaintances."

And the other figure had a tiny bird attached to the forefinger of her right hand, "that wagged its tail, flapped its wings, and opened its beak," and that she "attitudinized in a most fascinating manner, her eyes full of imagination, and irresistible."

Attitudinized! Now, there's a word you don't hear every day, meaning to "pose for effect," but let's not get sidetracked.

In fact, Babbage was so taken with the two exquisite ladies that years later he returned to the museum and purchased them for his own collection.

Could Babbage's visits to the museum, with its futuristic inventions, have helped to inspire the design of his *difference machine*, now recognized as the world's first computer?

No one knows.

Merlin was born and raised in Belgium. He attended the *Académie des Sciences* in Paris, France, where he was considered a prodigy, a young person of extraordinary talent.

At the age of twenty-five and on a first-name basis with the Spanish Ambassador to England, he moved to London where he befriended some of the most famous people of the era. This included Johann Christian Bach, the son of Johann Sebastian Bach and a distinguished composer in his own right; Thomas Gainsborough, best known for his painting, *Blue Boy;* Samuel Johnson,[2] the compiler of England's first dictionary; and art historian and antiquarian Horace Walpole, and others.

If you're willing to invest a little online time, run a browser search for the "John Joseph Merlin portrait by Gainsborough," and you'll be rewarded with a painting of Merlin, his right hand inside a bright red jacket, à la Napoleon Bonaparte.

One of Merlin's best-known inventions was a full-sized mechanical chariot (pulled by a real horse) that he often used to ride through the streets of London, especially the Hyde Park area. Within the chariot was a primitive odometer that told him how far he had travelled, and a mechanical whip that struck the horse each time he tugged a cord.

Another of his better-known creations was an automated Silver Swan with highly realistic life-like movements that can be seen today at the Bowes Museum in England, and on the internet.

Merlin also designed and built a highly maneuverable wheelchair for people with gout.

And along with British jeweler, James Cox, designed and manufactured a clock that rarely needed winding, ingeniously driven by a mechanism that used changes in barometric pressure to wind the clock's mainspring.

He also invented dozens of curious devices: scales, robots, an unusual Dutch oven, and a barrel organ.

By the way, Merlin was also a gifted musician and often performed for guests on the violin and harpsichord.

And he had a wicked sense of humor.

One of his inventions was a mechanical chair into which he built a device that could deliver a mild electrical shock. Merlin would dress in the costume of a quack doctor and anyone who approached him for medical advice could be assured of receiving, at a minimum, a few seconds in his mechanical chair, followed by, may we say, a shocking diagnosis.

But there was one invention, and one incident, that Merlin would prefer we not mention. It was his invention of inline roller skates, basically ice skates with wheels mounted in place of a skating-blade.

And now, for the embarrassing incident.

With regards to his inline skates, Merlin was an inventor with a problem. Getting up a head of steam on his skates was not a problem. But stopping, now that was a problem.

However, the invention was such a popular novelty, that despite his below average skating skills, he loved to dress in formal-wear and skate among the guests at social functions.

Sometimes he even cross-dressed as a barmaid and would glide in and around his guests, taking orders and returning with a tray laden with drinks.

He also loved to slither around party-goers while playing the violin, skating, swaying, and twirling in time with the music.

In attendance at an event sponsored by a Mrs. Cowley, was Thomas Busby, who wrote about the following incident:

> *One of his ingenious novelties was a pair of skaits contrived to run on wheels. Supplied with these and a violin, he mixed in the motley group of one of Mrs. Cowley's masquerades at Carlisle House.*

> *When not having provided the means of retarding his velocity, or commanding (his) direction, he impelled himself against a mirror of more than five hundred pounds value, dashed it to atoms, broke his instrument to pieces and wounded himself most severely.*

Then, Merlin's health began to falter near the close of the 1700s.

At the turn of the century he advised his friends, those who had patronized his museum, that his health had diminished to the point where he would soon be compelled to sell his collection and move from England to another location in Europe.

But it was too late.

Before he could start the process of selling off his collection of unusual inventions, he passed away.

Merlin died on May 4, 1803, in London, a brilliant and fun-loving genius known by the British as the *Ingenious Mechanick.*

He is interred at St. Mary's Church, Westminster, UK.

Stories from History's Dust Bin (additional reading):
   [1] Vol 3, Dec 26:   Featuring Charles Babbage
   [2] Vol 3, Sep 18:   Featuring Samuel Johnson

[3] Eyeglass, also called a Monocle: a circular single-lens magnifying glass that is kept in position by the muscles around the eye. Typically, attached to a cord or necklace, allowing it to be close at hand when not in use.

It's a strange world of language in which skating
on thin ice can get you into hot water.
Franklin P. Jones (1908-1980) Humorist

Jackie Mitchell

Born: Virne Beatrice Mitchell
The girl who struck out Babe Ruth.
Aug 29, 1913 (Chattanooga TN) - Jan 7, 1987 (Fort Oglethorpe GA)

B EATRICE "JACKIE" MITCHELL weighed just three pounds at birth, or about the same as the baseball glove she wore seventeen years later (April 2, 1931), when she struck out two of baseball's giants, Lou Gehrig[1] and Babe Ruth.

And if you're thinking that the Iron Man (Gehrig) and the Bambino (Ruth) gave her a pass because she was a girl, or that her appearance was a promotional stunt, something Chicago White Sox manager Bill Veeck[2] might pull off to draw fans into Comiskey Park, wrong!

As soon as she could walk, her father took her to a local baseball park where he taught her the basics of the game that would make Jackie Mitchell a household name during the 1930s.

It didn't hurt that the Mitchell's next-door-neighbor was Charles Arthur Vance, better known to baseball fans as "Dazzy" Vance.[3]   At the time, Dazzy, an impressive pitcher, was still in the minor leagues, but he would go on to lead the National League in strikeouts for seven consecutive seasons and wind up in Baseball's Hall of Fame.

Dazzy adored Jackie and the two became friends as he taught her how to pitch, including his signature *drop ball* pitch. That pitch, known today as a breaking ball, would look as if it were about to arrive over the plate at one level. But, just before reaching the plate, it would drop wickedly downward and to one side, the batter fanning the air in frustration.

To say that Dazzy was impressed with Jackie's skills would be an understatement. He told her that someday she would be a great pitcher. And with the full confidence of a little girl who loved her coach, she believed him.

At sixteen, she played for a women's team in Chattanooga and attended a baseball school in Atlanta. There, her pitching skills and baseball instincts came to the attention of Joe Engel, the chief scout for the Washington Senators and president of the Chattanooga Lookouts.

Engel had taken control of the Lookouts just before the stock market crash of 1929, and generating any kind of income during the depression required ingenuity and promotion, and Engel was good at both.

He once traded an error-prone shortstop for a 25-pound turkey. Several days later he served roasted turkey to a gaggle of Chattanooga sports reporters, telling them that "since they had been giving him the bird all season, he thought he'd return the favor."

In 1930, the economy hadn't improved, and wouldn't until the end of the decade. That's when Engel, remembering the talented girl he had seen at the baseball school in Atlanta, offered her a legitimate contract for the 1931 season.

On March 28, 1931, Jackie, only seventeen, signed the contract, right next to her mother's signature, and became a bona fide member of the *Lookouts*.

The signing made Jackie the second woman to sign a professional baseball contract,[4] and caused a few blue-nosed do-gooders to question the propriety of a girl playing on a men's baseball team. But Jackie's mother quickly put that issue to rest by announcing she would be accompanying her daughter on all road trips.

With spring-training over in Florida, it was time for the New York Yankees to pack up and head north, and as was their custom, they would stop in Chattanooga for their annual game with the Lookouts.

The game was played on April 2, 1931.

Jackie, a member of the team for only five days, was not the starting pitcher.

She watched as the Yankee lead-off batter hit a double and then scored when the next batter hit one up the middle.

She also watched as the third batter, the great Babe Ruth rose from the bench and began sauntering to the plate. That's when the manager of the Lookouts stood up, looked down his bench and, according to the *Baltimore Sun*, "signaled for the snip-nosed blue-eyed girl" to take the mound.

After a few warm-up pitches, Jackie faced the Babe. Her first pitch was a ball. Her next two pitches were curveballs, with Ruth swinging through both. Ruth stepped back and asked the umpire to inspect the ball. The umpire complied and assured the Babe that the ball was fine.

Jackie's next pitch was her Dazzy Vance Special, a blinding fastball that crossed the plate for a called strike. The Babe stood frozen, then glared and threw his bat hard and spinning across the dirt while verbally abusing the umpire for the call before being led away by teammates.

The crowd roared its approval.

The next batter was Lou Gehrig, the Yankee's clean-up hitter. Jackie struck him out on three consecutive pitches.

Then, after walking the next batter, second-baseman Tony Lazzeri, the Lookouts manager walked to the mound and he and Jackie chatted for a few seconds. Jackie smiled, handed Lazzeri the ball, and walked to the dugout to a thunderous, sustained roar of cheers, her head high, her feet feeling as though they were walking on air.

In case you're wondering about the final score, there wasn't a baseball fan in Chattanooga who cared that their Lookouts had taken a 14-4 drubbing at the hands of the Yankees.

In fact, there wasn't a soul anywhere near the state of Tennessee who cared a fig about the score. Jackie Mitchell became famous that day for having struck out two of the greatest players in baseball history.

Fan mail poured in, including one letter addressed only to *The Girl Who Struck Out Babe Ruth, Chattanooga, Tennessee,* and it was delivered.

About a week after Jackie struck out Ruth and Gehrig, baseball commissioner Kenesaw Mountain Landis voided her contract.

The reason?

Baseball, he said, was "too strenuous" for a woman.

Feel free to read between the lines of the commissioner's action. Everyone else did.

Disheartened with the ruling, Jackie joined the "House of David," a novelty men's baseball team famous for their long hair and beards.

By 1937, six years after famously striking out Ruth and Gehrig, Jackie, now twenty-three and tired of the House of David sideshow, disappeared from baseball to work in her father's optometry office.

In 1982, fifty-one years after striking out two of baseball's legends, she accepted an invitation to throw out the ceremonial first pitch for her old team, the Chattanooga Lookouts, and she did so to thunderous applause.

Chattanoogans are slow to forget people they like, and Jackie was one of those people.

Beatrice "Jackie" Mitchell died January 7, 1987, at the age of seventy-three.

She is buried in the Forest Hills Cemetery in Chattanooga.

Stories from History's Dust Bin (additional reading):
[1] Vol 1, Mar 2:   Lou Gehrig with Moe Berg
[2] Vol 1, Feb 9:   Featuring Bill Veeck, Jr.
[3] Vol 2, Jul 17:   Dazzy Vance with Dizzy Dean

[4] The first woman to sign a pro baseball contract was Lizzie Arlington who, in 1898, signed to pitch for the Reading Coal Heavers in a game against the Allentown Peanuts. Two-hundred curious women showed up to see what she looked like and what she wore. Reading won the game: 5-0.

Little League baseball is a very good thing because
it keeps the parents off the streets.
Yogi Berra (1925-2015) Baseball

Rick Monday

Born: Robert James Monday, Jr.
He made baseball's greatest play!
Nov 20, 1945 (Batesville AR) –

C HICAGO CUBS CENTERFIELDER, Rick Monday, is said to have made the best play in baseball history, and it didn't have anything to do with hitting one out of the park, being part of a spectacular game-saving triple play, or scoring from third on a perfectly executed double suicide squeeze.

It had to do with something that the national pastime is good at doing. And that's combining the best in athletes, with the best in fans. And in this case, of turning a disgusting attempt to burn the Stars and Stripes in a public place, into an unabashed display of good old-fashioned American patriotism.

On April 25, 1976, the fans at Dodger Stadium watched as a man in the stands, William Errol Thomas, ran onto the outfield carrying something under his arm, throwing it to the ground, squirting it with something from a small can, and then kneeling over what had now become apparent to players and fans alike, an American flag.

Moments later another person ran onto the field. It was Thomas's eleven-year-old son. He knelt next to his father and the dopey dad and his son huddled tightly over the lighter-fluid damp flag, trying desperately to shield the flame of a cigarette-lighter from the outdoor breeze in hopes of setting the flag on fire.

The dynamic-less duo was so intent on burning the flag that neither had the presence of mind to look up and survey their surroundings. If they had, they would have seen two men in baseball uniforms rapidly converging on them from opposite sides of the field.

Lumbering as fast as he could from his position near third base and cussing like an angry longshoreman was well-respected and well-fed base coach Tommy Lasorda; and bearing down like a hawk from his position in center field was fleet-footed Rick Monday, a ballplayer in excellent physical shape and a former Marine Corps reservist to boot.

Well, that's a race that Rick is going to win ten times out of ten, but that doesn't make Lasorda any less a hero. It just means he won't be remembered as often when the story is told.

So, when retelling the story, don't forget to mention Lasorda, whose hard-charging footfalls during his mad-as-hell dash from third base, were reportedly recorded by seismographs as far north as Dawson Creek, British Columbia.

Without breaking stride and a good fifty feet ahead of Lasorda, Monday swooped in from behind the flakey flag desecrators and in a single motion, grabbed the flag and continued running.

The disrespectful twosome never knew what hit them. There they were, sitting cross-legged on the grass with no flag to burn and nowhere to hide, dad holding a cheap cigarette lighter that obviously had more sense than he did.

To the mischief-making miscreants, it may have seemed like being in a nightmare where you're suddenly in the middle of a public place wearing nothing but an athletic-supporter and a pair of sweat socks. And you've just been caught trying to do something beneath the dignity of Larry, Curly, and Moe.

And even worse, a scowling ballplayer with a number seven on his jersey is holding the only means of covering your bare butt, an American flag, and he's not about to give it back to you. And while you and your son are looking at each other with stupid grins on your faces, 56,000 fans are wildly cheering baseball's play of a lifetime.

As the pathetic pair[1] were escorted off the field by stadium police, the large ballfield scoreboard posted the following message: *RICK MONDAY . . . YOU MADE A GREAT PLAY!*

What followed next was one of those spontaneous, faith-renewing responses that can't help but restore your faith in Americans of all stripes regardless of race, creed, or political party.

From what had become a very quiet ballpark, first from one part of the stadium, then from another, and another and another, softly at first, voices came together melding into a beautiful rendition of God Bless America.

The incident is now considered one of the top 100 moments in Major League Baseball history, and Rick Monday, whose swift reaction to a feckless father and his eleven-year-old son, has endeared him to Americans from all walks of life.

As Monday would later say about the incident, "I'm not sure of exactly what was on my mind, except that what they were doing was wrong!"

He further explained that he'd been in too many veterans' hospitals and seen too many broken bodies of the guys who had given so much to protect the flag, that "if you're going to burn the flag, don't do it around me."

The flag has been in Rick Monday's possession since the incident, safely under lock-and-key in a safe-deposit box.

A few years ago, he was reportedly offered $1-million for the flag but turned it down, saying, "The flag is not for sale. What this flag represents, you can't buy."

And if you're into collecting baseball memorabilia, no serious collection should be considered complete without a bobblehead of Rick Monday in stride, carrying his baseball glove with his left hand, the American flag tightly gripped in his right hand, and his face – the very serious face of a no-nonsense patriot – with, "Don't mess with this flag!" written all over it.

---

[1] William Errol Thomas was charged with trespassing, fined $60, sentenced to three days in jail, and given probation. His son spent a day or two in juvenile hall and was released, hopefully with more respect for the American flag.

Guys ask me, don't I get burned out?
How can you get burned out doing something you love?
I ask you, have you ever got tired of kissing a pretty girl?
Tommy Lasorda (1927-) Baseball

Earl "Madman" Muntz

Born: Earl William Muntz
Madcap marketing maven Madman Muntz
Jan 3, 1914 (Elgin IL) – June 21, 1987 (Ranch Mirage CA)

I F THERE'S SUCH a thing as a natural-born used car salesman, it was Earl Muntz. In 1929, after dropping out of high school, he went to work in his parents' hardware store. Five years later and twenty years old, he opened his first used car lot in his hometown of Elgin, Illinois. But since he was not yet twenty-one, he had to carry each sales contract to the hardware store for his mother to sign.

Who could possibly have guessed that within thirteen years (1947), he would become a used car phenomenon in the state of California with gross sales of $76-million!

Six years after opening that first used car lot, someone told Earl that California was used car heaven, so he moved to the city of Glendale and opened a used car lot there, and soon afterward, another in Los Angeles.

Then, after settling into a comfortable California lifestyle, he tipped the used car world on its ear by adopting an outrageous persona for himself, that of "Madman" Muntz, and he started an all-out used car media blitz that lasted a decade and turned him into a millionaire several times over.

And selling used cars was just one of the pots he stirred.

Was he successful?

As mentioned up front, in 1947 he enjoyed gross sales amounting to $76-million dollars, making him the largest volume used car dealer in the world.

Someone has suggested that had there been no Madman Muntz, today's used car salesmen might enjoy the perception of being honest, hard-working citizens instead of odometer-adjusting charlatans.

In all fairness, Muntz can't be blamed for the bottom-feeding perception of a few used car salesmen, as there is no evidence he ever cheated anyone out of anything.

But there is evidence, in spades, that he was nothing short of a marketing genius, a genuinely likeable, personable, smiling and friendly used car super salesman.

Was he recognizable?

Would people suddenly sit up and take notice should you begin appearing on a thousand billboards in your home state wearing nothing more than a crazed, wild-eyed grin, a pair of bright red long-johns, black boots and a Napoleonic hat sporting the initial of your surname? You bet they would!

Madman Muntz knew the power of self-promotion. Because he portrayed himself in such outlandish fashion during the era of his popularity, you would be hard-pressed to find one soul in California who didn't know who he was or what he did. And borrowing a line from comedian Red Skelton,[1] how well he dood what he did. The latter, because the tagline at the bottom of his billboards always proclaimed, "Outselling every other Automobile Dealer in America," and it was not an idle boast.

About those billboards. He was always presented in outlandish caricature wearing red long-johns and a Napoleonic hat, always leaving the impression that he was not quite right in the head, and the text on the billboards removing any remaining doubt. For instance, one of his freeway billboards read, *I buy 'em retail, sell 'em wholesale – It's More Fun That Way*. And when you exited the freeway, there he was, same red underwear, same weird hat, same wild-eyed grin, saying, *I wanna give 'em away – but Mrs. Muntz won't let me. She's Crazy!*

Thousands of cars on his California lots were purchased from dealers in the Midwest where their values were greatly depressed. For transporting the cars to Los Angeles, he hired military servicemen, paying them $50 to make the trip. It was a good deal for both. The servicemen got a cheap ride home, and Muntz got cars that in California, were worth double their Midwestern value.

Because of his outlandish billboards and equally funny radio ads, America's comedians such as Bob Hope, Jack Benny, and others always kept a Madman Muntz joke handy, which amounted to more free advertising and the sale of more cars.

When television became available in the late 1940s and early '50s, sets were expensive, but Muntz discovered another way to make money. He experimented with the sets, disassembling them one component at a time until the television set would no longer work, then he'd replace the last component removed.

In the pop culture of the 1950s and '60s, the process of reducing the complexity of something, such as removing marginally-needed vacuum tubes from a television set, became known as "muntzing," or, after something was once stripped of non-essential parts, it was said to have been "muntzed."

Muntz Television, built thousands of *muntzed* sets, and his retail stores carried the first television sets in America advertised at less than $100, complete with a certificate attesting to the fact.

He used skywriting to advertise his television sets, but when upper-level winds destroyed the first few letters of "television," he shortened the word to "TV," leading historians to credit Earl Muntz as the first to use TV as an abbreviation for television.

In fact, he liked the way "Tee Vee" sounded so much, that he named his only daughter Tee Vee Muntz.

He purchased the manufacturing rights to produce the Cadillac V8 powered Kurtis-Kraft sports car. He then extended the body by sixteen inches, added a removable fiberglass top, and renamed it the Muntz Jet. The car was in production from 1951 to 1954, selling only 400 units before the factory closed. Today, Muntz Jets are highly-prized collector cars.

Earl Muntz died of lung cancer in 1987, but he left a legacy of creativity not only in marketing used cars, but in the field of electronics as well. In 2001, Earl Muntz was posthumously inducted into the Consumer Electronics Hall of Fame.

Not too shabby for a high school dropout who became a caricature of himself in a pair of red long-johns, a Napoleonic hat, and a wildly-insane – crazy like a fox – grin.

[1] *Stories from History's Dust Bin* (additional reading):
   Vol 2, Jul 18:   Featuring Red Skelton

If it weren't for Philo T. Farnsworth, the inventor of television,
we'd still be eating frozen radio dinners.
Johnny Carson (1925-2005 Television host

William "Bull" Nelson

Born: William Nelson
Here I am. If you don't like me . . . .
Sept 27, 1824 (Maysville KY) - Sept 29, 1862 (Louisville KY)

MAJOR GENERAL WILLIAM NELSON of the Union Army was a big man, 6-foot-2, something north of 300 pounds, and built like a fireplug, a very big fireplug! Yet, it was said, he carried himself lightly and was genteel, well-bred and well-read.

To a stranger, his airy aristocratic bearing might cause one to wonder just which side of the Mason-Dixon Line his sympathies lay.

General Nelson hadn't always been an army man.

In fact, he had twenty years' service as a naval officer when, two days after Lincoln's first inauguration in 1861, he strode boldly into the Executive Mansion unannounced and said to the president, "Here I am. If you don't like me, the worse for you."[1]

You now have two impressions of General Nelson. The first is that of a gentle giant, a warm, chatty Southern gentleman, a ladies' man; and the second is that of an aggressive giant, of whom on occasion it might be said, was "full of himself."

Within that second impression, discounting the intimidation that comes with being a very large man with a no-nonsense nickname, the *Bull* was a self-assured and competent leader who expected of others what he expected of himself. And that's what those who served under Bull Nelson came to understand.

Yes, he could be tough, but there was a fairness in him not always present in men of authority, and for that he was respected by those who served under him.

The respect was evident in the way the Bull meted out discipline. Anyone, officer or enlisted man who fell short of his responsibilities was subject to his wrath, and when Bull Nelson was displeased, and discipline was forthcoming, it was not kept a secret.

Following the surprise meeting in the Executive Mansion, Lincoln, impressed by Nelson's naval record, his single-minded approach to any assigned task, and perhaps because they were both native Kentuckians, asked Nelson to assess what it would take to move Kentucky, a neutral state, into the Union column.

Two months later (May 3, 1861), Nelson returned to the Executive Mansion with a detailed plan acceptable to Lincoln, which included the distribution of 5,000 rifles to Kentuckians.

On July 1, 1861, Lieutenant Commander Bull Nelson, formerly of the Union Navy, became Lieutenant General Bull Nelson of the Army. And only two months later, September 16th, he was promoted to Brigadier General, and ten months after that (July 17, 1862), Lincoln promoted him to Major General and put him in command of the Army of Kentucky.

From July 1, 1861, when he received his first Army command, until August 30, 1862, when he was grazed in the neck by a Confederate bullet at the Battle of Richmond (Kentucky), General Nelson had fought in and survived battles at Pittsburg Landing, Shiloh, and the Siege of Corinth.

After a brief convalescence from his neck injury, he received orders to move his army to Louisville and to hold the city.

Enter now, Brigadier General Jefferson C. Davis of the Union Army, not to be confused with President Jefferson F. Davis, the leader of the Confederacy.

And of course, there was no way anyone could confuse General Jefferson C. Davis with General William "Bull" Nelson. Davis was a wisp of a man, 5-foot 8, and 130 pounds fully-clothed and soaking wet.

General Davis, like General Nelson, had fought at the Siege of Corinth. But after that battle, General Davis had complained of exhaustion and was granted twenty days of rest, after which he was ordered to Louisville to serve under General Nelson.

Upon arriving, Nelson put Davis in charge of preparing the citizens of Louisville to defend their city.

A short time later General Davis was asked to report to General Nelson for a briefing. When Davis arrived, he was hard-pressed to provide specifics to any of Nelson's questions.

"How many men have signed up so far?"

"I'm not sure. I'll check on it and let you know."

"How is the work progressing on a defensive perimeter?"

"I'll look into that and get right back with you."

Those were not the kind of answers that General Nelson was accustomed to hearing, and red-faced furious, the Bull ordered General Davis out of his office.

General James B. Fry who was present during the briefing, recorded the following:

> *Davis arose and remarked, in a cool, deliberate manner: "General Nelson, I am a regular soldier, and I demand the treatment due to me as a general officer." Davis then stepped across to the door to the Medical Director's room, both rooms being open . . . and said: "Dr. Irwin, I wish you to be a witness to this conversation." At the same time Nelson said: "Yes, doctor, I want you to remember this."*
>
> *Davis then said to Nelson: "I demand from you the courtesy due my rank." Nelson replied, "I will treat you as you deserve.... You are relieved from duty here and you will proceed to Cincinnati and report to General [Horatio] Wright." Davis said, "You have no authority to order me." Nelson turned to* (his aide) *and said, "Captain, if General Davis does not leave the city by nine o'clock tonight, give instructions to the Provost-Marshal to see that he shall be put across the Ohio River."* [2]

Davis didn't like it, but he went to Cincinnati as ordered and reported to General Wright.

At about the same time, another general officer, General Don Carlos Buell was ordered to assume command of Louisville from General Bull Nelson. General Wright, believing that with Buell now in command and Bull Nelson likely assigned elsewhere, that Davis could be returned to Louisville where military leadership was needed.

Davis returned to Louisville as ordered by General Wright, and reported to General Buell.

General "Bull" Nelson, who had not yet departed Louisville to report to his new command, walked into his old headquarters to find General Davis, whom he assumed was in Cincinnati, approach and once again demand from him an apology for the earlier incident.

Nelson responded by telling Davis he was, "a damned puppy that he wanted nothing more to do with."

The much smaller Davis, frustrated, took a piece of paper from a nearby desk, wadded it into a marble-sized ball and flipped it directly into Bull Nelson's face.

Instantly infuriated by the intentional disrespect, Bull Nelson slapped Davis with the back of his hand.

Davis then turned to Indiana Governor Oliver Morton who was present in the room and asked, "Did you come here, sir, to see me insulted?" Governor Morton replied, "No sir," and Bull Nelson briskly spun on his heel and started down the corridor toward his office.

General Davis borrowed a pistol from someone in the room and walked down the corridor to where Bull Nelson was now standing, facing toward him. In a single fluid motion, Davis raised the pistol, aimed and fired. The bullet struck Nelson near the heart. He died thirty minutes later.

General Davis was taken into custody and later released.

Those were desperate times and the Union Army could ill afford to lose one field commander, let alone two, and Davis was never required to pay for his crime.

---

[1] Not a direct quote, but wording from an essay written by Ralph Waldo Emerson (1803-1882) titled, *Here I am.*

[2] From *Killed by a Brother Soldier,* by General James B. Fry (1885).

War is Hell.
William Tecumseh Sherman (1820-1891) General

Leslie Nielson

Born: Leslie William Nielson
A modern-day master of deadpan.
Feb 11, 1926 (Regina, Canada) – Nov 28, 2010 (Ft Lauderdale FL)

L ESLIE GREW UP in the Northwest Territories where his father, Ingvard Nielson, a Royal Canadian Mounted Policeman and strict disciplinarian, didn't spare the rod when it came to raising his sons. "You damned-well better amount to something!" he would tell them, his voice and countenance demanding respect, and they knew they'd damned-well better not disappoint.

Leslie's brother, Erik Hersholt Nielson did just that, and for many years he represented the Yukon as a Member of the Canadian Parliament, and from 1984 to 1986 he was the Deputy Prime Minister of Canada.

But for the equally good-looking, but less politically-driven Leslie, Erik was not only a tough act to follow, he was an impossible act to follow.

If anyone had asked Ingvard where, on his ladder of careers, did the profession of acting fit, he would probably have told them "somewhere beneath the bottom rung."

But Leslie knew he was never cut out to be a lawman like his father, and there was no way he could ever follow in the footsteps of his politician brother Erik, so as soon as he was old enough to do so, he joined the Royal Canadian Air Force.

It was a choice that neither his father nor brother could fault. But for Leslie, it was a means of buying time, a way of holding his demanding father at bay until he could figure out what to do with his life.

He served honorably, but when his enlistment was over he immediately moth-balled his uniform and enrolled in the Lorne Greene Academy of Radio Arts in Toronto. There, his efforts were good enough to earn a scholarship to the Neighborhood Playhouse School of Theater in New York.

In New York, he fully expected to show up for class or rehearsal one day and be told what he already knew, that he had less talent than a busted stage prop.

But the day never came, and he landed a television role in a 1948 episode of *Studio One* alongside Charlton Heston, earning $75 for his effort. But more important to Leslie than the money, was the heady feeling that he had shared the stage with a major talent.

By 1950, he was being selected for minor roles, earning little, but as an actor, he had several important things going for him. He was tall and handsome, a serious-minded thespian with the chiseled profile of a leading man.

Thus, whether he was eating regularly or not, he had the look of success written all over him.

In 1956, he starred in *Forbidden Planet*, now considered a science-fiction classic. His co-star was the beautiful Anne Francis. His role was that of a competent no-nonsense spaceship captain. The movie surpassed all box-office expectations, elevating both Francis and Nielson in the process.

A year later, he landed the male lead opposite Debbie Reynolds and alongside Walter Brennan[1] in *Tammy and the Bachelor*, a romantic comedy giving Nielson an opportunity to stretch his acting legs.

Over the next dozen years, he received numerous supporting roles like his 1958 portrayal of Colonel Stephen Bedford in *The Sheepman* (starring Glenn Ford and Shirley MacLaine); and even a few leading roles such as that of Frank Dayton (with Rory Calhoun and Lainie Kazan) in *Dayton's Devils.*

In 1968, he played a major role in the television pilot for *Hawaii Five-O*, but only appeared in one of its regular episodes.

Leslie Nielson had become the actor that movie-goers knew they had seen before, somewhere, in some movie . . . but doggone it, what was the movie, and what was his name?

Sometime during the 1960s, Nielson's hair turned white, but instead of relegating him to grandfatherly roles, it gave him an even more distinguished appearance.

In 1972, he played Captain Harrison, the venerable skipper of an ill-fated luxury-liner in the *Poseidon Adventure* (starring Gene Hackman, Red Buttons, and Shelley Winters), an edge-of-your-seat disaster film about a ship overturned by a tsunami during its final voyage.

Then, along came the film that transformed Leslie Nielson from a good-looking, but dime-a-dozen male actor, to a one-of-a-kind comedic genius.

The year was 1980.

The movie was *Airplane!* in which he played a handsome, dignified, but medically inept physician aboard a Boeing 707 filled with passengers who were dying of food poisoning. The movie, with what should have been an impossible storyline for a comedy, must be seen to be believed.

It is off-the-wall funny!

Costing a mere $3.5 million to produce, it grossed over $83 million in North America alone.

After *Airplane!,* he was suddenly in demand for more films. And there was no question that his niche wasn't in the dramatic roles he'd been playing, but in comedy where he had the uncanny ability to turn the absurd into an art form.

In 1988 came *The Naked Gun: From the Files of Police Squad* and Nielson's portrayal as the straight-laced, straight-faced, clueless Lieutenant Frank Drebin. If you thought Peter Sellers as Inspector Clouseau was funny as a clueless detective, you'll love Leslie Nielson as Frank Drebin.

Nielson's star in Hollywood rose quickly. He was a distinguished-looking actor with a marvelously resonant voice and a gift for stupefying deadpan. And he had the remarkable ability to maintain his composure, and deliver serious-sounding lines, when surrounded by abject absurdity.

From somewhere in the heavens, you can be certain that Buster Keaton,[2] the comedy star of the silent movies and early talkies has reverently tipped his porkpie to Leslie Nielson.

In 1988, Nielson received a star on the Hollywood Walk of Fame.

In 2001, he was added to Canada's Walk of Fame.

In 2002, he was made an Officer of the Order of Canada.

In 2003, the Grant MacEwan College in Edmonton named its School of Communications after him, and in that same year, the Alliance of Canadian Cinema, TV and Radio Artists gave Nielson their Award of Excellence.

Yes Ingvard, your son Leslie amounted to something. And in doing so, he exceeded all expectations, yours, and even his own, for he became one of Hollywood's most recognizable and best-loved actors.

Leslie Nielson died November 28, 2010 of pneumonia.

He is interred at Evergreen Cemetery in Fort Lauderdale, Florida.

[1] *Stories from History's Dust Bin* (additional reading):
   Vol 3, Sep 21:   Featuring Walter Brennan

[2] See Buster Keaton in this book, pages 153-156, to learn more about Keaton's comedic deadpan genius.

The reason they call it 'golf' is that all the other
four-letter words were used up.
Leslie Nielson (1926-2010) Actor, comedian

Oofty Goofty

Born: Leonard Borchardt
The original Wild Man of Borneo.
Apr 26, 1862 (Berlin, Germany) – after 1923 (Unknown)

T HE LEGENDARY WILD MAN of Borneo was neither a wild man nor from the Asian island of Borneo. He was Leonard "Leon" Borchardt, a small, slightly-built Jewish-born German. In 1876, at the age of fourteen he stowed away on the *SS Fresnia* bound for America.

When the ship docked, but before he could disappear into the New York shadows, he was spotted, chased, caught, and forced to pay for his passage by working as a deck-hand for two years. It would be 1878 before he set foot in America.

Five years later, after drifting aimlessly in search of steady employment and desperately in need of money, he enlisted in the U.S. Cavalry. There, he was constantly harassed because of his dark complexion and short, five-foot-four stature.

On April 9, 1883, after being told that Indians scalped Jewish soldiers first, he walked away from his post and sold his rifle and horse to a local farmer. He was quickly caught, then, just as quickly, escaped.

Fully aware of the dim view the military took of deserters, he went in search of a career change, preferably one in which his dark complexion would not betray his identity.

And he found the perfect job, carnival side-show performer.

Overnight, Leonard Borchardt became the *Wild Man of Borneo*, performing on San Francisco's famed Market Street as an untamed, uncivilized, barely human creature, captured and brought to America at great expense.

To convince the public of his mutant status he slathered his body with tar, onto which he stuck great quantities of horsehair. He was then locked in a sturdy cage to protect the nickel-paying public.

Once enough nickels were collected, a protective curtain was drawn to reveal a hairy, wild-eyed, ferocious half-man, half-beast, of whom the show's manager would periodically silence by pushing chunks of raw meat between the bars of the cage.

The Wild Man would fiercely grab the meat and consume a portion of it as if he hadn't eaten in weeks. When finished, he would rattle the bars of his cage, growl menacingly at the curious crowd and grunt, "Oof! Oof! Oofty Goofty!" And thus, Leonard Borchardt became Oofty Goofty, even when his side-show career came to an end, which it did, and very soon.

After a couple of weeks of acting like a wild man, Borchardt became ill due to his body's tar-clogged pores and the inability of his skin to regulate body temperature through perspiration.

He was taken to a San Francisco hospital where medical students labored unsuccessfully for days to remove the tar and horsehair. It was only when he was placed on the sun-drenched roof of the hospital and painted with turpentine that the tar gave up its adhesive properties, allowing the skin to gradually resume normal function.

In June of 1885, Oofty was caught setting a house on fire.

He claimed the owner paid him $200 to start the fire so an insurance claim could be filed. During the court proceedings, the judge, learning that Oofty had once worked as a carnival side-show exhibit, demanded his birth name. When Oofty gave it up, his name caught the attention of the military. When the civilian court closed its case, the military court opened theirs, and Leonard Borchardt received a deserter's sentence of three years in a military prison.

To gain his freedom, the ever-resourceful Oofty feigned episodes of epileptic behavior in hopes of a prison release, which didn't work. Later however, but overestimating his aptitude for rational thought, and underestimating the distance to the ground, he jumped from a cliff with hopes of a medical discharge, which did work.

He was discharged on September 18, 1885, for injuries sustained from the jump.

Remembering his brief theatrical success as the Wild Man of Borneo, Oofty convinced the owner of the Bella Union, a San Francisco burlesque theater, that he was an actor. Bella Union's big draw, and we're talking ginormous here, was a woman known as Big Bertha.

A decision was made to feature the smallish Oofty and the super-sized Bertha opposite each other in a spoof of *Romeo and Juliet.*

The production was as true to Shakespeare's story as you would expect from a burlesque theater, with one major theatrical exception. Due to Bertha's enormous girth and weight and the lack of a theatrical crane, it was necessary in the play's most famous scene to have Romeo croon to Juliet from the balcony, while the jumbo-sized object of his affection giggled, jiggled and threw kisses from the stage below.

The production was a smash hit with Bella Union's clientele, which shouldn't come as a surprise as San Franciscans have never let a little insanity become an issue when it comes to the arts or politics. Consider the city's earlier support (1860-70s) of His Majesty, Joshua Norton, the Emperor of America.[1] Ah, but we digress.

When Bella Union's run of Romeo and Juliet closed, Oofty was out of a job, but not for long.

Fresh from his plucky portrayal as Romeo, he was hired to perform at Bottle Koenig's Beer Hall in San Francisco's rowdy Barbary Coast district.

On opening night, he danced and sang only one song before management and patrons alike, and with great ceremony, lifted his small body high above their heads and literally threw him through the swinging doors and onto the rock-hard cobblestone street – and straight into his next career.

When Oofty was able to stand up he discovered he had lost all feeling in his body. To make certain he wasn't dreaming, he sauntered back into the saloon and asked a customer to punch him as hard as he could. The customer, only too willing to oblige, delivered a powerful blow to Oofty's midsection.

Oofty thanked the man, doffed his hat in respect, and walked out of the saloon.

For a nickel or dime, he allowed people to hit, punch, slug, and kick him – and for a quarter, whack him with a baseball bat. All things considered, it was a decent living, that was until he let heavyweight champion John L. Sullivan bust a cue stick over his back.

The blow not only ruined a perfectly good pool cue, it fractured three of Oofty's vertebrae, and left him with a painful limp for the rest of his life. Even worse from a career standpoint, the blow had returned all feeling back to his body.

Now, unable to support himself as a human punching bag, he traveled to Houston where he entered quail-eating contests, which had become the rage at the close of the 1800s.

A report on one of those contests was printed in the January 10, 1897 *Houston Daily Post*:

> *St. George Hotel, Dallas – Leon Borchardt, better known as "Oofty Goofty," who has well-nigh finished his task of eating thirty quail in thirty days for a purse of $100, at the Oriental Hotel in this city, is an interesting study. "Oofty" is a German Jew, born in Berlin and . . . .*

The 1923, the Houston City Directory listed Leon Borchardt as a 61-year-old resident, but nothing more is known of his life, or when or where he died.

S*tories from History's Dust Bin* (additional reading):
[1] Vol 1, Jan 8:   Featuring Joshua A. Norton

Love all, trust a few, do wrong to none.
William Shakespeare (1564-1616) Playwright

Ötzi the Iceman

A 5,000-year-old man, give or take a century or two.
Discovered, Ötztal Valley, Alps: Sept 19, 1991.

O N SEPTEMBER 19, 1991, tourists Helmut and Erika Simon were hiking along the edge of a glacial snowfield at an altitude of 10,530 feet in the Ötztal Valley of the Alps, when they spotted a pile of debris likely discarded by an inconsiderate hiker. After hiking across the snowfield to pick up the trash, they were shocked to discover it wasn't a pile of trash at all, but a partially exposed human body.

The body was face down in a shallow gully of the snowfield, the lower extremities firmly embedded in the dense glacial ice.

The Simon's assumed the body to be that of a mountaineer, most likely a climber like themselves who had met with an unfortunate accident while challenging the mountain.

It's not always possible to recover the body of a climber whose final breath was drawn as he or she spiraled out-of-control across a glacial ice-sheet before tumbling into the maw of a deep abyss. And attempting to recover a body under such circumstances, as often as not, ends up with the mountain claiming yet another victim.

Helmut and Erika used the next-to-last image on their roll of film to photograph the remains, then they carefully recorded its location before continuing their hike to a mountain lodge where they stopped for something to eat.

They told the manager of the lodge about the body. He nodded knowingly, telling them that only three weeks previous, the bodies of a man and a woman who had disappeared fifty-seven years earlier had been found by hikers and recovered.

The manager wrote down Helmut and Erika's names as well as specific directions to the site, and assured the hikers that every attempt would be made to recover and identify the body.

The following day a small, but helpful contingent of volunteers and curious citizens, including a local policeman, ascended the mountain, found the body, and discussed ways in which they might remove it from the ice.

Unfortunately, the first attempts to extract the body didn't go well.

First, a long stick found near the body shattered in a futile attempt to leverage the body up and out of the ice. The stick was later identified as the primitive bow the man had been carrying prior to his death.

Then, some additional damage was done to the body when an attempt was made by the hikers to encircle the body and simply pull it up and out of the ice.

Next, the group tried to weaken the glacial ice around the man's lower body with an ice drill. The group regretfully put the drill away when they discovered all they had accomplished was to drill a hole in the man's hip.

Several days later, mountaineers Hans Kammerlander and Reinhold Messner hiked to the site with several experienced volunteers. With Hans and Reinhold directing the operation, the body was finally extracted from the ice without further damage and carried to the village along with the shattered bow and other artifacts uncovered during the removal process.

Once in the village, the body, whose left arm had been awkwardly thrust across the right shoulder by the action of the glacier, was being forced into the rectangular confines of an unforgiving casket.

It was a classic example of trying to fit a square peg into a round hole. With one last attempt to get the body into the casket, the man's arm, the one thrust across his shoulder, was cleanly broken off at the elbow.

By now, it was becoming more and more apparent that the frozen, well-preserved body wasn't of recent origin at all, but the mummified remains of an ancient man.

Thus, after surviving a remarkably intact burial in glacial ice for over 5,000 years, his discovery, trip down the mountain, and visit to a local village – all in less than a week's time – may have been more traumatic than the day he met his death on the snowfield.

That is, unless he was the victim of a murder or an attack by thieves, which just may have been what happened. During a post-mortem examination, trauma to his head was evident, and an arrowhead was discovered buried deep into his left shoulder.

A CT scan performed in 2005 showed the position and trajectory of the arrowhead was such that it could have severed an artery and may have been the cause of death.

When word spread of the existence of the "iceman," as he was now being called, photographers began showing up to take his picture.

In addition, scientific types, interested in his discovery began to descend on the village. That's when it was discovered that the body, now free from the protective glacial ice, was under attack again, this time from a fungus, a serious concern of the scientific community.

The iceman, named "Ötzi the Iceman" by Austrian journalist Karl Wendl in honor of the Ötztal Valley where he was found, was flown to the University of Innsbruck (Austria), where he was extensively examined, measured, and dated.

Here's what we know about Ötzi (rhymes with 'tootsie') today.

Despite the less-than-ideal removal from the glacier, and the broken arm he suffered at the hands of well-intentioned villagers, he is considered the world's best-preserved mummy, and Europe's oldest physically-intact human mummy.

He lived about 3,300 years before Christ, during the period known as the Copper Age. When those years are added to the 2,000-plus years since the birth of Christ, Ötzi is around 5,300 years old. That's older than the Egyptian pyramids and England's Stonehenge.

We know that Ötzi stood about five-foot-three, weighed about 120 pounds, had a total of sixty-one distinct body tattoos, and was approximately forty-five years of age at the time of his death.

Trauma to the side of the head as well as the arrowhead lodged in his shoulder suggest he was likely waylaid, murdered and left to die on the trail

His last meal, eaten about two hours before his death, was meat from an ibex (a type of goat), combined with venison, roots, and fruits, all of which were found in his stomach and intestines.

Also found in his stomach was the microbe *Helicobacter pylori* (H. pylori), an organism found only in the human intestine, and useful in tracing human migrations.

Genetic researchers have determined that Ötzi's H. pylori microbe is a close match to the people of Asia.

If true, Ötzi had migrated over time and for a reason (or reasons) unknown, only to be murdered on a glacial snowfield in the Alps of Europe, near the current border between Austria and Italy.

Ötzi, along with his clothing, shoes, and a pouch attached to his belt that contained a scraper, a crude drill, a piece of flint, a bone awl, and some dried fungus – along with his shattered bow, are on display at the South Tyrol Museum of Archaeology in Bolzano, South Tyrol, Italy.

A glacier will frequently move forward one foot
while retreating three feet, which reminds me a lot of myself.
Charles M. Schulz (1922-2000) Cartoonist

Jesse Owens

Born: James Cleveland Owens
The Buckeye Bullet
Sept 12, 1913 (Oakville AL) – Mar 31, 1980 (Tucson AZ)

W HEN NINE-YEAR-OLD James Cleveland Owens, known by his family as J. C., was asked his name during enrollment at a new school, he responded in his heavy southern accent with what sounded like "Jeh-Cee Ow'ens." The school secretary handling the enrollment heard "Jesse Owens," and James Cleveland Owens became Jesse Owens, a name he would use for the rest of his life.

It was also a name that one world leader would despise, and another ignore, but more about that later.

Jesse Owens was born in 1913 in America's segregated south. He was the grandson of a slave and the son of a sharecropper, the latter a way of life barely a step removed from slavery.

In 1933, Owens was a high school student at Cleveland's East Technical High School. There he equaled the world record of 9.4 seconds in the 100-yard dash, and he set a long-jump record of 24-feet, 9½-inches at the National High School Championships in Chicago. It was a dash and a jump that landed him on the Ohio State University track team, and what an athlete he was, busting one record after another and becoming the *Buckeye Bullet* to those who followed sports.

During the Big 10 Championships at Ann Arbor, Michigan on May 25, 1935, Owens set three world records and equaled a fourth in less than an hour, giving rise to what athletes, coaches, and the public have all called the greatest forty-five minutes in sports. It's also a feat that in 83 years (1935-2018) has never been equaled. Not even close.

He started by (1) running the 100-yard dash with a world record-equaling time of 9.4 seconds; then (2) setting a new world record of 26-feet, 8-inches in the long jump; then (3) setting a new world record of 20.3 seconds in the 220-yard race; and then (4) as quickly as the hurdles were moved into place on the same track where he had just run the 220-yard race, he set a new world record in the 220-yard hurdles.

Think about what Jesse had just done.

That last race required running the same 220-yards he had just ran, but with the added difficulty of consecutively flying over hurdle, after hurdle, after hurdle (ten hurdles in all), and he did it in a mind-boggling 22.6 seconds, only 2.3 seconds slower than he had run the same distance without hurdles!

You don't have to be an athlete to appreciate the difficulty of running four races in the space of forty-five minutes, and tying one world record and setting three new world records.

But it would be the following year, 1936, that Jesse Owens would tilt the sports world – and with it, the world's broiling political scene – on its axis.

Germany's dictator, Adolf Hitler, was looking to the Berlin Olympics to drive home the concept of Aryan (non-Jewish Caucasian) superiority and to flash on the world stage for all to see, a resurgent and powerful Nazi Germany. Hitler was so confident in his belief of a master race that he even barred his own country's non-Aryan athletes from competing.

And equally distasteful, or perhaps even more so to Hitler, was the hateful notion that a person of African heritage should be dignified as an athlete at all.

Hitler refused to acknowledge America's eighteen black Olympians, like Jesse Owens, by having them referred to in the German press, not as Olympians, nor even athletes, but as "America's Black Auxiliaries."

Then it was time to begin the games, and Owens won four gold medals, one each for the 100-meter sprint (10.3 seconds); the long jump with a leap of 26-feet, 5-inches; the 200-meter sprint (20.7 seconds); and the fourth as a member of America's sprint relay team that set a new world record (39.8 seconds).

On the first day of the games, Hitler, as leader of the host country, would only shake the hands of his Aryan victors, refusing to shake not only Owens' hand, but all others. When Olympic officials insisted that Hitler either shake the hands of all winners or pass on the hand-shaking part of the ceremony, he chose the latter option.

Hitler was noticeably upset by the superior athleticism of "the Negro Owens," as Jesse was called in the German press, and he winced in anger each time the Negro Owens received another gold medal. It wasn't what the Führer had expected.

When asked about athletes of African heritage, Hitler reportedly shrugged and said that since their bodies were inherently stronger than the bodies of "civilized people," they should be excluded from all future Olympic participation.

Jesse Owens returned to America and a New York ticker-tape parade in his honor.

The one blemish, however, on the 1936 Olympics came not from anything that happened in Berlin, but something that took place back home in America.

Although Owens had achieved national and international recognition, he was not invited to the White House, nor given the opportunity to shake hands with President Franklin D. Roosevelt as was traditionally done to honor achievements of national significance.

Why not?

Since 1936 was an election year, Roosevelt was advised by his re-election committee that an act of overt friendliness toward a black man would prove costly in southern states' votes, thus no such offer was extended to Owens.

Owens never said much, if anything, about the snub. But when some from Roosevelt's party later courted his support, Owens rejected the overture and publicly endorsed Alf Landon, Roosevelt's opponent, in the presidential race.

Late in life when asked how he achieved success as a track and field athlete, Owens gave up his secret, "I let my feet spend as little time on the ground as possible. From the air, fast down, and from the ground, fast up."

Owens died in Tucson, Arizona, on March 31, 1980.

He is buried in Oak Woods Cemetery in Chicago.

Awards become corroded, friends gather no dust.
Jesse Owens (1913-1980) Olympian

Satchel Paige

Born: Leroy Robert Page
Perhaps the best pitcher in baseball history.
July 7, 1906 (Mobile AL) – June 8, 1982 (Kansas City MO)

T OM MEANY, WHO began covering baseball in 1922, best explained why Satchel Paige is as popular today as he was during his forty years of playing professional baseball. His reason: "More fabulous tales have been told of Satchel Paige's pitching ability than of any other pitcher in organized baseball."

If you're a trivia expert, you might question the accuracy of the "forty years of playing professional baseball," statement, and you're right. He only played pro baseball for thirty-nine years. He started with the Chattanooga Black Lookouts of the Negro League in 1926, and finished with Major League's Kansas City Athletics in 1965, and sure enough that's only thirty-nine years.

But, if you'll allow the 1967 season in which he played with the Indianapolis Clowns, a team informally known as the *Harlem Globetrotters of Baseball*, could you find it in your little pointed heart to let him round out his career with an even forty years?

Thanks.

Satchel was more than just a very durable, very funny, and very human athlete. He was a walking encyclopedia of tips for all humankind. But before we carry his "satchel" or open the "paiges" of his book to reveal his down-to-earth philosophy of life, and how to make the most of it by getting along with others, let's look at the name he made famous.

You didn't think that John and Lulu Page, or anyone in their right mind for that matter, would name their infant son Satchel, did you? John and Lulu named their little boy, Leroy Robert, and his surname was spelled just like theirs, "Page." At least, that's how they spelled their surname when they got married.

According to Satchel, someone told his parents a surname like "Page" was ordinary and unimpressive, like the pages of a book. So, John and Lulu inserted the letter 'i' between the 'a' and the "g,' looked it over and decided that "Paige" looked more "high-tone" than the rather ordinary, "Page."

About his nickname, "Satchel," the monument that marks his grave at the Forest Hill Cemetery in Kansas City explains:

> *He began work carrying suitcases at Mobile Union Station and devised a sling harness for hustling several bags at once. The other Red Caps said he looked like a 'walking satchel tree,' thus Leroy Robert Page became Satchel Paige. And Satchel Paige became a legend.*

Satchel may not hold the record for the number of quotes attributed to one person, but his name would be right up there for the best all-around selection. Whether you need an inspirational quote for a talk in church, a motivational quote for a team that has trouble winning, or an encouraging quote for a senior citizen's group, Satchel Paige has you covered.

For the inspirational talk, "Don't pray when it rains if you don't pray when the sun shines."

For the losing locker room, "You win a few, you lose a few. Some get rained out, but you've got to dress for all of them."

For the care center crowd, "How old would you be if you didn't know how old you are?"

Satchel was also famous for his six basic rules on how to stay young.

Here, for your edification:

1. Avoid fried meats which angry up the blood.
2. If your stomach disputes you, lie down and pacify it with cool thoughts.
3. Keep the juices flowing by jangling around gently as you move.
4. Go very light on the vices, such as carrying on in society. The social ramble ain't restful.
5. Avoid running at all times.
6. Don't look back, something might be gaining on you.

Was Satchel Paige any good during those forty years of playing baseball?

His estimated career record stands at 2,600 games pitched with 300 shut-outs, and 55 no-hitters.

It's claimed that on a few occasions, he signaled his outfielders to sit on the grass during an inning, then he would step to the plate and strike out the next three players.

It's also claimed that he once deliberately walked two batters just to pitch to Josh Gibson,[1] considered the most dangerous hitter in black baseball – and struck him out.

Was he respected?

Joe DiMaggio said that Paige was the best pitcher he ever faced; legendary pitcher Bob Feller said that Paige was the best pitcher he ever watched; and Dizzy Dean once commented that "Paige's fastball made his own look like a changeup."

In 1949, Paige went from the Negro League's Philadelphia Stars to the Cleveland Indians, becoming the oldest rookie, forty-years' young, to play in a Major League season.

In 1965, playing with the Kansas City Athletics at the age of 59, he became the oldest player to pitch in a Major League game.

When asked if he wasn't getting a little too old to pitch in the major leagues, he came back with a typical Satchel Paige response, "Age is a question of mind over matter. If you don't mind, it doesn't matter."

In 1971, Satchel was the first player from the Negro Leagues to be elected to the National Baseball Hall of Fame.

He died of a heart attack on June 8, 1982, in Kansas City, Missouri, just twenty-nine days shy of his 75th birthday.

---

[1] Josh Gibson, the second player from the Negro Leagues elected to the National Baseball Hall of Fame, was often referred to as the "most dangerous hitter" in black baseball.

Ain't no man can avoid being born average,
but there ain't no man got to be common.
Satchel Paige (1906-1982) Baseball

Rosa Parks

Born: Rosa Louise McCauley
First Lady of Civil Rights
Feb 4, 1913 (Tuskegee AL) - Oct 24, 2005 (Detroit MI)

DECEMBER 1, 1955, was a chilly day in Montgomery, Alabama, and it was about to get chillier.

Forty-two-year-old Rosa Parks had put in a long day as a seamstress. Exhausted and looking forward to a pleasant evening at home, she pulled the collar of her coat tight about her neck and waited for the familiar yellow-and-white Cleveland Avenue city bus.

Furthest from her mind was that within the hour, she, Rosa Parks, a lowly seamstress, was about to initiate a new era in the quest for racial equality, and in the process, she would become an American icon and the world would forever be changed.

After the yellow-and-white bus pulled up to the bus stop, Rosa boarded and mindlessly made her way past the first ten rows of seats reserved for white passengers.

As she had done almost every day for countless years, she took a seat on the eleventh row alongside three other black passengers. Several stops later the bus was full, and although nothing seemed out of the ordinary for a cold December day in Montgomery, the next stop would become a place-marker in time for one of America's defining moments.

It happened when a white man stepped into the bus and the driver, James Blake, a black man, did what he had been doing for years, just as mindlessly as Rosa Parks' daily walk to the eleventh row. He asked the four blacks occupying the eleventh row to stand in the aisle, so the white man could take a seat.

Blake's request was legal, conforming to a segregation ordinance passed fifty-five years earlier, in 1900, that allowed drivers to assign seats based on race.

Three of the black passengers in the eleventh row wearily stood up and complied with Blake's request. It's just the mindless way things were done in Montgomery in 1955.

But Rosa, quite unlike herself, remained in her seat as she had never done before, knowing full well she was breaking the law and fully aware she would pay a penalty for her disrespect of the driver's request.

A member of the National Association for the Advancement of Colored People, Rosa had worked toward black equality in Montgomery. And although the only thing on her mind when she boarded the bus that afternoon was a desire to get home and get warm, she had felt an impulse of resolve from somewhere deep inside.

It was a feeling that something needed done.

Later, when asked about her decision, she thought for a moment before replying, "When I made that decision I knew that I had the strength of my ancestors with me."

When arrested, Rosa asked the arresting officer, "Why do you push us around?" His response was an honest one, "I don't know, but the law's the law, and you're under arrest."

Rosa was charged with violation of Chapter 6, Section 11 of the Montgomery City Code. This, even though she had been sitting in the section reserved for "colored" passengers.

Her crime? She hadn't complied with the driver's lawful request to stand.

Several months before the arrest of Rosa Parks, Joann Robinson, a black professor and activist in Montgomery had suggested the possibility of a boycott of the city's buses. It's not known whether Rosa knew of the professor's suggestions, but one woman from the community, when she learned it was Rosa Parks who had been arrested, commented, "They've messed with the wrong woman now."

Four days later Rosa appeared before the judge for her crime, failure to comply with the above-named city code. The appearance took less than a minute. She was found guilty and fined $14 ($10 fine, $4 court costs). Instead of paying the unimpressive fine, she appealed, challenging the legality of Montgomery's code regarding racial segregation, and the fight was on!

A group of black citizens met to discuss strategies.

To guide their effort, they selected the relatively new minister of the Dexter Avenue Baptist Church, a young man from Atlanta, Georgia, who had married an Alabama girl (Coretta Scott) and moved to Montgomery two years earlier, in 1953.

His name was Martin Luther King, Jr.

The Women's Political Council of Montgomery printed 35,000 handbills announcing a boycott of all city buses, and on Sunday every black church in Montgomery encouraged their parishioners to honor the boycott, and they did just that for an astonishing 381 days!

Considering that three-fourths of Montgomery's public transportation passengers were blacks, the boycott posed a serious economic threat to the city, to say nothing of the social threat to the city's long-standing segregationist policies, formal and informal, and to much of the city's white population.

Coloreds with equal rights on city buses?
Allow that, and what will be next?
Coloreds drinking from the same fountains as whites?
Using the same restrooms?
Shopping at the same stores?
Attending the same social events?
Sitting together at Little League games?
Eating in the same restaurants?
Imagine!
What's the world coming to?

On June 13, 1956, Alabamians were about to learn exactly what the world was coming to. That's when a federal District Court ruled that Montgomery's city code was unconstitutional.

The state of Alabama and the city of Montgomery appealed, and the case went to the Supreme Court.

On December 17, 1956, the Supreme Court upheld the lower court ruling and Alabama was ordered to desegregate its buses.

Rosa Parks, who only wanted to get home and get warm that cold December night, suddenly became the face of America's civil rights movement.

Then, nearly fifty years later, on October 24, 2005, at the age of 92, Rosa Parks died of natural causes.

Three days later, Montgomery announced that the front seats of each of its city buses would be adorned with black ribbons and held vacant until the day after Rosa's funeral.

Secretary of State Condoleezza Rice spoke at her funeral in Montgomery after which Rosa was driven 800 miles to Washington D.C., her body to lie in state in the hallowed rotunda of the U.S. Capitol building.

To make the cross-country trip from Montgomery, Alabama to Washington, D.C., her body was transported inside a yellow and white Cleveland Avenue city bus, very much like the one in which she had refused to give up her seat fifty years earlier, in 1955.

You must never be fearful about what you are doing when it is right.
Rosa Parks (1913-2005) Civil Rights

Sam Patch

Born: Samuel Patch
The Yankee Leaper.
1799 (Pawtucket RI) – Nov 13, 1829 (Rochester NY)

S AM PATCH THRIVED on danger and the public adoration
that came with tempting fate.

He was also fond of saying, "Some things can be done as
well as others," a quote that falls flat these days. But it must
have had some recognizable meaning in the early 1800s, as it
appeared often on the posters announcing another Sam Patch
event, guaranteeing another thrilling leap higher and more
spectacular – and more dangerous than the one before.

Then came the day he fell to his death. It's not known
whether Sam jumped, slipped, or tripped, but some who were
there that day say he appeared to stumble as he stepped onto the
special custom-built platform high above the Genesee River.

Born in 1799, well before the passage of child labor laws, he
worked as a scavenger in a textile mill.

Scavengers were small, nimble children who were paid
pennies a day to dart beneath the giant looms and retrieve wisps
of errant cotton for later use. It was a difficult and dangerous
job, and occasionally a child would lose a finger, a hand, or even
their life by crawling too close to the broad leather belts that
constantly slapped against the large wheels that powered the
huge looms.

When Sam wasn't working, he would go outside and climb
the zig-zag edge of the concrete millrace[1] as high as he dared.
Then, curling his toes around one of the millrace steps, he would
eye the deep swirling catchment below the bottom step.
Swaying slightly to get a feel for his center of balance, he would
bend his knees and thrust his body forward and outward, hoping
to clear the jagged concrete edge of the millrace and disappear
into the cold water.

As he grew older, he grew braver, always challenging the
height of his previous dive.

When he didn't feel like diving, he would climb to the top of the millrace, sit in the moss-slippery chute and let the rushing water carry him swiftly to the catchment.   There, powerful swirling eddies would force him deep into an underwater crater carved by the relentless cascading waters before regurgitating him into the calm water beyond the race.

He often stayed under water until his lungs were about to burst, just to heighten the tension of the onlookers, before surfacing to their applause.

Any miscalculation, any tentative action, or any simple slip at any level of the millrace would not end well. At a minimum, the outcome would have resulted in at least a broken bone, and the very real possibilities of paralysis or death could never be ruled out.

But there was something about the adrenaline rush, the accolades of those who watched, that pushed Sam to make each jump a little more daring than the last.

It was an overwhelming feeling of power over the limits of nature, and he found himself jumping from more and more demanding heights – towers, bridges, ledges, and even the masts of ships, each jump attracting more attention and larger crowds than before.

And Sam's fame spread.

On September 30, 1827, Sam jumped from the top of the 70-foot Passaic Falls in New Jersey.

The modest crowd that showed up to watch Sam jump was so enthusiastic and so loud in their cheers, that he repeated the jump several more times over the next few months – to larger and larger audiences.

Others, including news reporters, started showing up at his events and writing about his daring-do.

On August 11, 1828 Sam made a 100-foot jump at Hoboken, New Jersey, and this time the press elevated his growing fame by publishing an article that referred to him as *Sam Patch, the New Jersey Jumper* with the subtitle, "There is no mistake in Sam Patch!"

In 1829, Patch was the headliner for a special event designed to draw tourists to Niagara Falls. To the thrill of everyone present, Sam leaped from the falls into the Niagara River below, becoming the first person on record to do so.

When he didn't resurface right away as everyone expected, the crowd grew restless and feared the worst, but resurface he did, to a long and sustained round of energetic applause! He had played the tourists at Niagara, just as he had played his co-workers at the old millrace, and his fame spread.

On November 6, 1829, he walked to the edge of a specially constructed platform five feet above the top of the 94-foot Genesee River Falls, this time accompanied by his new best friend, a pet bear cub.

After tossing the cub into the churning water below, Sam jumped. As was becoming his style, he added seconds to his reappearance before resurfacing and then waving and smiling broadly to let his admirers know he had once again cheated the grim reaper.

While most reports don't mention the fate of the cub, at least one does, saying it survived and was seen swimming to the opposite shore. But one thing is certain. The cub wasn't with Sam for his next and most spectacular jump, a 123-foot leap into the freezing cold Genesee River on, of all days, Friday the 13th, November 1829.

A crowd estimated at 10,000 shivering spectators braved the weather to watch the amazing Sam Patch once again spit in the face of death.

Sam was no longer the *New Jersey Jumper*. Instead, with fame came painted advertisements on the sides of barns and even larger ads on the sides of commercial buildings all of them proclaimed him an American original, as *Sam Patch, the Yankee Leaper*.

High above the Genesee River a special ladder and platform had been constructed for the daring event, and Sam, never one to disappoint, waved and climbed to the top of the ladder.

It would be Sam's last leap.

There was a rumor he'd been seen drinking before the event, and there were those who refused to believe that Sam would take such a chance.

After waving to the crowd below, he began his walk to the far edge of the jumping-off platform where it appeared to some of the spectators, that he may have stumbled, or stubbed his toe.

Regardless of what happened, he failed to achieve his normal vertical, feet-first entry. It wasn't until St. Patrick's Day the following spring (1830) that his frozen body was discovered by a farmer breaking the ice on the Genesee River to water his horses.

A medical examiner found that both shoulders had been dislocated due to his awkward entry into the water, making it impossible, even if he had survived the jump, to swim to safety.

Sam's body was buried in a pauper's grave in the Charlotte cemetery near Rochester, New York.

A simple plank marker with the words, *Sam Patch – Such is Fame,* was erected at the time of his burial. But the marker soon disappeared, likely taken by someone who wanted a piece of Sam Patch memorabilia, or vandals lacking respect for the property of others.

President Andrew Jackson, inspired by Sam's bravado and deeds of daring, named his personal horse Sam Patch in honor of *The Yankee Leaper.*

In 1948, funds were raised by the students of Charlotte High School in Rochester, to erect a proper granite marker noting his name, the years of his birth and death, and on the reverse side of the marker, an engraved panel with the brief details of his life, his fame, and his death.

---

[1] A millrace is a structure designed to carry water rapidly downhill within a wood or concrete channel to turn a water wheel and thus produce power to run textile looms, grist mills (grinding grains), saw mills (cutting timber), cider mills (crushing apples), etc.

Whatever there be of progress in life
comes not through adaptation, but through daring.
Henry Miller (1891-1980) Author

236

Mary Pickersgill

Born: Mary Young
The inspiration behind America's anthem.
Feb 12, 1776 (Philadelphia PA) – Oct 4, 1857 (Baltimore MD)

M AJOR GEORGE ARMISTEAD distinguished himself during the capture of Fort George near the Niagara River on May 27, 1813. Following the victory, he gathered the captured British flags and personally delivered them to President James Madison.

Madison was so impressed with Major Armistead's leadership at Fort George, that he directed the major to take command of Fort McHenry, a fort built to protect Baltimore Harbor and to prevent unwanted ships from sailing up the Baltimore River.

Then, on the morning of September 13, 1814, four months after Armistead's arrival, British ships entered the harbor and the *Battle of Baltimore Harbor* had begun. The daytime shelling continued relentlessly throughout the night. In the pre-dawn of the following morning, Armistead ordered a new flag raised over the fort, one intended to send an unmistakable "no surrender" message to the British.

Across the harbor, an American lawyer was being held prisoner aboard a British ship. He had spent a restless night watching the bombardment of the fort when suddenly, as the morning dawn turned night to day, he saw a flag unlike any he had ever seen. It was an enormous flag, a flag so large that even from his location on the opposite side of the harbor, a harbor filled with the smoke of battle, that he could make out the stars and stripes.

And the prisoner, with little sleep, began to write.

Here is the back story to that event, and what it was that the prisoner wrote.

Fort McHenry was named for America's third Secretary of War, James McHenry. It was a "defensive fort," a star-shaped fort surrounded by an elaborate system of earthworks.

The fort controlled access to Baltimore Harbor, making it a crucial defensive location for the colonists, and a critical point-of-attack for the British who believed it provided their best opportunity to breach America's defenses.

According to Major George Armistead, Fort McHenry was prepared to defend an attack, except for one thing. After taking command, he discovered that the fort had no flag, and in a dispatch to Major General Samuel Smith of the Maryland Militia, he wrote:

> *We, sir, are ready at Fort McHenry to defend Baltimore against invasion by the enemy. That is to say, we are ready except we have no suitable ensign to display over the Star Fort, and it is my desire to . . . .*

A few years earlier, in 1807, following the death of her husband, the young widow Pickersgill returned to her hometown of Baltimore. To support herself, she opened a business designing, sewing, and selling "silk standards, cavalry, and division colors" of every description, including signaling and house flags for the Army, Navy, and the various merchant ships that sailed in and out of Baltimore Harbor.

Mary wasn't new to flag-making. Her mother, Rebecca Young, had long been respected as one of America's premiere flag-makers, and she had taught Mary well the art of the seamstress. Also, living in the house with Mary and her mother was Mary's daughter Caroline, an expert seamstress in her own right.

That's how it was on the day that Major Armistead, the commander at Fort McHenry, knocked on Mary Pickersgill's door, introduced himself, and told Mary he needed two flags.

He had also brought with him a signed contract authorizing payment of $168.54 for one flag and $405.90 for a second flag. The sum of the order, $574.44, was enough to cause Mary to gasp, and then call her mother and daughter into the room to see what it was that Major Armistead had in mind.

What the major had in mind was first, a standard military flag measuring 17 x 25-feet; and a second, non-standard flag measuring a whopping 30 x 42-feet in size. A flag, Armistead explained, that he intended to hoist high above Fort McHenry at the appropriate time.

When asked why the unusually large size, Armistead only said, "I want it to be so large that the British will have no difficulty seeing it from a distance."

"Could the women make the flags," the major asked, "and how quickly?" Mary assured the major they could indeed make the flags, and that they would commence work on them right away, but she wasn't sure how long it would take.

To put the task into perspective, here are the specifics for the large 30 x 42-foot flag. The flag would require 420 square yards of fabric and contain fifteen stars and stripes, one for each of the fifteen states in the Union. Each stripe would be two feet wide, and the fifteen five-pointed stars would measure two feet between star tips. When completed, the flag would require eleven men to hoist it to the top of a ninety-foot flagpole.

Mary signed the contract.

To help with the task, Mary not only brought her mother, Rebecca Young out of retirement, but she included her daughter, Caroline, two nieces, Eliza and Margaret Young, two African American servants whose names have been lost to history, and an unknown number of seamstresses, perhaps as many as a dozen, from the Baltimore area.

The small flag would be sewn at the residence, but for sewing the larger flag, Mary arranged with a local business, Claggett's Brewery, to spread the fabric out in the malt house, where the sewing would take place until it was completed.

As soon as Major Armistead was notified that both flags were ready for delivery, which they were on August 19, 1918, he had them picked up and delivered to the fort.

Thirteen months later, September 13, 1814, as noted in the opening paragraphs, the British engaged Fort McHenry in the *Battle of Baltimore Harbor*.

At 6:30 in the morning, the British opened fire on the fort while remaining beyond the range of the fort's weaponry.

Next, British warships moved in and began firing heavy mortar shells at the fort, but as the ships drew near, they came under extremely heavy fire from Fort McHenry's guns, enough that they were forced to back off.

The fight continued throughout the night and as the first rays of the sun began to light the morning sky, Major Armistead ordered the lowering of the fort's standard flag, and the raising of the grand flag made by Mary Pickersgill and her band of seamstresses.

Once raised, the flag was not only visible to every ship in Baltimore Harbor, but to the ships in the river as well, and that included the *HMS Tonnant*, the ship where a young lawyer by the name of Francis Scott Key[1] was being held prisoner.

Key had watched the uninterrupted shelling of Fort McHenry throughout the night.

And now, as his eyes adjusted to the dawn's early light, he saw a new flag flying over the fort. It was a star-spangled banner so large and so intimidating that when combined with the ineffectiveness of 24-hours of relentless bombardment, it was enough to convince the Royal Navy that it wasn't going to breach Baltimore Harbor – not this day, not this time.

And it was there, aboard the British ship, the *HMS Tonnant* that Francis Scott Key penned the poetic words that have since become America's National Anthem, an anthem that is as much a part of the efforts of Mary Pickersgill and her legion of flag-sewing warriors, as it was of those who took up arms to defeat the British during the War of 1812.

---

[1] *Stories from History's Dust Bin* (additional reading):
    Vol 2, May 3:   Francis Scott Key with Daniel Sickles
    Vol 2, May 27: Francis Scott Key with Robert Ripley

Then, in that hour of deliverance, my heart spoke.
Does not such a country, and such defenders of their country,
deserve a song?
Francis Scott Key (1779-1843) Lawyer, poet

Edna Purviance

Born: Olga Edna Purviance
She faked her way into Charlie's heart.
Oct 21, 1895 (Paradise Valley NV) – Jan 13, 1958 (Hollywood CA)

W HAT CAN YOU DO if you're wealthy, as Charlie was, after you find the girl of your dreams, and a romance doesn't work out as you had once envisioned?

And yet, your heart tells you that something memorable must be done to let the lady know just how deeply you cared. It must be something out of the ordinary. Something that says you're not just another guy who takes what he wants from a girl and disappears. That wasn't what happened. Charlie's head may have called off the relationship, but his heart still yearned for the lady.

Yearned! Yes, that's the perfect word. If you're Charlie and your situation is as described above, how about softening the ache by sending a monthly check to the lady for the rest of her life, no strings attached?

Never mind the cost, remember it's the act that's important. The lady already knows *who* you are. This is to let her know *what* you aren't, that you aren't like other men, and that's exactly what Charlie did.

Edna Purviance, born in 1895 to Madison and Louisa Purviance was the lady, and she received a check from Charlie every month from when they broke up in 1923, at the age of twenty-eight, until her death in 1958, at the age of sixty-two.

And here's the story of Edna Purviance and the lover who for 34 years, never quite quit caring.

When Edna was three, the family moved a hundred miles from Paradise Valley, Nevada, where Edna was born, to the town of Lovelock where they took over management of the Singer Hotel. Four years later, with the hotel in the throes of financial failure and their marriage on the rocks, Madison and Louisa divorced, with Edna remaining with her mother.

In 1904, Louisa married Robert Nurnberger, a plumber, and the family lived together until Robert's death in 1913.

Now eighteen and head-turning attractive, Edna packed her suitcase and traveled 300 miles west to San Francisco where she moved in with a married half-sister, Bessie, who helped her find employment as a secretary.

Thirty miles across San Francisco Bay, near the town of Niles, a man named Charlie and a crew of script-writers, set designers, and construction workers were in the beginning stages of building a theatrical set for the filming of a silent movie titled, *A Night Out.*

Everywhere there were things needing done in preparation for filming, from matching the visual imagery of the movie set to the never-ending litany of script revisions, to identifying the perfect actress to play the leading lady, but overall, the project was on track.

Returning to the construction site after spending the morning and noon hour across the bay, one of Charlies' associates was enthusiastically telling anyone who would listen, about the strikingly beautiful girl he had seen eating lunch by herself in a San Francisco café.

That's when Charlie asked his associate if he remembered the name of the café. He did, and Charlie tucked "Tate's Café" into his memory.

On the very next day, Charlie was in Tate's Café describing the girl to the owner, who may have responded by saying something like, "There's only one girl who comes in here with that kind of beauty, and that's Edna, a secretary from across the street."

Not wanting to be appear too forward to the young lady, Charlie asked the café owner if he would mind arranging a meeting, so he could meet Edna. The café owner agreed, and Charlie met Edna, and Edna did not disappoint!

She was stunning!

But she also presented a problem.

Charlie knew that without any acting experience, she would never make it as a leading lady. Still, she was so very easy-on-the-eyes, so naturally beautiful, that he arranged to have her hired as "window dressing," a theatrical term used to describe someone strategically placed on a movie set to add interest, or intrigue, or pathos, in fact, anything that might help the audience understand the screenplay, especially in a silent movie.

But Charlie was smitten, enamored, a goner, twitterpated, in love, infatuated, whatever descriptor you want to use, and Edna's face and her smile ran through his mind like an endless loop of celluloid.

A few days later Charlie received an invitation to a dinner party and he asked Edna if she would accompany him.

She said she would.

At some point during the evening, Charlie told Edna that he could hypnotize her, and do it in a matter of seconds. Edna laughed, saying she had never been hypnotized in her life, and she couldn't possibly be hypnotized now.

Charlie pressed the issue and challenged Edna to let him hypnotize her, and she relented.

Charlie quieted the room and announced he was about to prove to his date that he could hypnotize her, and do it quickly.

As the party-goers gathered around to watch, Charlie stood Edna against a wall, wiggled his fingers in front of her eyes while evoking some nonsense mumbo-jumbo, and then he leaned in close to her face and mouthed the words, "Fake it," and Edna collapsed as if she'd been shot through the heart, and in fact, she had to be carried to a couch.

Charlie was impressed!

Not only with Edna's ability to follow directions, but that faked collapse? He'd never seen it done better! It almost had him convinced, and with that, Edna had not only won Charlie's heart, but the role of his leading lady in the silent movie that was about to be filmed in nearby Niles.

The two became an *item* in lover's terms and were seen everywhere together, and many expected Chaplin – yes, Charlie was Charlie Chaplin[1] – to make Edna his permanent and very personal leading lady, but it wasn't to be, and it was Charlie who called off the relationship.

Later, he would question his decision and think about how he might let Edna know how much he cared for her, but what?

In addition to Edna's movie debut as the headwaiter's wife in Chaplin's, *A Night Out,* she was the farmer's daughter in *The Tramp,* Carmen in *Burlesque on Carmen,* the girl stolen by the gypsies in *The Vagabond,* and the immigrant in *The Immigrant.* In fact, she co-starred with Charlie in thirty-four movies.

If you're watching a Chaplin movie in which Edna has a role, and you're wondering which actress is Edna, ninety-nine percent of the time you'll be right if you pick the prettiest.

In 1923, after starring in *A Woman of Paris* (written, produced, and directed by Charlie Chaplin), Edna's movie career ended, but not her pay checks.

Even after she married Jack Squire in 1938, the checks from Charles Chaplin Productions kept right on coming and they never stopped until she passed away on January 13, 1958.

Charlie lived nineteen years beyond Edna's death, and in his autobiography, he says only, "I had reservations about Edna. I was uncertain of her, and for that matter uncertain of myself."[2]

But what Charlie proved, most certainly to Edna and now to you, was that the thing for which he was most guilty, was second-guessing with his mind, the feelings of his heart.

Granted, there may be times when second-guessing a relationship is the right thing to do, but you'd better be sure!

Because when second-guessing misses its mark, it doesn't matter whether you're famous like Charlie Chaplin, or virtually unknown like the rest of us, it shares a common name.

It's called loneliness.

And it hurts.

---

[1] *Stories from History's Dust Bin* (additional reading):
   Vol 2, Jun 16:   Charlie Chaplin with Stan Laurel
   Vol 3, Oct 13:   Charlie Chaplin with E. C. Segar

[2] *Charles Chaplin: My Autobiography,* Simon and Schuster, First Edition (1964).

Ever has it been that love knows not its own depth
until the hour of separation.
Kahlil Gibran (1883-1931) Poet, writer

Ernie Pyle

Born: Ernest Taylor Pyle

He told about war from the soldier's perspective.

Aug 3, 1900 (Dana IN) – April 18, 1945 (Iejima Island, Okinawa)

WHAT MADE ERNIE PYLE'S reporting different from every other war correspondent during World War II was perspective.

Ernie wrote, not through the eyes of the generals who had to out strategize the enemy, and then translate those strategies into battle plans for the men in the trenches, but through the tired, bleary eyes of the men in the trenches who rarely knew what was over the next hill, only knowing it wouldn't be easy.

They were the guys who lived in foxholes, saw their friends die in front of them, ate cold K-rations, wore the same pair of skivvies for weeks on end, and although exhausted beyond all that is human, stood tall and proudly saluted their commanders and the flag that joined them together.

You see, Ernie Pyle slogged his way through Africa, the Pacific, and Europe, right in step with those dog-faced men upon whose shoulders rested the fate of the world.

And he did it knowing full-well that regardless of where the fight would take place tomorrow or the next day, it would be accompanied with a sickening loss of American and allied lives.

Author John Steinbeck, who knew something about the struggles of the common man while growing up and working alongside the migrant workers around Monterey, California, defined Ernie about as well as anyone:

> *There is the war of maps and logistics, of campaigns, of ballistics, armies, divisions, and regiments. Then there is the war of the homesick, weary, funny, common men, who wash their socks in their helmets, complain about food, whistle at Arab girls, or any girls for that matter, and lug themselves through as dirty a business as the world has ever*

seen, and do it with humanity and dignity and
courage – and that is Ernie Pyle's war.

Pyle, who was the editor of the student newspaper at Indiana University, knew how to express himself in print.

After college he worked for the *Washington Daily News* as a reporter, and in 1932 became the managing editor, a position he didn't like except for the few extra bucks it paid.

In 1934, Pyle and his wife took a well-deserved vacation to California and upon returning he was asked to fill in for vacationing syndicated columnist Heywood Hale Broun. He agreed, writing eleven columns in all, and he was a hit. Not long after, he resigned his job as a managing editor and moved with his wife Geraldine to Albuquerque, New Mexico.

From Albuquerque, he and Geraldine began wandering around America, with him sending in daily columns about the out-of-the-way places they visited and the interesting people they met.

He did that, working as a roving reporter until 1940 when he took his pen, notepad, and writing skills onto the World War II battlefields as a war correspondent.

Living with the soldiers, he told his readers exactly what he saw with the same sensitivity, the same colorful prose, the same feeling of patriotism, and the same curious mix of urgency and pathos that the soldiers felt.

He described what it was like to be a soldier. To be as jittery as a rabbit knowing that at any moment an attack might light up the night sky, or dirt kicked up from an incoming shell might rain down your back.

He told what it was like to drift off, and for a dreamy minute believe you were back home in the arms of your mother, your sister, your wife or your girlfriend, only to be jarred back to reality by the dissonance of war and the hurried footsteps and shouts of men running past your foxhole.

Pyle's gift for letting the folks back home know what their sons, brothers, husbands, and loved ones were experiencing halfway around the world earned him national respect, and in 1944, a Pulitzer Prize.

Here are a couple of excerpts from his writing:

ALGIERS, December 1, 1942 – *The last of the comforts are gone. From now on you sleep in bedrolls under little tents. You wash when you can. You carry your food on your back when you are fighting. You dig ditches for protection from bullets and from the chill north wind off the Mediterranean. You see men washing mess kits and clothing in five-gallon gasoline cans heated over an open fire made from sticks and pieces of packing cases. They strip naked and take sponge baths in the heat of the day. In the quick cold of night, they cuddle up in their bedrolls. Swinging first and swinging to kill is all that matters now.*

TUNISA, May 2, 1943 – *We're now with an infantry outfit that has battled ceaselessly for four days and nights. The mountains aren't big, but they are constant and treeless, easy to defend and bitter to take, but we are taking them. I love the infantry. They have no comforts and in the end, they are the guys that wars can't be won without. A narrow path comes like a ribbon over a hill miles away, down a long slope, across a creek, up a slope and over another hill. All along this ribbon is a thin line of men. For four days and nights they have fought hard, eaten little, washed none, and slept hardly at all. Their nights have been violent with attack, fright, butchery, and their days sleepless and miserable with the crash of artillery. The men are walking. They are fifty feet apart, for dispersal. Their walk is slow, for they are dead weary, as you can tell even when looking at them from behind. Every line and sag of their bodies speaks of inhuman exhaustion.*

Then, on a warm spring day, America's newspapers carried this brief United Press release:

ALBUQUERQUE, NM, April 19, 1945 (UP) – *Mrs. Geraldine Pyle, "That Girl" in Ernie Pyle's stories, was grief-stricken today at her husband's death. Mrs. Pyle said she had been notified of his death before it was announced in Washington. Mrs. Pyle answered the telephone in a calm but very low voice. She said she had received no details of his death.*

Geraldine would soon learn that on April 18th, Colonel Joseph B. Coolidge and Ernie were in a jeep on Iejima Island, Japan, when a machine gun burst made them dive into a ditch.

After a few minutes of silence, both men cautiously raised up to survey their surroundings. Ernie asked Colonel Coolidge, "Are you all right?" At that instant, a sniper's bullet struck Ernie in the left temple, killing him instantly.

A sign was hastily fabricated and posted at the place where Ernie Pyle died. It read: *At this spot, the 77th Infantry Division Lost a Buddy. ERNIE PYLE 18 April 1945.*

Ernie was buried with his helmet on and laid to rest in a row of graves. A ten-minute service took place with representatives of the Navy, Marines, and Army present.

His body was later reinterred at the National Memorial Cemetery in Honolulu, Hawaii.

In 2007, the Ernie Pyle home and library in Albuquerque, New Mexico was designated as a National Historic Landmark.

If you go long enough without a bath,
even the fleas will leave you alone.
Ernie Pyle (1900-1945) War correspondent

Harriet Quimby

Born: Harriet Quimby
America's First Lady of the Air
May 11, 1875 (Arcadia MI) – July 1, 1912 (Squantum MA)

I N 1991, THE U.S. Postal Service issued a commemorative fifty-cent airmail stamp acknowledging Harriet Quimby as one of America's *Pioneer Pilots.*

Behind her image on the stamp is a fragile-looking, open cockpit, Blériot XI monoplane. It was the plane that Harriet was piloting when she and her passenger were literally tossed like rag dolls from the open cockpit and plummeted 1,500 feet to their deaths.

This would be a good time to take a break and check out that commemorative airmail stamp. Stick a marker in the book, go to your computer, and do a search on Harriet Quimby. You may have to check a few different websites as the stamp doesn't show up on all of the websites dedicated to the aviatrix[1] known as America's *First Lady of the Air.*

The extra surfing, however, may be a good thing.

Especially if you're expecting to see Harriet wearing overalls and her elbows and brow smudged with aviation grease. The daughter of a Michigan farmer, Harriet wasn't averse to work, but she was almost always photographed in feminine attire, often in the fashionable purple jumpsuit she designed for herself.

Harriet was movie-star beautiful and in fact, appeared in one movie before her death. She was also a model, a movie critic, and the author of seven screenplays, all accepted and directed by D. W. Griffith for the Biograph Company. And there's more. She was also an accomplished photo-journalist with over 250 articles to her credit.

Had she learned to fly a year earlier, she may have been the first woman in the world to receive a pilot's license, although that honor goes to Raymonde de Laroche[2] of France, an outstanding pilot and a very lovely lady herself.

Quimby was America's first licensed female pilot (August 1, 1911), a nice enough honor, and the first woman in the world to pilot an aircraft across the 21-mile English Channel (April 16, 1912), an international honor.

Here, in Harriet's own words, excerpted from an article about her crossing of the English Channel titled, "An American Girl's Daring Exploit," published in *Leslie's Illustrated Weekly* magazine on May 16, 1912.

By the way, Harriet's crossing of the Channel took place just six weeks before her untimely death.

> *It seemed so easy that it looked like a cross-country flight. I'm glad I thought so and felt so, otherwise I might have had more hesitation about flying in the fog with an untried compass, in a new and untried machine, knowing that the treacherous North Sea stood ready to receive me if I drifted only five miles off course . . . It was a cold 5:30 am when my machine got off the ground . . . I put my hand up to give the signal of release. Then I was off. . . . up fifteen hundred feet within thirty seconds. From this high point of vantage my eyes lit at once on Dover Castle. . . . In an instant. I was beyond the cliffs and over the channel . . . the thickening fog obscured my view. Calais was out of sight . . . . There was only one thing for me to do and that was to keep my eyes fixed on the compass . . . .*

Harriet never married, and during the final two years of her life she was a New York darling with her colorful writing and well-publicized aerial exploits. Shortly after receiving her pilot's license, she began touring and giving flying exhibitions in the United States and Mexico.

Instead of the drab browns, blacks, and white scarves preferred by male aviators, she designed what she called her "flying suit" to fit her personality. It was a purple satin jumpsuit with a hood, and as a functional accessory, large aviator goggles at the ready, resting casually on her forehead.

After her flight across the Channel in the spring of 1912, her stock went even higher. Her style and beauty, combined with her well-respected flying skills, allowed her to command lucrative fees for appearances at air shows.

It seemed that everyone in America wanted to see the flying lady who had successfully challenged the English Channel, and in doing so, showed the world that a woman could pilot an airplane as well as a man.

It was at one of those paid appearances at a small airport near Quincy, Massachusetts, that Harriett and the manager of the air show, William Willard, decided to fly over the bay.

The purpose?

It was an unplanned publicity flight to generate interest in the airshow by reminding everyone from miles around that the lovely and fearless Harriet Quimby and her bright yellow Bleriot XI monoplane had arrived, and it was almost time for the show to begin.

As people were milling around or setting up seats for the show, Harriet and air show manager William Willard decided to kick up the excitement a notch by going aloft before the planned show got underway.

That's when many of the show's spectators heard an aircraft engine roar to life. Shielding their eyes, they watched as Harriet's single-winged Blériot sped down the runway. Moments later, the airplane was airborne, carving a beautiful wide arc in the sky as it gained altitude, flying out to the lighthouse in Boston Harbor, then another bold, wide arc, and the plane beginning its return to the airfield.

Then, as the crowd was watching, the unthinkable happened!

The airplane suddenly lurched forward at a rakish downward angle, tumbling first William Willard and then Harriet Quimby from their open-air seats.

As Willard and Quimby tumbled 1,500 feet to their deaths, the pilotless plane magically righted itself and glided earthward as though nothing were amiss, coming to an undamaged upright rest in a damp patch of Massachusetts shoreline.

Not yet, but before long, seatbelts would be installed as standard equipment in aircraft.

Harriet Quimby, who had added her name to the history of flight, was dead less than a year after becoming America's first licensed female pilot and the country's sweetheart of the skies.

In addition to the commemorative postage stamp mentioned in the opening paragraph, she was inducted into the National Aviation Hall of Fame in 2004; and into the Long Island Air and Space Hall of Fame in 2012.

Harriet was thirty-seven years old.

Her remains are interred at Kensico Cemetery in Valhalla, New York.

---

[1] Aviatrix: Female pilot, combined from the Latin *avis* (meaning *bird*) and *trix* (feminine suffix, Latin). It was a term often used during the early days of aviation to denote gender [aviatrix: female pilot; aviator: male pilot]. Although the term is considered archaic, it is sometimes applied to a female pilot in an old-fashioned or romantic way.

[2] *Stories from History's Dust Bin* (additional reading):
Vol 2, Aug 22:   Featuring Raymonde de Laroche

If a woman wants to fly, first of all she must, of course, abandon skirts and don a knickerbocker uniform.
Harriet Quimby (1875-1912) Aviatrix

Jeannette Rankin

Born: Jeannette Pickering Rankin
First female member of Congress
June 11, 1880 (Missoula MT) – May 18, 1973 (Carmel CA)

M ONTANA'S JEANNETTE RANKIN was the first woman elected to the U.S. Congress. She served twice, once in 1916 and again in 1940.

In 1916, after breaking the "glass ceiling" of representative politics in America, she spoke words as true as any ever spoken, "I may be the first woman member of Congress, but I won't be the last."

Her road to the House of Representatives wasn't easy, partly due to that damned Whitehall incident! But, no lawmaker ever worked harder, and unlike some politicians, she stubbornly held principle above party line.

Was she loved by everyone in Montana? No, but mostly because she was a dove in a state full of hawks. The better question is: "Was she respected?"

And the answer to that is a definite yes.

Each state is allowed only two statues in Washington's Statuary Hall. Montana's are of cowboy artist Charles M. Russell and Congresswoman Jeannette Rankin.

Jeannette grew up in Missoula, the first of John and Olive Rankin's children. She was the favorite of her father who made certain his daughter learned all about ranching, and that included slopping the hogs, turning bulls into steers, and mending fences.

Jeannette's mother, who was perpetually pregnant, also suffered from a thyroid problem. Thus, the task of managing the home fell largely on Jeannette's shoulders, whose jobs included keeping the children fed, their clothes patched, and their studies current.

Jeannette's strong-willed father chose biology for his daughter, so she complied, graduating from the University of Montana with a degree in biology, but with little interest in the subject. While at college, the tall, slender, brown-haired girl received several marriage proposals, another subject in which she had no interest.

In 1902, there weren't a lot of options for girls growing up in Montana, so she tried her hand at teaching in a rural community outside of Missoula, and hated it.

The following year she signed a contract to teach in Whitehall, a railroad town thirty-miles east of Butte, and she loved it!

The rigors of teaching were offset by new friends, a mix of handsome railroad men who enjoyed dancing and pretty ladies who loved to organize dance parties. The town also hosted literary events, theater productions and concerts, all activities that Jeannette enjoyed.

Then, in the spring of 1904, something happened.

Speculating as to what may have happened serves no purpose here, but know that Jeannette was not invited back to teach the following year. It was an embarrassing blow to the attractive teacher and the kind of thing that then, as today, leads to rumor and insinuation. Jeannette quietly packed her suitcases and just as quietly, put Whitehall behind her.

Instead of looking for another teaching job, she enrolled at the New York School of Philanthropy and became a social worker. After being passed over for positions of increasing responsibility because of her gender, she moved to Seattle and enrolled at the University of Washington, supporting herself as a seamstress.

Then, one day she noticed an advertisement for volunteers to work for women's suffrage, a woman's right to vote, and that advertisement changed her life.

By 1909, only four states allowed women to vote: Wyoming in 1869, Colorado in 1893, and Utah and Idaho in 1896.

In 1909, the state of Washington was in a heated battle over suffrage. It was a made-to-order issue for Jeannette, perfectly suited to her stubborn, focused temperament.

Besides, it was the right thing to do!

She dug into the problem like a Montana grizzly tearing apart a rotten snag for grubs, and before long, every legislator in the state of Washington knew who Jeannette Rankin was, what she was going to do, and what she expected from them.

Within a year, voters approved an amendment to the state's constitution, and Washington became the fifth state to allow women to vote.

That same year, when asked to assist the ladies of New York, she was instrumental in establishing the New York Women's Suffrage Party.

By 1912, the Rankin name had become synonymous with women's voting rights, and that year she helped to advance the cause in Arizona, Kansas, and Oregon.

In 1914, after becoming the first woman to speak before the Montana legislature, and after three years of daily arm-twisting, *Rankin-izing* the legislators of both parties called it, Montana's lawmakers – with their wives firmly behind them – voted 53 to 47 to allow women to vote, the nation's 10th state to do so.

That same year, with the national spotlight illuminating her women's rights leadership, she began eyeing a run for political office herself, and three things made such a dream possible for Jeannette in the 1916 elections.

First, because of her untiring work on behalf of Montana's women, she believed, and rightly so, that she could count on the women's vote, and probably a lot of men's votes as well.

Second, Montana's population had grown to where the state now qualified for two Congressional seats. Since both seats were "at large," all she needed to do was to come in first or second in the voting.

Third, her younger brother, Wellington Rankin, a successful attorney was up to his eyeballs in the Republican Party, and she knew he would work as tirelessly as she in the campaign, and that's exactly what the brother-sister team of Rankin and Rankin did.

The press loved Jeannette's attractive face, her boundless energy, and her skill as a public speaker.

Oh yes, the opposition party renewed the whispers about an old scandal in the town of Whitehall where she had once taught school.

They reminded voters relentlessly, that she had left town in the middle of the night, insinuating she may have been pregnant, or had an abortion, or been involved in a damaging love triangle, and they asked the voters, "Do you want someone unfit to teach your child to be your voice in Congress?"

Jeanette ignored the relentless innuendo and apparently, so did most of Montana's voters.

While the other party was trying to make mud stick to Jeannette's campaign, Jeannette was becoming the darling of Montana's newspapers, and when the votes were cast and tallied,[1] she had become America's first woman to be elected to a national legislative body.

During six decades, including her two terms in the House of Representatives, she worked tirelessly on the legislation that became the 19th Amendment, granting unrestricted voting rights to all American women.

About her politics, remember the comment about her being "a dove in a state full of hawks?" In 1917, she voted against entering World War I; and in 1941, she was the only member of Congress to vote against declaring war on Japan following that country's sneak attack on Pearl Harbor.

So, she hated war and was a little myopic about the need to bring Japan to its knees.

But what she did in securing equal rights for women puts her in a class by herself, and since it was Montana's male legislators who chose to place Jeannette Rankin on a pedestal in Statuary Hall, well, that's all you need to know.

End of discussion!

---

[1] In the 1916 election for a seat in the U.S. House of Representatives, Rankin lost by 7,600 votes to Democrat John M. Evans, but defeated third place candidate, another Democrat, by over 6,000 votes, winning one of the two "at large" seats.

You can no more win a war than you can win an earthquake.
Jeannette Rankin (1880-1973) Suffragist, politician

George Reeves

Born: George Keefer Brewer
He wasn't faster than a speeding bullet.
Jan 5, 1914 (Woolstock IA) – June 16, 1959 (Benedict Canyon CA)

G EORGE REEVES, WHOSE ALTER-EGO was said to be faster than a speeding bullet, was dead at 45-years of age from a .30 caliber gunshot. It had been fired into his head at about two o'clock in the morning of June 16, 1959.

Reeves was best known for his portrayal as Superman in the 1950s television program, *The Adventures of Superman.* His death is officially listed as a suicide, but whenever there's a Superman shooting, there's bound to be controversy.

The timing of the suicide was unusual, just three days before George was to marry society playgirl Leonore Lemmon, the wedding following a breakup with his former girlfriend, Toni Mannix, a breakup she didn't appreciate.

On the night of the suicide (or murder), but earlier in the evening, George and Leonore had been out with friends William Bliss, screen-writer Rip Van Ronkel and his wife Carol, and author Richard Condon (*The Manchurian Candidate, Prizzi's Honor*, and others).

During the evening, an argument had erupted between Reeves and Condon and the group drove to Reeves' home for a nightcap. But George, still steamed over the earlier dust-up was in no mood for small talk, or a drink, so he excused himself and went upstairs, telling everyone he was going to bed.

By midnight the downstairs foursome, feeling no pain from endless rounds of cocktails, had become very noisy.

George, awakened by the downstairs din, got out of bed, descended halfway down the stairs, and in no uncertain terms told the revelers to "knock off the noise!"

The group, abruptly quieted, watched as George lumbered up the stairs and disappear into a hallway.

With the guests unsure about what to do next, and thinking that maybe they should leave, a well-oiled Leonore, not wanting to see an end to the evening's festivities, made light of the situation by saying about George, "Oh, he'll probably just go to his room and shoot himself."

And a short while later, a shot rang out.

Guest William Bliss raced up the stairs and found Reeves laying naked, face-up across the bed with a bullet hole to the right side of his head. Between his feet, which were touching the floor, a 9 mm Luger pistol.

Crime scene investigators found George's blood alcohol level at .27, well above the minimum for intoxication, but they were unable to find any fingerprints, not even George's on the murder weapon, nor any powder-burns on the body, thus the police report concluded that Reeves death "indicated suicide."

That was it.

His death was, well, an indicated suicide.

But now, more than a half-century later, people aren't quite so sure.

At the time of Reeves' death, few knew his secret, and those who knew it were loath to make it an issue.

Why?

Because of the impact it would have had on the squeaky-clean image he had cultivated as reporter Clark Kent, vis-à-vis Superman.

But, the secret was this.

Reeves' on-screen persona was a poor match for off-screen reality.

As the flesh and blood representative of the morally incorruptible Superman, Reeves, in real life, was much less virtuous and not unlike many, if not most, of his Hollywood colleagues. In other words, the Man of Steel was <sniff> a mere human!

Although Reeves had been acting since 1939 when he won the role of Stuart Tarleton in *Gone with the Wind*, it was the 1950s television hit as Superman that turned him into a star.

And it shouldn't come as a surprise to anyone that Lois Lane, the fictional ace reporter for the *Daily Planet*, wasn't the only woman in Metropolis, or Hollywood for that matter, to notice the well-defined abs and pecs he kept hidden under his costume.

Another admirer, and one who felt no competition from *Daily Planet* reporter Lane, was the wife of MGM executive producer Eddie Mannix.

Mrs. Eddie Mannix (Toni) and George Reeves had worked together to raise money for the Myasthenia Gravis Foundation, for which Reeves had been named national chairman. But it didn't take long before working together evolved into playing together and a full-blown relationship between Toni and George ensued.

Things like that are hard to keep under wraps. But for a Hollywood affair, the folks in the know did a good job of downplaying anything that might hurt Reeves' all-American image.

As far as the Mannix side of the equation was concerned, Eddie apparently knew about his wife's affair with Reeves, but found no reason to make an issue of it. After all, why rock a boat that might expose his own man-about-town activities?

Toni, in her fifties and eight years older than George, feared her two worst enemies, the Hollywood glut of beautiful young women who were as capable as she in charming the Man of Steel, and Mother Nature.

So, she compensated her aging beauty by adding wealth to the equation. She spent lavishly on George, giving him expensive gifts, and she even bought him a home in Benedict Canyon, not far from hers and Eddie's residence.

But still she worried about maintaining her hold on his affections.

And she was right.

It was 1958 and the day arrived when it became necessary for George to tell an angry Toni that he was in love with someone else, and not only that, but that he was about to be married.

And if that weren't enough to rock Toni's world, hubby Eddie tossed in the marital towel as well. Thus Toni, who had been playing in two sandboxes, was now locked out of both, and that didn't set well.

The new girl in George's life was Leonore Lemmon, young, single, and as beautiful and well-endowed as Toni had once been. George and Leonore set a date for their marriage, June 19, 1959, with a Tijuana honeymoon to follow.

Afterward they would live in Benedict Canyon, in the very home Toni purchased to keep George near her, and as you might imagine, that was another source of irritation for Toni.

And then, a mere three days before time to tie the knot.

The shot upstairs.

William Bliss's panicked race upstairs and down the hall to the bedroom where he found Reeves' body, face-up across the bed with a bleeding bullet hole to the side of his head.

So, by whose hand did Reeves die? There are three possibilities: Reeves accidentally shot himself; he intentionally committed suicide; or he was murdered by a hired hitman.

Hired by someone named Mannix? There were never any arrests. Eddie Mannix died in 1963, Toni in 1983, and now we're left with an unsolved mystery.

It sure sounds like a job for Superman, but with Clark Kent nowhere to be found, learning what really happened that night is as unlikely as finding a chunk of Kryptonite in the backyard of George Reeves' home in beautiful Benedict Canyon.

Reeves was buried at Forest Lawn Memorial Park in Glendale, California, in the same gray double-breasted suit he wore on the set as Superman's alter-ego, Clark Kent.

I think a hero is an ordinary individual who finds strength to persevere and endure in spite of overwhelming obstacles.
Christopher Reeve (1952-2004) The other "Man of Steel"

Residence Act of 1790

Establishing America's capital city
Signed into law by George Washington, July 16, 1790

A S YOU MIGHT RECALL from your High School American History class, prior to the Residence Act of 1790, the seat of government was all over the map. From 1776-1790, legislative sessions were held (not in order) in Philadelphia, Lancaster, and York, Pennsylvania; Annapolis and Baltimore, Maryland; Princeton and Trenton, New Jersey; and in New York City.

The Residence Act of 1790 put an end to the foolish hop-scotching from city to city by (1) establishing Philadelphia as the "interim" capital of the United States for a maximum of ten years, during which time, (2) legislators would select a piece of real estate for the nation's capital at a site near the Potomac River,[1] but outside the boundaries of any state,[2] and (3) providing authority for the president to hire a surveyor to specifically identify sites for the "Congress House" (the Capitol Building) and the "President's House (the White House) and to begin laying out the city.

While the legislators were busy legislating, one very famous surveyor was quietly setting up his transit on the banks of the Potomac. If you were paying attention in class, you might already know who that surveyor was.

What! You don't remember the teacher talking about the Residence Act of 1790? You must have been snoozing in class that day.

Here's what you slept through.

The genesis of a decision to locate the nation's capital outside the boundaries of any state occurred during the so-called Pennsylvania Mutiny of June 20, 1783. That's when, during a session of Congress, four-hundred unhappy men surrounded Independence Hall in Philadelphia to protest the size of their payments for having fought in the Revolutionary War.

While the protesters were noisily blocking the exits, and threatening to hold the law-makers hostage until their grievances were addressed, Alexander Hamilton was drafting a letter that was slipped to a courier and taken to Philadelphia's city fathers.

The letter stated that unless the city took steps to protect the legislators from the protestors, they would pack their bags, leave the city, and take their wallets with them. Okay, so that's not the exact wording of Hamilton's letter, but it was essentially the message.

The next day Hamilton met with John Dickinson, president of Pennsylvania's Executive Council and restated what he had written in his letter. Dickinson said he would meet with the state's militia leaders and report back the following day.

Dickinson appeared the next day as promised and shared the substance of his conversation with the leaders of Pennsylvania's militia.

"Unfortunately," said Dickinson (paraphrasing), *the militia doesn't want to upset the protesters, who were mostly military types claiming to have been short-changed in the amount of military pay they had been promised.*

With no assurance that they would be protected from the demonstrators, the congressmen did as they said they would do, they departed Philadelphia, and completed the congressional session in Princeton, New Jersey.

Because of the above incident, Congress refused to reconvene in Philadelphia until 1788 when Robert Morris, Chairman of the Pennsylvania Safety Committee, talked them into coming back for another session.

When they returned, Morris went into high-gear, pitching the advantages of a Philadelphia-based national capital, but the legislators had long memories and their interest in Morris's proposal ranged from "ho-hum" to complete indifference.

While all of this was taking place, the surveyor mentioned up front was strolling along the scenic banks of the Potomac, imagining a new nation's capital set within the beauty of the blossoming cherry trees that were everywhere in the area.

Now, if you know someone from Pennsylvania, nice folks that they are, you also know they can be long on stubborn, short on compromise, and that they rarely give in.

That description fit Robert Morris to a tee, and he remained convinced that once the home of the federal government had moved into Philadelphia, they would be so pleased with the arrangement they would stay.

After all, Morris and his group thought, why should the legislators go to the expense of building a new city when the nation's largest and most cosmopolitan city already exists?

When the legislators showed only minimal interest, Morris sweetened the deal by expanding Philadelphia's Congress Hall, and then, using his own property at 6th and Market Streets, he began a renovation project that he believed would become the "Presidential Palace."

But it didn't work out as Morris and the Pennsylvanians had hoped.

Instead, the members of Congress, serious about finding a permanent home for the seat of the nation's government, passed the Residence Act of 1790, dashing Philadelphia's hopes.

The Act allowed Philadelphia to serve as the nation's capital for a period, "not to exceed ten years," at which time Congress was required to have a permanent location selected "…on a parcel of land not to exceed 10 miles square and free of the jurisdiction of any state."

So, who was the former surveyor who had been looking at a piece of real estate alongside the Potomac? You already know he had surveying experience, and now you're getting ahead of the story.

That's right, it was George Washington,[3] who was in his first term as President of the United States.

But building a new city, and not just any city, meant having a surveyor, civil engineer, and architect of enormous talent, and fortunately such a man existed.

His name was Pierre Charles L'Enfant, a French-born American who had been with General Washington at Valley Forge, and who had once painted a portrait of the general. It was also L'Enfant, who at Washington's request, had designed the logo for the exclusive Society of the Cincinnati.[4]

Almost before the ink was dry following the passage of the Residence Act, President Washington appointed L'Enfant as city designer, a task he welcomed and begun immediately.

L'Enfant started work, and on June 22, 1791, he presented a plan to the President in which he had located within the boundaries of the new city, the specific locations for the Capitol Building and the White House (as they are known today), and the layout of the streets, including the diagonal avenues radiating out from the Capitol Building and many other uniquely Washington features.

By the early 1800s, that ten-square mile piece of land was simply referred to as the *Federal District,* and sometimes as *Federal City.* It was later renamed the *District of Columbia,* and eventually renamed for the last time as, *Washington, the District of Columbia,* in honor of the nation's first president. Today, it is informally referred to as Washington, D.C.

In honor of the man who laid out America's capital city, a beautiful complex of office buildings known as L'Enfant Plaza was dedicated in 1956.

A statue of Pierre L'Enfant has been completed by sculptor Gordon Kray in anticipation of eventually being granted a place in Washington's Statuary Hall.

Current law allows only the states to have statues, two per state, but legislative work has been underway since 2007 for an exemption to allow Washington, D.C. a single statue.

[1] The Act specified the location to be along the Potomac River, between the Anacostia and Connogochegue Rivers, consisting of no more than ten miles square on a side, for a maximum area of 100 square miles.

[2] The Act provided that the laws of the states from which land would be ceded (Maryland and Virginia) would apply to the "federal district" until the government established official residence, at which time the "federal district" would assume full authority over all matters within the district.

Stories from History's Dust Bin (additional reading):
[3] Vol 1, Feb 22:   Featuring George Washington
[4] Vol 2, May 13:   Featuring the Society of the Cincinnati

Washington is a community of southern efficiency
and northern charm.
John F. Kennedy (1917-1963) 35th U.S. President

Bobby Riggs

Born: Robert Larimore Riggs
He's famous for losing a tennis match.
Feb 25, 1918 (Los Angeles CA) – Oct 25, 1995 (Encinitas CA)

MOST ATHLETES BECOME famous for the games, tournaments, competitions, and matches they win. Bobby Riggs became famous for the one he lost, a wildly-hyped, nationally televised tennis match against a woman, Billie Jean King.

Bobby Riggs was born to play tennis, any kind of tennis.

As a pre-teen, he was an excellent table tennis player. That was, when he could talk someone into playing against him.

Most adults don't mind losing a game or two to a kid. We've all played to lose a race or a board-game, just to provide a youngster with some positive reinforcement.

But no one likes to lose every game without exception and the small scrappy kid wouldn't let you win, even if you were a relative and he liked you – a lot. And challenging Bobby to a rematch usually meant being embarrassed even worse the second time.

In 1930, twelve-year-old Bobby was practicing against the hitting wall in a Los Angeles tennis complex when Dr. Esther Bartosh, a professor of anatomy at the University of Southern California, walked by.

She stopped, watched, and did a double-take, amazed at the accurate strokes and the kid's uncanny ability to sense the angle of the returning ball as it rebounded off the wall. He was like a pool player knowing exactly how the cue and target balls were going to react to the angles of a cushion shot.

Most every young tennis player is lucky to get two, or maybe three whacks at the ball when they compete against the hitting wall.

But not this kid.

As Dr. Bartosh watched, it was Wham! Wham! Wham! Wham! Wham! Wham! Wham! and they weren't pussycat-strokes! Not at all. It was just Bobby playing table tennis with a standard tennis racquet and a fuzzy tennis ball against an uncomplaining opponent.

Bartosh asked Bobby if he'd like to learn more about the game and he said, "Sure."

Now, Dr. Bartosh wasn't your typical college professor.

She was also Southern California's 4th-ranked women's tennis player, and less than three months after taking Bobby under her wing, her young protégé reached the finals of Southern California's 13-years-and-under tournament.

She and Bobby continued working together and the following year he competed in the National Boys' Championships held at the Culver (California) Military Academy.

Under Dr. Bartosh's watchful eye, tennis know-how, and her ability to work with Riggs, the youngster quickly rose to the top of the talent-rich Southern California tennis circuit, winning the U.S. Junior Title in 1935, and a year later, the U.S. Clay Court Championship.

Moving ahead now, during the late 1930s and into the '40s, Bobby Riggs was ranked the world's number one men's tennis player three times, first as an amateur in 1939 and two more times as a professional in 1946 and 1947.

But, as the old maxim goes, fame is fleeting, and by 1970 virtually everyone had forgotten about Bobby Riggs. That was, until he came out of retirement at the ripe old age of fifty-five to challenge Margaret Court, the world's number one ranked female player.

The match was played on Mother's Day, 1973, and Riggs, using drop shots and lobs to keep Court off balance, won the match handily, 6-2, 6-1.

To use a term known mostly to folks familiar with the game of tennis, Bobby Riggs landed "trademark-side-up"[1] on the covers of *Sports Illustrated* and *Time,* and he was famous all over again.

And did he enjoy the limelight?

You bet he did!

You can say that again.

Riggs loved the limelight!

Heady and ready after defeating Court, Riggs challenged tennis great Billie Jean King to a nationally televised match. It was billed as the *Battle of the Sexes* with a prize of $100,000.

King was the same age as Court (30), in excellent physical shape, and a former number one ranked women's player. She had also won thirty-nine Grand Slams, twelve singles titles, and more.

King was strong competition.

Riggs, overconfident and intoxicated by his lop-sided victory over Court, taunted King during every broadcast and every sports magazine interview he got.

But King played it smart. She didn't say much, just smiled her fabulous smile and played it cool.

The day of the televised match, September 20, 1973, arrived.

More than 30,000 fans, celebrities, and the curious attended the match at Houston's Astrodome.

An estimated ninety-million Americans watched the match on their television sets.

The months of professionally-orchestrated hype all came together as the players made their grand entrances.

Billie Jean entered the Astrodome first, Cleopatra style, carried aloft in a chair held high by four bare-chested athletes, members of Rice University's men's track team dressed as Roman slaves.

As soon as the applause died down, Bobby entered the Astrodome, seated in a rickshaw surrounded by a bevy of scantily-clad lovelies he referred to as his bosom buddies.

Riggs presented King with an enormous multi-colored lollipop.

King returned the favor by presenting Riggs with a piglet named "Larimore Hustle," Larimore being Riggs' middle name.

And the match was on!

But, the once ageless Riggs was no match for the matchless King.

Studying and learning from Court's mistakes, King returned Rigg's lofty lobs and his dreaded drop shots with placements that simply ran Riggs ragged, and the $100,000 prize went to Billie Jean in three straight sets: 6-4, 6-3, 6-3.

Riggs tried to get Billie Jean to agree to a rematch, but she coyly refused, leaving the impression she didn't have time for such foolishness.

But not all was lost.

The publicity surrounding the Battle of the Sexes surpassed the publicity Bobby received during his career as one of the world's top-ranked tennis players, and it also netted him a cushy $100,000 a year job as the resident tennis pro at the Tropicana Hotel and Casino in Las Vegas.

Over the years, the differences between the two athletes mellowed, and Bobby Riggs and Billie Jean King became friends.

She was one of the last persons Bobby visited with, via telephone, on the eve of his passing on October 25, 1995.

The last thing Billie Jean told Riggs during that phone call was, "I love you."

Riggs was seventy-seven years old.

---

[1] Tennis racquets display a trademark on only one side of the racquet throat. In determining initial service, one of the players will say, "trademark." The other player will then place the head of the racquet against the playing surface and give the racquet handle a twist. The racquet will spin momentarily before coming to rest on the playing surface. If the racquet comes to rest "trademark-side up," the player who called "trademark," will begin the match by serving first.

Tennis is a perfect combination of violent action
taking place in an atmosphere of total tranquility.
Billie Jean King (1943-) Tennis

James Whitcomb Riley

Born: James Whitcomb Riley
Ain't he a funny ol' Raggedy Man?
Oct 7, 1849 (Greenfield IN) – July 22, 1916 (Indianapolis IN)

W HEN THE LITTLE GUY arrived on that cold blustery October day in 1849, his father, Reuben Riley, a member of the Indiana House of Representatives, was so certain his son would follow in his footsteps that he named him after a politician friend, Indiana governor James Whitcomb.

Well, little Jimmy may have spent some time walking in his strutting father's footsteps, but it would never have anything to do with becoming a politician. Not even remotely so.

Believing that James would face learning difficulties in school, his mother worked patiently with him for months before enrollment time. She taught him the alphabet and the basics of reading, hoping that somehow her loving investment in his future would give him enough of a head start to at least stay even with his classmates.

With worrisome hopes, she enrolled James in school where he performed just as she feared. Poorly. That is, except for a love of poetry and literature from listening to the town librarian read to the students.

But of what practical value are poems and stories?

None.

Even James knowed that nobody kin eat pomes and stories. Shoot, ever body knowed that!

His school attendance was sporadic at best.

Showing up at school usually meant he was in trouble at home for a misdeed committed there. But what he lacked in spelling, ciphering (arithmetic), and social studies, he more than made up for in persistence.

In fact, persistence was James' long suit. For instance, although his lackadaisical pattern of attendance never improved, he persisted, graduating from the eighth grade in 1869, at the age of twenty.

So, what was next for James?

He bummed around during the 1870s and '80s.

Wrote a few poems when he felt like it, sold a few Bibles, did some acting, painted signs, did odd jobs – lots of 'em – why shucks, he even hawked patent medicines.

Once, he claimed to have been born blind, but was miraculously cured by the very elixir he was holding in his hand, perhaps telling the crowd something akin to:

> *That's why I'm here today my good friends, and you are my good friends, to share with you my story, as the Good Book tells us in Hepzibah chapter 8, verse 13, 'There will come among you, one who holds the key to improve, yea, even to restore the sight of the believer.'*
>
> *An' friends, like yourselves, I do believe in the Good Book!*
>
> *Now, if one of you out there would be so kind as to hold up some fingers – I'll tell you how many. I see three fingers. Am I right? A year ago, my friends, I couldn't have seen this man's head, let alone his fingers!*

Selling nostrums, quack cures for real and imagined illnesses, consisting of colored water laced with alcohol was not what his well-respected politician father had envisioned of his first-born.

But, dear reader, don't give up too quickly on the lad from Greenfield, Indiana.

James would eventually make his father proud. But for the present, he would do what he could to eat and stay alive, and in his spare time he would write, mostly poetry, a seemingly odd interest for a guy whose brain wuz empty of grammar skils and what cood hardly spel the werds he needed for his pomes.

James liked to write about the places and the people he met as he wandered the country, and his writing, as he would later explain, "… 'flected the language as I herd it and as bees' I could writ it."

In 1883, he published a couple of poetry collections, *The Old Swimmin' Hole*, and *'Leven More Poems,* and in 1890, he published, *Rhymes of Childhood*, and there would be more.

You've heard his poetry, of course you have.

Each selection is full of fun-to-read local dialects, with titles like *The Raggedy Man, Romancin', When the Frost is on the Punkin, The Runaway Boy, Little Orphant Annie,* and . . . . and you say you can remember your mother reading *Little Orphant Annie* to you, but you can't remember the words, or exactly how it goes.

Well, it's like most of James Whitcomb Riley's fun-to-read and fun-to-listen-to poems.

And, there's a secret to the reading.

It's best to read the verses in their entirety, aloud and with feeling, to a grandchild or two. All of you snuggled together under a quilt, in the dark, at an hour when the "Gobble-uns" in your house just might bump into a wall, or make a creaking sound in the attic.

Here's a verse from *Little Orphant Annie*:

Wunst they wuz a little boy wouldn't say his prayers, --
An' when he went to bed at night, away up-stairs,
His Mammy heerd him holler, an' his Daddy heerd him bawl,
An' when they turn't the kivvers down, he wuzn't there at all!
An' they seeked him in the rafter-room, an' cubby-hole, an' press,
An' seeked him up the chimbly-flue, an' ever'-wheres, I guess;
But all they ever found wuz thist his pants an 'roundabout: --
An' the Gobble-uns 'll git you
Ef
    You
        Don't
            Watch
                Out!

As you might imagine, *Little Orphant Annie* became a favorite read-aloud poem at Halloween, and it still is. It was also made into a silent film in 1918, with Riley on the screen, delivering the narration by means of superimposed captions.

In the 1920s, the poem was the inspiration for the comic strip *Little Orphan Annie*.

And another of Riley's poems, *The Raggedy Man*, was the inspiration for the *Raggedy Ann* doll.

Here's a verse from *The Raggedy Man*:

An' The Raggedy Man, he knows most rhymes,
An' tells 'em, ef I be good, sometimes:
Knows 'bout Giunts, an' Griffuns, an' Elves,
An' the Squidgicum-Squees 'at swallers the 'rselves:
An' wite by the pump in our pasture-lot,
He showed me the hole 'at the Wunk's is got,
'At lives 'way deep in the ground, an' can
Turn into me, er 'Lizabuth Ann!
Er Ma, er Pa, er The Raggedy Man!
Ain't he a funny old Raggedy Man?
Raggedy! Raggedy! Raggedy Man!

At the time of his death in 1916, the kid from Greenfield, Indiana, who struggled mightily at school, and who didn't finish the eighth grade until he was twenty years old, but who wrote about the places he traveled – and the people he met – in the language he heard – had become the wealthiest writer of his era.

Yes, James' father, the politician, would be proud!

It is no use to grumble and complain;
it's just as cheap and easy to rejoice;
When God sorts out the weather and sends rain –
Why, rain's my choice.
James Whitcomb Riley (1849-1916) Author, poet

Fred Rogers

Born: Fred McFeely Rogers
Would you be his neighbor?
March 20, 1928 (Latrobe PA) - February 27, 2003 (Pittsburgh PA)

D ID YOU KNOW that Mister Rogers of children's television fame was once a Marine sniper who could pick off an enemy soldier at 1,500 meters?

That he had twenty-five confirmed kills as a Navy Seal.

That he could, in hand-to-hand combat, disarm or kill another man in a heartbeat.

That he is never seen without a long-sleeved shirt or sweater because his arms are covered with erotic tattoos.

That he was once charged with child molestation.

Now, and this is going to come as a shock to all but the most internet savvy of you, but a whole lot of what you can find on the internet – isn't true! None of the above is. Yet it's there.

What is true is that Fred Rogers was the exact same guy off-camera as he was on-camera, a simple, friendly, caring man who loved children, and who was loved and respected by a nation of children and grown-ups in return.

A native of Latrobe, Pennsylvania, he was a graduate of Rollins College in Winter Park, Florida (1951) and the Pittsburgh Theological Seminary (1963).

He was an ordained Presbyterian minister with an interest in serving a congregation. But the leadership of his church suggested he could serve a higher calling by continuing with his work in children's television, and he did just that, making a difference in more young lives than anyone will ever know.

Working as the floor director for a television station in Pittsburgh, he was offered the job of co-hosting a children's program called, *The Children's Corner,* when no one else on the staff showed any interest in the project.

The show, a low-budget program by the station, left the construction of what few props were needed to the co-hosts.

Rogers did the best he could, and the resulting small, primitive puppets wouldn't have won any awards for artistic value, but the response from the kids who loved Mr. Rogers and co-host Josie Carey was overwhelmingly positive.

Those early hand-made puppets stayed with Mr. Rogers, eventually moving into the *Neighborhood of Make-Believe* when he was offered his own children's show.

And do you know what?

Fred Rogers served as the puppeteer and the voice for nearly all of the puppets in the *Neighborhood of Make-Believe*."

And do you know what else?

Those little puppets were named for members of his family. Queen Sara (the wife of King Friday XIII) was named for his wife, Sara. The school teacher, Harriet Elizabeth Cow was named for his aunt, Harriet Elizabeth Rogers, and cranky Lady Elaine Fairchilde was named after his adopted sister, Elaine.

His own show, *Mister Rogers' Neighborhood,* began in 1968 and ran for 905 episodes, the final show airing in 2001.

That's thirty-three years of continuous interaction with America's children.

That's the better part of two generations of pint-sized viewers who learned to respect not only each other, but themselves. Now! That's a legacy! Or, as the leadership of his church, and others might say, a long-running ministry.

The format for the show was simple, warm, and predictable, all important elements for small fry. Every show began with Mister Rogers entering his home singing his theme song, *Won't You Be My Neighbor?*

He always changed into a pair of sneakers and donned a cardigan sweater, while talking to his viewers about something of interest to them – on their level.

By the way, about those sneakers and that cardigan?

When he started in television, it was as a floor director, a job that demanded "quiet on the set," and the best way to insure quiet was by wearing sneakers.

He continued to wear sneakers on *The Children's Corner,* and when he became *Mister Rogers,* it made little sense to change footwear. Sneakers were quiet and consistent with his wardrobe. And if you think the kiddos cared whether he wore a pair of thousand-dollar Christian Louboutin oxfords or a pair of $19.95 Wal-Mart specials, well, then you just don't know kids!

And those sweaters he changed into as he began each show? Every one of them was knitted, with love, by his mother.

On each show, there was always a visit to his *Neighborhood of Make-Believe* on board a miniature trolley that chugged along with its own theme song.

Most early episodes ended with a song titled, "Tomorrow." Later episodes closed with the song, "Feeling."

Rogers' awards are too numerous to list, but here are a few:

The Presidential Medal of Freedom (2002); and both the U.S. Senate and the U.S. House of Representatives passed resolutions to honor "his legendary service to the improvement of the lives of children."

Upon his death, the Presbytery of Pittsburgh observed "a memorial time for the Reverend Fred McFeely Rogers for his profound effect on the lives of millions of people."

There is also a Fred Rogers Memorial Statue not far from Heinz Field in Pittsburgh.

And even the scientific community recognized his worth by naming an asteroid, "26858 Misterrogers," in his honor.

The key to Mister Rogers' success was in his in his ability to communicate with children.

He didn't need an outlandish costume, silly makeup, or a funny hat.

Children loved him for the sensitive adult authority figure he was, someone who didn't talk down to those who looked up to him.

And although it might seem a minor point to some people these days, he wasn't *Fred.* With never needing to say so, or to explain why, he instilled into the very souls of his small charges, a respect for adults.

He was always, *Mister* Rogers.

To love someone is to strive to accept that person
exactly the way he or she is, right here and now.
Fred Rogers (1928-2003) Children's television

Nipsey Russell

Born: Julius Russell
Poet Laureate of Television.
Sept 15, 1918 (Atlanta GA) – Oct 2, 2005 (Manhattan NY)

N IPSEY RUSSELL KNEW how to make people laugh and he never failed to have one of his famous four-liners available whenever he appeared on a celebrity roast, a game show panel, or as a guest on a late-night show. And those famous four-liners never failed to bring a lighthearted smile.

What's the secret to eternal youth?
The answer is easily told;
All you gotta do if you wanna look young,
Is hang out with people who are old.

Nipsey began entertaining at the age of three as a member of a children's dance team called the *Ragamuffins of Rhythm.*

At the ripe old age of six, he became the master of ceremonies for another children's song and dance troupe, this one run by jazz musician Eddie Heywood, best known for his recording of "Canadian Sunset" and the piano version of "Begin the Beguine."

Nipsey tells that at the age of nine he was taken to see an African-American tap dancer named Jack Wiggins. Wiggins, perhaps the most elegant tap dancer of his time, so impressed young Nipsey that he later wrote:

> *He came out immaculately attired in a well-dressed street suit and he tap-danced. As he danced, he told little jokes in between graceful moves. He was so clean in his language and was lacking any drawl, he just inspired me. I wanted to do that.*

Well, Nipsey did just that, but without the tap dancing.

He became a world-class entertainer, an elegant yet playful comedian, funny without profanity, and he may well have done his share of inspiring as well.

He made America laugh with an endless stream of very funny, and very relatable, four liners. Four liners that he invariably found a way to introduce into his appearances on comedy shows, and all would agree that a Hollywood celebrity roast without Nipsey on the dais was hardly a roast at all.

Here's a week's worth of Nipsey Russell four liners:

Children:
> When sounds are heard around the house
> Of little kids and their toys,
> We know children were sent from heaven
> Cause the Lord couldn't stand the noise.

Teenagers:
> The young people are very different today;
> And there's one sure way to know,
> Kids used to ask where they came from;
> Now they tell us where to go!

Solutions:
> Before we lose our autonomy
> And our economy crumbles to dust,
> We should attack Japan, lose the war,
> And let Japan take care of us.

Women:
> A woman's age is like an odometer
> On a second-hand car.
> We all know it's been turned back,
> We just don't know how far.

Dating:
> I'm a bachelor and I will not marry
> Until the right girl comes along;
> But while I'm waiting, I don't mind dating
> Girls that I know are wrong.

Entertainment:
> I just saw a movie about a mermaid.
> Did I like it? I don't know why!
> There's not enough woman to make love to,
> And too much fish to fry.

Dying:

> If you're not drinking and smoking,
> If you're not out having a ball,
> When you pass away, the doctor will say,
> "You died from nothing at all."

Nipsey loved America and its diversity, once commenting that, "America is the only place in the world where you can work in an Arabian home in a Scandinavian neighborhood and find a Puerto Rican baby eating matzo balls with chopsticks."

He was never seen without a smile and he was always ready with a head full of seemingly impromptu poems, each perfect for poking a little fun at a thousand human foibles and situations.

It was his apparently endless supply of short, humorous poems that led others in the entertainment industry to begin referring to him as the *Poet Laureate of Television*, a spot-on title for one of America's favorite sons.

Nipsey Russell died of stomach cancer on October 2, 2005.

He was a youthful eighty-seven years old.

His ashes were scattered in the Atlantic Ocean.

It was a little Gypsy tea room,
A fortune-telling place,
A lovely Gypsy read my mind
And then she slapped my face.
Nipsey Russell (1918-2005) Comedian

Carl Sagan

Born: Carl Edward Sagan
Billions and Billions
Nov 9, 1934 (Brooklyn NY) – Dec 20, 1996 (Seattle WA)

D URING ONE OF astrophysicist Carl Sagan's many appearances on Johnny Carson's late-night show, the immensity of the universe came under discussion. Carson may have asked Sagan the number of visible stars in the night sky, or the distance in light years to the furthest star. Regardless, Sagan began by explaining to Carson and the audience, the difference between a million and a billion. To make his point, he emphasized the "**b**" sound in "**b**illion," and added length to the word, as in "**b**illlllions." Thus, "millions and millions" remained "millions and millions," but "billions and billions" became "**b**illlllions and **b**illlllions."

Sagan had such a youthful enthusiasm about the wonders of the universe, the enormity of space, and of worlds beyond our own, that just listening to him was inspiring.

Whether watching him on the Johnny Carson show, or catching his Public Broadcasting Service television series, *Cosmos: A Personal Voyage*,[1] he was a skilled communicator.

During the 1980s, the above-mentioned television series, which Sagan co-wrote and narrated, was the most widely watched series in the history of American public television with an audience estimated at more than 500 million people from over sixty countries.

Never talking down to his audience, he made viewers feel worthy to be watching a show about a subject they may not fully understand or appreciate. His non-condescending presence and ability to talk about technical things in every-day language won him an audience as great as his universe.

Carl Sagan was not only a scientist's scientist, but a lay person's scientist as well. He was an astrophysicist and cosmologist with world-wide name recognition and a professor of astronomy at Cornell University where he was the director of its Laboratory for Planetary Studies.

He was also known for his scientific research into the possibility of extraterrestrial life. He wrote over 600 scientific papers and authored over 20 books, including *The Dragons of Eden* that won a Pulitzer Prize. He also wrote *Contact,* a novel that became a movie and won the 1998 Hugo Award presented for the best science fiction or fantasy work of the previous year.

One might wonder how someone with a scientific mind so finely attuned to the science of physics and outer space could possibly relate to those of us with our feet so firmly planted on *terra firma.* In the case of Sagan, the answer might have something to with his childhood.

He was the son of a Russian immigrant garment worker who earned extra money ushering at a local movie theater, and a New York mother who grew up homeless. Both parents, he said, gave him the right amount of skepticism and wonder. Thus, it might be that he thought if he could explain other-worldly concepts to his parents, he just might be able to explain them to those of us who stayed up at night to watch the Johnny Carson show.

Returning now to Sagan's reference to *billlllions and billlllions.*

As soon as Carson heard those words, his mind instantly recognized their comedic value. So, each succeeding time that Sagan appeared on the show, Carson made certain that those words came into play at an opportune time during the late-night banter, and Carl Sagan, the world-famous astrophysicist, could do nothing but *smilllle* and *plaaaay* along.

Carson even did a few sketches on his show impersonating Sagan, complete with a Sagan-esque wig, a Sagan-like turtleneck sweater underneath a corduroy sports jacket complete with leather elbow-patches and then, over-emphasizing for laughs, the phrase *billlllions and billlllions* to clarify a point.

To illustrate:

Ed McMahon (as straight man): *Have you earned much income from the sale of your books?*

Carson (appearing as Sagan): *I've made billlllllions and billlllllions.*

Sagan always came prepared to discuss some aspect of his work, such as his preparation of the "messages from earth" plaques and recordings that accompanied the *Pioneer* and *Voyager* space probes into deep space. It was his hope that they might be intercepted by extraterrestrial intelligences, who in turn would learn a thing or two about us Earthlings.

He also talked about red dwarfs, white dwarfs, nebulas, time warps, black holes, supernovas, and other spacey things, always knowing that Carson would find a way to generate some laughter.

It was obvious to everyone who watched the two men interact, that not only did they enjoy the banter, but they genuinely held each other in high regard.

Sagan's final years were a long fight with myelodysplastic syndrome, a type of cancer in which the bone marrow cannot produce enough healthy blood cells to support the body.

Just prior to his death in 1996, Sagan published his final book, and as if to show the world he held no ill feelings about the catchphrase that had become so identified with his name, he titled the book, *Billions and Billions: Thoughts on Life and Death at the End of the Millennium*.

And to assure its readers that the title was his idea, the book opens with a friendly discussion of how the catchphrase came into being.

Carl Sagan, the friendliest, most recognizable, and easily the best understood astrophysicist on the planet passed away December 20, 1996. And in his honor, the landing site of the unmanned Mars Pathfinder spacecraft was renamed the *Carl Sagan Memorial Station*.

[1] *Cosmos: A Personal Voyage* aired on television from September 28 to December 21, 1980. Variations of the original broadcast, including computer animated sequences, have been added over the years, most recently in 2014, and hosted by astrophysicist Neil deGrasse Tyson.

The universe is not required to be
in perfect harmony with human ambition.
Carl Sagan (1934-1996) Astronomer, cosmologist

Saint Nicholas

Nikolaos – Sinterklass – Santa Claus
Mar 15, 270 (Patara, Lycia) – Dec 6, 343 (Myra, Lycia)

Y ES VIRGINIA, AND to all the kids of the world
regardless of age, heritage, ethnicity, or creed, there
really is a Santa Claus, and his name was Nicholas.[1] History
tells us he was a real man, a bishop of the Eastern Orthodox
(Catholic) Church in Myra, Lycia[2] with a reputation for secretly
giving gifts to good children. And because of his love of
children, and for other reasons, the Catholic Church has
recognized him as one of its saints.

So, how did Saint Nicholas find his way to America?

Without stretching the historical record any further than
necessary to stay within sight of a few historical boundaries, but
embroidering where necessary for the sake of the world's
children who love to believe, it happened this way.

Saint Nicholas was born March 15, 270 in Patara, Lycia.

At some point in history, Saint Nicholas's *spirit* traveled to
Holland, a province of the Netherlands where, in the language
of the Dutch, he was known as Sinterklass.

In 1624, the *spirit* of Sinterklass traveled to the New World
(America) as a member of an immigration colony established by
the Dutch West India Company. The group called their small
settlement New Amsterdam, in honor of the capital city of the
Netherlands from which they had just departed.

Forty years later, English colonization under the direction of
the Duke of York assumed control of the Dutch colony, and on
September 8, 1664, the name of New Amsterdam was officially
changed to New York.

And, that's when the kindly, child-loving Sinterklass
anglicized[3] his name to Santa Claus. And that, my little one, is
how Santa Claus came to America.

If you're too much of a historical purist to accept the above
few paragraphs at face value, discard what you don't like and go
with what you can handle. Find a kid who needs more of an

explanation, and you've found a kid who will find a lump of coal in his stocking Christmas morning.

So, how did all of this come about?

The Emperor Constantine, who ruled the Roman Empire from 306-337 AD, converted to Christianity midway through his reign (313). After his conversion, he proclaimed that December 25th of each year would be observed as "Christ's Mass" in celebration of the birth of Christ.

On December 6, 343, Nicholas, the Bishop of Myra died. When his miraculous acts were acknowledged by the Catholic Church, and the appropriate amount of time had passed since his passing, he was named a Catholic saint, with his feast day to be observed on the day of his death, December 6th.

Now, sainthood isn't merely a cushy job with an honorific title, it comes with numerous responsibilities, and St. Nicholas was named the saint-in-charge of marriageable maidens, brewers, archers, pawnbrokers, merchants, perfumers, repentant thieves, sailors, orphans, and <whew!> children.

Although it couldn't have been supposed at the time, the proximity of Christ's Mass (December 25th) and St. Nicholas' feast day (December 6th) lent itself to the eventual intermixing of celebration, including the giving of gifts, especially to children, alongside the more solemn and holy aspects of the day, the worship of the birth of Christ.

For Christians, not of the Catholic faith, a great deal of borrowing has taken place over the centuries, a good thing, to not only bring the warmth and kindness of Saint Nicholas into their homes, but to acknowledge his great love of children and his fondness for making them happy, a worthy achievement for people of all faiths to emulate.

There are many stories about Saint Nicholas and of the good things he did, especially for children during the years he was Bishop of Myra, and from out of those kind deeds, many traditions have grown.

One such story tells of a man with three loving and kind daughters. In those days, a young maiden stood little chance of being wed unless her father had a dowry[4] to present to the groom at the time of the wedding.

Unfortunately, the man with the three daughters was very poor and when it seemed unlikely his daughters would marry, three bags of gold from an unknown benefactor were tossed into the family home, each bag miraculously landing next to each of three pairs of stockings left to dry before the hearth.

The gold served as the needed dowry, and the girls married well and lived happily ever after. This led to the custom of children hanging their stockings near the hearth in hopes of finding a gift from St. Nicholas in the morning.

It's also important to mention that Saint Nicholas (Santa Claus) is also known for leaving something unpleasant, typically a small lump of coal, for those children who fail to say their prayers, mind their parents, or are naughty in other ways.

How does Santa Claus know who gets the nice gifts and who gets the lump of coal these days?

He checks his email daily, sometimes twice, and that my little sugar-plum, is how he knows who's been naughty or nice.

---

[1] Nicholas was originally spelled *Nikolaos,* and that spelling can be found in the earliest accounts, but know that *Nikolaos* and *Nicholas* are the same man.

[2] Lycia: a geopolitical region on the Southern coast of today's Turkey.

[3] To Anglicize means to adapt a foreign word, or phrase, to English usage, e.g. to anglicize *Juan* to *John.*

[4] Dowry: Traditionally, money or property that a bride, or her family, gives to the bridegroom at the time of the wedding, intended to help bond the bride and groom's families together.

He who has not Christmas in his heart
will never find it under a tree.
Roy L. Smith (1887-1963) Methodist minister

Harland Sanders

Born: Harland David Sanders
Persistence and one heck of a recipe.
Sept 9, 1890 (Henryville IN) – Dec 16, 1980 (Louisville KY)

H ERE'S A QUESTION that will stump ninety-nine percent
of you. That's because the answer, which should be
obvious, isn't. "In what state did Harland Sanders award his
first Kentucky Fried Chicken franchise?"

Here's a hint. It wasn't Kentucky. If you don't know the
answer, you'll be surprised as you read about the man who built
a finger-lickin' good empire from a pint-sized restaurant inside
a Kentucky service station. So, do drop in, sit a spell, and enjoy
the story of one of America's most successful entrepreneurs.

Harland was the eldest of three children born to Wilbur and
Margaret Sanders, a family eking out a living in a four-room
shack on eighty acres of hardscrabble Indiana farmland. Wilbur
farmed until he broke his leg; afterwards becoming a butcher.

Then, one day in 1895, Wilbur left the butcher shop early
and went home complaining of a high fever.

He was dead by nightfall.

Margaret, desperate, had to find work fast and she did,
leaving five-year-old Harland with the responsibility of caring
for and feeding his siblings.

When he was twelve (1902), his mother remarried, and the
family moved to Greenwood, Indiana. Although the marriage
lightened Margaret's load, Harland and his step-father never
bonded, and Harland quit school and became a live-in farmhand
for a neighbor.

When relations with the neighbor went south, Harland
moved out and worked odd jobs. He painted carriages, cared for
mules, and in 1906 he lied about his age (16), enlisted in the
army, and was sent to Cuba. Three months later the underaged
soldier was back in Indiana, scavenging for work.

In 1909, and nineteen years old, he married Josephine King.
They had three children and lots of arguments. The marriage
was over when Harland called Josephine while on a business trip

to tell her he'd been fired for arguing with his boss. She sold the furniture to pay the bills, and moved herself and the kids into her parents' home.

Harland took a mail-order law course and became a lawyer in Little Rock, Arkansas. His career as an attorney lasted less than three years, ending when he got into a courtroom brawl with his own client.

From there, he worked for a railroad, then sold insurance for Prudential and Mutual Benefit Life of New Jersey before setting up a ferry boat operation on the Ohio River (1920). His company made money and in 1922 he took a second job with the Columbus, Indiana, Chamber of Commerce, but resigned for unknown reasons a few months later.

He sold his ferry boat and used the money to grubstake a venture assembling acetylene lamps, which quickly went bankrupt.

In 1923, he moved to Kentucky and went to work for Michelin Tires. The job lasted until Michelin closed the store a year later.

He managed a Shell station in Nicholasville, Kentucky, until it went bankrupt in 1930.

Now, after years after getting nowhere, of bouncing from job to job, life was about to change for Harland Sanders.

With the closing of the station in Nicholasville, Shell offered Sanders a service station in Corbin, Kentucky, under a unique arrangement. The station came with attached living quarters, and Shell offered it to Sanders to manage, rent free, with Shell taking a percentage of the gas and petroleum product sales.

Before long, Harland, who had been preparing meals since the age of five, turned the attached living quarters into a roadside restaurant serving country steak, ham, and fried chicken.

Because the tiny kitchen was so cramped for space, he improvised and used a pressure cooker instead of a frying pan to prepare his chicken, and the customers loved the finger-licking result.

Harland's unique pressure-cooked fried chicken, seasoned to perfection and so tender it fell from the bone, made *Sanders Shell Station and Café* a popular place to dine in Corbin.

Even Kentucky governor Ruby Laffoon liked his cooking, and in 1935 he commissioned Harland Sanders a "Kentucky Colonel," an impressive-but-honorary Southern title.

In 1939, nationally-respected food critic Duncan Hines stopped by, sampled the Colonel's pressure-cooked chicken, and included the service-station café in his *Adventures in Good Eating* guide.

Now, there's not room to take you from 1939 to 1951, but know that during those years, Harland became a very successful businessman.

Remember the question that opened this story? In what state did Colonel Sanders award his first Kentucky Fried Chicken franchise?

Well, stand by, you're about to be surprised.

In 1951, two men who had never met were destined to do just that, and it would lead to a life-long friendship.

Harland Sanders and Pete Harman were at a restaurant convention in Chicago, an event packed with hundreds of cigar-smoking men, loud ties, and dozens of questionable convention parties.

That's when Sanders and Harman, neither of whom owned a loud tie, smoked, drank, or caroused, ended up sharing a quiet dinner together. They learned that each owned a restaurant, Sanders, the *Sanders Shell Station and Café* in Corbin, Kentucky, and Harman, the *Do Drop Inn* at 3900 South State Street in Salt Lake City, Utah.

A year later, on August 3, 1952, Sanders stopped in Salt Lake to visit his friend, Pete, before continuing to Australia.

Pete and his wife Arline treated Sanders to a tour of the city, including a visit to the beautiful Mormon Temple and a drive to the breathtakingly large Bingham open-pit copper mine.

There, overlooking the copper mine, small talk turned to shop talk and Pete casually mentioned that he and Arline had been searching for a specialty dish for their restaurant.

A short time later, Sanders suggested he repay Pete and Arline for their hospitality by cooking dinner for them. After leaving the copper mine, Harland stopped and purchased a pressure cooker, some herbs and spices, and a chicken – and you're getting ahead of the story.

The chicken that Harland prepared for dinner that night was the most tender and most flavorful that Pete and Arline had ever tasted, and the after-dinner conversation culminated with an agreement and a handshake that made Pete Harman, Harland Sanders' first franchisee.

Harland continued to Australia and on his return trip, Pete and Arline drove him to the *Do Drop Inn* where the words, "Featuring Kentucky Fried Chicken" had been added to the restaurant's signage.

The following year, 1953, Pete and Arline changed the restaurant's name to *Harman's Café – featuring Kentucky Fried Chicken*, and just inside the door to greet each customer, was a life-size cardboard cut-out of Colonel Harland Sanders.

Today, in Salt Lake City on that 3900 South State Street site, is a modern restaurant and a museum honoring Colonel Sanders.

But, before you go inside, stop and admire the two larger-than-life statues of Colonel Sanders and Pete Harman, standing side-by-side as they did for the remainder of their lives, and notice that neither is wearing a loud tie.

And just inside the door of that modern restaurant is a life-size reproduction of the Colonel, greeting customers today, just as the cardboard cut-out had done in 1953.

Pete Harman died November 19, 2014, at the age of 95.

Harland Sanders died December 16, 1980, at the age of 90 and is buried at the Cave Hill Cemetery in Louisville, Kentucky, wearing his familiar white suit and black western string tie.

At the age of 65, Sanders said: *My life isn't over and I'm not going to sit in a rocking chair and take money from the government.*
Harland Sanders (1890-1980) Restauranteur

Santos-Dumont

Born: Alberto Santos-Dumont
Did he fly before the Wright Brothers?
July 20, 1873 (Palmira, Brazil) – July 23, 1932 (Guarujá, Brazil)

SANTOS-DUMONT IS a national hero in Brazil. There, in his home country, he is recognized as the first to have achieved heavier-than-air flight, having done so in 1906, three years *after* – that's right, *after* – Orville Wright's[1] historic flight at Kitty Hawk in 1903. And his supporters have reason to feel the way they do.

As an affirmation of his status as a national hero, Santos-Dumont City in the Brazilian state of Minas Gerais is named for him, as are hundreds of streets, buildings, and other tokens of recognition throughout Brazil.

There is also the Santos-Dumont Airport in Rio de Janeiro; the Rodovia Santos-Dumont (Santos-Dumont Highway) in the state of São Paulo; the Santos-Dumont Medal of Merit is awarded by the Brazilian Air Force to aviation heroes; and Brazil's presidential aircraft is named the "Alberto Santos-Dumont."

Internationally, the Office of Naval Research in San Diego named one of their research aircraft the "Santos-Dumont," and a lyceum in Saint-Cloud, France is the Lycee Polyvant Santos-Dumont.

In 2013, *Flying Magazine* listed Santos-Dumont as #8 in its "51 Heroes of Aviation" edition, just ahead of 9th place honoree Amelia Earhart. For trivia buffs: Charles Lindbergh[2] was listed at #3; Orville and Wilbur Wright at #2; and Neil Armstrong[3] at #1 on the list. Thus, Santos-Dumont, if you've not heard of him before, is among stellar company.

And Santos-Dumont was not only an aviator, but a fashion trend-setter as well. Prior to Santos-Dumont, any Brazilian man worth his XY chromosomes carried a pocket watch and wouldn't be caught dead wearing an item as blatantly feminine as a wristwatch!

Here's the Santos-Dumont story and why there are some who feel that he – not that pair of bicycle mechanics from Dayton, Ohio – should be recognized as the first to fly a heavier-than-air aircraft.

Santos-Dumont was born into an affluent family, the owners of a plantation so vast that his father was often referred to as the Coffee King of Brazil. Thus, he was assured a bright future educationally and financially, especially as it pertained to his interest in flight, an interest he claimed was revealed to him in a dream.

In 1891, his father suffered a paralyzing accident, sold the plantation, and sent his seventeen-year-old son to France to complete his education. There he was taught by private tutors at the *Colégio Cutto à Ciência,* a school strongly oriented toward the sciences.

In 1897, Santos-Dumont made his first balloon ascent. Thrilled with the experience, he paid the pilot to teach him the basics of flying such a craft.

He then purchased a balloon of his own that he named the *Brazil.* It was small compared to the balloon in which he learned to fly (a 4,000-cubic foot envelope versus a 26,000-cubic foot envelope), but it carried him aloft and a photo of him in a wicker basket sailing just above the French treetops can be found on the internet.

Although balloons were exciting to fly, they were subject to the whims of the wind, and he began working on a steerable balloon (a dirigible). He was not the first to tackle the problem of balloon steerability as Henri Giffard[4] had successfully done so in 1852, but his 350-pound steam engine that generated a measly three-horsepower required calm weather only.

Also, engineers Arthur Krebs and Charles Renard had successfully built a steerable balloon in 1884, but had to end their work when their funding ran out.

Santos-Dumont would not have that problem.

From 1898 to 1905 Santos-Dumont built and flew a total of eleven dirigibles, including the Santos-Dumont #3 that circled the Eiffel Tower successfully several times before landing at nearby Bagatelle field.

In 1901, the French offered a cash prize of F100,000 francs to anyone who could depart Saint-Cloud, circle the Eiffel Tower, and return to the starting point in under thirty minutes. Santos-Dumont won the prize piloting the Santos-Dumont #6.

In 1904, a year after Orville Wright made his first successful flight at Kitty Hawk, Santos-Dumont, who was as well-known as the Wright brothers at that time, shipped his Santos-Dumont #7 to St. Louis. The purpose, to compete for $100,000 dollars in prize money for "any flying machine that could make three round-trips over a 15-mile course and land without damage to craft or crew."

Unfortunately, when the Santos-Dumont #7 arrived in St. Louis, it was damaged in shipment, some think it was sabotaged, and Alberto, unable to repair the dirigible, returned to France empty-handed.

But by now he was the toast of Paris. Parisian men copied his style of dress from his floppy Panama hat to his high dress collar and ultra-narrow necktie.

In 1905 and no longer interested in dirigibles, he built an aircraft that resembled a series of strung-together box kites supported on the ground by two narrow wheels. He gave the craft the odd name, *14-bis*.

After numerous failed attempts to fly the *14-bis* during the latter part of 1905 and for most of 1906, he finally achieved success.

On October 23, 1906, in front of a large audience, including officials from the Fédération Aéronautique Internationale, Santos-Dumont started the craft's 50-horsepower Antoinette engine, rolled down a dirt runway, and flew into the Fédération's record books.

He traveled for 200 feet at an altitude of about ten feet, earning a prize of F3,000 francs for being the first to achieve a *heavier-than-air* flight of at least 25-meters (82-feet).

With this flight, the Fédération formally acknowledged Santos-Dumont as the first man to fly a heavier-than-air aircraft.

Why not Orville Wright?

Because, according to the rules of the Fédération, the flight had to lift off under its own power, something not achieved by Orville and Wilbur Wright who used a launching skid and human push-power to get their 1903 aircraft airborne, and they were still using a skid in 1906, after Santos-Dumont made his first heavier-than-air flight.

And what about the fashion idea that wristwatches were ladies' apparel only?

During Santos-Dumont's numerous practice trials, it was important that he accurately time his airborne intervals. Doing so by pulling a watch from a vest (or pants) pocket while piloting his aircraft was not only counter-productive, but unsafe.

So, he visited a friend of his who knew something about timepieces, a fellow named Louis-François Cartier,[5] and had him create a manly wristwatch that made timing flight intervals as easy as turning the wrist.

And when fashion trend setter Santos-Dumont, a man whose masculinity could not be challenged, was seen wearing a wristwatch, well, you know how guys are. All the rest of the fellows had to have one as well.

Alberto Santos-Dumont, who became depressed after being diagnosed with multiple sclerosis, hanged himself on July 23, 1932.

He is buried in São João Batista Cemetery in Rio de Janeiro, Brazil.

Stories from History's Dust Bin (additional reading):
[1] Vol 1, Feb 8:   Orville Wright with Thomas Selfridge
[2] Vol 2, May 27: Charles Lindbergh with Robert LeRoy Ripley
[3] Vol 1, Mar 11:   Neil Armstrong with Philo T. Farnsworth

[4] See Henri Giffard in this book, pages 106-109, to learn more about the first steerable balloon (dirigible).

[5] Louis Cartier, although not the first to create a wristwatch, that honor belongs to Patek Phillippe for an 1868 ladies' wristwatch, Cartier created the first wristwatch for men, the *Santos,* in honor of Santos-Dumont.

I never thought that my creation
would allow brothers to kill brothers.
Santos-Dumont (1873-1932) Aviation

Alexander Selkirk

Born: Alexander Selkirk
Was he Daniel Defoe's Robinson Crusoe?
1676 (Fife, Scotland) – Dec 13, 1721 (Cape Coast, Ghana)

I N 2008, THE *Society for Post-Medieval Archaeology* noted the find of a 300-year-old campsite on the small uninhabited Argentinian island of Aguas Buenas, 470 miles off the coast of Chile.

Recovered at the site were a pair of rusted navigational dividers, a tool useful only to a ship's navigator. Could this be the campsite of Alexander Selkirk, a man who would have known how to use a pair of navigational dividers, and could Selkirk have been the inspiration for a fictional castaway?

Read and decide for yourself.

Selkirk, born in 1676 in Fife, Scotland, was the son of a hide-tanner and shoemaker. But young Alex had no desire to follow in his father's shoe making footsteps; instead, he dreamed of becoming a seafaring man.

As an adult, Selkirk was a big man, surly and quarrelsome and not well-liked in his hometown.

In 1700, a display of indecent behavior in church resulted in a summons from the presbytery asking Selkirk to appear before an ecclesiastical court known as a Kirk Session. Alex, not the least bit interested in attending a church-court hearing, never bothered to show up.

Few in town were disappointed, most welcoming his decision to take up residency elsewhere.

A year later he was back in town and it wasn't long before his name again came before the local presbytery for discipline, this time for nearly beating his brothers to death.

It's not clear whether the presbytery formally initiated another Kirk Session, but what is clear is that Selkirk decided to leave Scotland for good, and to follow his seafaring dream.

From 1701 to 1703, he worked aboard a pirate ship flying the skull and crossbones.

In 1703, with some sailing and navigational experience, he joined a British privateering expedition as a ship's navigator and was pleased with the job. After all, the work wasn't all that different, as privateering was mostly a legal form of pirating.

The major difference being that pirates were somewhat self-governed, if that's possible; while privateers sailed privately-owned ships commissioned by a government to fight, harass, or capture pirate ships.

After capturing a pirate ship, the fate of the pirate crew was left up to the leader of the privateers, but know that the rules regarding life on the high seas and the disposition of pirate cargo were hard to enforce.

Conversely, if the privateers were defeated and captured by the pirates, the result was at least as rough and often worse. There was always plenty of rope to host (or hoist, if you prefer) as many hangings as might be deemed necessary for an evening of sport and frivolity. Everyone invited.

Such was Selkirk's cup of Scottish tea, at least at first.

A man named William Dampier, charged with outfitting a privateering expedition, hired Selkirk as a ship's navigator and assigned him to the *Cinque Ports*, a ship with a crew of ninety under the command of sailing master Thomas Stradling.

On September 11, 1703, Stradling and his crew set sail from Kinsale, Ireland, heading toward the South Seas looking for a fight.

In February 1704 at Cape Horn, one of the most treacherous stretches of water on the planet, the *Cinque Ports* engaged the *St. Joseph,* a well-armed French ship. But the best the two ships could achieve in the angry waters of the Cape was a draw, and the *St. Joseph* departed the fight to sail elsewhere, leaving Selkirk and his shipmates with no vessel to plunder.

The privateers, determined to pillage something, decided the Panamanian gold mining village of Santa Maria looked like easy pickings. But the townsfolk of Santa Maria, who had been invaded several times before, prepared a welcoming ambush for the ship's crew.

Those from the *Cinque Ports* who were not killed or badly wounded in the foiled attack, limped or crawled back to the ship empty-handed. There is no record regarding the forty-eight men who were unable to return to the ship, but imagine a highly-motivated citizenry with lots of rope and a sincere interest in putting a stop to future raids.

In September 1704, Captain Stradling and a seriously reduced crew of forty-two arrived at a place known in the 1700s as Más a Tierra,[1] one of the uninhabited islands that form the Juan Fernández Archipelago. The island, about 470 miles off the coast of Chile, offered the weary privateers a chance to rest, to take on fresh water, and to enjoy the island's plentiful fruit.

The ship, however, was in bad condition and not just from the beating it had taken at Cape Horn. The ship's hull had become seriously worm-infested, and as they were about to lift anchor, Selkirk tried to talk Captain Stradling into making some needed repairs before heading back out to sea.

In no mood to listen to the oft-cantankerous Selkirk, Stradling told the crew they would stay no longer and to prepare to lift anchor.

That's when Selkirk spoke to the captain, perhaps saying something along the lines of:

> *Stradling! You dumb son of a brainless worm-infested piece of dogwood! I'd rather take my chances, as slim as they may be, on this crappy, uninhabited island than to sail aboard this ship on the high seas with the sorry likes of your ugly face at the helm!*

Stradling was delighted.

That was all he needed to hear!

He had Selkirk physically removed from the ship and taken ashore, allowing him a musket, a ration of gun-powder and balls, a hatchet, a Bible, a cooking pot and a few personal items, which, as the ship's navigator, may well have included a pair of navigational dividers.

As the men in the landing boat began rowing back to the *Cinque Ports*, a suddenly sober Selkirk waded into the water, waving his arms frantically and pleading for Stradling to forgive him for his rashness, but the Captain, likely smiling broadly, only waved to him in return.

That was October 1704.

On February 2, 1709, four years and four months after being stranded on the island, Alexander Selkirk was rescued by the *Duke,* a privateering ship captained by Woodes Rogers and piloted by none other than William Dampier, the man who had originally hired Selkirk back in 1703.

Selkirk's tale of survival for four years on an uninhabited island brought with it a certain amount of fame and prestige, and yes, even a modest amount of fortune.

Alexander Selkirk died December 13, 1721 while on an anti-piracy patrol off the west coast of Africa. He was buried at sea.

And wait!

There's more to the story.

Alexander Selkirk (1676-1721) was a contemporary of a fellow named Daniel Defoe (1660-1731).

Defoe was the author of *The Life and Surprising Adventures of Robinson Crusoe,* a book published April 25, 1719, three years prior to Selkirk's death.

Although the stories of Selkirk and Crusoe differ and are set in different locales (Selkirk off the coast of Chile, and Crusoe in the Caribbean), there are many who believe that Selkirk's real-life experience provided the inspiration for Defoe's famous fictional character.

---

[1] Más a Tierra island is today known as Aguas Buenas island, or by the Spanish as Isla Róbinson Crusoe. This island is the largest of the Juan Fernández Archipelago off the coast of Chile.

It is never too late to be wise.
Daniel Defoe (1660-1731) Author

Eugene Shoemaker

Born: Eugene Merle Shoemaker

The man in the moon, literally.

Apr 28, 1928 (Los Angeles CA) – July 18, 1997 (Alice Springs, Australia)

I N THE DOZEN or so photographs of Gene Shoemaker on the internet, most capture the face of a man having way too much fun being one of America's preeminent scientists.

For instance, there's a photo of Gene poking holes in the air with the handle of a rock pick while explaining the use of the tool to the Apollo Astronauts.

On another webpage there's a photo of Gene seated at a stereo-microscope, his eyes twinkling, but instead of wearing the white lab coat of a scientist, he's much more casual, wearing an open-neck shirt and a southwestern bolo tie.

And here's another, this one showing a grinning Gene gripping the handle-bar controls of a Bell Rocket Belt, the kind used to power a person up and over obstacles, and the common thread throughout every photograph of Gene is that he looks like he's having more fun than a kid in a candy store.

Like a lot of American boys, Gene dreamed of becoming an astronaut, of leaving something of himself, an imprint of his boot perhaps on the surface of the moon[1] while adding to man's knowledge of the universe.

By adulthood he possessed the qualifying intellectual criteria needed for the job, in spades. But a 1963 diagnosis of Addison's disease meant that becoming an astronaut wasn't going to happen, so he did the next best thing. He became a trainer of astronauts, that is, when he wasn't doing other groundbreaking science stuff.

If you haven't guessed it by now, Gene was neither a typical instructor nor a typical scientist.

In fact, Gene wasn't a typical anything.

He was special!

At the age of eleven, the intellectually-gifted youngster was supplementing fifth-grade social studies and long-division with college-level night classes in biology and mineralogy at New

York's Museum of Science. He was also accompanying college students twice his age on field trips, and probably helping them with their homework as well.

Gene graduated from high school a month after his fifteenth birthday and the very next day he was accepted at the California Institute of Technology (CIT) in Pasadena, California.

Then, in May of 1947, a mere month after his 19th birthday, he graduated from CIT with a bachelor's degree, and a year after that he received his master's degree, also from CIT, walking across the graduation stage with his ever-present grin.

His master's thesis!

The Petrology of Precambrian Rocks.

After graduation, he went to work for the U.S. Geological Survey (USGS). There, while searching for uranium deposits in areas of prehistoric volcanic activity in Colorado and Utah, and making numerous trips to Arizona's famous Meteor Crater near Flagstaff, he developed some new theories regarding the origins of the moon's craters.

His 1956 paper, coauthored with Robert Hackman and titled *A Stratigraphic Basis for a Lunar Time Scale,* is considered a landmark scientific work in deciphering the history of the moon.

In effect, as someone afterward observed, with that 1956 paper Gene wrested the planets from the grasp of astronomers and handed them to the geologists.

After a few years of practical field experience. he enrolled at Princeton, completed his doctoral coursework, took his oral and written exams, and defended a doctoral dissertation on Arizona's Meteor Crater.[2]

In 1961, the newly minted Dr. Eugene M. Shoemaker, once again went to work for the USGS, but this time in Flagstaff, Arizona, where he introduced an entirely new field of science, *astrogeology,* the geologic mapping of the moon.

He worked his way into the U.S. space program with a plan to study the craters of the moon up close and personal. Then, in 1963 and only thirty-five years old, Gene was diagnosed with Addison's Disease, dashing his hopes of becoming an astronaut-scientist.

But, typical of Dr. Shoemaker, there was no whining about things beyond his control. No complaining. No hanging his head, curling his lower lip and moaning, "Why me?"

So, what did he do?

He established the *USGS Center of Astrogeology* in Flagstaff, Arizona, and as its chief scientist, he developed a highly-specialized geology curriculum for astronauts-in-training. It was Gene's way of saying if he couldn't make the trip and leave something of himself on the moon, those that could would do so taking a piece of his intellect with them.

Gene retired in the early 1990s along with his workmate wife, Carolyn Spellman Shoemaker, and the two of them spent their time traveling the world studying impact craters. Then, in Australia on July 18, 1997, he and Carolyn were involved in a head-on collision on a primitive road. Gene died on impact. Carolyn, severely injured, survived.

And here's the truly beautiful part of Gene's story.

On July 31, 1999, two years after his death, a remarkable tribute was paid to the ever-smiling scientist who had always wanted to go to the moon.

Planetary scientist Carolyn Porco, one of Gene's former colleagues, led the way in arranging to have some of Gene's ashes carried to the moon aboard the Lunar Prospector. She also helped design the capsule that carried his ashes and assisted in writing the announcement that was sent to the various wire services on January 6, 1998.

It reads (in part):

> *Tonight, the ashes of Eugene M. Shoemaker are to be launched in a memorial capsule aboard Lunar Prospector to the moon.*
>
> *The polycarbonate capsule, one-and-three-quarters inches long and seventh-tenths of an inch in diameter, is carried in a vacuum-sealed, flight-tested aluminum sleeve mounted deep inside the spacecraft.*
>
> *Around the capsule is wrapped a piece of brass foil inscribed with an image of Comet Hale-Bopp, an image of Meteor Crater in northern Arizona, and a passage from William Shakespeare's enduring love story, Romeo and Juliet:*

And, when he shall die,
Take him and cut him out in little stars,
And he will make the face of heaven so fine
That all the world will be in love with night,
And pay no worship to the garish sun.

To date, Gene Shoemaker has the distinction of being the only person to have his ashes interred on the moon.

And, it is only fitting that scientist-friend-mentor, Dr. Eugene Merle Shoemaker, the man who had helped so many others leave their boot prints on the moon, has become himself, quite literally, the man in the moon.

[1] *Stories from History's Dust Bin* (additional reading):
    Vol 2, Aug 25:   The moon with The Great Moon Hoax

[2] The exact title of Dr. Shoemaker's doctoral dissertation is: *Impact Mechanics at Meteor Crater, Arizona.*

To look out at this kind of creation
and not believe in God is to me impossible.
John Glenn (1921-2016) Astronaut, senator

The Shortest War in History

Don't blink while reading or you might miss the war.
Aug 27, 1896 (9:02 EAT) – Aug 27, 1896 (9:40 EAT)[1]

L ET'S BEGIN WITH a refresher of your high school World History class, as if you could possibly forget the excellent report you presented in class on the 1890 Heligoland-Zanzibar treaty between Germany and Britain. And you're right! The treaty did give control of the Heligoland archipelago to Germany, and control of Zanzibar to Great Britain. And you're also right that the latter two countries, Zanzibar and Great Britain, were soon engaged in what is now known as the *Shortest War in History.*

You do know your history!

With the signing of the above 1890 treaty, Zanzibar became a protectorate of the British Empire. This included British control over the selection of Zanzibari sultans (rulers), a cultural deviation not appreciated by the ruling class.

In 1893, the British elevated the sultan of their choice, a political puppet named Hamad bin Thuwaini to lead Zanzibar's government. From Great Britain's point-of-view, Hamad was an excellent choice as he did exactly as he was told, no more, no less, and thus Zanzibar enjoyed three years of peace.

Then, on August 25, 1896, just as his administration was beginning its fourth year of so-called "directed governance," Hamad bin Thuwaini died suddenly of a very suspicious illness.

Within hours of Hamad's death, and almost before his body had cooled, his cousin, Khalid bin Barghash declared himself Sultan Khalid bin Barghash, and moved, lock, stock, and harem, into the palace.

As you might imagine, Khalid's unexpected and forceful claim as the new sultan, in direct opposition to the above-mentioned treaty, didn't sit well with the British.

In fact, the leader of Britain's diplomatic corps, Sir Basil Cave, quite undiplomatically told Khalid *to pack up his family, his harem, and his servants and to not let the palace doors smack his rear-end as he exited the building*, or words of similar sentiment.

Cave then issued a written ultimatum set to expire two days hence, August 27th, at precisely 9:00 EAT.[1]   And if there's one thing the Brits are good at doing, it's being punctual when it comes to cleaning out someone else's palace.

The next two days were a whirlwind of activity.

The self-appointed Sultan bin Barghash had no intention of moving to a less opulent residence. He liked being right where he was, and to make his point, he ordered 2,800 guardsmen to surround the palace.

He then placed several artillery pieces at strategic locations. And to let the Brits know he wasn't a namby-pamby push-over like his recently deceased cousin – may he rest in peace – he ordered the Royal Yacht to be fully armed and readied for battle, and anchored in the harbor.

Across the street, Sir Basil Cave had no intention of turning the palace over to Khalid, or anyone else not approved by the British crown. After issuing his ultimatum, he ordered three cruisers, two gunboats, and 150 marines and sailors into strategic positions, all within striking distance of the palace.

And if that weren't enough, he ordered an additional 900 Zanzibaris to stand "at the ready" to storm the palace. A task, that if carried out, would literally have had grave consequences for the soldiers of both camps.

To cover his earlier decisions and to secure approval, Cave telegraphed the authorities in London with this question: "Are we authorized in the event all attempts at a peaceful solution prove useless, to fire on the Palace from the men-of-war?"[2]

In the early morning hours of the August 27th deadline, two additional British warships entered the harbor, and as they were easing into position, Cave received the following response to his earlier telegram: "You are hereby authorized to adopt whatever measures you may consider necessary, and you will be supported in your action by Her Majesty's Government. Do not, however, attempt to take any action in which you are not certain of being able to accomplish successfully."

At 8:00 a.m., one hour before the deadline, Khalid sent this message to Diplomat Cave: "We have no intention of lowering our flag and we do not believe you will open fire on us."

Immediately after receiving Khalid's message, Cave restated the British position in typical British stiff upper lip fashion, saying he didn't relish firing upon the palace, but that "unless you do as you are told, we shall most certainly do so."

At precisely 9:02, the British ships in the harbor opened fire, the first volley destroying all of Khalid's artillery and seriously damaging the entire front of the palace, which was constructed of wood. Within minutes, the front of the palace was gone, as was Khalid, who had slipped out the back door leaving nearly 3,000 persons, including his harem, to fend for themselves.

A short time later, Khalid was furiously banging on the door of the German consulate pleading for political asylum. When the British demanded that Khalid be turned over to them, the Germans refused and smuggled Khalid into German East Africa where he was given political asylum.

But the British have very long memories and twenty years later (1916) Khalid was captured and exiled to Saint Helena, a small, volcanic island in the South Atlantic Ocean.

Back at the palace, after just over thirty minutes of constant bombardment, the noise stopped and the flag that had been flying atop the palace was replaced by the British Union Jack.

The shortest war in history was over, lasting exactly thirty-eight minutes.

---

[1] EAT refers to East Africa Time, the time zone for Zanzibar.

[2] Man-of-war/Men-of-war: an armed naval vessel(s) of the Royal Navy. A ship carrying armed soldiers was called a "man-of-war ship" from the 16th to the 19th century. Over time, the word "ship" was dropped, and "man-of-war" came to mean any warship of the British Navy. As spoken by Diplomat Cave, the plural "men-of-war" referred collectively to the five warships (3 cruisers and 2 gunboats) in the harbor.

War is God's way of teaching Americans geography.
Ambrose Bierce (1842-1914) Journalist, satirist

Freddie Spencer
Born: Fred W Spencer
A world-class athlete and role model.
Aug 9, 1902 (Westfield, NJ) – Feb 9, 1992 (Rahway, NJ)

M RS. LAURENT, A TEACHER at the Madison Elementary School in Rahway, New Jersey, was always on the lookout for special guests to surprise and energize her fifth-grade class.

Near the end of the 1953 school year she told her students that she had arranged for a special guest to visit the class on the following day. The classroom conversation that followed may have sounded like this:

> *"Who," the students asked, tossing out a few famous names. "Joe DiMaggio? Jerry Lewis? Mr. Wizard?"*
>
> *"Nope! Nope! Nope!" Mrs. Laurent responded.*
>
> *"President Eisenhower?" continued the guessing.*
>
> *"Now you're just being silly," Mrs. Laurent said, shaking her head, "It's someone you already know. Mr. Spencer?"*
>
> *The classroom grew silent, and then someone asked, "Do you mean Mr. Spencer, our janitor?"*
>
> *"Yes. Mr. Spencer, our janitor," smiled Mrs. Laurent, "and he's bringing something very special with him."*

The following day, school janitor Fred Spencer walked into the classroom carrying a thick, impressive and well-worn scrapbook. As the students formed a big circle, he opened the scrapbook, and there on the first page was an aging photograph of a handsome, well-built athlete dressed in an early 1900s bicycle racing uniform.

The students couldn't believe their eyes. It was a very young Mr. Spencer receiving a big medal from someone important, the caption reading, "World Bicycling Championship."[1]

While turning the pages and looking at the pictures and clippings, Mr. Spencer told the students that in the 1920s and '30s, when he was young, bicycle racing was one of the world's most popular sports. He told of how he had competed in 102 six-day races over a fifteen-year period, winning twenty-two of them and setting five world records in the process.

He went on to say that races were often cheered on by movie stars and other famous people, and that the best racers earned up to $50,000 a year, an enormous sum in the 1920s and more money than sports greats like Babe Ruth earned.[2]

"Wow," the students gasped.

Then the room grew quiet as one of the students, in typical straight-from-the-lip, fifth-grade fashion, asked, "Well, if you made so much money, why are you a janitor?"

Mr. Spencer neither frowned nor blinked. He explained that he had invested his winnings in building bicycle racing tracks around the country, then something happened that everyone called the Great Depression, and he lost everything.

He went on to say that he didn't have any regrets. "Bad things happen in life," he told the students quite matter-of-factly. Then, with a warm smile, he told the students how much he enjoyed being around them and how he considered it an honor and a privilege to be the janitor of their school.

By class end, he had become much more than just a janitor. He had become a special friend.

Nearly sixty years after the classroom event, someone familiar with the above experience, perhaps one of Mrs. Laurent's former fifth grade students, posted the story on a personal website.[3]

That person put everything in perspective, saying that without the students knowing it, Mr. Spencer had taught them one of life's most important lessons, that even when it seems we have lost everything, we can continue to live and work with dignity.

It's a safe bet to say that Mrs. Laurent's fifth-graders never forgot the day that school janitor Mr. Fred "Freddie" Spencer was their special guest.

All of us would have been blessed to have had a teacher like Mrs. Laurent, and a janitor like Mr. Spencer.

Freddie Spencer died February 9, 1992, at the age of 89. He was laid to rest at the Hillside Cemetery, in Scotch Plains, New Jersey.

[1] According to Bill Shannon's Dictionary of New York Sports, Category: Bicycle Racing, "During the last Golden Era of bicycle racing in America, no star was bigger than Fred Spencer." The entry shows Spencer: (1) winning both the American Pro Sprint Championship and two six-day races in 1925 (the same calendar year), a feat never repeated; (2) in 1926, winning the Chicago six-day race; (3) winning the Madison Square Garden six-day races in 1927, 1928, & 1932; (4) in 1928, setting a world record for the half-mile in the Newark Velodrome; (5) in 1929, setting four world speed records in one day at the New York Velodrome, for 10 miles, 15 miles, 20 miles, and 25 miles; and (6) he repeated his 1925 U.S. Pro Sprint win with two more sprint wins, 1928 and 1929.

[2] According to the *Bicycling in Plainfield* (NJ) website, "By the peak of his career in 1934, he (Freddie Spencer) had won twenty-two six-day bicycle races . . . in addition to holding five world records. He was the highest paid athlete in the country at one time, earning over $100,000 a year. He left racing in 1938, and retired in Rahway, NJ."

[3] Sometime during 2011-14 the author found the referenced website while doing research for the *Stories from History's Dust Bin* series. The "Freddie Spencer" story, however, along with almost 300 other stories, never became a part of the series and the author's notes were filed away. When work on this book commenced in 2016, the author reopened the Spencer file, which contained a copy of Spencer's racing statistics and the original story draft based on the previously mentioned website. However, an internet search failed to find the original website, thus the above story is based on the author's original story draft and his memory of the website contents.

Life is like riding a bicycle. In order to keep your balance, you must keep moving. I thought of that while riding my bicycle.
Albert Einstein (1879-1955) Physicist

Belle Starr

Born: Myra Maybelle Shirley
The Bandit Queen
Feb 5, 1848 (Carthage MO) - Feb 3, 1889 (near King Creek OK)

B ELLE STARR MIGHT have been relegated to an asterisk in the history of the west except for two things. First, she was a woman in a world where most outlaws were men; and second, her 1889 obituary found its way into the hands of a freelance writer named Alton B. Meyers, whose colorfully cobbled account of her life sparked the beginning of an enduring legend.

Seated at a small table in a run-down apartment house, Meyers read and re-read Belle's obituary, fascinated by the story's possibilities.

He then began writing, em-*Belle*-ishing the obituary account with fanciful stories that have since swirled around the lady outlaw, and in due time there appeared in the *National Police Gazette* a story titled, "Belle Starr, the Bandit Queen," by Alton B. Myers that begins:

> *Of all the women of the Cleopatra type, since the days of the Egyptian queen herself, the universe has produced none more remarkable than Belle Starr, the Bandit Queen.... She was more amorous than Anthony's mistress, more relentless than Pharaoh's daughter, braver than Joan of Arc, and . . .*

. . . and although Meyer's version is more dime-store sensationalism than fact, the true unvarnished story of Belle Starr is almost as exciting, and with an equally sad ending.

So, welcome to the real world of Belle Starr, who was born Myra Maybelle Shirley in a log cabin on the outskirts of Carthage, Missouri, in 1848. She was one of six children, and the only daughter of John and Elizabeth Hatfield Shirley.[1]

When Belle, who was known as Myra throughout her youth, was eight years old (1856), the family moved into the town of

Carthage where they bought and operated the Carthage House Inn, a livery stable, and a blacksmith shop. There, the family prospered and Myra, known for her independent spirit, grew up in relative comfort.

She attended the upscale Carthage Female Academy, where she studied classical languages and learned to play the piano.

She also loved the outdoors and spent much of her time with an older brother, John Allison "Bud" Shirley, who taught her how to ride a horse and handle a firearm, and she was a natural, excelling at both.

Life for the Shirley family changed, however, with the outbreak of the Civil War. Bud joined the infamous group known as Quantrill's Raiders,[2] a decision that the family proudly supported. Bud, who knew the area well and was a quick thinker, rapidly rose to the rank of captain.

In June of 1863, the Shirley family received word that Bud had been killed during a raid on a home near Sarcoxie, Missouri. It was a devastating blow to the family who then sold their property and business interests in Carthage and moved to a farm near Scyene, Texas, a small town southeast of Dallas.

On November 1, 1866, eighteen-year-old Myra married Jim Reed, a man she had known in Missouri and who had also relocated to Scyene.

Their first child, Rosie Lee, known throughout her life as Pearl, was born in 1868. But finding work was tough and Reed became involved with a notorious outlaw family known as the Starr Clan.

Then, in August of 1874, Reed was killed by lawman John T. Morris who tried to arrest him as he was eating dinner at a way station near Paris, Texas.

With Reed's death, Myra felt the need for a new identity, so she stopped using "Myra," dropped "May" from "Maybelle" and became Belle.

Six years later (1880) she wed Sam Starr, the leader of the Starr Clan, thus becoming Belle Starr, and the duo became quite the team. She scheduled and coordinated the thievery while Sam supervised the on-the-ground rustling and bootlegging.

Life was good, business boomed, and if a gang member was caught and locked up, well, Belle knew exactly who and how to bribe.

In 1882, Sam and Belle were caught and charged with stealing horses, with some historic accounts throwing in a few cows as well. In March of 1883, they were brought before Judge Isaac Parker, the notorious Hanging Judge, who convicted both and sentenced them to prison.

Belle received a soft-slap-on-the-wrist sentence, and shortly after charming the warden and becoming his "assistant" for a brief period, she received an early release.

As you might suppose, Sam lacked Belle's ability to charm, and he ended up serving a full year of hard labor.

On December 17, 1886, Sam and Belle attended a Christmas party. Also invited to the party was lawman John West, and it wasn't long before the two men were exchanging angry words.

As the situation worsened and feelings heated up, Starr and West drew their guns simultaneously, each firing a single round, and as the old western saying goes, both men died of lead poisoning. West was dead almost before he hit the floor. Starr hung on painfully for an hour or two before closing his eyes for the last time.

But, the widow Starr didn't stay single for long.

In early 1889, she married for a third time, this time to Jim July Starr, an outlaw fifteen-years her junior, and who was either a cousin or an adopted brother of her deceased husband. Regardless of the relationship, it was a marriage that would literally become the death of her.

After a quarrel in which Belle accused her new husband of having an affair with a Cherokee girl, Jim July offered another outlaw $200 to kill Belle. When the outlaw refused, July reportedly yelled, "Hell, I'll kill the old hag myself and spend the money on whiskey!"

As you might imagine, the marriage between Belle and Jim July lost its luster and it was all downhill from there. On February 3, 1889, just two days before her 41st birthday, Belle was ambushed as she was riding home from a Sunday visit at a neighboring ranch.

The first shotgun blast hit her squarely in the back, knocking her off her horse. A second blast was fired directly into her face at close range, likely as she attempted to raise herself to a sitting position on the trail.

The prime suspect was her husband, Jim July Starr, who had been arrested a week or two earlier for trying, unsuccessfully, to steal a horse. When Belle cussed him out in front of his friends for either stealing the horse or for getting caught, she openly refused to pay his bail. Some believe it was Jim July who waylaid her on the trail in return for his public embarrassment.

Another suspect in Belle's murder was Edgar Watson, a neighbor whose cabin was within shouting distance of where she was killed. It was no secret that Belle and Watson didn't like each other, having long fought over an unmarked property line and water rights.

In addition, Watson, although not certain, was suspicious that Belle knew about his past, that he was an escaped murderer from Florida, a suspicion that Watson worried about daily.

After Belle's burial, her daughter Pearl had a stone carved with the inscription found below.

The stone marker still graces Belle's grave in the front yard of her cabin at Younger's Bend, Oklahoma.

[2] Elizabeth "Eliza" Hatfield Shirley, the mother of Myra Maybelle (Belle Starr) Shirley, was a relative of William Anderson Hatfield (1839-1921), the patriarch of the Hatfield side of the infamous feuding Hatfield and McCoy families of West Virginia and Kentucky.

[3] Stories from History's Dust Bin (additional reading):
   Vol 2, June 6:   Featuring William Quantrill

Shed not for her the bitter tear;
Nor give the heart to vain regret;
'Tis but the casket that lies here,
The gem that filled it sparkles yet.
Pearl Starr (1868-1925) Daughter of Belle Starr

Casey Stengel

Born: Charles Dillon Stengel
Baseball was more fun than pulling teeth.
July 30, 1890 (Kansas City MO) – Sept 29, 1975 (Glendale CA)

U NLIKE MOST BOYS who dream of playing in the big leagues, Charlie Stengel never thought of baseball as a career.

It's true he was a good athlete who performed well in high school, and when offered a minor-league contract with the Kansas City Blues, he signed, but his motivation wasn't what you might expect. Signing meant tuition money to pay his way into the profession he did dream about, and it had nothing to do with baseball.

For two years (1910-11), Charlie played in the minors, saved his money, and attended college in the off-season. In the minors, he was traded often, starting with the Kansas City Blues, then playing for the Kankakee Kays, Shelbyville Grays, Maysville Rivermen, Aurora Blues, and the Montgomery Rebels.

The Rebels, owned by the Dodger organization, liked what they saw in Stengel. His batting average was a respectable .290, he had stolen more than his share of bases, and at season's end, they offered him a major league contract worth a whopping $2,100.

The offer was simply too good to pass up. College in Missouri was placed on hold (Stengel would never return), and before long he was a starter for the Brooklyn Dodgers.

Charley made his major league debut on September 17, 1912, as the Dodger's starting center fielder. In a profession where nicknames are rampant, it wasn't long before someone called him *Dutch,* a nickname common in the early 1900s for almost anyone of German (Deutsch) descent.

But he didn't remain Dutch Stengel for long. When someone hollered at him using his hometown (Kansas City) initials, he became K. C. Stengel, which evolved into Casey Stengel.

Some historians suggest the evolution was in part because of the popularity of Ernest Thayer's[1] famous poem, *Casey at the Bat*. But over time, the mere mention of "Casey" when talking major league baseball meant only one person, Casey Stengel.

In 1914, Casey's former coach from Kansas City, Bill Driver, who had accepted the football and basketball coaching jobs at the University of Mississippi, helped Casey land the job as the university's baseball coach prior to spring training with the Dodgers. Stengel did well, coaching the Ole Miss baseball team to a 13-9 record, earning himself another nickname when he showed up at spring training, the *Ol' Perfessor*.

During 1915-1916, Stengel helped the Dodgers win the National League pennant, and because baseball is a business, he was traded the following year to the Pittsburgh Pirates.

When World War I interrupted life in America, he enlisted in the Navy. When the war was over, he returned to the Pirate organization, and then began a series of trades, each contributing to his baseball skills, and without knowing it, to his future as arguably the finest manager baseball has known.

As competent a player as Stengel was, and as great and tough a manager as he would become, Casey was also well-known for his often light-hearted and comic approach to the game.

On one occasion, he unobtrusively lifted the lid to a manhole in the outfield and lowered himself out-of-sight where he watched the game, his eyes barely above ground level. When a fly ball was hit in his direction he seemed to appear out of thin air, catching the ball to a standing ovation.

Once, after hitting a home run, Casey stopped at second and again at third base to dust off each bag with his hat before continuing his way to home plate.

And what about this insightful piece of baseball wisdom from the fertile mind of Casey Stengel, "Good pitching will always stop good hitting and vice-versa."

When Stengel played for Pittsburgh, he was mercilessly taunted by the fans of his former team, the Brooklyn Dodgers.

Somewhere near the dugout Casey captured a sparrow, put it in his baseball cap, and placed bird and cap on his head before walking to the plate amidst a chorus of boos. Turning to the crowd, he waved, tipped his cap, and out flew the sparrow. The catcalls turned to cheers as Stengel won over his former fans.

In 1923, Casey scored another first. His team, the Giants, had made it to the World Series where they were facing the Yankees in old Yankee Stadium.

Believe it or not, no one up to that year, including Babe Ruth[2] who started with the Yankees in 1920, had ever hit a home run in the old stadium during World Series play. Casey hit two home runs during that series, one in Giants Stadium, the other being the first-ever World Series homer hit at the old Yankee Stadium.

At season's end, Casey was traded to a second-division team, a matter that never sat well with him. Years afterward he would tell people, "I'm lucky I didn't hit three home runs in that series or Manager John McGraw would have traded me to a third-division team."

So, what was it that Charlie Stengel had originally wanted to become, enough that he saved two years of minor-league earnings to help finance his dream?

Here's a clue.

The college he attended during the off-season was the Western Dental College in Kansas City.

He never returned to dental school, and when asked why not? In typical Casey Stengel fashion, he blamed it on the lack of left-handed dental instruments.

Stengel died of cancer on September 29, 1975. He was laid to rest next to his wife, Edna, in the Forest Lawn Memorial Park Cemetery in Glendale, California.

He was one of America's best known and best loved baseball managers.

Stories from History's Dust Bin (additional reading):
  [1] Vol 2, Aug 21: Featuring Ernest Thayer
  [2] Vol 1, Mar 2:   Babe Ruth with Moe Berg

All right everyone, line up alphabetically according to your height.
Casey Stengel (1890-1975) Baseball

Melville Stone

Born: Melville Elijah Stone
Melville's once-in-a-lifetime idea.
Aug 22, 1848 (Hudson IL) – Feb 15, 1929 (New York NY)

I N 1875, TEN YEARS after the Civil War, Melville Stone founded Chicago's first penny newspaper, the *Chicago Daily News*. It was a four-page, five-column daily that he hoped would be affordable to the poor, appreciated by everyone, and of course, profitable.

But despite its extremely reasonable cost, the newspaper struggled. That was, until he had a "once in a lifetime" idea, an ingenious plan that not only saved his newspaper, but helped to alleviate a retail sales problem that was driving the downtown Chicago merchants nuts!

But first, who was Melville Stone?

Melville Stone was the son of an itinerant Methodist minister born thirteen years before the start of the Civil War.

According to Stone's biography, *"M.E.S.": His Book, a Tribute, et.al.,*[1] it was the Methodist Rule of Itinerancy that kept this "rolling stone" family from gathering any moss, as Methodist ministers of that era were required to relocate after a maximum of two years of service to any one congregation.

The biography also states that the Reverend Stone rarely earned over $300 a year for his preaching, so to make ends meet, he supplemented the family income by making and selling *Stone's Chinese Liniment – Good for Man and Beast*.

Thus, did young Melville learn about marketing and the value of a penny.

In 1860, the family moved to Chicago where the Reverend Stone was appointed minister of the Des Plaines Street Methodist Church. There, Melville attended West Division High School and met classmate John F. Ballentyne, the son of the editor of the *Chicago Tribune*.

The elder Ballentyne, impressed with his son's new friend, offered him a summer job as a cub reporter. Melville, who had his heart set on becoming a lawyer, accepted the offer to earn needed college money.

Not yet seventeen, Melville was at home when he learned of the assassination of President Lincoln. He rushed to the *Tribune* office and worked tirelessly alongside Mr. Ballentyne before going outside to glean whatever news he could amidst the flurry of street confusion. And in the excitement of the moment (gathering news, writing copy, and seeing his efforts in print), the thought of becoming a lawyer gave way to a serious interest in journalism.

That same year, Melville went to work for the *Chicago Republican*, a newspaper on financial life-support, so he quit and went to work for the *Chicago Times*. When he learned that his father was deathly ill, he returned home to help with his care.

Those were difficult times for young Melville, but printer's ink was now flowing in his veins.

When his father died, he tried publishing a newspaper of his own, a too narrowly-focused product named *The Sawyer and Mechanic*. It died a quick death.

In 1869 he married Martha McFarland, and invested in the Lake Shore Iron Works, a business he hoped would provide a steady income for his family. But, it wasn't to be. The business burned to the ground in the Great Chicago Fire of 1871.

In need of a job, he went back to doing what he knew best, journalism.

He went to work for Jacob Bunn who had just purchased the failing *Chicago Republican,* renaming it the *Chicago Inter-Ocean.* The year was 1872 and Stone was thankful for the job.

But now, more than ever, he had his mind set on owning his own newspaper, and the pennywise son of a thrifty Methodist minister would soon make headlines with a new approach to marketing a newspaper.

Three years later, on Christmas Day 1875, Stone had newsboys on the streets of Chicago handing out free copies of his newspaper, the *Chicago Daily News,* to the parade of ladies and gentlemen strolling by in their new Christmas finery. It was Stone's way of introducing his four-page, five-column daily, that beginning a week hence, New Year's Day, 1876, would be available to everyone, rich and poor, for a penny.

Well, we're right back at the place where we began this story, with Melville Stone determined to make a penny newspaper profitable, and here's the story behind his once in a lifetime idea.

Despite the low cost of a penny per issue, the newspaper struggled.

Why?

Because pennies were not widely circulated following the Civil War, thus the cost of store-bought products were usually priced in 5¢ increments, and dollar items were, well, generally marked at a dollar.

In a meeting with downtown merchants, Stone learned that they were experiencing problems with sales clerks putting the customers' dollars in their pockets, instead of in the cash register.

It was a revelation that gave Stone an idea.

He convinced the merchants that theft would be reduced if they lowered the price of items marked at a dollar to 99¢.

Why?

He explained that if a clerk had to make change, he or she would have to keep the dollar visible while they opened the cash register, and with the customer waiting for their penny in change, the clerk would be more likely to place the dollar bill in the register, than in their pocket.

Merchants experimented with the idea and found Stone's suggestion sound, and besides, marking an item at 99¢ gave customers the sense they were getting a bargain, so store and customer both benefited from the lower price.

Now, as shop patrons left the various stores with a penny in hand, and as Stone's newsies were hawking the *Chicago Daily News* for a penny right in front of their noses, customers were inclined to toss the newsy the penny they had just received in exchange for a paper.

Stone's *Chicago Daily News* gradually pulled out of the red and into the black, and the penny newspaper became the foundation for Melville Elijah Stone's financial empire.

And, oh yes, to help the merchants out, because of the scarcity of pennies during those post-Civil War times, guess who purchased barrels and barrels of the small copper coins directly from the mint?

Right!

And Stone provided the same to Chicago's downtown merchants on an even 100 pennies for one-dollar basis.

Stone was foremost a businessman, and a frugal one at that, who turned his idea-of-a-lifetime into a small fortune, one penny at a time.

As Stone's newspaper empire grew, so did his stature among others in the newspaper business, and he became head of the Associated Press in 1893.

Melville Elijah Stone died in 1929 and is interred at Chicago's Graceland Cemetery.

---

[1] The full 27-word title of Stone's biography is: *"M.E.S.,"*: *His Book, a Tribute and a Souvenir of the Twenty-Five Years, 1893-1918, of the Service of Melville E. Stone as General Manager of the Associated Press.*

The difference between burlesque and the newspapers
is that the former never pretended to be performing
a public service by exposure.
I. F. Stone (1907-1989) Investigative journalist

John Sutter

Born: Johann August Suter
Life was good, and then . . . gold!
Feb 15, 1803 (Kandern, Germany) – June 18, 1880 (Washington DC)

J UST WHEN EVERYTHING was running its smoothest, the worst of all things happened. At least, that's how Colonel John Sutter would assess the situation, once he could clearly look back on the historic turn of events. January 24, 1848, was the beginning of the end of his dream, and the problem was a most unlikely one, gold, and too much of it.

Johann August Suter was a dreamer.

Born in the Swiss-German border town of Kandern, Germany, he attended school in Switzerland where he became proficient in Spanish, English, and Swiss-French along with his native German.

In his late teens he joined the Swiss Army, rising to the rank of captain of an artillery unit.

At twenty-three (1826), he married Annette Dübold and tried to settle down. But Johann Suter, the dreamer, had a problem. He preferred spending money to earning it, and by 1834 he was so deeply in debt he needed to do something, and do it fast.

Facing serious charges of financial impropriety, Suter was nowhere to be found on the day of the trial that would have landed him lock, stock, and reputation in debtor's prison.

The first thing he did after missing his court date was to change his given name, Johann, to "John," alter his middle name from August, to "Augustus," add a second "t" to his surname Suter, to become "Sutter," add a meaningless but nice-sounding "Captain" to the front of his name, and choose a profession.

Thus, literally overnight, Johann August Suter, a deadbeat fugitive, became Captain John Augustus Sutter, successful businessman.

Then, barely one step ahead of the law, but armed with a French passport, he sailed to New York, arriving July 14, 1834, promising to bring the rest of his family to America once he was settled, a promise he would keep.

From New York, he went to St. Louis where he joined a group of thirty-five Germans traveling west to Santa Fe, New Mexico Territory.

Four years later (1838), he joined up with a mixed group of trappers and missionaries on their way to the Pacific Coast via the Oregon Trail. When the trappers reached their destination, the far west headquarters of the Hudson Bay Company at Fort Vancouver, Washington, Sutter departed the group as well.

From Fort Vancouver, he boarded the ship *Columbia* and sailed to Honolulu, Hawaii Territory, arriving on December 9, 1838. From Honolulu, he sailed to the Russian colony of New Archangel (today: Sitka, Alaska), and a month later he was in the struggling mission town of Yerba Buena (today: San Francisco).

It was now 1839. He hadn't seen his family for five years, and for the first time in his life, he may have taken time to take stock of himself and to do a little introspective thinking about the future.

Whether that happened or not, he settled down, moved eighty miles inland from Yerba Buena where he made friends with the Miwok and Maidu Indians. Using Miwok and Maidu labor, he built a residence and some out-buildings, all enclosed within an eighteen-foot high wall.

The resulting complex became known as Sutter's Fort.

Since the real-estate upon which he built his fort belonged to Mexico, the only way he could take possession of the land was to become a Mexican citizen.

Sutter never blinked.

He filled out the appropriate documents for citizenship, agreed to live on the property for at least a year, said *muchas gracias* to the clerk who counter-signed his paperwork, and he took up residency.

On August 29, 1840, Sutter became a citizen of Mexico.

Now, besides simply being Captain John Sutter, he added a reference to his days in the Swiss army, and became Captain John Sutter of the Swiss Guard. Using his somewhat impressive title, he befriended Mexican Governor Juan Bautista Alvardo, to whom he presented a plan to establish a colony near his fort.

Governor Alvarado saw the idea as useful in buttressing the frontier against encroachment by Indians, Russians, Americans, and the British, and in 1841, he awarded Sutter title to an incredible 48,827 acres of land surrounding the Fort. That's right, nearly fifty-thousand acres, which computes to just over 76 square miles. Sutter named the acreage Nueva Helvetia, meaning New Switzerland.

At around this time, Sutter's wife and children had successfully immigrated to America and completed a long overland trip to the rustic, but surprisingly pleasant accommodations at Sutter's Fort.

Captain Sutter, never bashful about advancing himself in the eyes of others, promoted himself to the rank of Colonel, and by every standard, he was becoming wealthier by the day.

But even more than the wealth, Colonel Sutter enjoyed the power and influence he wielded at New Helvetia, once stating: "I was everything, patriarch, priest, father, and judge."

Life was good, and Sutter's Fort became an important way station, with immigrants, trappers, pioneers, traders, merchants, lumberjacks and losers, all putting down roots, with houses and cabins springing up everywhere.

On January 24, 1848, one of Sutter's employees, a carpenter named James Marshall, was building a sawmill on the American River near Coloma.

During a cleaning of the millrace, he noticed some small yellow rocks remaining after the wash. An assayer confirmed they were indeed gold nuggets and just about that fast (snap your fingers here) – the California Gold Rush was on!

From Marshall's discovery of gold on January 24, 1848, until the end of 1849, an estimated 100,000 people arrived with dreams of striking it rich.

They ranged from ministers to misfits, from gold-seekers to gold-diggers, most with little concept of property rights, many with no conscience, and all of them overrunning Sutter's Nueva Helvetia like a swarm of angry locusts, destroying everything in their path.

Despondent, Sutter gave the land to his son, John Augustus Sutter, Jr, who would envision a new world, eventually laying out a new town he would name after the Sacramento River.

As an aside, among those who became wealthy was the Gold Rush's first millionaire, Samuel Brannon, who owned the only store between San Francisco and Sutter's Fort on the way to the gold fields. After gold was discovered, Brannan reportedly bought every gold mining pan available, and profited $36,000 by selling 15-cent pans for $15.00 dollars each, and that's just for starters.

In 1871, John Augustus Sutter, showing his age and in failing health, moved with his wife to Lititz, Pennsylvania to take advantage of the reputed healing qualities of Lititz Hot Springs.

For fifteen years, he had petitioned Congress for $50,000 in financial restitution for land and property lost during the gold rush.

On June 18, 1880, two days after receiving the final rejection to his claim, he died in a Washington, D.C. hotel room. His body was returned to Pennsylvania for burial.

There is an upside to the story, if only meaningful to the rank-conscious John Augustus Sutter.

Engraved on the marble slab that marks his grave at the Lititz, Pennsylvania, Moravian Brotherhood Cemetery, is the name with which he was laid to rest: *General John A. Sutter.*

He would have been proud!

The internet is like a gold-rush;
the only people making money are those who sell the pans.
Will Hobbs (1947-) Author

Lucy Hobbs Taylor

Born: Lucy Beaman Hobbs
First American woman to earn a dental degree.
Mar 14, 1833 (Constable NY) – Oct 3, 1910 (Lawrence KS)

L UCY HOBBS WAS a maverick. During the mid-1800s, when societal expectations were such that women were either kept-in-their-place or flatly told they were incapable of doing much beyond cooking, cleaning, and having babies, Lucy refused to listen.

She wasn't about to accept the status quo.

She knew what she wanted, and she was resourceful, even if it required breaking a few rules. And in so doing, she became the first American woman to earn a medical degree in dentistry. But the road wasn't an easy one.

Did we mention she was a maverick?

Refusing to sweat the small stuff like graduating from dental school first, and then opening a dental practice, Lucy was quite literally, ahead of her time. But not everyone felt good about her encroachment into what was then considered a man's world.

Looking back on her experiences after she had finally earned an accredited dental degree, she wrote:

> *People were amazed when they learned that a young girl had so far forgotten her womanhood as to want to study dentistry.*

You see, in the mid-1800s, things like being a woman and being a dentist were considered mutually exclusive options, and not just among men; this attitude prevailed even among the most progressive of women's groups.

A woman could be a teacher, which is where Lucy began her career, but could a woman be a doctor or a dentist? C'mon now, do you really think a woman's frail and naturally weepy nature could handle those kind of occupations, what with the likelihood of getting someone else's blood on your hands? Why, a woman's delicate constitution should never be subjected to the like!

Lucy taught school for ten years in Michigan, but she had always been interested in medicine and at first, she had planned to become a doctor.

In 1859, there was only one college in America that admitted female candidates to the study of medicine, and it was in Cincinnati, Ohio. It went by the odd-sounding name of the *Eclectic College of Medicine.*[1]

She applied to the college for acceptance, only to be informed that the school had recently adopted a policy of non-admittance to women. Her letter of non-acceptance advised her to look elsewhere, that she consider the field of dentistry, suggesting that as a woman she would be better suited to practicing "a less stressful form of medicine."

Unhappy with the refusal letter but still determined to get into medical school, she found support in the person of Dr. Samuel Wardle, the dean of the *Ohio College of Dental Surgery.*

He introduced her to a dentist in private practice who agreed to train Lucy as his apprentice. After gaining confidence in her abilities, and feeling she now had a medical foundation sufficient to compete against men, she filed an application for admission. But even with Professor Wardle's endorsement she was refused admittance because she was a woman.

So, what did she do?

It was now 1861 and Lucy, twenty-eight years old and unable to find a dental school that would admit her, decided to take matters into her own hands. She rented an office in Cincinnati, hung a shingle above the entrance, and began practicing dentistry with neither a college degree nor a license.

A year later she moved to Iowa, first to Bellevue and then to McGregor, where, in 1865 and after having successfully practiced dentistry for four years, the Iowa State Dental Society accepted her into their ranks. This provided her with full professional recognition, but still she hadn't graduated from college, let alone a dental school.

This prompted the *Ohio College of Dental Surgery*, the same school that had earlier denied her admission because of gender, to admit her as a fourth-year student, accepting her four years of having successfully run her own dental practice as "practical" college credit.

She studied, passed their exams, and a year later (1866) became the first woman in the United States, and quite possibly the world, to receive a legitimate, medical school-based degree in dentistry.

Also, around this time, she met and married James M. Taylor, a Civil War veteran.

Rather than have her husband matriculate through a standard multi-year dental program, Lucy taught him the procedures, finer points, and nuances of dental science.

In 1868, they purchased an empty lot at 809 Vermont Street in Lawrence, Kansas where they built a combination residence and dental office and went into practice together.

Moving thirty years into the future, 1900, there were about a thousand women dentists in the United States, a number that quite assuredly would not have been possible without Lucy Hobbs Taylor's pioneering efforts to break the gender-barrier in medical dentistry in the 1860s.

Since 1983, the *American Association of Women Dentists* has recognized outstanding females in the field of dentistry by honoring one of their own with the annual *Lucy Hobbs Taylor Award* that "empowers women in dentistry to drive change and deliver success through networking, innovation, and giving back."

James Taylor died in 1886, after which Lucy Hobbs Taylor retired from her dental practice.

Lucy died October 3, 1910 and was laid to rest next to her husband at the Oak Hill Cemetery in Lawrence, Kansas.

---

[1] The term "eclectic," as used in the *Eclectic College of Medicine,* meant a medical program designed to draw from the best of several differing approaches to medicine.

My husband goes to a female dentist just for the novelty
of hearing a woman tell him to open his mouth.
Unknown source

Moulton Taylor

Born: Moulton Burnell Taylor
The patron saint of the flying car.
Sept 29, 1912 (Portland OR) – Nov 16, 1995 (Longview WA)

M OLT, AS HE WAS KNOWN to his friends, grew up during the barnstorming days, an era when men flew biplanes held together with baling wire and prayer – mostly prayer.

Pilots in open-cockpit planes hopscotched from town to town, buzzing main streets, flying so low you could see the colors of their good luck scarves as they whipped in the plane's prop-wash.

After "buzzing" a small town's Main Street a couple of times, the pilot would ease back on the stick and the plane would climb dizzily until gravity overcame thrust. Then came the few seconds that the plane seemed to teeter on the very edge of space before beginning its descent, cutting wide arcs and perhaps a figure-eight in the sky before bouncing to a safe landing on the ground.

The flight always gathered a crowd, sod-busters and city-slickers alike, all wondering why a handsome young man would risk his life in such a flimsy machine, challenging a branch of physics that none of them, not even the pilot, understood.

Protected by what?

A silk good luck scarf?

To make barnstorming a paying proposition, the pilot had to apply a little psychology. He soon learned that a guy with a girlfriend often had more bravado than good sense, and was thus more likely to part with a few quarters for the privilege of taking a bouncy, potentially vomit-inducing ride high above the town's farms and orchards.

"What a thrill!" the boyfriend would tell his adoring lady upon his return from the sky, "You bet, honey, I'd do it again in a heartbeat! But for now, I just want to sit down and hold your hand . . . but I think I'll go to the men's first and comb my hair. Windy up there you know."

Few who went up once were interested in a second flight.

Molt was fourteen when he climbed aboard an airplane for the first time, and he neither threw up, nor forgot the magic he felt during that first flight.

Imagine, he may have asked himself, *what would it be like if every-day regular people like me could travel from place to place through the sky."*

He knew right then that airplanes would become a part of his life.

Two years later, while his friends were learning to drive their flivvers on Oregon's dirt roads, Molt was learning to fly. Later, when his friends were taking their driver's license tests, he was a thousand feet in the air over a remote corner of the county, logging solo flight time toward a pilot's license.

At the University of Washington, he earned a degree in engineering and signed on with the U.S. Naval Reserve Cadet Program, so he could receive training as a military flight officer.

In September of 1939, he established a light plane radio manufacturing business, *Taylor Airphone Products*, which he ran until 1941 when he was called into duty in World War II.

As a lieutenant in the Navy with an engineering degree and an interest in aeronautics, he was assigned to work on the development of radio-controlled aircraft for use as assault weapons.

Three years later he became the first person to control a surface-to-surface missile and was assigned to work with the Navy's pilotless aircraft program, the precursor of today's missile program.

His work earned him the Navy's Legion of Merit medal and at the time of his discharge in 1946, he held the rank of Commander and was overseeing the Navy's Pilotless Aircraft and Development Program.

He had no sooner hung up his naval uniform for the last time when he was hired by a firm that was trying to contract with the federal government for the delivery of civilian airmail by pilotless aircraft,[1] an idea that was so far ahead of 1940s technology that it couldn't be delivered, and the program was scrapped.

Now, and this is pure conjecture, but as early as 1947 Molt Taylor may have begun pondering, as he had done after that barnstorming ride in 1926, about what it would take to build an aircraft simple and safe enough for every-day people to fly.

Then, why not a *car-plane,* a vehicle of blended automotive-aircraft design that could be used to either drive from place-to-place, or if runways were available, to fly from place-to-place, or to do both on a cross-country trip.

In 1948, Americans were in an upbeat post-war, we-can-do-anything frame of mind and Taylor, with the financial backing of believers like himself, established the *Aerocar Corporation* in Longview, Washington.

It was the perfect marriage of a passionate believer in what he could do aeronautically; with what his investors could do financially; and what both believed the public would embrace enthusiastically.

By December of 1950, the first Aerocar (the Model I)[2] had been designed, built, and approved for flight by the Civil Aeronautics Authority. It was a truly innovative piece of genius with foldable wings that could be removed, placed in a trailer, and towed when the Aerocar was being driven as an automobile.

With its wings unfolded and attached, and given a runway or a deserted stretch of highway to power itself into the air, it could fly at over 100 miles per hour and travel 500 miles on 32 gallons of fuel, roughly 15 miles per gallon.

Taylor built into the aircraft some failsafe features, such as not allowing the engine to start unless each of the plane's components were securely locked in place; and if the aircraft's engine experienced difficulties in flight, the Aerocar's horn would honk to alert the pilot to the problem.

One of those to purchase an Aerocar was Hollywood actor-pilot Bob Cummings,[3] star of television's *The Bob Cummings Show,* a situation-comedy about a pilot-playboy sponsored by Nutra-Bio, a vitamin company.

As Taylor was delivering Cummings' Aerocar to the actor, he spotted an Earl Scheib Auto Paint business, stopped, and had the Aerocar painted yellow and green to match the colors used on the labels of Nutra-Bio products.

Cummings was so pleased with his futuristic car-plane that he had his scriptwriters write the Aerocar into some of the show's weekly situations, giving viewers a chance to see for themselves what the weekly magazines were touting as Molt Taylor's vision of the future.

Unfortunately, the Aerocar never got off the ground, market-wise, and only six units were produced, each slightly different than the previous as improvements were literally being made on the fly. Thus, assembly-line production of the hybrid never took off.

Six days before Taylor's death in 1995 at the age of 83, he was inducted into the Experimental Aircraft Association Hall of Fame, and what was once known as the Kelso-Longview Regional Airport, in Kelso, Washington, is now known as Molt Taylor Field.

[1] *Stories from History's Dust Bin* (additional reading):
 Vol 2, Jun 8: Featuring Missile Mail

[2] The first Aerocar built can be seen these days at the EAA AirVenture Museum in Oshkosh, Wisconsin. Also, the Aerocar originally delivered to Bob Cummings in 1960, is still airworthy, still yellow and green, and is owned and maintained by Ed Sweeney at the Kissimmee Gateway Airport in Kissimmee, Florida.

[3] See Bob Cummings in this book, pages 61-64, to learn about the pilot/actor/movie star, who legally changed his name to Robert Orville Cummings in honor of his aviation hero, Orville Wright.

There are two gifts we should give our children;
one is roots, the other is wings.
Hodding Carter (1907-1972) Author, journalist

Jim Thorpe

Born: Wa-Tho-Huk (Sac–Fox meaning *Bright Path*)
English name: James Francis Thorpe
The greatest athlete of the 20th Century.
May 28, 1887 (Pottawatomie OK) – Mar 28, 1953 (Lomita CA)

I N 1941, TWELVE YEARS before his death at the age of sixty-five, Jim Thorpe returned to his alma mater, the Carlisle Indian School in Pennsylvania, and wearing street clothes, stood in the center of the fifty-yard line holding one football in his hands, and a second football resting at his feet.

Turning to face the goal posts at one end of the field, he drop-kicked[1] the ball fifty yards dead-center through the uprights. Then, picking up the ball at his feet, he spun on his heel and did the same thing to the goal posts at the other end of the field. Back-to-back fifty-yard field goals – in his street shoes!

In a 2012 poll, ABC Sports asked fans to select from a list of fifteen names the person who best meets the criteria as the "Greatest Athlete of the Twentieth Century." By the way, the list included names like Muhammad Ali, Babe Ruth, Jesse Owens, Wayne Gretzky, Jack Nicklaus, Michael Jordan, Jim Thorpe, and eight others.

The winner was Jim Thorpe, a Native American (Sac and Fox) from Oklahoma whose best years as an athlete were from 1915 through 1928.

So, how good was Thorpe?

He was a virtual a one-man track and field team.

Prior to the 1912 Olympics he had run the 100-yard dash in 10 seconds; the 200 in 21.8 seconds; the 440 in 51.8 seconds; the 880 in 1:57; the mile in 4:35; the 120-yard high hurdles in 15 seconds; and the 220-yard low hurdles in 24 seconds.

He had also long-jumped 23-feet 6-inches; high-jumped 6-feet 5-inches; pole-vaulted 11-feet, threw the shot 47-feet 9-inches; threw the javelin 163-feet; and threw the discus 136-feet.

Assuming you're not a track and field expert, know that every one of those times and distances are very, very good.

When Thorpe competed in the U.S. Olympic trials for both the pentathlon (five events) and the decathlon (ten events), he won both easily.

At the 1912 Olympics, he took the gold by winning 4 of 5 pentathlon events, and in the only one he didn't win, the javelin throw, he placed 3rd.

On the same day that he competed in the pentathlon, he qualified for the high jump by placing fourth, and in the long jump by placing seventh.

And here's something that a lot of people never knew or would have forgotten. On the opening day of the Olympic games, before he had competed in a single event, he discovered that someone had stolen his athletic shoes. Rummaging through garbage cans outside the Olympic dressing rooms, he found a used pair that "fit pretty good," and he competed in them.

Thorpe's final event was the Olympic decathlon (ten events). It was the first time he had ever competed in the event. Sweden's Hugo Wieslander was considered the favorite. When the decathlon was over, Thorpe had defeated Wieslander by over 700 points. In all, during the 1912 Olympics, Thorpe had amassed 8,413 points, a record that stood for nearly twenty years.

Upon his return from the Olympics he was honored with a ticker-tape parade on Broadway, to which he commented, "I heard people yelling my name, and I couldn't realize how one feller could have so many friends."

But there is something else for which Thorpe is remembered and it was a controversy that resulted in the loss of his Olympic standing and medals.

The controversy centered on his having played professional baseball for two years (1909-1910), during which time he received between $2 and $35 per game (about $50 and $900 in 2018 dollars).

His 1912 results were removed from the official Olympic records and he was stripped of his medals.

In 1982, seventy years after the 1912 Olympics, and twenty-nine years after his death, the International Olympic Committee (IOC) declared Thorpe as *co-champion* with Sweden's Hugo Wieslander, and his medals were returned to his children. A year later, 1983, his amazing results from the 1912 Olympics were once again made a part of the Olympic record.

Here's an interesting aside to the Jim Thorpe story.

In 1953, the year of Thorpe's death, a series of events led to the combining of two tiny Pennsylvania towns, Mauch Chunk and East Mauch Chunk, into a single small town. The two tiny towns, in addition to serving as the gateway to the Poconos, are about a hundred miles from where Jim Thorpe began his athletic career at the Carlisle Indian School.

When Jim passed away in 1953, his widow Patricia lobbied Oklahoma, Jim's birth state, to erect a monument in honor of her husband's legacy.

When her efforts failed to find support, and after learning about the two small Pennsylvania towns, Patricia approached the town's leaders with an idea for a unique and creative way to boost the local economy. Combine the two tiny towns into one town and name the new town Jim Thorpe, and that's exactly what the people voted to do.

And when the paperwork was signed and delivered, the U.S. Postal Service assigned the town of Jim Thorpe, Pennsylvania its own ZIP code, 18229.

And that's not all!

The new Pennsylvania municipality, with Patricia Thorpe's blessing, obtained the athlete's remains and erected a red marble monument to the Oklahoma native. The monument is not only inscribed with King Gustav V of Sweden's comment to Thorpe at the 1912 Olympics: "You, sir, are the greatest athlete in the world," but it is inset with four bronze images showing Jim competing in track, field, baseball, and football.

And there are two larger-than-life statues near the memorial, one of him carrying a football in a Heisman-like pose, and a second of him throwing the discus.

And finally, his tomb rests on a special mound of soil, half of it imported from the stadium in Stockholm, Sweden, where he competed in 1912; and the other half hauled in from his home state of Oklahoma.

Then, as with all good things, Oklahoma, and others, have found a way to honor the memory of Jim Thorpe.

Today, there are two statues of Jim Thorpe in Oklahoma. There is one at the entrance to the Oklahoma Sports Hall of Fame; and another at the Jim Thorpe Museum.

Thorpe is a charter member of the Professional Football Hall of Fame; a U.S. Postal Service stamp was issued in his honor in 1998; and the *Jim Thorpe Trophy* is awarded annually to the best defensive back in college football.

And here are a couple of brief stories for trivia buffs.

In 1912, the Carlisle Indian School defeated Army 27-6. During the game, Thorpe ran 92 yards for a touchdown, only to have the play nullified by a penalty. On the very next play, Thorpe ran 97 yards for a touchdown.

On another occasion, during a game in which Thorpe was making life miserable for the Black Knights of the West Point Military Academy, West Point coach Ernie Graves sent cadet and future U.S. president Dwight D. Eisenhower into the game with specific instructions to "Stop that Indian!"

Eisenhower tried his best, only to be run over as he tried to tackle "that Indian."

---

[1] In football, a "drop kick" is exactly as its name implies. It is a kick that involves a player holding the ball at arm's length from his body, dropping it, and then kicking it when it bounces off the ground. In the early days of football (1800-1930s), the drop kick was a common way of kicking a football. Prior to 1934, the American football was closer in shape to the "football" used in rugby, and the rounder-shaped ball lent itself to being dropped before being kicked, as is still done in rugby. In 1934, the shape of America's football officially took on a "pointier" shape, and the drop kick virtually disappeared from the game.

Thanks, King.
[Thorpe's reply to King Gustav V of Sweden, when
the King praised him as the greatest athlete in the world.]
Jim Thorpe (1887-1953) Olympian

Harry S Truman

It's just an 'S' – no period. Period!
May 8, 1884 (Lamar MO) - Dec 26, 1972 (Kansas City MO)

I N 1905, AT THE AGE of twenty-one, Harry joined the
Missouri National Guard signing his name as it appeared
on his birth certificate, *Harry S Truman,* with no period after the
middle initial. After all, the 'S' was just an 'S' and nothing
more.

When Harry was born, it was John and Martha Young
Truman's way of being respectful, by allowing the "S" to
represent the given name of either Shipp Truman or Solomon
Young, their newborn son's grandfathers.

But, throughout Harry's life, nearly everyone except Harry
had a problem with his "period-less" middle initial.

Then, sixty-one years after his birth, on April 12, 1945 to be
exact, Supreme Court Justice Harlan F. Stone administered the
presidential oath of office to America's 33rd President by
saying:

I, Harry Shipp Truman <*pause*> do solemnly swear. . . .

To which Truman, who may have paused a second longer
than usual, responded:

I, <*p a u s e*>Harry S Truman do solemnly swear . . . .

Early in his presidency, the problem of the president's
period-less middle initial became an issue.

That is, should the president's typed name beneath his
signature be *Harry S Truman* or should it be *Harry S. Truman*?

A look at the signature he had used for most of his sixty-plus
years wasn't any help. It was a running together of his name in
the manner of *HarrySTruman*, the nib of his pen never leaving
the paper.

Generally, when typing the president's name, civil service
secretaries followed Harry's 'S' with a period, unaware that the
'S' was but a simple stand-alone letter of the alphabet intended
to represent "Shipp" and "Solomon" equally, in honor of both
grandfathers.

Now, and you may find this difficult to believe – or maybe not – but there are government officials who view resolving a thorny issue such as a questionable period following the middle initial in a presidential signature, as a prime opportunity to standout at Performance Evaluation time.

After all, Washington has wasted millions on projects of less consequence, such as studying the mobility of shrimp by placing the little crustaceans on treadmills and recording their dismount preferences as they become exhausted.

Silly shrimp studies and their ilk, make research into the question of whether a period after a presidential middle initial is vital to the welfare of the nation, take on an aura of extreme importance.

Ask any Washington bureaucrat, "Why doesn't someone just make a decision?" and you'll hear something like: *No! No! No! In Washington, we take decisions very seriously. We've already invested ten-thousand on a university study, and just last week we submitted an RFP* (Request for Proposal) *to bring a high-priced consultant on board.*

At any rate, with someone's recommendation in hand, a committee of government functionaries settled the issue by suggesting that omitting a period after a middle initial would set a bad example for America's youth, thus a period was officially added to the president's signature.

Now, no one wants to be responsible for a decline in the moral fiber of America's youth, especially the president, so from that point on, Truman's signature took on a different look. The run-together *HarrySTruman* was discarded in favor of a distinct three-part signature, including a period, as in *Harry S. Truman.* The two versions different enough in appearance to have been penned by two different persons – or presidents.

Thus, not satisfied with the decision rendered in the 1940s, the author opened a copy of what many consider the best American English grammatical guide available today, *Words into Type* (Prentice-Hall).

Inside the guide, the section on "Punctuation" includes a sub-heading titled, "Period," which is further subdivided to include the sub-topic, "Abbreviations." There, in black-and-white it reads, "In some proper names, initials are used without periods."

That statement is followed by six representative examples of proper names with period-less initials, the fifth of which being, "Harry S Truman."

Eureka!

Finally!

Substantive authoritative resolution that there should be no period after the "S" in President Harry S Truman's full name.

Thus, as "Give 'em Hell Harry" might have said, referencing the famous sign that graced the top of his Oval Office desk, "The Buck Stops Here!"

As an aside to the story, except for a run of bad luck, Harry S Truman might never have become an American president at all.

Just prior to his military service, Harry and three friends leased 320 acres of land near Augusta, Kansas. With all geologic indicators pointing to the likely existence of oil underneath, Harry and his friends drilled one dry hole after another, right up to the time their money ran out, and then they sold the lease to another speculator.

In 1919, after a nine-year courtship, Harry married Bess Wallace, and with army buddy Eddie Jacobson, they bought a men's clothing store, or as they were called in those days, a haberdashery. When the haberdashery failed, Harry refused bankruptcy and spent several years paying off his share of the store's debt.

He then enrolled in law school, but couldn't manage the tuition and dropped out.

Next, with the backing of Eddie Jacobson's uncle, political boss Tom Pendergast, Harry was elected judge in Jackson County, Missouri.

Although Truman couldn't have known it at the time, he would become a U.S. Senator and Franklin D. Roosevelt's[1] running mate in the 1944 presidential campaign.

Roosevelt won a fourth term in 1944, but eighty-two days into the term, he collapsed while sitting for a portrait and died of a cerebral hemorrhage, and Harry S Truman became America's 33rd President.

Remember the 320 acres of supposedly oil-rich land once leased by Harry and his friends? The man to whom they sold their lease did find oil, a lot of it, and one of America's largest oil companies, Cities Service, was born, and later renamed Citco.

If Harry and his buddies could have hung in there a little longer, and drilled a little deeper, someone else would have been in line to take Franklin D. Roosevelt's place.

As it turned out, it was Vice-President Harry S Truman who became president, and the country would have to wait eight years, until 1953, to find out if the next president would be someone needing a period after their middle initial.

It just so happened that the next president, Dwight D. Eisenhower, did need a period following the initial of his middle name, the "D" being an abbreviation for his father whose given name was David.

Thus, in 1953, the world of civil-service secretaries and typists returned to normal, and balance was restored to the political universe.

[1] *Stories from History's Dust Bin* (additional reading):
    Vol 1, Feb 24:   Franklin D. Roosevelt with Battle of Los Angeles.
    Vol 3, Sep 28:   Franklin D. Roosevelt with Max Schmeling

If you want a friend in Washington, get a dog.
Harry S Truman (1884-1972) 33rd US President

Harriet Tubman

Born: Araminta Ross
A 19th Century Moses
c. 1820 (Dorchester County MD) – Mar 10, 1913 (Auburn NY)

T HERE SHOULD ONLY be a handful of Americans, high-school age or older, who haven't heard of Harriet Tubman. She is a special lady in American history and there's a possibility she will become better known to all Americans sometime in the future, but you'll need to read on to find out why.

Depending upon your understanding of American history, you already know, or will soon learn that this remarkable woman was instrumental during pre-Civil War days in leading an unknown number of enslaved people to freedom. And you might also know that she was involved with something called the Underground Railroad. Such responses would be worth at least a "C" on your report card.

Now, if you know that the Underground Railroad wasn't a railroad at all, but the familiar name of a broad network of secret routes, clandestine meeting places, and safe-houses supported by abolitionists, former slaves and others, black and white, who served as "conductors" from one secret location to the next, well, you're worth a solid "B."

But if you know that upwards of 100,000 people escaped slavery via the railroad during its twenty years of operation prior to the Civil War; and that Harriet Tubman, the best known of the railroad's conductors, made countless trips between her home in Maryland to Niagara Falls, Canada; and that her code name was "Moses," because like Moses of the Bible, Harriet delivered people to "the promised land," then you've earned an "A-plus."

And finally, if you know that this giant of a woman stood barely five-foot tall and suffered from seizures and narcoleptic[1] episodes, you can add "with honors," to your A-plus.

Harriet Tubman was born Araminta Ross, and grew up as "Minty," one of nine children born to slaves Harriet 'Rit' Green and Ben Ross.

The Ross family, however, was the property of plantation owner Mary Brodess and her son Edward. Rit and Ben Ross tried desperately to keep their family together and were devastated when Edward Brodess sold three of their daughters to another slaveowner.

Later, when Brodess tried to sell one of Rit and Ben's sons, Rit boldly confronted Brodess and the prospective buyer, telling them there would be no sale! Young Minty watched as Edward Brodess and the buyer stomped toward the slave quarters to seize the boy.

The fleet-footed Rit arrived first and stood unyielding in the doorway with an axe, "You want my son; but I tell you, the first man that comes into my house, I will split his head open." The sale didn't take place and young Minty, who had never attended a day of school in her life, had just received, in five minutes, the education of a lifetime in the power of resistance.

When Minty was six, she was put in charge of a newborn and told that each time the baby cried she would be "whupped." She was whupped five times before breakfast and carried the scars across her back for the rest of her life.

As she grew older she grew stronger, in part because of the work demanded of her. Although a diminutive girl, she did field work, split wood, plowed, and drove oxen. But, of all her personal traits, there was one that really stood out. She was stubborn! She would rather take a beating than give in.

Once, as a teenager, she encountered a slave owner who was having difficulty getting his slave to stand still so he could whip him. The slave owner demanded that Minty assist him, so he could administer the lashings. When she refused, the slave shook free and took off running. The slave owner was so furious with Minty's disobedience that he threw a rock at her, striking her in the head. From that injury, Minty suffered periodic seizures for the remainder of her life.

At the age of twenty-four, she married a free black man, John Tubman, and changed her name from Araminta to her mother's given name, Harriet, thus becoming Harriet Tubman.

But, being a slave, even though she was married to a free black man, meant that any children born into the union would belong not to her and her husband, but to her owner.

Her owner, the afore-mentioned Edward Brodess, tried a few times to sell the tiny woman, but because of her seizures and her well-established reputation as stone-solid stubborn, she was unmarketable and Brodess took his anger out on her family.

According to Sarah Hopkins Bradford, author of *Scenes in the Life of Harriet Tubman*, Tubman prayed, asking the Lord to make Brodess change his ways.

When it didn't happen, she prayed, "Oh Lord, if you ain't never going to change that man's heart, kill him, Lord, and take him out of the way." A week later Brodess died and Tubman, convinced she had contributed to his death through her prayer, often expressed regret for her words.

In 1849, Harriet ran away, making her way along the Underground Railroad from Maryland to Pennsylvania and freedom.

Later, Harriet would recall:

> *When I found I had crossed the line* (into Pennsylvania) *I looked at my hands to see if I was the same person. There was such a glory over everything; the sun came like gold through the trees, and over the fields, and I felt like I was in Heaven.*

With that awesome feeling of freedom always fresh in her heart, she began making regular Underground Railroad runs, each time guiding others safely to freedom.

She became so well known within the system that William Lloyd Garrison, editor of the abolitionist newspaper, *The Liberator*, gave Harriet the code name "Moses" since she, as Moses of old had done, was leading her people out of slavery and into freedom. She was also known by others of the Railroad as "General" Tubman.

In the 1890s, and still suffering from periodic seizures, she underwent brain surgery at Boston's Massachusetts General Hospital. Without anesthesia, she bit down on a bullet while a doctor opened her skull, and the strong-willed lady survived the operation.

On March 10, 1913, frail and ill with pneumonia, she told friends surrounding her bed, "I go to prepare a place for you," and soon afterward, her spirit departed her body. She was an estimated 93 years old.

As mentioned up front, you will now learn why Harriet Tubman may become better known to all Americans sometime in the future.

It's because there is currently (2018) a plan being floated in Washington to place Harriet Tubman's portrait on one of America's paper currencies, perhaps the $10 or $20-dollar bill, or a bill of a different denomination, or a newly released $2 bill, or perhaps upon a coin.

The idea for replacing one of America's current historical figures with a portrait of Harriet Tubman was initiated by President Barack Obama at the end of his term in 2016. The proposal has received some support in Washington and is currently under consideration.

Harriet Tubman was the first African-American woman to be honored on a United States stamp, and was the first honoree in the Black Heritage series in 1978.

All of this is a reminder that Harriet Tubman was a truly remarkable lady!

---

[1] narcolepsy: a rare condition characterized by sudden and uncontrollable episodes of deep sleep.

I was the conductor of the Underground Railroad for eight years,
and I can say what most conductors can't say;
I never ran my train off the track and I never lost a passenger.
Harriet Tubman (c. 1820-1913) Humanitarian

Bob Uecker

Born: Robert George Uecker
Mr. Baseball
Jan 26, 1934 (Milwaukee WI) –

B OB UECKER IS A one-of-a-kind baseball guy. You know, someone who comes on the scene once in a blue moon to add something to the sport that makes it more exciting, safer to play, or just more interesting. It's to the latter category that Bob Uecker has been contributing to the sport of baseball for over forty years.

There are the superstars who have contributed to America's love affair with baseball, players whose surnames are household words whether you follow the sport or not: Aaron, Bonds, Cobb, DiMaggio, Gehrig, Mantle, Mays, Paige, Robinson, and Ruth, to name a few.

And there are those who are better known to baseball fanatics and trivia players than to the casual fan.

Take for instance, club owner Bill Veeck, Jr.[1] who drilled shallow holes in his wooden leg, so he was never without an ashtray; Moe Berg[2] who used baseball as a cover to gather pre-World War II intelligence; Pete Gray,[3] baseball's only one-armed major leaguer; Frederick Koenig who pitched over 3,000 games with never a windup; and Ray Chapman,[4] whose death from a pitched ball inspired the "Chapman Rule" that requires umpires to frequently replace balls as they become dirty or scuffed.

And there are those who played the game, and when their on-the-field careers were over, became even more famous as sports announcers, such as Dizzy Dean[5] and Bob Uecker.

Dean's playing days were numbered when he was struck in the head by a ball that rendered him unconscious. Hospitalized as a precaution, St. Louis' fans smiled, and then heaved a collective sigh of relief when a newspaper headline the next day revealed: *X-ray of Dean's Head Shows Nothing.*

That's when the popular and colorful Dean went from pitching balls and strikes to calling them from an announcer's both.

And he was good!

Then, there is pitcher-turned-catcher Bob Uecker, who once hit a home run off a very good pitcher.[6] That's about it.

Although Uecker might make a point of reminding you that he lasted in the majors six years longer than some of the less talented guys.

Then came Uecker's big break! It was 1975, just four years after his retirement. That's when he was offered a job on Milwaukee radio, calling the games for his hometown Brewers.

Uecker, of whom Johnny Carson facetiously referred to on the air as *Mr. Baseball,* has been baseball's clown prince ever since taking that radio job, and what a broadcasting career.

Today, forty-three years later (1975-2018), Uecker is still going strong, combining a serious player's knowledge of the game with his own quirky brand of self-deprecating humor.

In fact, his on-air calling of Brave's games has generated a broad base of fans from well beyond Milwaukee. This includes a sizeable following from fans of other teams, who tune him in just for the fun of listening to his colorful play-by-play, and endless rattling of stories that cover the gamut from serious baseball insights to comments that are obviously tongue-in-cheek.

So, what is it about Uecker that makes him unique?

His career batting average of .200 (one hit for each five times at bat) is below par, and his 14 home runs spread over six seasons (Barry Bonds hit 73 home runs in one season) is bland and uninspiring.

But as Uecker might explain, it's all in interpretation.

He might point out that in 1967, and despite playing in only 59 of 162 games, he led the league in "passed balls."

Now, if you're not a student of baseball, you might think that leading the league in anything is a good thing. But what it means here is that of the number of pitches that Uecker was expected to catch, he allowed more balls to get past his catching glove than anyone else in the major leagues.

Yes, Bob Uecker's astonishing league-leading record for passed balls has stood the test of time. In the past 51 seasons (1967-2018), the record has never been seriously challenged, and may never be broken.

Each year the Baseball Hall of Fame hosts the Ford C. Frick Award, given annually to a broadcaster for major contributions to baseball.

On July 27, 2003, Bob Uecker won that award. Here is an excerpt from his acceptance speech, and some insight into the quirky mind of Mr. Baseball, Bob Uecker:

> *"My first sport was eighth-grade basketball. And my dad didn't want to buy me the* (athletic) *supporter, you know, to do the job. So, my mother made me one out of a flour sack. And the tough thing about that is ...."*

[At this point, Uecker appears to be side-tracked, rattling on about something else, until he says . . .]

> *"You know, everybody remembers their first game in the major leagues. For me it was in Milwaukee. My hometown, born and raised there, and I can remember walking out on the field and Birdie Tebbetts was our manager at that time. And my family was there: my mother and dad, and all of my relatives.*
>
> *And as I'm standing on the field, everybody's pointing at me and waving and laughing, and I'm pointing back. And Birdie Tebbetts came up and asked me if I was nervous or uptight about the game. And I said, 'I'm not. I've been waiting five years to get here. I'm ready to go'"*
>
> *"He said, 'Well, we're gonna start you today. I didn't want to tell you earlier. I didn't want you to get too fired up.'"*
>
> *"I said, 'Look, I'm ready to go.'"*
>
> *"He said, 'Well, great, you're in there. And oh, by the way, the rest of us up here wear that supporter on the inside.'"*

And another story.

In Milwaukee's Miller Park where the Braves play, are a group of seats officially known as the Uecker Seats, the least expensive seats in the stadium, available at only a dollar each.

But even Bob Uecker would tell you, "you get what you pay for." The seats are on the fourth deck behind home plate, with many of the seats behind the massive beams that support the ballpark's retractable dome roof where it's almost impossible to see the entire playing field.

And yet another story.

Uecker tells about his first pitching opportunity in the majors, when his family and friends came to watch him play.

> *The manager came out to the mound to take me out of the game. I didn't want to be relieved because I was embarrassed. I said, 'Let me face this guy one more time because I struck him out the first time I faced him.'*
>
> *He said, 'I know, but it's still the same inning, and I've got to get you out of there.*

And finally, when asked how he knew his baseball career was over, he said, "It was when my baseball card came out with no picture."

Stories from History's Dust Bin (additional reading):
[1] Vol 1, Feb 9:   Featuring Bill Veeck, Jr.
[2] Vol 1, Mar 2:   Featuring Moe Berg
[3] Vol 1, Mar 6:   Featuring Pete Gray
[4] Vol 2, Aug 17:   Featuring Ray Chapman
[5] Vol 2, Jul 17:   Featuring Dizzy Dean

[6] That "very good pitcher," was pitcher Sandy Koufax who, at the age of 36, became the youngest player ever elected to the *Baseball Hall of Fame*. After Uecker's home run off Koufax, he said he expected that homer would probably keep Koufax from being elected into the Hall of Fame.

I spent three of the best years of my life in the 10th grade.
Bob Uecker (1934 -) Athlete, sportscaster

Jimmy Van Heusen

Born: Edward Chester Babcock
Would you like to swing on a star?
Jan 26, 1913 (Syracuse NY) - Feb 6, 1990 (Rancho Mirage CA)

T HERE'S SOMETHING ABOUT Jimmy Van Heusen's past that few people know about, and it's not how he re-packaged himself from Edward Chester Babcock, the name he was born with, to Jimmy Van Heusen. It's something he did that few of us would associate with the light-hearted composer of over 800 songs, although one of his songs, the one he wrote especially for Frank Sinatra[1] titled, *Come Fly with Me,* is a very good clue. But first, how did Chester Babcock become Jimmy Van Heusen, the guy who wrote over 800 songs?

Here's the story.

Chester "Chet" Babcock didn't feel his birth name conveyed the star quality he wanted for his disk jockey show.

As he and a friend were driving around, bouncing a bunch of fancy-sounding names off each other, they saw a billboard ad for Van Heusen shirts. Babcock liked the name. He pronounced it several times, each time altering his voice inflections as he sometimes did during his radio broadcasts: "Van Heusen." "Van Heusen?" "Van Heusen!*"*

The name had a first-class, upscale sound, and Chet and his friend both agreed it had star-quality written all over it.

And the "Jimmy?" Well, as Chet tells it, he just liked the way "Jimmy" rolled off the tongue with Van Heusen. "Jimmy Van Heusen." "Jimmy Van Heusen?" "Jimmy Van Heusen!"

Exit now, Chet Babcock <*sound of an opening and closing door*> and welcome to the world of non-stop music and light-hearted talk, your host <*drum roll*> Jimmy Van Heusen.

Hello out there! This is Jimmy Van Heusen mike-side, spinning all of your favorites for your listening pleasure, and now, for you and your lady's star-lit evening on the town – the swinging sound ... of Les Brown ... and his Band of Renown.

That's how it all started for Chet Babcock, who became
Jimmy Van Heusen, who went from spinning records on the
radio to becoming one of America's most prolific songwriters.

Every composer and songwriter would love to have one song
nominated by the Academy for Best Original Song. Jimmy Van
Heusen had sixteen nominated, with four winning the Oscar!

Here are the titles, the year they won, and if you're over
sixty, a few phrases from each to help you liberate some of those
wonderful pent-up memories.

Swinging On A Star (1944)
Would you like to swing on a star;
Carry moonbeams home in a jar;
And be better off than you are;
Or would you rather be a mule.
A mule is an animal with long funny ears . . .

All the Way (1957)
When somebody loves you;
It's no good unless he loves you – all the way;
Happy to be near you;
When you need someone to cheer you
All the way . . .

High Hopes (1959)
Just what makes that little old ant;
Think he'll move that rubber tree plant;
Everyone knows an ant, can't –
Move a rubber tree plant;
But, he's got .. high hopes, he's got .. high hopes,
He's got high .. apple pie .. in the sky .. hopes . . .

Call Me Irresponsible (1963)
Call me ... irresponsible.
Yes, I'm ... unreliable.
But it's ... undeniably true ...
That I'm ... irresponsibly mad for you . . .

And, as if he needed to prove himself in more than one entertainment venue, in 1955 he also took home an Emmy (television's counterpart to the Oscar) for the song *Love and Marriage*.

So, you've heard the songs, at least a few of them, but you've never heard of Jimmy Van Heusen?

Well, a lot of people love a lot of songs and can identify the band, group, or the vocalist in a heartbeat, but couldn't come up with the name of the composer if their life depended on it.

Take for instance, that Emmy-winning song, *Love and Marriage*. Adjust your crooning voice to your best Frank Sinatra impersonation, and sing along:

> *Love and marriage ...*
> *Love and marriage ...*
> *They go together like a horse and carriage ...*
> *This! I tell you brother!*
> *You can't have one without the other.*

That's a Jimmy Van Heusen song, and you sang it like you've been practicing all day.

Maybe it's because it was the theme song for the long running (1987-97) sitcom, "Married . . . with Children."

As mentioned up front, the light-hearted song-master Jimmy Van Heusen has composed over 800 songs, 50 of which are already considered classics and standards.

His songs have been featured in over 200 movies.

He also wrote the scores for five Broadway musicals, including *Thoroughly Modern Millie*, and he was inducted into the Songwriters Hall of Fame in 1971.

Remember in the first paragraph, mention was made about something in Jimmy Van Heusen's past that might seem out-of-character for a guy who could turn out award-winning song after award-winning song?

Would you have guessed that the same guy who wrote *Come Fly with Me, A Pocketful of Miracles,* and *Thoroughly Modern Millie* also served his country during World War II as a test pilot?

That's right!

Chester "Chet" Babcock was a World War II test pilot for Lockheed Aviation.

He was a nerves-of-steel patriot, a man who was as much at home in the cockpit of an experimental aircraft as he was on the cushioned seat of a piano, composing many of America's most enduring songs and lyrics.

Jimmy Van Heusen died February 6, 1990 at the age of 77.

He is buried near his friend, Frank Sinatra, at Desert Memorial Park in Cathedral City, California.

His grave marker notes his name, and then reads, *Swinging on a Star.*

[1] *Stories from History's Dust Bin* (additional reading):
    Vol 1, Feb 29:   Frank Sinatra with Dinah Shore

After silence, that which comes nearest
to expressing the inexpressible is music.
Aldous Huxley (1894-1963) Writer, philosopher

Cornelius Vanderbilt

Born: Cornelius Vanderbilt
The Commodore
May 27, 1794 (Staten Island NY) – Jan 4, 1877 (New York NY)

A MERE EIGHT YEARS (1873) after the Civil War, *Union* supporter Cornelius Vanderbilt bought a piece of land in the former *Confederate* state of Tennessee for the construction and endowment of a university that would bear his name.

By the time you've finished this historical vignette, you'll know why he built and endowed that university, and the reason speaks volumes about his values, his patriotism, and his love of country.

The Vanderbilt name represents one of America's oldest families. Cornelius Vanderbilt's great-great-grandfather, Jan Aertson, emigrated from the small village of De Bilt in the Netherlands to New York as an indentured servant in 1650. That's a mere 30 years after the pilgrims landed at Plymouth Rock; and a full 126 years before George Washington's army defeated the British to win America's independence in 1776.

Great-great-grandfather Aertson eventually cleared his debt, but at a rate that would be considered criminal today. It's not known for how many years he was a slave to the man who held his Contract of Indenture, but once his years of servitude were over, the Aertson's put down roots in the virgin soil of a sparsely populated piece of land called Staten Island.

Sometime during the 144 years between 1650 and 1794, the old-country name of Aertson gave way to a surname based on the family's village of origin, "De Bilt." But, to be useful as a surname, De Bilt needed to be preceded by the prefix, "van der," which means, "of the." Thus, the father of the subject of this story was known in his community as Cornelius van der De Bilt, that is, Cornelius of the village of De Bilt.

On May 27, 1794, Cornelius's wife, Phebe, gave birth to a son whom they honored by naming him after his father, thus you are introduced to the subject of this story.

Then, during the lifetime of the elder Cornelius, or soon after the birth of their son Cornelius, the van der De Bilt surname was further anglicized[1] to the now familiar Vanderbilt.

But back then, the Vanderbilt name meant nothing as far as prestige and fame were concerned. The family's beginnings were no different than hundreds of other struggling immigrant families.

The elder Cornelius supported his family by farming and when he wasn't growing produce, he was busy hauling it by boat across the bay that separated Staten Island from Manhattan Island.

As a lad, the younger Cornelius worked alongside his father, quitting school at the age of eleven to devote full time to helping provide for the family.

By fifteen, young Cornelius had become an accomplished navigator of his father's *pirogue*, a small two-mast draft boat suitable for ferrying produce.

Imagine for a moment that it's 1809 and you're fifteen-year-old Cornelius, and your father is telling you what your 'tomorrow' is going to be like. "Son, be at the wharf by morning light, load the pirogue with all of the produce you can carry, take the load across the upper bay, unload and sell the produce, and you better be home before dark if you know what's good for you!"

After working hard for his father for five years, Cornelius borrowed a hundred dollars, enough to buy his own pirogue. Thus, sixteen-year-old Cornelius Vanderbilt started his first business, hauling carrots, cabbages, and corn across Upper New York Bay.

By living and spending frugally, he eventually owned a fleet of pirogues and various other small boats. But he didn't only own boats, he learned how to manage money wisely, and by working twice as hard as his competitors, he acquired more money to invest in more things.

Cornelius wasn't your average young man. He was a young man driven by purpose. Because of his boundless energy and the eagerness with which he vied for business, often challenging the status quo, he sometimes forced others out of business by simply outperforming them.

Over time, because of his dynamic personality, leadership, and remarkable business acumen, along with his ever-expanding fleet of multi-purpose boats and small ships, he came to be known as the "Commodore," a nickname that remained with him for the rest of his life.

He would go on to become the wealthiest man in America, expanding his holdings and his interests from pirogues, to steamships, to railroads, to shipping and various businesses, and Cornelius Vanderbilt was an unabashed patriot.

If you're interested in knowing more about Cornelius Vanderbilt, the businessman who gave away more money for philanthropic purposes than some countries were worth, there are numerous resources for that purpose. But we'll end here with a single story that illustrates the love he had for his country.

At the beginning of the Civil War, Commodore Vanderbilt offered his largest steamship, the *Vanderbilt* (built at a cost of $1-million in 1850s dollars) to the Union Navy to use as they saw fit.

The gift was refused, in part, because the Union's War Department didn't have the funds to outfit the ship for war and even if it did, it didn't have the money to operate the ship afterward.

When the powerful Confederate ironclad, the *Merrimack*, began blasting holes in the Union blockade at Hampton Roads, Virginia, something needed to be done, and fast. That's when President Lincoln[2] and Secretary of War Edwin Stanton knocked on the Commodore's door.

As soon as the men were seated, President Lincoln began a lengthy prepared introduction to the purpose of the visit, but he didn't get far.

That's because the Commodore not only raised his hand and interrupted the president and then donated the use of the *Vanderbilt* to the Union cause, but he went one better!

At his expense, he outfitted the ship with a battering ram off the bow, selected the officers, paid the salaries for the officers and crew, and furnished the fuel to power the ship.

After the *Vanderbilt* helped to defeat the *Merrimack* at Hampton Roads, the Commodore paid to have the ship converted to a cruiser for hunting down the Confederate raider-ship, the *Alabama.*

Now, it's time to answer the question posed up front. Why Union supporter Cornelius Vanderbilt built a university bearing his name in a former Confederate state.

Before his death in 1877, Vanderbilt authorized a $1-million-dollar endowment fund to establish a university in the former Confederate state of Tennessee, in hopes that doing so would help to heal the sectional wounds inflicted by the Civil War.

The Commodore was a true American patriot, one who saw through the fog of political differences, and then took action to do his part in helping to reunite the country.

Since the founding of Vanderbilt University in 1873, the students have honored their benefactor by calling themselves the *Vanderbilt Commodores.*

---

[1] To Anglicize means to adapt a foreign word, or phrase, to English usage, e.g. to anglicize *Juan* to *John.*

[2] *Stories from History's Dust Bin* (additional reading):

Vol 1, Feb 12:	Featuring Abraham Lincoln
Vol 2, Jun 7:	Abraham Lincoln with Edwin Thomas Booth
Vol 2, Jul 20:	Abraham Lincoln with Laura Keene
Vol 3, Dec 14	Abraham Lincoln with Joseph Lane

I have always served the public to the best of my ability. Why?
Because, like every other man, it is to my best interest to do so.
Cornelius Vanderbilt (1794-1877) Businessman, philanthropist

Jules Verne

Born: Jules Gabriel Verne
The Father of Science Fiction.
Feb 8, 1828 (Nantes, France) – Mar 24, 1905 (Amiens, France)

A LTHOUGH LIKELY MORE fiction than fact, the story is told that at the age of eleven, Jules Verne secretly hired on as a cabin boy for a trip to the West Indies. Before sailing from France, the ship had to make one last stop to take on supplies and passengers at a place called Paimbœuf.

As the vessel slowed to a stop, there on the dock stood Pierre Verne, Jules' father, who not only put an end to his son's youthful escapade, but made the boy promise to hereafter "travel only in his imagination."

Whether true or not, young Jules did one better. He became the author that illuminated the traveling imaginations of millions with his uncanny knack for futuristic thinking.

Pierre Verne was a successful attorney and in 1847, hoping his son would follow in his footsteps and someday take over his law practice, he sent Jules to law school in Paris. Jules passed his first-year law exams, returned home, fell in love with Rose Herminie Grossetiére and quickly turned out thirty poems in her honor.

Rose's parents, unsure that an unproven attorney who wrote poetry would ever amount to much, saw to it that Rose married well, but not to Jules!

Jules, devastated, would later become an author whose books include a significant number of women who were forced to marry against their will.

Jules returned to law school where he did well but found himself more and more drawn to the world of literature.

An uncle in Paris, Francisque de Chatêaubourg, introduced him to the city's literary salons, gatherings of intellectuals in science, literature, and other disciplines, and Jules found just the environment he had been looking for.

To please his father, he passed the bar in 1851, but he knew his interest lay not in writing briefs regarding legal matters, but in writing books that provided brief glimpses into the future.

When it became evident that Jules wasn't going to open a law office, his disappointed father cut off his allowance.

In the literary salons, he met Alexandre Dumas, author of *The Three Musketeers,* and he went to work as a secretary at Dumas's Lyric Theater. There, he wrote over twenty plays, of which two were produced at the Lyric.

But neither turned a profit nor sparked much interest in French literary circles.

In 1856, he fell in love with Honorine de Viane Morel, a widow. But, barely earning enough to support himself, let alone a wife, it was Honorine's brother who came to the rescue with a job for Jules at a stock exchange, and the couple exchanged vows on January 10, 1857.

Jules started each day arising very early and spending four or five hours writing before downing a quick breakfast and heading for the exchange. It was a grueling schedule, but in 1863 an old friend and fellow author, Alfred de Brehat, introduced him to his publisher, Pierre-Jules Hetzel. Hetzel liked Verne's manuscript, *Five Weeks in a Balloon,* and agreed to publish it.

It wasn't a best seller, but it was good enough for Hetzel to contract with Verne for two stories a year and in 1871, he published Verne's *20,000 Leagues Under the Sea,* a story that indeed, captured the imagination of its readers.

Thus, as someone might point out, at the age of forty-three and after twenty-three years of spending untold hours of grinding out one disappointing manuscript after another, Jules Verne had finally become an overnight success.

It's reported that after the publication of *20,000 Leagues Under the Sea,* Jules stood on the steps of the stock exchange where he worked and announced to his co-workers:

My boys, I believe I'm about to desert you. I had the kind of idea Émile Girardin[1] says every man must have to make a fortune. I've just written a new kind of novel, and if it succeeds, it will be an unexplored gold mine.

*In that case I'll write more such books while you're
buying your stock. And I think I'll earn the most money!
Laugh, friends and we'll see who laughs longest.*

The above account provides an excellent way to close the
book about a man who tried to please his father, but couldn't;
and then worked tirelessly to please himself, and did. And in
the process, took his readers on one heck of a literary ride into
the future.

Here are some unusual parallels, a century apart, that should
give you a sense of just how in-tune Verne was in imagining
what the future might be like.

Verne wrote *From the Earth to the Moon* in 1865.

It tells the story of three people, a gun club president named
Impey Barbicane; a man from Philadelphia named Captain
Nicholl; and a French poet named Michel Ardan who travel to
the moon and back in the year 1869.

According to the story, the three men were launched in a
bullet-shaped projectile named *Columbiad* from an enormous
cannon constructed at a place called Stone's Hill, Florida, and
upon their successful return, they splash down in the ocean.

Exactly 100 years later, in 1969, three men named Neil
Armstrong, Buzz Aldrin, and Michael Collins were launched in
a space capsule named *Columbia* from a place called Cape
Canaveral, Florida, and upon their successful return, they too
splashed down in the ocean.

And here's a nice touch with which to conclude our story.

On the return trip of the *Columbia*, astronaut Neil Armstrong
made mention of the flight that preceded theirs, by saying to
Mission Control, "A hundred years ago, Jules Verne wrote a
book about a trip from the . . .."

In 1961, a large impact crater on the far side of the Moon
was named *Jules Verne Crater* in honor of the Earth's earliest
science-fiction writer.

The name of the crater is quite unusual in that it is one of the
few lunar craters given the honoree's full name, rather than the
surname only.

Forty-seven years later (2008), the European Space Agency launched a spacecraft named the *Jules Verne ATV* on a mission to deliver supplies to the International Space Station. In addition to its cargo of Space Station supplies, it carried two handwritten manuscript pages from Verne's personal files and two early editions of Jules Verne's moon-based science-fiction, *From the Earth to the Moon* and *Around the Moon,* both published during Verne's lifetime (1865 and 1870 respectively). Verne died at the age of seventy-seven on March 24, 1905. He is buried at La Madeleine Cemetery in Amiens, France.

[1] Émile Girardin (1806-1881) was an innovative French journalist, known as the Napoleon of the press.

With happiness, as with health; to enjoy it,
one should be deprived of it occasionally.
Jules Verne (1828-1905) Novelist, playwright

Vlad III, Prince of Wallachia

Born: Vlad III (the son of Vlad II)
Bram Stoker's inspiration for Dracula
Nov 1431 (Wallachia) – Dec 19, 1476 (Wallachia)

W HEN VLAD III, the Prince of Wallachia, decided to cleanse his kingdom of unwanted subjects, the destitute, dissidents, and those beyond the age of productivity, he invited them to join him for a great banquet in the city of Târgovişte, Wallachia.[1] There, sparing no expense, he hosted a lavish banquet and afterwards asked those present if they would like to never experience the hopelessness of hunger again.

Their response was an enthusiastic, "Yes!"

Moments later, those same smiling and enthusiastic citizens felt their hearts sink in horror as they heard Vlad order his men to secure the exits and allow no one to leave. The scene that followed can only be imagined as the structure was set ablaze.

There were no survivors.

Stories of Vlad's cruelty have survived the ages, telling of his having impaled hundreds of his own citizens along the road to his kingdom as a way of discouraging criminals and foreign travelers from passing through his land.

There is available on the internet a centuries-old woodcut of Vlad sitting alone at a lavishly-spread outdoor table, enjoying dinner and wine amidst a backdrop of anguished impaled souls. It was Vlad's penchant for watching the living die in this horrible, unspeakable manner, that gave rise to his shiver-inducing nickname, *Vlad the Impaler*.

In 1459, Pope Pius II initiated a crusade against the Ottoman (Turkish) Empire, which claimed Wallachia as part of its territorial holdings. The Sultan Mehmed II sent an envoy to Vlad to demand from him tribute, a tax for protection, not unlike the "protection money" collected by the mafia bosses of 1920's and '30s America.

The Sultan not only wanted the demanded tribute, but he also expected Vlad to provide his envoy with a fresh army of 500 young men.

Vlad, as you may suppose, was neither impressed with the Sultan's request for tribute, nor his need of soldiers. He arose, smiled broadly at the Sultan's representative, and then expressed disappointment that the entire delegation seated before him had failed to remove their turbans in his, Vlad's, royal presence.

The representative explained that Turkish tradition requires the turban be worn always. It would be an unforgivable insult, the representative explained, for a Turkish man to remove his turban in the company of a man as great as Vlad III, the noble Prince of Wallachia.

Vlad smiled and nodded approvingly.

He commended the Turkish men for their devotion to their culture, and then he gave the order for his men to surround the delegation. He told the nervous visitors that he was sympathetic to their beliefs, and that from this day forward their turbans would forever remain on their heads. He then directed his men to nail each Turk's turban firmly to his skull.

As you might imagine, news of Vlad's treatment of the delegation was not appreciated by Mehmet II, who then successfully forced Vlad into exile in Hungary in 1462.

During Vlad's exile, his brother Radu converted to Islam, and with help from Vlad's nemesis, Mehmet II, he became the ruler of Wallachia.

When Radu died in 1475, Vlad III either escaped or was freed from his Hungarian prison and once again became the ruler of Wallachia. But his second rise to power was doomed from the start.

There was no way that Sultan Mehmet II was going to allow the man who had ordered the nailing of his envoy's turbans to their heads to rule Wallachia. In less than a year, Vlad III was dead, killed by Mehmet II's soldiers in an ambush.

Although Vlad III enjoyed a dozen ways to impose painful deaths upon his victims, from boiling to disembowelment to driving nails into the heads of his victims, his favorite method remained impalement.

In closing, here is a genealogical note about Vlad III, and why it is believed he may have served as the model for Bram Stoker's[2] literary character known as Dracula.

When Vlad the Impaler was born in 1431, King Sigismund, Emperor of the Holy Roman Empire, knighted his father, Vlad II, and conferred upon him membership in the "Order of the Dragon." In accordance with custom, knighting brought with it a new surname, "Dracul," meaning "Dragon" in the ancient Wallachian language.

As Vlad II's son was passing through adolescence, in addition to being known as "Vlad III, the son of Vlad II," he was also known as "Drăculea," a diminutive form of "Dracul" meaning, "the son of Dracul." Then, as Vlad III grew into manhood, the diminutive form, Drăculea, gave way to its adult form, Drăculeşti.

The Irish author, Bram Stoker, who spent a considerable amount of time in studying European folklore and mythological stories about vampires, likely used the story of Vlad III Drăculeşti as the inspiration for the main character in his 1897 Gothic novel, *Dracula*.

But as you can see from the above, the real Dracula was far worse, far more inhumane, than the Dracula from Bram Stoker's fertile mind.

[1] Trivia: During the 1400s, the era of Vlad III, Wallachia was one of three neighboring principalities, the others being Moldavia and Transylvania. In 1859, Wallachia joined with Moldavia to form the state of Romania. Following World War I, Transylvania joined Romania, reunifying the three former principalities.

[2] *Stories from History's Dust Bin* (additional reading):
Vol 1, Apr 15:   Bram Stoker with Edward Gorey
Vol 2, Aug 7:   Bram Stoker with Elizabeth Bathory

No man knows till he has suffered from the night
how sweet and dear to his heart and eye the morning to be.
Bram Stoker (1847-1912) Author

Lew Wallace

Born: Lewis Wallace
Military officer; prolific author
Apr 10, 1827 (Brookville IN) – Feb 15, 1905 (Crawfordsville IN)

L EW WALLACE, BORN in Brookville, Indiana in 1827, was one of the Union army's youngest and brightest generals. He led troops during the Civil War battles of Shiloh, Fort Donelson, and Monocacy Junction.

At Monocacy Junction his command of 5,800 men successfully delayed Confederate General Jubal A. Early's advance toward Washington.

Those were the kinds of things that General Wallace would prefer to be remembered for, his skill as a military commander, rather than for being an author.[1]

Although Wallace wrote many books, there is only one title remembered today, and he wrote that one in his spare time.

A multi-faceted man, Wallace was more than a military man and an author, he was also a lawyer. Admitted to the Indiana bar in 1849, he served as the prosecuting attorney for the state's First Congressional District. And you can add successful politician to the list as he was elected to the Indiana State Senate in 1856.

Following the assassination of President Lincoln[2] on April 15, 1865, Wallace served as a military judge in the trials of the Lincoln conspirators. He also served in the same capacity in the trial of Andersonville Commander Heinrich "Henry" Wirz.

And yet, about the only thing people remember about Lew Wallace today, was the book he wrote in his spare time.

Wallace also served his country for four years as the U.S. Ambassador to the Ottoman (Turkish) Empire.

And, during a time of conflict in the New Mexico Territory, a dust-up known as the Lincoln County War, he was sent to Santa Fe to serve as the Territorial Governor.

In fact, although he had begun work on his famous book years before and elsewhere, it was while serving as governor of the New Mexico Territory that he finished it. He did so during the infrequent lulls that occurred while conducting territorial business, which on at least one occasion, included sitting down with the well-known outlaw, Billy "the Kid" Bonney.[3]

The "sit down" with the Kid involved a possible pardon if he agreed to testify before a grand jury about a killing he had witnessed. Although Billy kept his word, the "exemption from prosecution" never happened, but that's a story for another day.[4]

So, what's the name of the famous book that Lew Wallace finished while sitting in the governor's chair in Santa Fe?

You've surely heard of the book, you may have even read it, and it's likely that at some time in your life, you saw the movie.

The full title of the book is *Ben-Hur: A Tale of the Christ*, first published on November 12, 1880.

The state of Indiana, like every state, is allowed two statues in Washington's Statuary Hall. Lew Wallace is one of Indiana's two offerings, making him one of many military figures to grace Statuary Hall, but the only novelist so honored.

And what about Wallace's story, *Ben-Hur?*

Ben-Hur became the best-selling American novel of the 19th century, surpassing Harriet Beecher Stowe's *Uncle Tom's Cabin*. It remained the nation's top selling novel for over fifty years, until the publication of Margaret Mitchell's[5] *Gone with the Wind* in 1936.

In addition:

Ben-Hur debuted as a lengthy, 3½-hour stage production at the Broadway Theater in New York on November 29, 1899 starring Edward J. Morgan (1st season – 194 performances) and western movie star William S. Hart (2nd season).

Ben-Hur was produced in 1907 as a silent, one-reel, movie, again starring William S. Hart.

The *Ben Hur* six-cylinder touring car was built by the Ben-Hur Motor Company in 1916.

Ben-Hur was produced as a silent movie for a second time in 1925 starring Ramon Novarro.

The *Ben Hur* trailer was a 1-ton military cargo and water carrier produced during World War II for the military.

Ben-Hur was produced by Metro Goldwyn Mayer in 1959, starring Charlton Heston as Judah Ben-Hur and won eleven Academy Awards.

Ben-Hur was produced as a television miniseries in 2010.

Ben-Hur is considered the most influential Christian novel of the 19th century.

The novel, *Ben-Hur* has never been out of print and has been translated into twenty foreign languages.

Ben-Hur wasn't the only book Wallace wrote, but it was the only one that caught the imagination of a nation.

And if the above is not enough, there are towns named Ben Hur in Arkansas, California, Texas, and Virginia.

Not a bad legacy for a military general who used his spare time to do what?

To write a novel that captured the imagination a nation for over half a century.

And, oh yes, he was an outstanding general as well.

[1] Wallace wrote many novels and biographies, including a narrative poem, *The Wooing of Malkatoon: Commodus* (1898). In addition to his most famous novel, *Ben-Hur: A Tale of the Christ* (1880), he was the author of *The Fair God, or the Last of the Tzins: A Tale of the Conquest of Mexico* (1873); *Battles and Leaders of the Civil War* (1887); *The Boyhood of Christ* (1888); and *The Prince of India* (1893.

Stories from History's Dust Bin (additional reading):
[2] Vol 1, Feb 12:   Featuring Abraham Lincoln
[3] Vol 3, Nov 7:   Featuring William "Billy the Kid" Bonney
[5] Vol 2, Aug 16:   Featuring Margaret Mitchell

[4] In a letter dated March 15, 1879, Governor Wallace promised to exempt Bonney "from prosecution" if he would testify in the matter of a murder he had witnessed. However, post-testimony arrangements could not be settled. The exchange of letters is available on the internet.

My greatest personal satisfaction was due to discovery
of the fact that in the confusion and feverish excitement
of real battle, I could think.
Lew Wallace (1827-1905) General, author

Gertrude Chandler Warner

Born: Gertrude Chandler Warner
The lady behind the Boxcar Children.
Apr 16, 1890 (Putnam CT) – Aug 30, 1979 (Putnam CT)

*O*N A WARM NIGHT *four children stood in front of a bakery. No one knew them. No one knew where they had come from.*

Thus, begins the first of Gertrude Chandler Warner's classic stories about the adventures of four homeless children and a dog who lived by themselves inside a deserted railway boxcar.

If those first three sentences didn't tug at your heartstrings, know that the original story, and the numerous stories that followed, have tugged at the pure feelings of countless children. Stories that have fired their imaginations, built their confidence, and, oh yes, helped to improve their reading skills for numerous decades now.

In fact, if you've ever read any of the boxcar books, you might even recall the names of the four siblings who lived in the boxcar – along with the unusual name of their pet dog, and if your memory isn't what it used to be, you'll meet them all again in just a few paragraphs.

In 1918, with World War I in full swing and no qualified teachers remaining in her small New England hometown, twenty-eight-year old Gertrude Warner, with a tenth-grade education, was approached by the local Board of Education to serve her community as a teacher.

Here is how she described that request many years later:

I was asked or begged to take this job because I taught Sunday School. But believe me, day school is nothing like Sunday School, and I sure learned by doing! I taught in that same classroom for thirty-two years, retiring at sixty to have more time to write.

Teaching was fine, and she enjoyed it. It was also a good way to put food on the table, but she could never remember a time when she didn't want to become an author. Even as a child she wrote stories for her grandfather, presenting him with a different original story every Christmas.

Then came the day that changed the world!

Okay, so it didn't change everyone's world, but it sure changed Gertrude's world, and the world for millions of children who would come to know those four homeless ragamuffins, Henry, Jessie, Violet, and five-year-old Benny[1] Alden, and their faithful dog.

Gertrude had been too sick to go to work that day, and fearing her illness might be contagious, she reluctantly stayed home. Staying home when she should be in her classroom wasn't easy for the dependable New Englander, but the illness and recovery at home allowed her to drift into the netherworld of her youth.

She thought about the days when she would stand in her backyard and watch the trains clatter down the tracks. And she remembered once stealthily peeking inside a caboose where she saw a small stove with a tin coffee pot, its dented spout facing the window into which she was peering. There was also a little table upon which rested several cracked and hopelessly stained cups.

That's when she began to imagine what it would be like to be a child with no home, only a deserted boxcar with its little table, stove and its cracked and stained cups, and a great big and often confusing adult world outside.

She began to write about the adventures of four children, orphaned by the death of their parents and wary of a wealthy, but worrisome grandfather. They were children who stayed together because they belonged together. They would collect dishes and other needed items from a nearby garbage dump, and survive on the strength of their collective wits, making their own decisions and learning from the outcomes.

She tested the stories against the language skills of her students, many of whom were not native speakers of English, and it wasn't long before the adventures of the Boxcar Children took on a life of its own.

In 1942, with several well-written and child-tested stories in hand, she found support in the Scott-Foresman Publishing Company, a major source of instructional resources and a publisher of children's books.

It wasn't long before children across America knew about the resourceful Alden children, their boxcar home, and of the difficulties they experienced living on their own.

As you might imagine, the success of the books caught the attention of a few critics who sensed a crumbling of modern civilization because school children were enjoying stories about four, very clever young truants.

"Those stories about childhood self-sufficiency will encourage childhood rebellion!" cried the critics, waving their advanced college degrees in the air.

"That's exactly the reason the children enjoy the stories," responded author Warner, "because the children are in charge."

And amidst it all, the Boxcar Children have shown remarkable resilience to the decades of time since Gertrude Chandler Warner first brought them to life seventy-six years ago (1942-2018).

To this day, Henry, Jessie, Violet, and Benny Alden, and their faithful dog, continue to explore an ever-changing world. They continue to solve new problems consistent with today's world, delighting millions of children along the way.

Children who love to read about their adventures, and their enterprising and ingenious minds and their willingness to help others, including your children and your grandchildren to improve their reading skills.

In addition to the nineteen *Boxcar Children* books written by Warner, supporting authors have added another 126 books to date, plus twenty-one Boxcar Children Specials, each new title featuring the byline, *Created by Gertrude Chandler Warner*.

And yes, to let you know that everything worked out fine, the children and their once worrisome grandfather have come to understand and appreciate each other.

But don't tell your young readers who should discover that for themselves.

And do you know what?

You just might make a few memories yourself by reading the stories aloud to your own children or grandchildren.

Couldn't hurt, and the kiddos will love the stories.

Guaranteed!

And, oh yes, as promised, the name of the Boxcar Children's dog? It's not Spot, Lassie, Benji, or Toto.

It's "Watch."

That's right! The name of their faithful dog is "Watch." Think about it.

---

[1] Benny, the youngest of the four Alden siblings is five-years-old, the only child that author Warner specifically provided an age. The eldest child is Henry, and it is assumed he is in his early teens, probably 13 to 15 years of age. Of the two girls, Jessie and Violet, Jessie is the oldest, likely a year or two younger than Henry.

I believe that children are only beneath me in years,
I find in some, my superiors.
Gertrude Chandler Warner (1890-1979) Author

Robert Watson-Watt

Born: Robert Alexander Watson-Watt
The man who invented radar.
Apr 13, 1892 (Brechin, Scotland) - Dec 5, 1973 (Iverness, Scotland)

S IR ROBERT WATSON-WATT came from good stock, the son of a carpenter and a direct descendant of Scottish chemist and mechanical genius James Watt, the man who invented the first practical steam engine.

But Robert Watson-Watt wasn't interested in steam, he was interested in radio waves and he was responsible for one of the most important inventions of World War II.

Watson-Watt also loved light-hearted doggerel, and he had a great sense of humor as evidenced when his invention was used against him, quite literally, by a Canadian lawman.

But first, the story behind Watson-Watts' invention.

After graduating in 1912 from University College in Dundee, Scotland, with a degree in engineering, he received an assistantship to study wireless telegraphy, or radio, as it would later be known.

That's where he was on July 28, 1914, the day that World War I broke out, busy studying the physics of *radio frequency oscillators* and *wave propagation*.

Two years later, after completing his assistantship, he applied for a job in communications with the British Ministry of Defense.

When told that nothing was available, he went to work as a meteorologist at the Royal Aircraft Factory in Farnborough, Scotland. There, applying his knowledge of radio waves, he discovered he could pinpoint the location, speed, and movement of thunderstorms, thus leading to improved methods of forewarning pilots of weather dangers.

After World War I he went to work at the Radio Research Station at Slough, Scotland.

In 1933, he became head of the National Physics Laboratory where, still researching radio waves, he wrote a report titled: *The Detection of Aircraft by Radio Methods.*

The report caught the eye of Henry Tizard, Chairman of the Committee for the *Scientific Survey of Scotland's Air Defense System.*

Tizard, impressed with Watson-Watt's work, asked him to demonstrate his ideas before a group in Daventry, Scotland. He did so on February 26, 1935, demonstrating that radio waves could be used to detect aircraft in flight, just as they had been used to detect the presence and movement of thunderstorms.

That demonstration led to Watson-Watt's appointment as Superintendent of the Bawdsey Research Station in Felixstowe, England, and it was there that he invented an aircraft detection system that he named, *Radio Detection and Ranging.*

Then, in 1939, just prior to the beginning of World War II, Watson-Watt was asked to supervise the installation of his aircraft detection system along a corridor of weather stations on the Southern and Eastern coasts of England.

Following the defeat of France by Nazi Germany in 1940, Adolf Hitler wanted his military to immediately land 160,000 German soldiers along a 40-mile stretch of Southeast England.

It would have happened except that enough of Hitler's generals, concerned that the Royal Air Force could inflict heavy casualties during such an attempt, convinced the Führer to put the invasion on hold until the *Luftwaffe* (German Air Force) had sufficiently weakened or destroyed the Royal Air Force.

But what the Germans hadn't counted on was Watson-Watts invisible *Radio Detection and Ranging* system with its ability to silently detect the presence of aircraft.

During the numerous air battles that followed, the German Luftwaffe lost 1,389 aircraft to the Royal Air Force loss of 792 aircraft. An almost two-to-one lopsided victory margin that must have infuriated the Fürher to no end!

Today, we know Watson-Watts' invention, *Radio Detection and Ranging* by its familiar acronym, RADAR,[1] formed from the initial letters of its full name: **Ra**dio **D**etection **a**nd **R**anging.

Years later, Sir Robert Watson-Watt, who was knighted in 1942 for service to his country, learned the hard way that his invention could detect more than aircraft.

It all happened when he was given a speeding ticket by a Canadian radar-gun toting officer. The ticket prompted Watson-

Watt to introduce himself to the lawman with the tongue-in-cheek message, "Had I known what you fellows were going to do with it (radar), I'd never have invented it."

When he returned to his native Scotland, he must have been smiling as he sat down and penned the following, titled "Rough Justice."

> *Pity Sir Robert Watson-Watt,*
> *strange target of this radar plot,*
> *And thus, with others I can mention,*
> *the victim of his own invention.*
> *His magical all-seeing eye,*
> *enabled cloud-bound planes to fly,*
> *But now by some ironic twist,*
> *it spots the speeding motorist*
> *And bites, no doubt with legal wit,*
> *the hand that once created it.*

Sir Robert Watson-Watt died in Iverness, Scotland in 1973 at the age of 81.

He was buried next to his wife Katherine Trefusis Forbes,[2] in the churchyard of the Episcopal Church of the Holy Trinity at Pitlochry, Scotland.

Sir Robert Watson-Watt was the right man at the right time, and his work and his life made a difference for the cause of freedom for mankind, for which we are all indebted.

---

[1] *Stories from History's Dust Bin* (additional reading):
    Vol 2, Jul 19:   Radar mentioned with Percy Lebaron Spencer

[2] Sir Robert Watson-Watt's wife, Katherine Forbes, was the founding Air Commander of the Women's Auxiliary Air Force, the female support group of the Royal Air Force.

> *Every time I look into the eyes of an animal, I see life;*
> *the force of life and the beauty of creation.*
> Gary Burghoff (1943-) Played Radar O'Reilly on M*A*S*H

Gustave Whitehead
Born: Gustav Albin Weisskopf
Could he have been the first in flight?
Jan 1, 1874 (Leutershausen, Bavaria) – Oct 10, 1927 (Bridgeport CT)

W ITH THIS STORY, it's good to keep in mind that in a state full of Connecticut Yankees, all things are [almost] possible, including the rewriting of aviation history.

As a German boy growing into his teens, Gustav Weisskopf, showing a serious interest in flight, was not your typical teenager. He captured birds, measured the surface area of their wings, experimented to see how much weight they could lift and still become airborne, and kept track of the information.

He also experimented with tissue paper parachutes, built models, and in 1887 at the age of thirteen, he confidently, albeit foolishly, jumped from the roof of his house with a homemade pair of bird-like wings strapped to his body.

And as only possible when one is young, foolish and inquisitive, he survived with nothing more than a bruised ego.

That same year, he was orphaned. His father had died the previous year and it's not known if Gustav had scared his mother to death with his leap from the roof, or if she had been ill, but shortly after his unwise jump, she died, and life changed for young Gustav.

He lived with one relative after another until he was old enough to receive an apprenticeship as a machinist at the Rudolf Diesel[1] Company in Angsburg. Bavaria.

Around 1889, with a case of 15-year-old wanderlust, he told his relatives he was going to America, but instead, he ended up traveling to Brazil.

He stayed in Brazil for several years working as a sailor and, perhaps because of his earlier experiments with birds and how they achieved flight, he became aware of the effect that the play of the wind had on the sails of ships.

Four years later and in his nineteenth year (1893), Gustav departed Brazil for America. Once in America, he anglicized[4] his name as a way of showing the depth of his commitment to his new country. He added a final "e" to his given name and since the literal translation of Weisskopf into English means *Whitehead,* he became Gustave Whitehead.

Once settled into a place to live, he went to work for a toy manufacturer where he built huge kites and took up an interest in model gliders.

A year later, because of his kite and model-making skills, he was hired by Dr. William Pickering[2] of Harvard University to build some experimental weather kites. From that association comes the first known photograph of Gustave. He is shown as a young man testing a large weather kite for Dr. Pickering at Harvard's Blue Hill Weather Observatory.

While working for Dr. Pickering, Whitehead met James Means who had just published a book titled *Manned Flight.*

Means shared with Whitehead his plans to form America's first aviation organization, the Boston Aeronautical Society, which he did the following year (1895).

Means had been corresponding with a German scientist named Otto Lilienthal, who is today considered the *Father of Wing Aerodynamics,* and he had in his possession, several letters from Lilienthal, technical letters written in German that he needed to have translated into English. Thus, Whitehead became the Society's official translator, a task he enjoyed and performed well.

Incidentally, Otto Lilienthal's research was also being closely monitored by a couple of bicycle mechanics in Dayton, Ohio, named Orville and Wilbur.

From 1896-1898, Whitehead and one of the Society's mechanics, Albert B. C. Horn, built a Lilienthal-designed glider and a strange-looking contraption they called an ornithopter.

The latter, it was hoped, would fly by flapping its wings like a bird. While Whitehead reportedly made several successful non-powered flights in the glider, he was never able to get the doggone ornithopter to fly into the history books, and the project died an unflappable death.

In 1899, per a 1934 affidavit signed by a man with the surname of Darvarich, he and Whitehead made a one-half mile flight in a steam-powered aircraft at Pittsburgh's Schenley Park.

In the affidavit, Darvarich states that they flew at an elevation of 25-feet above the ground before crashing into a brick building. No newspaper article or other evidence that might prove the veracity of that claim has ever been uncovered.

There is another story, also without collaboration, that was carried in the June 9, 1901 edition of the *New York Sun* in which Whitehead supposedly made an unmanned test flight of a powered, heavier-than-air flying machine.

The story states that Whitehead flew his machine about a half mile before crashing into a tree. Also in the article, Whitehead made a point of saying it was his intent to keep the location of his experimental flights secret to avoid drawing a crowd.

And there is yet another story, one in which Whitehead's supporters claim that their man, not those bicycle mechanics in Ohio, should be recognized as the first to fly a powered and controlled heavier-than-air aircraft.

It tells of a Whitehead-designed aircraft named the "Condor" that sported a distinctive pair of fanciful scalloped condor-esque wings. The flight was to have taken place in Connecticut on August 14, 1901, more than two years before the Orville Wright[3] flight at Kitty Hawk, North Carolina on December 17, 1903.

The story received renewed traction in 2013 when a respected magazine, *Jane's All the World's Aircraft*, resurfaced the Wright Brothers – Gustave Whitehead controversy.

The story is based on marginal evidence at best, but is tongue-in-cheek enough that on June 5, 2013, the Connecticut State Senate passed House Bill 6671 proclaiming a yet to be determined date as "Powered Flight Day" in honor of Gustave Whitehead. The Bill (in part) reads:

The Governor shall proclaim a date certain in each year as Powered Flight Day to honor the first powered flight by Gustave Whitehead and to commemorate the Connecticut aviation and aerospace industry.

On June 25, 2013, Governor Dannel P. Malloy signed HB 6671 into law (Public Act 13-210), specifically noting that *Powered Flight Day* cannot result in an impact to state funds.

At first blush it may seem that Connecticut dissed Orville Wright in favor of Gustave Whitehead, but a careful reading of the Bill's language shows only that the day honors, "the first powered flight by Gustave Whitehead," or stated another way, *Gustave Whitehead's first powered flight*, not necessarily that Whitehead's flight was the first by a *heavier-than-air* aircraft.

Thus, with tongue-in-cheek, aviation historian John Brown added that, "At least in Connecticut, aviation history now appears to have been rewritten," afterward, expressing doubt that the state's elementary and high school history books could be "reprinted in time for the start of Fall classes."

Finally, you may want to note that alongside the passage of HP-6671, two other decrees were passed to impact Connecticut life. First, a decree that the *Ballroom Polka* be named the state's official State Polka, and a decree that the *Beautiful Connecticut Waltz* be deemed the "second state song."[5]

Imagine, three decrees with such far-reaching consequences being passed with a single stroke of the gavel.

Only in Connecticut.

Stories from History's Dust Bin (additional reading):
[1] Vol 1, Mar 18:   Featuring Rudolf Diesel
[2] Vol 2, May 15:   William Pickering with Williamina Fleming
[3] Vol 1, Feb 8:   Wright Brothers with Thomas E. Selfridge

[4] To Anglicize means to adapt a foreign word, or phrase, to English usage, e.g. to anglicize *Juan* to *John*.

[5] Fake news: There is no plan at the present to replace Connecticut's state song, *Yankee Doodle*, with the 1939 song, *Connie's Got Connections in Connecticut*.

Both optimists and pessimists contribute to the society.
The optimist invents the airplane; the pessimist the parachute.
George Bernard Shaw (1856-1950) Playwright

Harvey Wilcox

Born: Harvey Henderson Wilcox
He envisioned a model city; not a city of models.
1832 (Monroe County NY) – Mar 19, 1891 (Los Angeles CA)

IN 1883, IN CALIFORNIA'S Cahuenga Valley, former Kansas real-estate developer Harvey Wilcox purchased 160 acres of land for $24,000.

The cost was considered high for undeveloped property. But Wilcox was well-heeled and besides, his wife Ida, thirty years his junior, had fallen in love with the beautiful rolling hills, especially the free-growing stands of bright English holly that everywhere graced the landscape.

It was Harvey's intention to produce apricots and figs on the land, so he subdivided the land into orchards, figuring the fruit trees would thrive in the 300-plus days of yearly California sunshine.

The sun did shine for the requisite number of days each year, maybe even more, but the topsoil was so thin and nutrient poor that coaxing fruit from the trees in his orchards was, well, pardon the pun, fruitless.

After four years of doing his best to raise fruit and finding the venture a bust, he decided to do what he had done in Topeka, establish a real-estate company and turn the orchards into a town, complete with businesses and beautiful residential areas.

It was now 1887 and Harvey knew that the property, dotted by young, albeit poorly producing fruit trees and the previously mentioned stands of English holly that Ida loved, would be the perfect place to create a new kind of community.

He wasn't interested in the typical speculator's approach, that of throwing together a mindless cluster of cookie-cutter homes that could quickly be turned for a profit.

As an outspoken member of a no-nonsense temperance society, he imagined an exemplar community. A beautiful town that would serve as a wholesome model for Christian living.

It would be, as Harvey envisioned, a town whose name might one day be known around the world. A town without saloons, dance halls, casinos or brothels; a town devoid of loud music, exotic dancing, slick-talking men, and ladies of the night.

Yes sir! It would be a community based on heavenly ideals and sober religious principles.

Building lots were sold to teetotalers only, a non-negotiable rule, for $1,000 per lot.

The lots sold, homes were built, and the city turned out just as Harvey and Ida had imagined. Ida laid out the landscaping for much of the town and created most of the street names.[1]   It was a truly tranquil setting, a place of peace and sobriety and so free of crime the town never even bothered to build a jail.

Then, on March 19, 1891, Harvey Wilcox, age 59, died, leaving Ida a 29-year-old widow.

Four years later, Ida met and married Philo J. Beveridge, a businessman, and the son of former Illinois governor John L. Beveridge.

They continued to develop the town, perhaps not with Harvey's outgoing religious zeal, but with great civic pride. Ida and Philo donated land for churches and public parks, and paid for the town's first sidewalks.

And life was good in California.

But before continuing with Ida and Philo, we now shift our attention to something taking place three-thousand miles to the east, in Menlo Park, New Jersey.

In Menlo Park, Thomas Edison[2] had just invented the first practical motion picture camera. He called it a *kinetoscope,* and in 1889 it became one of 1,093 patents that Edison would hold at the time of his death in 1931.

Edison claimed that the *kinetoscope* would "do for the eye what the phonograph does for the ear." But before the world could fully appreciate the magic of his marvelous invention, someone had to invent a flexible alternative to the heavy glass photographic plates that were being used in photography.

George Eastman of Rochester, New York solved the problem in 1893 by inventing "roll film, " coating one side of a strip of clear celluloid with a fine layer of silver nitrate.

Still, it would be another 17 years (1910) before the first motion-picture would play before an audience.

That first-ever motion-picture was a 17-minute offering that we would call a short subject today. It was titled *In Old California,* a silent-movie melodrama depicting life in a small Mexican village, produced and directed by D. W. Griffith[3] who would become legendary for his silent era epics.

The location selected by Griffith for shooting that very first motion-picture was on the outskirts of a town known for its friendly people, beautiful scenery, and the bright green plant that dotted the rolling hills, the plant that Ida liked so well, English holly.

In fact, one legend claims it was that very plant that inspired Ida Wilcox to suggest to her husband that they name their small emerging town, *Hollywood.*[4]

Over the long haul, Hollywood may not have ended up as the idyllic Christian community that Harvey and Ida Wilcox had once envisioned, but Harvey was certainly right about one thing.

The town that he and Ida founded, is today, certainly known around the world.

[1] Perhaps the most famous street named by Ida Wilcox is the one known as *Sunset Boulevard.*

Stories from History's Dust Bin (additional reading):
[2] Vol 2, Jul 10:   Thomas Edison with Nikola Tesla
[3] Vol 3, Oct 14:   D.W. Griffith with Lillian Gish

[4] The naming of *Hollywood* is the subject of multiple legends. One legend tells of Ida meeting a woman on a train whose estate in Ohio was named *Hollywood,* and Ida liked the name. Another suggests that Ida first heard the word *Hollywood* when used by a neighbor who lived in nearby Holly Canyon. And of course, there's the version used in the above story. Regardless, when Harvey Wilcox submitted a grid map of his proposed town-site development to the Los Angeles County Recorder's Office on February 1, 1887, the document listed the name of the new town's first residential subdivision as *Hollywood.*

Strip away the phony tinsel of Hollywood and
you'll find the real tinsel underneath.
Oscar Levant (1906-1972) Composer

John T. Wilder

Born: John Thomas Wilder
The businessman warrior
Jan 31, 1830 (Hunter NY) – Oct 20, 1917 (Jacksonville FL)

J OHN T. WILDER was intelligent, personable, independent, and a quick thinker, qualities that had served him well in business.

Prior to the Civil War, he and his wife Martha lived in a beautiful home in Greensburg, Indiana, and were the parents of nearly enough children to populate a small state. He owned a successful foundry and held several patents on hydraulic machines as well as a unique water wheel.

At the outbreak of the Civil War in 1861, John did the patriotic thing. He enlisted as a private in the 1st Indiana Battery. He would have happily remained a private, but because of his reputation as a successful businessman who knew how to get things done, he was elected captain by the men in the Battery. In those days, the men in a military unit could elect their captains.

With only two months' experience as a military captain and no battlefield experience, Indiana Governor Oliver P. Morton commissioned Wilder a Lieutenant Colonel and assigned him to the 17th Indiana Infantry.

In 1862, Colonel Wilder and his men got their first taste of fighting at the Battle of Shiloh. The 17th Indiana Infantry performed beyond expectations and Wilder was given command of a brigade.

With virtually no military training, yet flushed with success and a quick rise in rank, the business end of his personality began to override the military way of doing things.

It would be his independent thinking and his decision to fight as he best knew how, as a businessman, that would turn him into a Civil War legend.

In August of 1862, Colonel Wilder and a garrison of less than 2,000 soldiers were charged with protecting a crucial bridge over the Green River near Munfordville, Kentucky.

On the other side of the river stood Confederate General James R. Chalmers and a similar-size army whose task it was to wrest the bridge away from the Union forces. And marching toward the bridge was Confederate General Braxton Bragg with his *Army of the Mississippi*, as his troops were called. Bragg needed control of that bridge to continue his offensive into Kentucky, and he wasn't a man to be trifled with.

On September 13, 1862, General Chalmers sent a message across the river to Colonel Wilder demanding that he surrender his garrison.

The following day, Wilder sent a remarkably casual message back to Chalmers stating that he and his men would instead, "try fighting for a while."

When Chalmers received Wilder's note, he was infuriated, and ordered his men to take control of the bridge at all costs.

Well, it turned out to be an expensive battle for the Confederates who counted 283 casualties to only 37 for the Union. And even worse from General Chalmers' point-of-view, that blankety-blank bridge was still under Union control!

Colonel Wilder had out-strategized, out-positioned, and out-thought an experienced Confederate general.

But it wasn't over!

Wilder, although able to secure a few additional soldiers, had become aware that something unusual was happening within the Confederate encampment.

What was happening was that General Bragg's *Army of the Mississippi* was quietly flowing into the area. It didn't take Colonel Wilder long, as the business side of his brain might have stated it, *to realize he had insufficient information upon which to make an informed decision.*

He didn't want to surrender the bridge; but neither was he willing to engage his men in a costly battle they couldn't win. What Wilder did next may be a first in the annals of military warfare. He decided to ask the enemy what they would do if they were in his shoes.

Before the Confederates initiated another assault, they made one final attempt to get the Union soldiers to surrender, and to their surprise, Colonel Wilder himself stepped onto the bridge and began walking forward with a white flag.

Midway across the bridge, he was approached, blindfolded, and escorted to the tent of Major General Simon Bolivar Buckner. There, he told a surprised Major Buckner that the white flag was not a "flag of surrender," but rather a "flag of truce."

He explained that he had come to discuss an assessment of each army's potential to control the bridge. From all accounts, it was a respectful discussion, and when the talking was over, Major Buckner turned Colonel Wilder over to General Bragg for a tour of the Confederate ranks.

When Wilder saw the seemingly endless rows of tents accommodating Bragg's Army, an estimated 25,000 men, he gasped in disbelief. At that point, General Bragg asked him to continue the walk and to count the number of cannon already trained on the Union position.

After counting forty-five cannon placements aimed toward his Union forces across the river, Wilder stopped, paused for a few seconds in considered thought, looked General Bragg in the eye and said, "I believe I'll surrender," and he did.

Colonel Wilder spent two months in a Confederate prison before being released as part of a prisoner exchange.

When he returned to the Union lines, he was given another brigade. His assignment was to protect Union supply lines with foot soldiers. The assignment sparked his imagination and he went on to create the best-known fighting brigade of the Civil War, a fighting unit that you've likely heard about.

The first thing he did was to request, cajole, argue, and ultimately receive permission to put his foot soldiers on horseback. It was a totally new concept, a mounted infantry, where before only officers were mounted.

Next, he wanted his men to have the best possible weapons, so he ordered 900 Henry rifles. When the manufacturer couldn't deliver in a timely manner, he turned to Christopher Spencer who had just invented the Spencer .52 caliber repeating rifle, but they weren't cheap.

When the government balked at purchasing an expensive $35-dollar rifle for each man, Wilder personally contracted with Spencer for 1,400 rifles. Then, after demonstrating the rifle's efficiency to his men, he handed each a rifle asking only that they repay the $35.00, roughly three months' military pay, when the war was over and they were back on their feet.

The government, exasperated by Wilder's non-military approach to getting things done, grudgingly paid for the rifles so the men wouldn't have to do so.

The first engagement of Wilder's new brigade was so fast and so efficient that it became known as the *Lightning Brigade*, and it would go on to score victory after victory after victory.

Colonel Wilder was brevetted to Brigadier General at war's end, but like Lucius Quinctius Cincinnatus,[1] the Roman statesman-general of old, he resigned his commission, moved his family to Tennessee, established another foundry, built a couple of blast furnaces, and settled into civilian life until his death in 1917 at the age of eighty-seven.

Stories from History's Dust Bin (additional reading):
[1] Vol 2, May 13: Featuring the Society of the Cincinnati

In the end, you're measured not by how much you undertake,
but by what you finally accomplished.
Donald J. Trump (1946-) 16th U.S. President

Xerography/Chet Carlson

Born: Chester Floyd Carlson
A story worth copying.
Feb 8, 1906 (Seattle WA) – Sep 19, 1968 (New York NY)

Y OU WON'T RECOGNIZE Chester "Chet" Carlson's name unless you're conducting research on the history of photocopying.

But he is worthy of remembrance.

Not only because he eliminated the purple smudges that ended up on secretaries' noses and starched white blouses prior to his wonderful invention, but because his invention could make an unlimited number of copies, each as sharp as the original.

Prior to Carlson's machine, making even one copy as sharp as the original was impossible. But copies so clearly reproduced that not even your boss could tell a copy from the original? Well, that would take a miracle.

Unless you were a secretary during the "before Xerox" era, you probably don't know how hard it was to make really good handouts for your boss's Board of Directors' meeting.

Oh, there were options.

You could (1) stick a half-dozen sheets of paper, each separated by a carbon paper into a typewriter and strike the keys forcefully enough to imprint an image onto each sheet of paper, or (2) use a mimeograph machine that forced ink through a "stencil master" onto blank sheets of paper; or (3) use a spirit duplicator that used "spirit masters" and relied on a thin coating of solvent to transfer the purple inked characters (or drawings) onto a blank sheet of paper.

Now for an incredible story of perseverance with the most primitive of tools and an unwavering belief in oneself.

How Chet Carlson ever found the time to invent anything is a tribute to the man.

From the time he was born, he never knew a healthy parent. His father had long suffered from tuberculosis and his mother the same from malaria.

At eight, Chet worked odd jobs. As a teen, he worked before school at a local print shop before pedaling his bike home to wash up, grab his sack lunch, and rush to school.

Unable to earn the number of high school credits required by California law, he couldn't graduate with his classmates. So, did he say, "poor me" and give up? Nope. He repeated his senior year, earned the needed credits, and graduated. But unfortunately, not in time for his ill mother to watch him walk across the stage.

Determined to receive a college degree, Carlson attended Riverside Junior College on a work-study program, working and attending classes during alternating six-week blocks.

He began as a chemistry major, added a second major, physics, and worked an extra job to cover the rent on a small apartment for himself and his invalid father.

Even after working virtually full-time and caring for his father, he was able to keep his grades high enough for acceptance at the California Institute of Technology, but not quite good enough to cut the $260 yearly tuition.

Did Chet say, "poor me" and give up? Nope. He worked at a cement factory long enough to pay off his $260 tuition debt.

After graduating from Cal-Tech in physics, he sent 82 résumés to 82 companies and received 82 rejections. Needing a job, and fast, he became a patent clerk for Bell Laboratories. It wasn't what he had gone to college for, but it came with a regular paycheck and his father needed regular medications.

Being a patent clerk required endless hours of typing carbon copies of patent applications to which were attached pages of specifications. Even worse, every application change, every amendment made during the approval process required a new set of carbon copies for the various reviewers, and woe to the reviewer who received a fifth or sixth generation copy.

When his father died in 1933, Chester married, divorced, and married a second time.

Life was never easy.

The tedious day-after-day copying in Bell's patent office was wearisome with no end in sight. He enrolled in night school to study law, but couldn't afford the textbooks.

Did he say, "poor me" and give up? Nope. He went to a public library after work and hand-copied the court cases and legal decisions needed for the next day's classes before going home, spent and exhausted.

The routine was hard on his new marriage, but Chet had never quit anything in his life and he wasn't about to quit now.

In 1936, he received his law degree.

Suddenly, his interest in chemistry and physics returned and he began visiting the library to peruse the technology and science stacks. It was during one of those visits that he read an article by Hungarian physicist Paul Selényi. Selényi was an expert in electrostatic imagery, and Chet's brain, infused with a new idea, lit up like a halogen lamp.

Motivated by his monotonous patent-copy workload and Selényi's article, but to the dismay of Dorris, his wife, Chet took over the kitchen in the tiny apartment to test a few theories.

Imagine Chet melting sulfur over the family stove, his wife glaring at him with crossed arms and a softly tapping foot. Then, Chet pouring the liquid sulfur onto a zinc-coated plate, only to have the sulfur and zinc ignite, filling the apartment with the acrid smell of rotten eggs.

Now, if you've never experienced the sneeze-inducing, pungent rotten-egg odor of burning sulfur,[1] you cannot fully appreciate the force with which Dorris Carlson's once soft-tapping foot hit the floor!

But, as unlikely as it might seem, it was Chet's mother-in-law who came to the rescue. As the owner of several rental properties in Astoria, New York, she allowed Chet to turn one of those vacant apartments into a primitive physics lab.

Elated, Chet hired an unemployed Austrian physicist named Otto Kornei as an assistant.

It would be in that small apartment, in what would be hard-pressed to pass as a scientific laboratory, and using low-tech equipment such as a common hot-plate, a handkerchief and a reading lamp, that one of the world's greatest advances in printing would be invented.

Just know that between moving into that small apartment and experiencing success, Chet and Otto logged hundreds, perhaps thousands of hours of exhausting research.

Then it happened!

On October 22, 1938, Chet recorded in his journal that Otto had prepared a sulfur coating on a zinc plate, then printed the date and place, *10.-22.-38 Astoria*, on a glass microscope slide. After darkening the room, Otto rubbed the sulfur-coated surface vigorously with a handkerchief to create an electrostatic charge, then laid the glass slide, momentarily, under the reading lamp. When the slide was removed, on the surface of the zinc plate was a near-perfect duplicate of the notation, *10.-.22.-38 Astoria.*

Chet and Otto named the process *Electrophotography*.

That discovery and more years of hard work led Chet to the Haloid Company, who renamed the invention *Xerography*, a word formed from two Greek words, *xero* meaning "dry" and *graphia* meaning "writing."

That word, *Xerography*, would become the basis for one of the world's best-known brand names, *Xerox*.

In 1959, the Haloid Company introduced the world's first dry photocopier, the Xerox 914.

Unlike most inventors whose inventions are refined after their death, Chester Carlson lived long enough to see for himself how he had made the world a better place.

How, with a simple push of a button, a perfect high-quality copy could be made without leaving a purple-smudge on a single nose or starched white blouse.

On September 19, 1968, Chester Carlson died of a heart attack in New York, but not before anonymously donating over $150 million to philanthropic purposes.

---

[1] Sulphur (Hydrogen Sulfide), when burned produces a gas that smells like rotten or decomposing eggs, hence it's common name, rotten-egg gas.

You are successful the moment you start moving
toward a worthwhile goal.
Chester Carlson (1906-1968) Inventor

Alvin York

Born: Alvin Cullum York
"Well, I got a tolerable few."
Dec 13, 1887 (Pall Mall TN) - Sept 2, 1964 (Nashville TN)

O NCE, WHEN TELLING some friends how they hunted turkeys in Tennessee, Alvin York explained that if six turkeys come runnin' out of the bushes, you always teched off the last turkey first, then you teched off the next-to-last turkey, then the fourth, and so on. That way, the front turkeys don't know the back ones been teched, so they just keep a comin' 'til you get 'em all.

On another occasion when explaining how they held turkey shoots in Tennessee, York explained, "We tied the turkey behind a log and ever time it bobbed its head, we let fly. If we hit the turkey's head, we kept the turkey." As everyone in Pall Mall would tell you, Alvin got dang good at techin' the turkey's head off, right clean, on the first shot.

In 1917, Alvin was drafted to fight in World War I.

The family pastor suggested he apply for "conscientious objector" (non-combatant) status, but as Alvin later explained, "I knew I had plenty of brothers to look after my mother and I never was a conscientious objector. I didn't want to go and fight and kill, but I had to answer the call of my country."

Alvin answered the call and became a Sergeant York, a member of the Army's 82nd Infantry Division.

Then, on October 8, 1918, in the middle of the dense Argonne Forest, German machine gun nests had stopped the allies from advancing. That's when Sergeant York and four squads of men cautiously worked their way behind German lines, surprising fifteen Germans, including a major, eating breakfast.

"Put 'em up!" barked York, and the Germans ceased their chatter, put their coffee cups down, and raised their hands. York assigned a squad to guard the prisoners while he and the other three squads left to put an end to those pesky machine gun nests.

As York and his men rounded a corner, a German machine gun opened fire, killing everyone except Alvin and six others, leaving Alvin in command of a fighting force of seven.

Alvin, in his own words:

I had no time nohow to do nothing but watch them German machine gunners and give them the best I had. Ever time I seed a German I teched him off, jes like in the turkey matches in Tennessee. ... I jes couldn't miss ... at that range. An' I didn't. Besides, it weren't no time to miss nohow.

I knowed that in order to get to me – they would have to raise up to see where I was. Ever time a head come up I done knocked it down. They would sorter stop for a moment and then another head would come up and I'd knock it down too.

I was in the open and the guns were spitting fire something awful. But they didn't seem to be able to hit me. I stood and begun to shoot off-hand, my favorite position.

A German officer and five men done jumped out of a trench and charged me with bayonets ... and they were a comin' right smart. I only had a half clip in my rifle; but I had my pistol. I done flipped it out and ... teched off the sixth man first; then the fifth; then the fourth; and so on. That's how we shoot wild turkeys at home ....

Then I returned to the rifle, and kept right on after those machine guns. I knowed I had 'em if I didn't run out of ammunition. I hollered for them to give up. But they didn't know my language.

I got holt of the (earlier captured) *major after he seed me stop the six who charged, an' he asked, 'English?' I said 'American' and he said 'Good!' Then he said, 'If you won't shoot anymore I'll make them give up.' He blew a whistle and they came and threw down their guns and belts. All but one who threw a hand grenade which burst in the air. I teched him off and the rest surrendered without trouble.*

Alvin and his small army lined the prisoners in two columns with the major in front and Alvin right behind with the barrel of his pistol touching the back of the major's head. A lieutenant counted 132 captured Germans, then, shaking his head in disbelief, said, "Sergeant York, you've captured the whole dang German army!"

York drawled in response, "Well, I got a tolerable few."

A return to the battle site found twenty-eight dead Germans and thirty silent machine guns.

After the war, Alvin returned home to marry Gracie Loretta Williams, a girl who had promised to wait for him. They became the parents of eight children, most of whom were named after historical American figures, such as Woodrow Wilson York, Sam Houston York, Betsy Ross York, Andrew Jackson York, etc.

A modest patriot, he turned down numerous offers for endorsements, always stating, "This uniform ain't for sale."

He did receive royalties from a book that was made into a movie of his life, *Sergeant York*, starring Gary Cooper (1941). But he wasn't comfortable keeping the money for himself, so he and his wife used the royalties to fund schools in his native Tennessee mountain country, and earnings from the movie were used to establish an interdenominational Bible school.

In 1919, he received the Congressional Medal of Honor.

York died of a cerebral hemorrhage at the Veterans Hospital in Nashville, Tennessee, on September 2, 1964, at the age of 76.

Several public buildings have been named for Alvin, including the *Alvin C. York Veterans Hospital* in Murfreesboro, Tennessee and the 82nd Airborne Division's movie theater (*York Theater*) at Fort Bragg, North Carolina.

For trivia buffs: the rider-less horse used in the funeral procession for President Reagan was named *Sergeant York.*

What you did was the greatest thing accomplished by any
private soldier of all of the armies of Europe.
Field Marshal Ferdinand Foch (1851-1929) French General

Frank Zamboni

Born: Frank Joseph Zamboni, Jr.
He's from where? . . . Who'd a thunk it!
Jan 16, 1901 (Eureka UT) - July 27, 1988 (Paramount CA)

W HEN SOMEONE UNFAMILIAR with the sport of hockey is asked if they know what a *Zamboni* is, guesses might range from an exotic deli sandwich, to a Himalayan mountain, to the capitol of Zimbabwe. Wrong on each count!

But you'd be hard-pressed to find a bona fide hockey fan who doesn't know what a Zamboni is.

Assuming for the moment you're not a hockey fan, you've probably seen a Zamboni yourself while surfing the sports channels. You just didn't know that the strange-looking contraption had a name. It's that four-wheeled, slightly larger than jeep-sized machine that shaves, cleans, and resurfaces the ice between hockey game periods.

By the way, someone on the internet with more time than good sense, claims that every time a Zamboni does its job, it shaves enough ice from the rink to make 3,661 snow cones. There's no evidence, however, that the same ice shaved from a hockey rink has ever been used to make a snow cone.

But still, we're talking hockey fans here, so a cautionary note might be appropriate. If you're wearing a sweater with the visiting team logo emblazoned on the front or back, you might want to cover it with a friend's jacket before you head toward the refreshment stand to buy one of the frozen treats.

But, back to the Zamboni.

It's best not to ask a hockey fan what that four-wheeled, ice-resurfacing machine is. That's because if you do, you'll see an incredulous grin just before you're told in a voice intended to embarrass you, "Geez! I can't believe you've never heard of a Zamboni!"

And if the fan is Canadian, right after he or she lifts their toque[1] to scratch their head: "I can't believe what I'm hearing aye. You're telling me aye, that you've never heard of a Zamboni?" Aye?

But now, you're within seconds of knowing what many hockey fans don't know. You see, while every hockey fan on the planet knows what a Zamboni is, rare-as-hen's-teeth is the hockey fan who knows the history behind the machine, or anything about its inventor.

Now, because someone loved you enough to give you a copy of this indispensable book of little known facts, get ready to stun your hockey-loving friends.

In 1922, twenty-one-year-old Frank Zamboni and his older brother Lawrence went into the ice-making business in California. When it became apparent in the 1930s that electric refrigerators were not going away, they combined their existing refrigeration equipment with some new equipment and built the Iceland Skating Rink in Paramount, California.

The year was 1940, and the rink was no small project.

It was one of the first large-scale indoor ice-skating rinks in the United States with 20,000 square feet of surface ice.

And that's a lot of ice!

But, there was a problem and it had to do with the science of freezing. You see, unlike everything else on the planet that contracts when it freezes, water expands. And water frozen into ice by rows and rows of under-the-surface refrigerant lines leaves an annoying and unsafe rippling effect on the skating surface. That was a problem that Frank Zamboni would apply his inventive genius to – and solve.

Smoothing the ice each day in preparation for the ice-skating public required an army of workers with snow shovels, long water hoses to prep and patch surface holes and cracks, and then the wait for the freshly applied water to freeze.

Ice upkeep was both expensive and time intensive.

As soon as the rink was finished, Frank began working on a solution to the ice-prepping problem, especially the rippling effect caused by the under-the-ice refrigerant lines.

By 1946, he had figured out a way to shave the ice, and he patented the machine. In so doing, he had cut the labor force for daily resurfacing of the ice from dozens of snow-shovel wielding workers to a mere handful, but the process still took a full ninety minutes to complete.

Three years later his improved ice-resurfacing machine required only one man and fifteen minutes' time, and it resembled something out of a Rube Goldberg comic panel.

The machine used aircraft hydraulics, an oil derrick chassis, a Jeep engine, a wooden box to catch ice-shavings, and far too many belts and gears to count.

At first, he thought of the invention as simply something to help the bottom line of the family's Iceland Skating Rink, but when the Chicago Black Hawks heard about it, they wanted one for their hockey facility, and then figure-skating great Sonja Henie wanted two of the machines.

Orders were placed, Frank built the machines, and the first of many future sales were in the book.

In 1953, after more refinements, he mounted the ice-shaving, water-cleansing, and ice-resurfacing components onto a stripped-down Jeep CJ-3B chassis and named it, what else, the *Zamboni Ice Resurfacer,* giving it Serial Number 001, as if he would ever make and sell 999 of the machines.

It wasn't long before the demand for the ice-smoothing Zamboni went through the roof, and manufacturing the strange-looking machine shifted into high gear.

In April of 2012, the Montreal Canadiens took delivery of the 10,000th Zamboni.

And now it's time for you to further impress your hockey friends with your seemingly endless knowledge of all things Zamboni.

Start by throwing in a couple of trivia-worthy facts, such as in 2000, a miniature of the *Zamboni Ice Resurfacer* became an authentic Monopoly® board game token in the NHL version of the game.

In 2004, the NHL's Tampa Bay Lightning buried one of those tiny pewter Monopoly Zamboni's at center ice for good luck during the Stanley Cup Finals and won the Cup!

There is also a *Cheers* television episode in which Carla's hockey-playing husband Eddie (played by Jay Thomas) "died a noble death" after being struck and run over by a Zamboni while trying to save a hockey fan.

And now for the promised coup de grâce.

Not even the most ardent hockey fan will know that Frank Zamboni, the man who invented the Zamboni ice-resurfacing machine, was born and grew up in Utah, a state where more residents would recognize the face of world-renowned chef Wolfgang Puck, than could correctly identify a photograph of a hockey puck.

Frank Zamboni died of a heart attack on July 27, 1988 in Paramount, California. He is at rest at All Souls Cemetery in Long Beach.

Frank was posthumously inducted into the National Inventors Hall of Fame in 2007, and the U.S. Hockey Hall of Fame in 2009.

[1] Toque. The knit cap worn by Canadians during cold weather.

There are three things in life that people like to stare at: a flowing stream, a crackling fire, and a Zamboni clearing the ice.
Charlie Brown (Initial appearance in Peanuts - 1948) Lovable loser

Index

Chapter headings are shown in UPPER CASE, such as the first entry, that of JOHNNY ACE. If a chapter heading is followed by a single numeral, that will be the page number for the beginning of that story. If the chapter heading is followed by multiple numerals, the numeral in brackets will be the page number for that story.

For instance, the first chapter heading with multiple page numbers is for CUMMINGS, BOB, with two numbers, 61 and 326. The first number is set in brackets, e.g. [61], thus Bob Cummings' story begins on page 61. The other number, 326, references a page where Bob Cummings appears in another story.

64754986R00236

Made in the USA
Middletown, DE
17 February 2018